P9-CIU-018

THE MAN WITH THE GOLDEN TYPEWRITER

BY THE SAME AUTHOR

Amaryllis Fleming
Barrow's Boys
Killing Dragons
Ninety Degrees North
The Sword and the Cross
Cassell's Tales of Endurance

The Explorer's Eye (ed.)
The Traveller's Daybook (ed.)

THE MAN WITH THE GOLDEN TYPEWRITER

Ian Fleming's

James Bond Letters

Edited by

FERGUS FLEMING

BLOOMSBURY

NEW YORK · LONDON · OXFORD · NEW DELHI · SYDNEY

Bloomsbury USA
An imprint of Bloomsbury Publishing Plc

1385 Broadway
New York
NY 10018
USA

50 Bedford Square
London
WC1B 3DP
UK

www.bloomsbury.com

BLOOMSBURY and the Diana logo are trademarks of Bloomsbury Publishing Plc

First published in Great Britain 2015
First U.S. edition 2015

© The Ian Fleming Estate and Fergus Fleming, 2015

The Letters of Ian Fleming © The Ian Fleming Estate
www.ianfleming.com

The James Bond novels © Ian Fleming Publications Ltd

Ian Fleming®, the Ian Fleming signature®, and the Ian Fleming logo and bird device™
are trademarks owned by The Ian Fleming Estate.

THE IAN FLEMING ESTATE

James Bond and 007 are registered trademarks of Danjaq LLC, and used under
license by Ian Fleming Publications Ltd.

Unless credited otherwise, images reproduced in this book are © The Ian Fleming Estate

All rights in third party copyright material quoted in this book are reserved
to the respective copyright holder.

Every reasonable effort has been made to trace copyright holders of material reproduced in this book, but if any
have been inadvertently overlooked the publishers would be glad to hear from them. For legal purposes
the Acknowledgements on p. 382 constitute an extension of this copyright page.

All rights reserved. No part of this publication may be reproduced or transmitted in any form or by any means,
electronic or mechanical, including photocopying, recording, or any information storage or retrieval
system, without prior permission in writing from the publishers.

No responsibility for loss caused to any individual or organization acting on or refraining from action
as a result of the material in this publication can be accepted by Bloomsbury or the author.

ISBN: HB: 978-1-63286-489-5
ePub: 978-1-63286-490-1

Library of Congress Cataloging-in-Publication Data has been applied for.

2 4 6 8 10 9 7 5 3 1

Typeset by Newgen Knowledge Works (P) Ltd., Chennai, India
Printed and bound in the U.S.A. by Thomson-Shore Inc., Dexter, Michigan

To find out more about our authors and books visit www.bloomsbury.com. Here you will find extracts,
author interviews, details of forthcoming events, and the option to sign up for our newsletters.

Bloomsbury books may be purchased for business or promotional use. For information on bulk purchases please
contact Macmillan Corporate and Premium Sales Department at specialmarkets@macmillan.com.

To R. K. G

My love

This is only a tiny letter to try out my new typewriter and to see if it will write golden words since it is made of gold.

Ian Fleming to Ann Fleming, 16th August, 1952

Contents

Introduction

I N THE 1963 edition of *Who's Who*, by which time he was virtually a household name, Ian Fleming summarised his achievements in four words: 'several novels of suspense'. It was a modest description of a career that not only gave the world its most famous secret agent, James Bond, but was conducted at breakneck speed. Between 1952 and his death in 1964 Fleming wrote fourteen Bond books, three works of non-fiction – *The Diamond Smugglers*, *Thrilling Cities* and *State of Excitement* (unpublished) – as well as a three-volume children's story *Chitty-Chitty-Bang-Bang*. On top of which he worked as Foreign Manager for the *Sunday Times*, to which he contributed numerous articles as well as being instrumental in creating its (and Britain's) first colour supplement; was motoring correspondent for the *Spectator*; directed a small publishing house, Queen Anne Press; operated the North American Newspaper Alliance (NANA); wrote several film treatments; and managed a magazine for bibliophiles, *The Book Collector*.

To this hectic schedule was added what *Who's Who* listed as 'Recreations'. These were, in Fleming's words, 'First Editions, spear fishing, cards, golf'. When it came to spear fishing, he had by 1963 become keener on observing fish than killing them, but over the years he had acquired a close knowledge of oceanic life – particularly when it came to predators and the more poisonous tropical specimens – and for a while kept a journal of his underwater exploits which he titled 'Sea Fauna or the Finny Tribe of Golden Eye'. Cards were another fascination, not only in the way they fell on the gaming table but in their mathematical progression (as well as being an enthusiastic gambler he was an avid bridge player). Golf, meanwhile, had been a favourite sport since he was a teenager. To these three items should have been added two others:

cars and treasure-hunting. He was gripped by the mechanics, the sensation and also the *look* of speed, to which end he acquired whenever possible the latest, smartest and fastest automobile on the market. As for treasure, it had been a fascination ever since he was a boy, and would feature prominently both in his novels and non-fiction.

Diving, cards, golf and cars were passions that he passed on to Bond (along with women, tobacco, Martinis and scrambled eggs) and when his novels were translated into film they became his hero's hallmark. But he drew the line at 007 being interested in First Editions. Although not often advertised, Fleming was an ardent book collector and from the 1930s, with the assistance of expert Percy Muir, amassed a library of first editions charting the advent of thoughts and practices that were relevant to modern life. It was an eclectic collection, ranging from *The Communist Manifesto* to the birth of computing and the rules of billiards, but was considered of such national importance that it was evacuated from London during the Blitz and in 1963 formed the largest private contribution to the British Library's seminal exhibition, 'Printing and the Mind of Man'.

Underpinning this activity was an equally energetic output of letters. In an age of instant electronic communication, it is hard to appreciate the vitality of postal services during the 1950s. In Britain, letters were the thrum of life, with at least two collections a day and maybe more if you lived in a big city: the weight of London's letters was so great that it had an underground network devoted solely to the transmission of mail. People may have been tempted to use the telephone (Fleming's office number was Terminus 1234) but the crackling reception combined with the omnipresent threat of crossed lines made it an uneasy means of communication. Anyway, why use the phone if you were a writer? With post you could be guaranteed delivery by the next or even the same day. Despite being an advocate of modern technology – and a dab hand at telegramese – Fleming chose to write letters.

The following selection charts the progress of his literary career from a January holiday in Jamaica to a September memorial service in London. It is not exhaustive: many of the letters mentioned in the two major biographies* have proved untraceable; Fleming's stepdaughter

* John Pearson's *The Life of Ian Fleming* (1965) and Andrew Lycett's *Ian Fleming* (1995).

Fionn Morgan,* with a view to publishing a memoir of her own, has understandably withheld the majority of Fleming's correspondence with his wife Ann; unfortunately almost all correspondence with his siblings has been lost, including what his brother Peter called the 'nit-picker' letters which he sent after reading each manuscript; and no doubt whole bales of vital and informative material will come to light the moment this book is published. Nevertheless, it offers a glimpse of Fleming's life as a writer and, importantly, it is written mostly by himself.

To put the contents in perspective a potted biography may be helpful. Ian Lancaster Fleming was born on 28 May 1908, the second son of Valentine and Eve Fleming. Val was the eldest son of a self-made Scottish banker; Eve a musically talented, snobbish yet contrarily bohemian English rose. After Val's death in action on the Western Front in 1917 Fleming and his three brothers – Peter, Richard and Michael – were raised by their mother, who in 1925 gave them a half-sister, Amaryllis, courtesy of the artist Augustus John. The terms of Val's will put his family in a peculiar situation. Under its provisions Eve would inherit Val's considerable funds provided she did not remarry, whereupon the money would go to their children, leaving her with only a stipend. So despite the occasional dalliance, she preferred to remain single, and although her children were brought up amidst the trappings of wealth they were left in no doubt that they had to make their own way. Which they did, with considerable ability,† but the fear of financial insecurity and the desire to succeed would dog Fleming throughout his life.

He was educated at Eton College, where he excelled at athletics and produced a small but profitable magazine called *The Wyvern*. After a failed attempt at the diplomatic service and an unsuccessful spell at the Royal Military Academy, Sandhurst, he went for a while to Munich to

---

* Ann's two children from her first marriage to Lord O'Neill were Raymond (b. 1933), who inherited both the title and the family seat in Northern Ireland, and Fionn (b. 1936), who took her husband's name on her marriage to John Morgan in 1961.

† Peter (1907–71) was an acclaimed travel writer, Richard (1911–77) a prominent banker, Michael (1913–40) a successful businessman until his death at Dunkirk, and Amaryllis (1925–99) one of the nation's foremost cellists.

brush up his German and then to the Austrian Tyrol where, at Kitz-
bühel, he studied under the ex-spy Ernan Forbes Dennis and his wife
Phyllis Bottome – a novelist who inspired him to write his first short
story, 'A Poor Man Escapes'. He later joined Reuters, where he learned
how to write fast and precisely, and in 1933 was sent to Moscow to cover
a notorious spy trial involving the firm Metro-Vickers. His ingenuity in
delivering reports ahead of his competitors became something of a
legend in journalistic circles, as did his attempt to obtain an interview
with Joseph Stalin.* But, worried that he was not making enough
money, he quit Reuters for the City. Spells with two major finance
houses proved unsuccessful and, as war loomed, he felt his experience
of both Germany and Russia might be of use to the nation.

His thoughts on Germany were expressed in a letter to *The Times*
which was published in September 1938.

TO THE EDITOR

Sir,

Since the immediate future of Europe appears to depend largely on
Herr Hitler's intentions, it is most important that we should have a
clear knowledge of exactly what those intentions are. The present crisis
has shown that to be forewarned is not necessarily to be forearmed, but
it may be argued that fore-arming did not appear necessary when the
warning was so incredible. Doubts are dispelled, and it may now be of
interest to your readers to learn the exact details of the National-
Socialist Party Programme as circulated to members of the party and
others on February 24, 1920, four years before "Mein Kampf" was
written.

The original 25 points were issued from Munich in the form of a circular which is now extremely rare. I know of only one other copy, in the
Nazi archives at the Brown House.

---

* Although the scoop failed he did receive an apology signed by the dictator
himself.

This is a literal translation, from an original copy in my possession, of the preamble and the first three points:

"The Programme of the German Workers'
Party is a 'Time-Programme' (*Zeit-Program*).
The Leaders will abstain from setting up new
goals, after the attainment of the goals set out
in the Programme, with the sole object of per-
mitting the continued existence of the Party by
artificially stimulating the appetite of the
Masses.
"(1) We demand the union of all
Germans within a Greater Germany on the
grounds of the right of peoples to self-
determination.
"(2) We demand equality of rights for the
German people *vis-a-vis* other nations, and
repeal of the Peace Treaties of Versailles
and St. Germain.
"(3) We demand land and soil (colonies)
for the feeding of our people and the
emigration of our surplus population."

The remaining 22 points deal with racial questions and other internal matters, and, although they do not concern the purpose of this letter, it is remarkable with what minute fidelity each of these 22 points has been adhered to. One might say with justice that only the above three points remain to be carried out to the letter [...]

Then, in April 1939, he submitted a confidential report headed 'Russia's Strengths: some cautionary notes', in which he outlined the pros and cons of relying on Russia as an ally. He judged, correctly, that for all its administrative incompetence the Soviet Union would prove a potent military power: 'When the moment comes for action [we] will realise that these tough, grey-faced little men (the average height of the Army is 5ft. 5in,) are a vastly different force from the ill-equipped gun-fodder of 1914.' At the same time, he advised caution: 'Russia would be an exceedingly treacherous ally. She would not hesitate to stab us in the back the moment it suited her'. Perspicaciously, he added, 'When the Soviet Government has more leisure it will certainly redirect its energies towards World Revolution. The threat of a territorial world war should not blind us to the ideological struggle which will have to come one day.' While personally fond of Russia he detested the Soviet regime.

Fleming's efforts drew him to the attention of Rear-Admiral John Godfrey, head of Naval Intelligence, who, on the outbreak of war, made him his personal assistant with the rank of commander. Fleming's war-time career was one of ingenuity and daring. Although he never engaged in active combat he engineered numerous covert operations, some of which had a major impact and others – such as recruiting the assistance of black magician Aleister Crowley – did not. But they were notable for their imagination and despite various changes of command his input was considered so valuable he was retained at his post until 1945. As the war entered its final stages, his parting coup was to organise a team of commandos, 30AU, whom he called his Red Indians, to retrieve vital documents left behind by the retreating Nazi forces.

The Second World War left him with two ambitions. The first was to build a house in Jamaica, which he had visited during operations. The second was, as he declared, to write the spy story to end all spy stories. He managed the first quite swiftly, constructing a bungalow on the north coast that he named Goldeneye. Guests complained that the furniture was hard, the windows unglazed, the plumbing unpredictable and the food (cooked by his housekeeper Violet Cummings) even more so. The bedrooms were small, with cast-iron beds whose legs rested in saucers of water to keep ants at bay. Noël Coward, who built a house nearby, Firefly, thought it looked like a clinic and christened it 'Gold-eneye-nose-and-throat'. But it did have a small beach fringed by a coral reef over which Fleming hovered for hours on end with goggles and snorkel. His second goal, to become a thriller writer, would take a little longer. In the interim he found a job as Foreign Manager of the *Sunday Times*, instigating a news service called 'Mercury' that employed ex-intelligence personnel who provided information from every corner of the world but, most valuably, from the borders of the Iron Curtain.

He retained, too, many of his espionage contacts who kept him abreast of covert activities as the Cold War gradually unfolded. His journalistic assignments for the paper would later supply inspiration and background detail for many of the Bond novels.

The terms of his contract with press baron Lord Kemsley, who owned the *Sunday Times*, were extraordinarily lenient, allowing him two months holiday every winter in Goldeneye. So, in January he would fly to New York where he caught up with old acquaintances such as Sir William Stephenson, erstwhile head of British Intelligence in North America, plus his childhood friend Ivar Bryce, a charming but wilful millionaire based in Vermont.* And from there he would fly to Jamaica, where at Goldeneye he kept open house for his friends. Among them, in 1948, was Ann,† the wife of Esmond, 2nd Viscount Rothermere, proprietor of the *Daily Mail*. She and Fleming had been conducting an on-off affair since the 1930s and by 1951 they agreed that they were quite incompatible. Whereas Fleming preferred a coterie of close male friends such as Noël Coward, Somerset Maugham, Ivar Bryce and others (mostly from the golfing or London club fraternity), Ann was a saloniste who preferred the intellectual scene. She couldn't stand Fleming's hankering after nature, activity and the open air; and he was unable to abide what he considered to be her brittle lifestyle. On which understanding they agreed to marry.

'We are of course totally unsuited,' he wrote from Goldeneye to Ann's brother Hugo Charteris on 23 February 1952.

> I'm a non-communicator, a symmetrist, of a bilious and melancholic temperament, only interested in tomorrow. Ann is a sanguine anarchist/traditionalist.
>
> So china will fly and there will be rage and tears.
>
> But I think we will survive as there is no bitterness in either of us and we are both optimists – and I shall never hurt her except with a slipper.

* John F. C. 'Ivar' Bryce (1906–85), who married the American heiress Jo Hartford, had first met Fleming in 1917 on a beach holiday. They remained inseparable companions and would become involved in a variety of uncertain enterprises.

† Née Charteris, Ann was the widow of Lord O'Neill, who had been killed in the Second World War.

These are disjointed thoughts which I must now take into the grey valleys of the sea.

China did fly, and their marriage was never smooth. They were both unfaithful, Fleming could be particularly heartless at times, and it was perhaps only at the end that they reconciled their differences. In 1961 Fleming had a heart attack, and, although he maintained an outward appearance of vigour, mortality loomed. He became increasingly weak and died of a second heart attack in 1964 aged only fifty-six.

A short word about how this opusculum (to use one of Fleming's favourite words) has been arranged. Each chapter concentrates on a single Bond novel and follows the sequence in which they were written. To muddy the situation, however, Fleming also wrote a children's book and several non-fiction books whose creation spanned several years – *Chitty-Chitty-Bang-Bang*, for example, was written in 1961 but not published until 1964. Furthermore, Fleming's correspondence concerning one novel might well spread across the years when he was writing others and the more books he wrote the more this became the case. A few chronological hiccups are therefore inevitable.* As to content, some chapters are thinner while others are fuller depending on the material available (there is a particular dearth when it comes to *Thunderball*, possibly because the correspondence went missing during the legal wrangles that followed its publication). Letters *to* Fleming, as opposed to those *by* him have, with the exception of a few stand-alone sections that give both sides of the conversation, been restricted to those from his publishers and one or two close friends such as Noël Coward and Somerset Maugham, though the gist of other exchanges (where available) are supplied in the commentaries. As some of the archive material consists just of carbon copies, salutations (My Dear Michael, etc.) have been included only where they are known.

While the vagaries of Fleming's spelling have been standardised in the editorial text, these and other typewritten quirks have been retained in the letters themselves.

* A list of the works of Ian Fleming with dates of original publication can be found on page 379.

1

Casino Royale

'I REALLY CANNOT remember exactly why I started to write thrillers,' Fleming recalled in 1956. 'I was on holiday in Jamaica in January 1951* [. . .] and I think my mental hands were empty. I had finished organising a Foreign Service for Kemsley Newspapers and that tide of my life was free-wheeling. My daily occupation in Jamaica is spearfishing and under-water exploring, but after five years of it I didn't want to kill any more fish except barracudas and the rare monster fish and I knew my own under-water terrain like the back of my hand. Above all, after being a bachelor for 44 years, I was on the edge of marrying and the prospect was so hor-rifying that I was in urgent need of some activity to take my mind off it. So, as I say, my mental hands were empty and although I am as lazy as most Englishmen are, I have a Puritanical dislike of idleness and a natu-ral love of action. So I decided to write a book.'

Thus Fleming described the genesis of *Casino Royale*. His wife-to-be, Ann, put it more simply in her diary: 'This morning Ian started to type a book. Very good thing.'

Fleming liked to say that *Casino Royale* wrote itself, but in fact it was the product of hard work and discipline. Every morning, for three hours, he sat at his desk and typed 2,000 words. He then put the sheets of dou-ble-spaced foolscap aside, and took the afternoon off. He repeated the process the next day, and the next, until by 18 March the book was fin-ished. Occasionally he and Ann lit off on a spree: there was an outing to the Milk River Spa – 'the highest radio-activity of any mineral bath in

---

* Actually it was 1952.

the world', according to Fleming – and an abortive foray to shoot alliga-
tors at midnight when 'their red eyes shine in the moonbeams'. But he
always returned to the task. 'I rewrote nothing and made no corrections
until my book was finished,' he said. 'If I had looked back at what I had
written the day before I might have despaired at the mistakes in gram-
mar and style, the repetitions and the crudities. And I obstinately closed
my mind to self-mockery and "what will my friends say?" I savagely
hammered on until the proud day when the last page was done. The last
line "The bitch is dead now" was just what I felt. I had killed the job.'

He also killed his bachelordom. He and Ann were married on 24 March
1952, with little pomp and much hilarity in Port Maria. The ensuing festivi-
ties were dear to his heart, with copious amounts of goodwill from a select
guest list that included his neighbour Noël Coward. The evening was illu-
minated by Fleming's personal concoction: Old Man's Thing. (Take a glass
bowl. Peel, but do not break, an orange and a lime. Put them in the bowl,
add a bottle of white rum and light with a match.) The next day they flew to
Nassau and then New York for further celebrations. At the beginning of
April the newly-weds finally returned to London where they moved into
Fleming's Chelsea apartment, 24 Carlyle Mansions, to be joined by Ann's
children, Raymond and Fionn, plus a talking parrot called Jackie.

Amidst this new-found domesticity, Fleming pondered the manuscript. Compared to his later output *Casino Royale* had involved little
research and was taken from imagination and experience. It introduced
the world to agent 007, licensed to kill, whose first fictional mission was
to confront a Soviet agent, Le Chiffre, and bankrupt him at the gambling
tables of a small French resort named Royale-les-Eaux. The resort was
based on Deauville, which Fleming had often visited, and the idea of
bankruptcy by casino was one that he had deployed during the war in
neutral Portugal when he played against a Nazi operative in a futile
attempt to deplete the Abwehr's exchequer. There was drama, high-
explosives, cocktails, secret weaponry, a car chase, torture, a double-
agent heroine and, of course, the famous first line: 'The scent and smoke
and sweat of a casino are nauseating at three in the morning.' It was
exotic fare for readers in post-war austerity Britain, but what really made
it stand out was the immediacy and freshness of the writing.

Fleming was faintly appalled. 'I did nothing with the manuscript,' he wrote. 'I was too ashamed. No publisher would want it and if they did I would not have the face to see it in print. Even under a pseudonym, some-one would leak the ghastly fact that it was I who had written this adolescent tripe.' Instead he busied himself with publishing matters. As a wedding present his employer, Lord Kemsley, had appointed him Managing Director of a new imprint, Queen Anne Press. He delighted in the role. After a failed attempt to acquire an unpublished book by Proust, he turned to one of Ann's friends, the acerbic novelist Evelyn Waugh, who at first agreed to a collection of reviews called *Offensive Matters*, which Fleming suggested he embellish with 'a short introduction on the virtue of being offensive and the decline of the invective', but settled in the end for a discursion on the Middle East titled *The Holy Places*.* He also wrote to travel writer Patrick Leigh Fermor, whose study of monasticism, *A Time for Silence*, he published the following year. For both projects he used his wartime friend Robert Harling† as designer. Less successful was a proposal to his *Sunday Times* colleague Cyril Connolly that he produce a 10,000-word novella. In the same period he also acquired from Lord Kemsley *The Book Collector*, a respected but ailing magazine for bibliophiles which he ran with the assistance of Percy Muir, John Carter and John Hayward, the friend and muse of T. S. Eliot. The first issue under Fleming's stewardship was published by Queen Anne Press and came out that August.

Fleming was also distracted by matters of golf. He had long hankered after Noël Coward's recently vacated house White Cliffs in St Margaret's, near Dover. There was nothing exceptional about it: the wallpaper

---

* Waugh was not impressed when it came out later that year. 'Ian Fleming's idiot printing firm', as he described it, had made 'a great balls-up of a little book of mine.'

† Robert Harling (1910–2008), author, publisher and typographer. He had worked for the Admiralty during the Second World War and had been a member of Fleming's 'Red Indian' commando unit, 30AU, in the closing stages of the war. He later joined Fleming at the *Sunday Times*, as typographical adviser. Among his many typographical innovations was the font 'Tea Chest', which would become a hallmark of the Bond dust jackets.

was sun-stained, with dark patches where once there had been pictures, and repairs were needed where Coward had damaged the brickwork by removing a statue of Mercury. But it had a view of the sea, was in Fleming's favourite county, Kent, and most importantly was within easy reach of the Royal St George's, one of England's premier golf courses. After much bickering about damages he took the lease in mid-May. Only then did he muster the courage to do something with *Casino Royale*.

His approach was oblique. Over lunch at the Ivy restaurant with his friend William Plomer,* who happened also to be a reader for Jonathan Cape's publishing house, he asked him how to get cigarette smoke out of a woman once you had got it in. 'All right,' he said. 'This woman inhales, takes a deep lung full of smoke, draws deeply on her cigarette – anything you like. That's easy. But how do you get it out of her again? Exhales is a lifeless word. "Puffs it out" is silly. What can you make her do?'

Plomer, himself a novelist, looked at him sharply: 'You've written a book.' Fleming pooh-poohed the idea, saying it was hardly a book, merely a *Boy's Own Paper* story, but was grateful when Plomer asked to see the manuscript. All the same, it took several months and a reminder from Plomer before he actually sent it off. 'He forced Cape to publish it,' Fleming wrote. And it was true: although the decision was eventually carried by a majority, Plomer pushed it through in the face of strong opposition. Jonathan Cape disliked thrillers in general,[†] and his editorial director, Michael Howard, was repelled by this one in particular: 'I thought its cynical brutality, unrelieved by humour, revealed a sadistic fantasy that was deeply shocking.' Howard acquiesced with an uneasy conscience, and when he met Fleming in October forbore to mention that the very idea of being associated with its publication gave him sleepless nights.

Plomer would remain Fleming's mentor throughout his literary career, providing detailed and encouraging comments. Notwithstanding his first opinion, Michael Howard also came round to the notion

---

* William Plomer (1903–73), author, editor, poet and librettist. Born in South Africa, he travelled to Japan and beyond before settling in the drab environs of post-war London. He pronounced his name 'Ploomer'.

[†] Cape's only previous foray into thrillerdom had been James M. Cain's *The Postman Always Rings Twice* (1934).

of 007 – albeit his remarks were sharper and less generous than Plomer's. Together with Howard's father Wren (aka 'Bob'), Cape's other reader Daniel George, and briefly Cape's son David, they formed a group that Fleming called the Capians, or Bedfordians (Cape was based in Bedford Square) whose input and approval he trusted implicitly. He addressed some of his most lively correspondence to them and it is fair to say that without their input the Bond books would not have been as finely tuned as they were. Others who bore the brunt included Al Hart of Macmillan in New York, Tom Guinzburg of Viking and the long-suffering Naomi Burton, his agent on the East Coast.

Once accepted, Fleming threw himself into every detail of the book. He liked to joke that he was Cape's hardest working author, and to an extent this was true. He had made a career in journalism, ran a network of foreign correspondents and was, indeed, a publisher himself. There was little Cape could tell him that he didn't know already. 'I enjoyed his enthusiastic interest in the technicalities of production,' wrote Michael Howard with surprise – which soon turned to alarm when it became clear that Fleming had more in mind than simply delivering a manuscript. He designed the covers, organised reviews, invented sales tactics and cast a steely eye over the finances. At one point, to everyone's horror, he airily suggested he should take a stake in the company. It was an unorthodox approach that took some getting used to and would trouble Cape for as long as they published him.

Behind the confidence lay a measure of uncertainty. Fleming had always longed for success, but failing that would settle for the trappings. So, in anticipation, he ordered a gold-plated typewriter from New York to congratulate himself on finishing his first novel. It was a Royal Quiet de Luxe, cost $174, and to avoid customs duty it was smuggled in by his friend Ivar Bryce as part of his luggage when he visited on the *Queen Elizabeth* later that year. It wasn't a custom-made machine – Royal had produced several of them – and his literary acquaintances considered it the height of vulgarity. Fleming did not care. It was the sheer, ridiculous delight of the thing. He owned a Golden Typewriter!

The shiny prize arrived shortly after a milestone in his life: the birth of a son, Caspar, on 12 August 1952. For a short while he was uncertain how to spell Caspar (he wasn't very good with his wife's name either) but to have a family gave his life a dependability it had previously lacked.

By modern standards he was a distant parent, and by any reckoning he was an unreliable spouse: within a few years both he and Ann were conducting extra-marital affairs. Yet however tempestuous their relationship they did indeed love each other, and the fact of being both husband and father provided Fleming with a solid platform from which his imagination took flight for the next fourteen years.

TO IVAR BRYCE, ESQ., (address unknown)

In the early 1950s Ivar Bryce and his wife Jo made the transatlantic crossing four times a year and Fleming often asked them to smuggle items past customs. On one occasion, Bryce recalled, he wrote, 'Could you execute one chore for me? I badly need a .25 Beretta automatic and I can't find one in London. Could you pray purchase one in New York and bring it over in your left armpit?' In 1952, however, Bryce was detailed to carry a particularly important item.

May, 1952

Dear Ivar

Now here is one vital request. I am having constructed for me by the Royal Typewriter Company a golden typewriter which is to cost some 174 dollars. I will not bother for the moment to tell you why I am acquiring this machine. Claire Blanchard* has handled all the negotiations and I would be vastly indebted if you would advance her the necessary dollars for the machine and also be good enough to slip it in amongst your luggage, possibly wrapping it up in Jo's fur coat and hat!

TO NOËL COWARD, ESQ., Goldenhurst Farm, Nr. Aldington, Kent

After much to and fro about the state in which White Cliffs had been left, for which Fleming insisted that repairs would cost at least £100, Coward replied with an offer for £50. In the spirit of playful banter that marked their correspondence, he added the words: 'If you do not want it I can give you a few suggestions as to what to do with it when you come to lunch on Sunday.'

* A wartime intelligence operative and Fleming's one-time girlfriend, she now worked for the Kemsley Group in America.

15th May, 1952

Dear Messrs Noël Coward Incorporated,

The mixture of Scottish and Jewish blood which runs in my veins has been brought to the boil by your insolent niggardliness.

Only Ann's dainty hand has restrained me from slapping a mandamus on your meagre assets and flinging the charge of bottomry, or at least barratry, in your alleged face.

Pending the final advices of Mann, Rogers and Greaves, my solicitors, I shall expend your insulting 'pourboire' on a hunting crop and a Mills bomb and present myself at one o'clock exactly on Sunday morning at Goldenhurst.

I shall see what Beaverbrook* has to say about your behaviour at lunch today.

Tremble.

FROM JONATHAN CAPE, 30 Bedford Square, London w.c.1.

Writing to congratulate Fleming on the birth of Caspar, Cape was ambivalent about his new author's capabilities either as a parent or a writer. He had little interest in thrillers, believing them to be short-run phenomena that rarely covered their costs. Nor did he think much of their authors, and suspected that Fleming was a dilettante. Remarkably, Casino Royale *was the only Bond book he ever read.*

13th August, 1952

My dear Ian,

The Times this morning tells me of the good fortune that has come to you and to your wife with the birth of a son. My congratulations and best wishes. You have succeeded I should imagine brilliantly, and I hope and believe that you will be equally successful when you have done a

---

* William Maxwell Aitken, 1st Baron Beaverbrook (1879–1964), business tycoon, politician, press magnate and owner of the *Daily Express* which, for a while, had the largest circulation of any newspaper in the world.

thorough job of revising the MS which I have read and about which William [Plomer] is corresponding with you. You are entitled to a certain amount of congratulations on the MS at this stage and I look forward to you having as much success as a novelist as it would seem you are likely to have as a parent.

To which Fleming replied, more or less cheerfully, on 16 August:

My dear Jonathan,

It was very kind of you to have sent me such a charming note on the birth of my son, but it was not so friendly of you to commit me to such a heavy holiday task.

The story was written in less than two months as a piece of manual labour which would make me forget the horrors of marriage. It would never have seen the light of day if William had not extracted it from me by force.

However, in view of your interest I am now at work on it with a pruning and tuning fork and we will see what it looks like in a week or two. At the present moment it is indeed a dog's breakfast and I am ashamed that William passed on to you such a very rough and slovenly version.

Already the corpses of split infinitives and a host of other grammatical solecisms are lying bloody on the floor.

We will see.

Again with many thanks for your note.

On the same day he wrote to Ann, using his golden typewriter.

My love

This is only a tiny letter to try out my new typewriter and to see if it will write golden words since it is made of gold.

As you see, it will write at any rate in two colours which is a start, but it has a thing called a MAGIC MARGIN which I have not yet mastered so the margin is a bit crooked. My touch just isn't light enough I fear.

You have been wonderfully brave and I am very proud of you. The doctors and nurses all say so and are astonished you were so good about all the dreadful things they did to you. They have been simply shuffling you and dealing you out and then shuffling again. I do hope darling Kaspar [sic] has made it up to you a little. He is the most heavenly child and I know he will grow up to be something wonderful because you have paid for him with so much pain.

Goodnight my brave sweetheart.

TO JONATHAN CAPE

Following a meeting with Jonathan Cape, Fleming outlined the contract as far as he understood it. Wren Howard, who had little time for such impertinence from an author whom he privately considered a 'bounder', added his comments [in square brackets] for Cape's attention.

18th September, 1952

Dear Jonathan,

It was very nice of you to be so patient with me yesterday and here is a note of the points I think we covered.

1) <u>Royalties</u>

10 per cent on 1 to 10,000;

15 per cent on 10,000 to 15,000;

17½ per cent on 15,000 to 20,000;

20 per cent thereafter.

If you are feeling in a more generous mood today, for symmetry's sake you might care to include 12½ per cent on the 5,000 to 10,000, but I will not be exigent. *[NO]*

2) <u>Print</u>

A first print of 10,000 copies.

I hope this figure will not give you sleepless nights. You may be interested to know that Nicolas Bentley's first thriller, "The Tongue-Tied

Canary," published by Michael Joseph in 1949 – a very moderate and conventional work – sold 13,000 and is still selling. *[It is pointless & most surely unnecessary imposition upon publisher in recent circs & in a falling paper market & with quick facilities for reprint. Especially in view of point 11, I should decline.]*

3. <u>American Publication</u>

I suggest that our efforts in this direction should be mutual, but whether I am successful or you are, the publisher will receive 10 per cent of all monies resulting. *[OK]*

4. <u>Serial Rights and Film and Theatre Rights</u>

The same applies as with the American rights. *[First serials, certainly, but we want joint control over 2nd sers.]*

5. <u>Television, Broadcasting Rights, etc.</u>

The same applies. *[and after joint control]*

6. <u>Advertisement and Promotion</u>

I hope you would agree to consulting with me on the text of anything you publish regarding the book. *[May be quite impracticable if he is e.g. in Bermuda]*

7. <u>Design</u>

I will submit some designs for a jacket and for the binding of the book (conforming with your very high standards), to which I hope you would give sympathetic consideration. *[yes, but NO MORE]*

8. <u>Blurbs</u>

I will submit text for the inside flap and biographical material and a photograph for the back of the wrapper. *[OK]*

9. <u>Publication Date</u>

Shall we aim at 15th April? (The "Royale" in the title may help to pick up some extra sales over the coronation period). *[RATS]*

10) <u>Copies For Personal Use</u>

For the fun of it and to make useful copy for gossip paragraphs, etc., I would like to suggest that I toss your secretary double or quits on the trade price for any additional personal copies I may require. (The odds will be exactly even for either side!) *[OK up to Dep.]*

11 <u>Next Book</u>

I would prefer to make my decision on this when the time comes, but all things being equal naturally I would first submit my manuscript to you. *[See under (2) above]*

12 <u>Proofs</u>

I shall return to you my corrected manuscript within a week and it would be most helpful if proofs could be forthcoming as soon as convenient thereafter and if I could have three spare copies, since I shall have an early opportunity of having it read in Hollywood. *[OK]*

13 <u>Page Proofs</u>

As I shall be going to New York about 15th January, would there be any possibility of having page proofs available by then? *[possibly]*

I do hope you won't find any of these suggestions unreasonable since I am only actuated by the motives of:

a) making as much money for myself and my publishers as possible out of the book; and

b) getting as much fun as I personally can out of the project.

Finally, I am sincerely delighted that you are to be my publisher and I hope we will both enjoy the adventure.

P.S. I return William's report which doesn't give me many hints on improving my style.

Presumably this means it is already impeccable.

TO JONATHAN CAPE

29th September, 1952

Dear Jonathan,

Many thanks for your letter of September 22nd, although it casts rather a cold douche on my adventurous spirit.

I suggested a first printing of ten thousand because it was a figure you agreed to when we discussed the point.

My own feeling is that the life of a book of this sort is not long, and that it is most important to make the maximum use of any initial impulse it may get from reviews.

For various reasons this book should be reviewed far more heavily than most and I am naturally anxious that this send-off should not be wasted.

I agree with you that sale or return is not satisfactory, but I think we can rely on Smith's displaying the book well, which I expect you will agree is very important.

Anyway, when the time comes I am sure you will be as anxious as I to get another edition printed very quickly if the initial reception appears to be favourable.

On the subject of American publication, Harcourt Brace are very anxious to see the manuscript, as a result of their Mr Reynal hearing of it from a friend of mine.

Assuming that Scribners are not the right publishers for it in Jamaica, do you think Harcourt Brace would be right? I am not quite clear why serial and film rights should be handled through your office. What is the object of this? And I am not quite clear what "joint control" means in your paragraph five.

Personally, I should have thought that a flat 10% to the publisher on all rights would be fair.

I don't want to have to employ an agent,* although I am everywhere advised to do so and, for the sake of happy relations between us and an

---

* He did, however, employ Naomi Burton of Curtis Brown agents on the East Coast of America who successfully placed *Casino Royale* with Macmillan in New York.

absence of subsequent argument, I hope you will agree to a round figure.

Regarding your paragraph six, whether I am in England or not, I am constantly available by cable through my office.

I should think I will be back in England by about March 20th. Will that allow sufficient time for arranging reviews, etc. if publication date is April 15th?

Perhaps we should discuss this point before I leave for Jamaica.

I shall look forward to tossing for the eighteen copies, and I only hope your Trade Manager is as pretty as your secretary!

About the next book, so be it.

So far as our contract is concerned, I shall ask you to sign this with the company which owns the copyright and other rights of this book and I will send you its name in a few days' time.

I am this company and will be signing for the company, so it is merely a question of adjusting the wording of the contract.*

TO JONATHAN CAPE

20th October, 1952

Dear Jonathan,

If you don't think my chapter headings are terribly old-fashioned, I will do my best to provide some when I can get my duplicate typescript back. Unfortunately Paul Gallico† has borrowed it with Hollywood in mind and I shall probably not see it back before the end of the week.

I am not in favour of reducing the price of the book to 10/6d. Hardly a novel is published today under 12/6d. and I think it would be a mistake for your first "thriller" to seem to be given away. Moreover, it would

---

* For tax reasons, and perhaps with a canny eye to the future, Fleming transferred the copyright in his work to a company called Glidrose.
† Paul Gallico (1897–1976), novelist and sportswriter. One of Fleming's many journalistic contacts, he had won international fame for his novella *The Snow Goose* (1941).

whittle down still further my already meagre financial expectations from the book.

I have designed a jacket of exquisite symmetry and absolute chastity and I am using my visual features studio here to prepare the finished product which should be ready today. When it is I will speak to Michael Howard.

I bet your other authors don't work as hard for you as I do.

TO JONATHAN CAPE

21st October, 1952

Dear Jonathan,

I have arranged to see Michael Howard on Friday afternoon and in the meantime here is a possible jacket.

I think the idea is good, namely that the nine of hearts which plays such an important part in the book should provide the basic design and that the meaning of this card in gypsy lore should appear somewhere, as it is also perhaps appropriate to the general theme of the book. I also like the colour scheme.

On the other hand, the hearts as shown are a little too lush and perhaps too heavily outweigh the Fry's Decorated which I have used for the type.[*]

I have shown it to Leonard Russell[†] who is delighted with it, but suggests that the title should be made much stronger and the hearts correspondingly reduced. We both think the ribbon design round the central heart could be improved.

I have also found the original draft of the book and have done some chapter headings from it. On the whole I think your idea of using them is a good one.

[*] The font came to Fleming's notice thanks to his friend Robert Harling who had used it for the Queen Anne Press colophon.
[†] Leonard Russell (1906–74), Literary Editor of the *Sunday Times*. Married to journalist and author Dilys Powell.

TO JONATHAN CAPE

29th October, 1952

Paul Gallico asked to read the manuscript and here is his verdict which he has sent from Rome:-

"The book is a knockout. I thought I had written a couple of pretty fair torture scenes in my day, but yours beats anything I ever read. Wow!

It's a swell thriller, and I am confirmed in what I told you at the Savoy that it is more than just a thriller and deserves a better publisher than just one known for the thriller-type of book. I am now talking of U.S. publishers. It goes in frankness and detail far beyond any American-type thriller and could have a big sale.

May I write to Swanson* in Hollywood about it? I can tell him from earnest conviction that here is a rip-snorter which would make a mar-vellous movie. No-one has EVER had the bright idea to couple gambling with espionage and economic sabotage and this gimmick of yours would film marvellously. Yeow, what tensions can be built up for that game of baccarat. It's a hell of a scene and you've done a first-class job. My heart-felt congratulations. Get out of that office, kid, and write because you can.

Am returning the MSS to you under separate cover."

Perhaps you will find this encouraging.

If you agree, I suggest we choose Harcourt Brace as the first pos-sible American publisher. Is there any news of their Mr Reynal arriving?

I had a most helpful conversation with your excellent Mr Michael Howard and I am falling in with his various suggestions for the jacket and so forth.

I very much like the specimen pages and I am much impressed that page proofs can be expected within a few weeks.

* 'Swanee' Swanson was Fleming's West Coast agent in the US.

TO MICHAEL HOWARD, 30 Bedford Square, London, W.C.1.

Casino Royale came out on 13 April (not, as Fleming had hoped, on 15 April to coincide with the coronation of Queen Elizabeth II), an Easter launch that would set the pattern for all future Bond books. The first print run of 5,000 copies sold out within a month, and as Cape geared up for a second run of 2,000 (which went equally swiftly) Fleming exhorted them to print even more.

22nd April, 1953

Dear Mr Howard,

In the course of the innumerable editions of "Casino Royale" which will now, I presume, flow from your presses, could you please correct a rather attractive misprint on page 96, line 13, and make the "Ace of Spaces" into the "Ace of Spades"?

Incidentally, although I know this won't wring anybody's withers, a friend of mine told me this afternoon that he had tried three bookshops, including Hatchards, and that they had all run out of the book.

Of course, it is better this way than that their shelves should be bulging with unsaleable dozens but, as I told Jonathan, obviously it is no good getting plenty of reviews if the book is not available.

So please tell Jonathan with my compliments, that he might as well swallow his pride and print the 10,000 he originally said he would.

TO JONATHAN CAPE

3rd June, 1953

Dear Jonathan,

Thank you very much for your letter of May 29th.

I am very surprised to hear you have already spent £200 on advertising "Casino Royale". Could you tell me how this is accounted for, as I have only seen two solus advertisements and brief mention amongst other Cape books.

Regarding further advertising, I simply don't think it is fair to ask me to go fifty-fifty.

I accepted your cut in my royalties under 10,000 copies. I accepted your reduction in the price of the book. And I accepted the fact that you halved the print from the original 10,000 agreed.

Is it not now your turn to be generous, particularly as you say in your letter of May 14th that you think that the splash of advertising might now be useful?

Regarding the next book, I am having twenty-percents dangled in front of my eyes from another quarter which has not even read the manuscript. I expect this is what usually happens in the publishing world when a new author has an initial success, but it will be obvious to you that I cannot ignore such terms if I intend to make money out of writing books.

To be specific, I have in mind 15% to 5,000 copies, and 20% thereafter.

Perhaps we could have a final discussion on the problem before I leave on June 11th.

TO JONATHAN CAPE

9th June, 1953

Dear Jonathan,

Many thanks for your letter of June 8th, and I am so sorry that the doctors are trying to get their claws on you. Personally I should have said that you were as strong as the Cape of Good Hope, and I am sure they will also agree with me after examining the structure.

Thank you very much for the details of the "Casino" advertising. As to the future, I will be happy to put up £60 if you will put up £140.

If this is acceptable to you, perhaps some sort of a scheme and some text could be prepared to try and get the book moving again before everyone goes away in August.

Regarding the new book, I am terribly sorry but I am afraid I must remain adamant on 15% to 5000 and 20% thereafter. I would certainly agree to you having the first offer of the subsequent book, but I could not commit my muse further than that.

I shall quite understand if you feel that these terms are not acceptable to your firm, and I can assure you that there will be no hard feelings on my side if you turn them down.

With very best wishes for an early escape from the London Clinic, where I can only tell you there was one pretty nurse in 1935. Alas, she will be twenty years older by now, but perhaps there are some new recruits.

TO JONATHAN CAPE

6th October, 1953

Many thanks for your royalty report for CASINO ROYALE.

In due course would you please ask the Accountant to make these and all other future cheques out in the name of Glidrose Productions Limited and send them to me at 16 Victoria Square.*

Incidentally, I must come over sometime and toss your Sales Manager double or quits on those extra copies, and see if I can't reduce the debt balance by a few shillings.

FROM JONATHAN CAPE

21st October, 1953

Dear Ian,

I understand that you and Michael Howard matched each other on Friday afternoon to see who should pay for the first eighteen copies of CASINO ROYALE which you bought. I haven't heard where the gambling took place, but it would be fitting if it was in the Café Royal, but as it was in the afternoon it would probably be the wrong time. I hope such an operation, which is entirely against my principles, did not take place in

* The London home to which he and Ann had recently moved.

the hallowed precincts of Thirty Bedford Square! I don't know on what basis you were tossing, but Michael tells me that it resulted in a cost to you of eight more copies than you actually had. It has been suggested by Michael Howard that you and David [Cape] might have a poker game when it comes to charging your copies of LIVE AND LET DIE.* I am as much against this as I am against any other form of gambling. It goes entirely against my Quaker origins. However, I realise that time moves on and things are not what they were. O tempore! O mores!

TO JONATHAN CAPE

28th October, 1953

When I think how you fought against my suggestion that I should toss your firm double or quits for the author's copies of CASINO, I wonder you are not ashamed to accept those eight copies!

There is something mysterious about the way the law of averages was set at naught in the office of Michael Howard, and the next time I come over to your gaming rooms in Bedford Square I shall bring my own coin.

TO AL HART, The Macmillan Company, New York

Al Hart, Fleming's editor at Macmillan,† was concerned about the book's more explicit passages.

27th November, 1953

On the whole you have been kinder to me than Naomi [Burton]. We had a splendid argument about the relative impropriety attached to the front and back of a woman. She was sweet but firm and I have been as pliant in her shapely hands as I have been in your calloused ones.

It was fine to see you and to take up so much of your time to get answers to my idle questions.

---

* Fleming's second Bond novel, which he had delivered that spring.

† Macmillan would publish all the Bond novels until Fleming moved to Viking in 1959.

Alas, I shall only be in New York for, at the most, three days in January, but I will get in touch and hand over the strings of my promotion machine.

TO AL HART

7th December, 1953

Many thanks for your note and in return I am making you a present of the attached letter from Paul Gallico who, as you can see, gives us two or three splendid quotes, of which "the best gambling thriller I have ever read" and "fabulously exciting" seem the most desirable words.

I also enclose for you to retain the letters to members of my "apparatus".

I have addressed these where I was able to do so but perhaps your secretary could fill in the gaps.

These are intended to be retained by you and then forwarded with a copy of the book to the addresses early in March or as appropriate.

I fancy most of them will come off so I hope you will ensure that the machine doesn't start working until there are sufficient copies on the bookstalls, since I imagine that in America as here people's memories are apt to be short. I should be sending you on another one to the News Week people in a day or so.

I am sure you have never had an author who takes so much trouble over such a puny masterpiece!

I am longing to see a proof of the cover which sounds most exciting. Alas, I shall not now be coming through in January so it would be angelic if you would put one into the post for me.

You are very lucky indeed having a newspaper strike and I only hope you don't have a bookstall strike around March.

TO N. LINGEMAN, ESQ., 14 Eaton Terrace, S.W.1.

'Being entirely bi-lingual,' wrote Mr Lingeman, 'I feel like starting a private war against the all too prevalent use of incorrect French terms in English writing.' He raised several matters, one of which concerned a gangster who said 'Allez!' instead of 'Allez-y!' or the more colloquial 'Vas-y!'. Separately,

he wanted to know if Fleming had worked alongside William Stephenson* *during the war.*

18th January, 1956

Thank you very much for your letter of January 15th and I am delighted that you and your wife enjoyed the books.

I quite agree with you about accuracy in foreign languages and I pride myself on being a stickler on all matters of factual detail. It did occur to me to write "allez-y" but I thought this a trifle prosy in the mouth of this tough character. I thought he would dispense with the "y" and just bark out the one word. Perhaps I was wrong but I gave thought to the question.

Yes, I was a frequent visitor to Rockefeller Centre during the war. As a matter of fact I am flying off to New York this afternoon and shall be seeing "Little Bill" tomorrow or the next day.

TO F. A. TAYLOR, ESQ., Landfall, Instow, Nr. Bideford, N. Devon

Another francophone reader wrote to advise Fleming that, rather vitally, he *had got the title wrong.*

3rd April, 1959

Thank you for taking the trouble to write to me and I can see you are a stickler for the French language.

So am I.

The points you make are legitimate but, to take "Casino Royale" first, the name of the town was Royale les Eaux and the owners decided to use the final 'e' so as to identify the casino with its town. This was deliberate.

Crime de la Crime was said by an illiterate gangster and is a clumsy joke of his on the expression Crème de la Crème. If he had said crime du crime it would have meant equally little and the joke would not have come off.

But thank you nevertheless for the mild rap over the knuckles.

---

* Sir William Stephenson (1897–1989), Canadian soldier, aviator, businessman, inventor and spymaster. Colloquially, 'Little Bill' as against 'Big Bill' Donovan, head of the US Secret Service. He had first met Fleming while head of British Intelligence in North America and their friendship continued after the war. Fleming liked to say that whereas Bond was a romanticised version of a spy, Stephenson was the real thing.

2

Live and Let Die

'YOU SHOULD CLEAR a wide space round January 16th–20th and write the dates in toothpaste on your shaving mirror,' Fleming told his friend Ivar Bryce. 'We shall be flying over and then taking the Silver Meteor on the night of the 20th to St Petersburg, Florida, where I want to inspect a live worm factory. We then fly from Tampa to Jamaica.' Work on the second Bond novel had begun in earnest.

Fleming was on a roll at the start of 1953. His marriage was still fresh, he had an infant son and the family had recently moved into a new London home, 16 Victoria Square. He was holding down a steady job at the *Sunday Times*. He ran his own publishing company, Queen Anne Press. And, best of all, in James Bond he had found an outlet for both his imagination and his restless ambition.

The novelist Michael Arlen had advised him not to hesitate: 'write your second book before you see the reviews of the first. *Casino Royale* is good but the reviewers may damn it and take the heart out of you.' Heeding his words, Fleming completed *Live and Let Die* before its predecessor had even been published. As with *Casino Royale*, he wrote it in his Jamaican home, Goldeneye, and did so with such discipline that he managed to cram it into the gaps of his wife's busy social calendar. The island was awash with literary and artistic grandees that year, but while Fleming could handle a certain amount of socialising he resented any disruption to his writing schedule. Not only did Ann's father and his new wife come to stay, but so did the artist Lucian Freud who arrived in pursuit of his latest inamorata armed with little more than a ten shilling note. His capital being deemed insufficient by the port authorities, he was permitted entry only on Fleming's intervention.

'Ian's temper quite remarkable considering the heat and provocation,' Ann wrote to Evelyn Waugh after they had stood surety for Freud to get through immigration. She described their stay as 'a time of sunshine, black slaves, and solitude save for occasional intrusions by celebrities'. Their friend Peter Quennell,* who wasn't there, imagined it more accurately: 'The Commander groans quietly under the horror of his unwanted guests.' Nevertheless, Fleming typed on resolutely and when he and Ann returned to London in March he had the first draft in his briefcase.

As against *Casino Royale*, a novel that he wrote from memory and the soul, *Live and Let Die* was a professional affair. Set in New York, Florida and Jamaica, its plot centred on the smuggling of pirate treasure and had at its heart Mr Big, a Jamaican gangster working for the Soviet Union, who used voodoo rituals to enforce his reign of terror. Agent 007 was despatched to investigate. Moving from the nightclubs of Harlem, to the swamps of Florida, to the Jamaican lair of Mr Big, the book glittered with exoticism. It included Felix Leiter, Bond's stalwart CIA ally, who was thrown into a shark tank before being returned, half-dead, with the warning note 'He disagreed with something that ate him'. It also featured 'Solitaire', the latest in a series of beautiful women whom 007 would rescue from jeopardy.† The final scene, in which Bond successfully planted a limpet mine on Mr Big's boat, before he and Solitaire were dragged behind a paravane across coral reefs, to be saved at the last moment by the mine's detonation, was a masterpiece of sensation.

The book was researched with a diligence that would become Fleming's hallmark. He had already explored Harlem's nightlife on a trip to America in December 1952; information on gold doubloons and Spanish treasure was supplied by Spink, London's premier coin dealers; and the scenes in Florida were taken from his own visit at the beginning of 1953. (As he wrote on the flyleaf of his personal copy, with an ill-disguised

* Peter Quennell (1905–93), biographer and man of letters.
† It would not, however, always be a matter of jeopardy. Fleming's female characters were often a match for his hero.

shudder, 'St Petersburg [Florida] is just like I say it is'.) Jamaica, mean-while, was all around him.

Although Fleming spent much of his time swimming the coral reefs off Goldeneye, the underwater sequences in *Live and Let Die* were given verisimilitude by a *Sunday Times* assignment shortly after his return to Britain. On 5 April 1953 Ann wrote to Evelyn Waugh: 'we are going on a secret mission to France for the next two weeks.' The 'secret mission' was a fortnight with Jacques Cousteau who was investigating a Greek galley that had sunk in 250 BC off a small island near Marseilles. Cousteau was a daredevil after Fleming's own heart. The father of scuba diving, and an indefatigable exponent of underwater exploration, he had a Gallic sense of style – his ship, *Calypso*, contained a one-ton stainless steel vat of wine from which each crew member drew at least a pint per day. The assignment excited Fleming tremendously, particularly when he persuaded Cousteau to let him join one of the dives. From a depth of twenty-five fathoms, while rescuing artefacts untouched for almost 2,000 years, he looked up through his mask at the sky. He saw the mercury ceiling of the sea, through which shone a bead of sapphire that was the sun and 'wished I had done something like this before'.

A couple of months later, again working for the *Sunday Times*, he was at Creake Abbey in Norfolk with a team of Royal Engineers where, by accounts, he was the first person to use a mine detector (ERA No. 1, Mark 2, to be precise) as a tool for finding buried treasure. After a long, hot day that turned up thirty nails, a frying pan, an oil drum and a hundredweight of scrap iron he abandoned the search. He wasn't bothered: it was the adventure that mattered. Quoting Mark Twain, he wrote, '"There comes a time in every rightly constructed boy's life when he has a raging desire to go somewhere and dig for buried treasure,". . . In me that particular boy has never died.'

August saw him in the French Pyrenees with pot-holer Norbert Casteret at the gulf of the Pierre St Martin cave. Casteret had made his name as a cave explorer in the 1920s and 1930s, and although in his sixties was still going strong. His day job was Public Notary, which probably influenced the single, cautious quote Fleming got out of him: 'The whole affair is very dangerous.' Six thousand feet above sea level, the

Pierre St Martin cave lay in a spot which Fleming described as 'mile-wide stony amphitheatre that might have been blasted by an atom bomb'. The place was not only desolate, but had a bad history. One of Casteret's colleagues, Marcel Loubens, had fallen 1,000 feet to his death the previous year when his cable snapped. Casteret's 1953 expedition achieved a record depth of 728 metres and opened about a mile and a half of new passages, but was unable to retrieve Loubens' body. They commemorated him with a cross of phosphorescent paper and an inscription on the cavern wall. 'It was the impression of this knowledge,' Fleming wrote, 'the awareness of the puny bodies enclosed in the mammoth viscera of this mountain that awoke in most of us, as we sat comfortably above on the surface of the world in the bright light among the Alpine flowers, a deep loathing for this great cave.'

If he had no love for 'this gloomy antechamber to Hell', the experience still stirred his sense of wonder. And wonder, alongside adventure, was what sparked his writing. But of the year's events what really caught him was the devotion Cousteau commanded from his team. 'Each dive is a new adventure,' said one man. 'And we will go anywhere with the Commandant.' It was a perfect description of Bond's attitude towards M – also of the relationship between Bond and his creator.

By now Fleming had established a routine that would set the pattern for his career. In January and February he wrote a novel at Goldeneye; over the following months he addressed Cape's editorial points, while checking details and maybe doing more research; and towards the end of the year he reviewed the proofs. By this time he had amassed enough material for a new book and when he flew to Jamaica the creative process started anew.

TO JONATHAN CAPE

Fleming was so intrigued by Cousteau's expedition that he skipped Casino Royale's *launch on 13 April 1953 in favour of a trip to the Mediterranean. He subsequently spent several weeks in France. But when he came home he wasted no time telling Cape what to do with the commodity he had on his hands.*

8th May, 1953

Since you are the best publisher in England, and I am said to be the best thriller writer since Eric Ambler, I feel it would be very unadventurous if we did not set our sights high!

We certainly seem to have got off to a good start – I seem to have hit on a formula which attracts the critics, and you have produced a handsome book and have marketed it superbly.

I am, of course, delighted and I willingly accept the fact that my income from this first book will be slight.

But one does not often score a grand slam with the reviewers, and I think it most unlikely that I will ever do so again, and I am wondering whether we would not be well advised to spend some of the profits we have made on this book on advertising it solus.

I am perfectly prepared to bear a fair proportion of the cost, and I am by no means suggesting that your profits should be milked for my benefit alone, but I do think we have some very good ammunition which it would be a pity to waste if I am to progress into the Cheyney class,* which is presumably our ambition.

Please do not say to me "I have heard that record before". The field of thriller writers is extremely bare. There is a vacuum to be filled and I really do not see why we should not fill it. I shall be giving my next one to William Plomer next Tuesday, and I have a plot for a third in my head. So you will see that I am a very willing horse and I am only hoping that my stable will show an equal zest!

Shyly I enclose a draft of the sort of advertisement which I think would push the book far enough to create a really fine platform for the next one. When the sales start to droop, or whenever you think appropriate, should we not have a modest solus campaign using something on these lines?

There are no more good reviews to come. Despite certain complications, I think the "Mail" will mention it briefly and, if I can catch Max

* Reginald Evelyn Peter Southouse Cheyney (1896–1951), British crime writer. His hard-boiled American-style novels were enormously popular in their day. In 1946 alone he sold more than 1,500,000 copies worldwide.

Beaverbrook in the right mood, he may do something, but we have now cleaned up on the leading serious book critics.

Everything you say about books following their own course and so forth is obviously true about anything in the class of THE CAINE MUTINY, but that is a solid work in the great tradition and will go on selling for years. This thriller business is a fly-by-night affair – a light-weight read with a probable selling of around 10,000 copies, unless it can be pushed into the Cheyney class.

Whether this can be done with your servant's works in the next year or two remains to be seen, but these astonishingly handsome reviews do, I think, weigh the odds sufficiently in our favour to have a go at the best seller stakes.

The Defence rests!

TO JONATHAN CAPE

A week later, having secured the offer of a three-book deal, Fleming threw emol-lience to the winds and told Cape what he thought of him and his royalties.

15th May, 1953

I am very mystified by your writing paper. Why does your typist have to type "from Jonathan Cape" over the address each time? And why don't you have this warning engraved into the letter-head? However –

Alas, I cannot manage lunch on Wednesday. I am taking the day off to joust in the Old Etonian Golfing Society's Annual meeting.

But perhaps I could come round at some convenient time – What about Tuesday afternoon? – when you could summon your cohorts, and we could all confer. Please let me know if this would suit.

It is very nice of you to offer me a contract for three future books and, in principle, I would like to be tied to your apron strings. I have had two tempting flies thrown over me obliquely by publishers who go in for this sort of book, and I would be much happier if I were out of temptation.

But, only yesterday, I was talking to a Cape author rather younger than myself, who had been granted a flat 20% on his <u>first</u> book with you.

This was a severe blow to my "amour propre", which could only be healed by someone acting with equal generosity towards my own productions.*

The truth is that in order to free myself to write more books for you, I simply must earn more money from them. My profits from "Casino" will just about keep Ann in asparagus over Coronation week, and I am praying that something may be forthcoming from one of the reprint societies, or the films, to offset my meagre returns from what has turned out to be a successful book.

This is not a moan, or a petty display of ingratitude for your splendid handling of the book. It is just the usual statement of the author's point of view.

Thank you for your helpful suggestions on the question of advertising. I am sure a careful campaign will be helpful to both of us. Would it really be fair for me to pay 50% of the cost? A comparison of our respective profits on a sale of, say, 10,000 copies, might, I hope, suggest to you that the ratio could be more generous to the author.

Whether we go for the higher, or lower, figure, I must leave to your judgement and your views on the whole question of advertising this type of book.

Michael Joseph's [the publisher] remarks the other day were rather negative on this point!

When we meet, do you think we could examine suggested campaigns on the two levels, and your proposed text for the campaign?

I think the media we should include are THE BRIDGE WORLD or whichever is the leading card players' journal, with a good solus position in THE FINANCIAL TIMES. The latter might be very helpful, but we would need to stock up the City booksellers before it appeared. If they appeared reluctant, perhaps we could venture to supply them on a "Sale or return" basis.

---

* The book in question was *Eastern Approaches* by Fitzroy Maclean (1911–96), author, soldier and politician. A friend of Fleming, who served as a commando during the Second World War and later wrote knowledgeably about espionage, Maclean has since entered the list of characters upon whom Bond is supposed to have been based.

Although you may not know it, the name of my family firm in the City, Robert Fleming & Company, has magical properties.

THE MOTOR or THE AUTOCAR might also be useful if we plugged the motor-chase. Their readers eat this sort of stuff up.

Finally, I hope you think all these suggestions are helpful and that you do not despise this extra shoulder behind the wheel of this and future books.

But I do hope you will sympathise with my financial aspirations which, I am afraid, are serious.

FROM WILLIAM PLOMER, 29 Linden Gardens W.2.

On the same day Fleming castigated Cape for his niggardliness William Plomer put the following critique of Live and Let Die *in the post.*

15th May, 1953

My Dear Ian,

The new book held this reader like a limpet-mine & the denouement was shattering. I have had palpitations & "tensions" from the moment I began the story & they show no sign of diminishing now that I've finished it.

If I'm any judge, this is <u>just the stuff</u> – sexy, violent, ingenious – most ingenious – & full of well-collected detail of all kinds. The Harlem nightclub – the scene of the fight among the fish-tanks – & the excellent stuff about St Petersburg, Fla. – these are among the things I enjoyed best. Obviously you'll have to go through the typescript with your fine-tooth-comb for superficial grooming, e.g. I think you oughtn't to use a word like "feral" or an expression like "sensual mouth" more than <u>once</u> in a book of this length.

What I particularly like is the Bond's-eye-view of America. It is very rare nowadays to get any kind of book with fresh observation of the ordinary or extraordinary details of American life by an English eye. The whole thing is done with great dash & one believes in it most of the time as one believes in a highly disturbing dream. I shall now put in a glowing report on it, & I hope there won't be too much Wet Blanketry in other quarters. It is now high time you got busy on the *next* book. . .

Live and Let Die seems to me just the title for this one – better than Paravane Lost, for instance.

There will be a heavy mortality among your "oldster" readers, from sheer agitation – I speak as an oldster myself, with one foot in the bone-yard. Meanwhile I take off my hat to the Supersonic Buchan.

Wm.

FROM JONATHAN CAPE

24th July, 1953

Dear Ian,

The matter of the agreement for THE UNDERTAKER'S WIND* seems to have been hung up. However, here is an agreement which I think you will find satisfactory. The riders which are typed in and attached will need to be initialled by you, also the deleted clauses. So will you besprinkle this with your initials, or get whoever signs on behalf of Glidrose to do so, sign the agreement and return to me. I will then send you a duplicate carrying my signature, and also duly initialled.

Publishing for you has its particularly interesting side. This agreement, and the one for CASINO ROYALE, will serve as historical exhibits when in a hundred years' time the Editor produces a new edition of Mumby's history of PUBLISHING AND BOOKSELLING.

Conning over your proposed agreement with The Macmillan Company [in the USA], I was interested to see the very modest scale of royalties which you are evidently prepared to accept from your American

---

* Fleming's working title, *The Undertaker's Wind* (named after the Jamaican term for a strong evening breeze), was eventually consigned to a chapter head. He tried several alternatives before settling on *Live and Let Die*.

publishers. Perhaps it is not so easy to be tough at three thousand miles distance, and working through an agent.

To which Fleming gave a tart response on 29 July: 'Yes, the royalties I accepted from Macmillans were very modest but then they have given me a present of $750 which is rather more, I guess, than I shall recoup on the English edition. If it is a success in America you will be surprised how tough I shall be over "Live and Let Die"!'

TO D. J. CROWTHER, ESQ., Messrs. Spink & Son Ltd., 5–7 King Street, St. James's, S.W.1.

29th July, 1953

I am very sorry to trouble you again with my light-hearted affairs but I am afraid the names of the coins you chose for me will, after all, not fit in. The dates are wrong, due to a slip of my own.

Would you be very kind and choose me four more with the following characteristics: romantic or exciting names; gold, worth to the collector between £10 and £20; and minted between about 1550 and 1650. There should definitely be one minted around 1650.

In fact I could really use the ones you gave me if you will add to the number a suitable coin minted around 1650.

Please forgive me for bothering you like this. Your reward will be a thriller containing everything except the kitchen sink.

TO GEORGE H. HAWKES, ESQ., "Truth" and "Sportsman" Ltd., Keystone House, Red Lion Court, Fleet Street, E.C.4.

Hawkes was the London representative of an Australian magazine publisher. Australia had recently hosted an atom-bomb test which, along with the toxic aftermath of the Korean War, may have led Fleming to suggest his books were an antidote to 'the future of the world'. No less pertinent was his mention of America's racial tensions.

22nd March, 1954

Thank you very much for your letter of the 19th, and I am delighted that you like the book. From all accounts it is just what people want in order to keep their minds off the future of the world!

The American rights have sold handsomely, which is rather remarkable as they generally fight very shy of anything touching the colour problem, however remotely, and they don't generally like to accept "Americanese" used by English writers.

I should think it's just the stuff for your full-blooded readers and because of my eight years' relationship with your Group, I have told Cape's to refuse all other enquiries from Australia until your people have made up their minds.

By the way, the "Star" wished to make it their "Thriller of the Month" but stipulated that we should put on a paper binder to that effect, which Cape's were not willing to do now that the book is already out for review and appearing Monday week.

TO VARIOUS, undated, 1954

A sample of the many letters that Fleming wrote to drum up publicity for the American edition of Live and Let Die.

TO MR. MALCOLM MUIR,* Newsweek, 152 West 42nd Street, New York 36, N.Y.

Here is the second volume of my autobiography and I hope that you and Mrs. Muir will enjoy it.

If you feel it wouldn't scarify the readers of NEWSWEEK I would be vastly grateful if it could find its way to your Literary Editor for mention if a dull week comes along.

I am sorry to keep missing you when I come through New York, but I hope I will catch up with both of you again this year.

---

* Malcolm Muir (1885–1979), editor and president of *Newsweek* magazine.

TO MRS. FLEUR GARDINER COWLES,* Cowles Syndicate, 488 Madison Avenue, New York 22, N.Y.

Here is the second volume of my collected works and you were so sweet about giving CASINO ROYALE a fine send off in LOOK that I wonder if you would continue to make my fame and fortune by passing LIVE AND LET DIE with your blessing, to the Literary Editor.

If not, I should be proud to have the book go into that very handsome waste paper basket of yours.

TO RT. HON. SIR WINSTON CHURCHILL, K.G., Chartwell, Westerham, Kent

Winston Churchill ranked high in the pantheon of Fleming's personal heroes. Not only had he led Britain to victory in the Second World War but he had been a close friend of Fleming's father, Valentine. The two men had served in the same regiment and when Val died in the trenches in 1917 Churchill wrote his obituary for The Times.

1st April, 1954

Since I have had the presumption to steal from "Thoughts and Adventures" your dramatic tribute to the Secret Service, which my publishers have printed on the jacket of my book, I am now also presuming to send you a copy.

It is an unashamed thriller and its only merit is that it makes no demands on the mind of the reader.

I hope you will accept it and forgive my theft of a hundred words of your wonderful prose.

With my kindest regards and best wishes,

---

* Fleur Cowles (1908–2009), writer and editor. An oft-married and colourful presence on the US publishing scene. *Look* magazine was owned by her third husband whom she divorced in 1955.

On the jacket flap of Live and Let Die *Fleming included the following quote from Churchill's* Thoughts and Adventures: *'In the higher ranges of Secret Service work the actual facts in many cases were in every respect equal to the most fantastic inventions of romance and melodrama. Tangle within tangle, plot and counter-plot, ruse and treachery, cross and double-cross, true agent, false agent, double agent, gold and steel, the bomb, the dagger and the firing party, were interwoven in many a texture so intricate as to be incredible and yet true. The Chief and the High Officers of the Secret Service revelled in these subterranean labyrinths, and pursued their task with cold and silent passion.'*

TO DR. ALAN BARNSLEY, 374 Loose Road, Maidstone, Kent

A doctor from Maidstone complained that Cape had sent him a copy of Live and Let Die. *'Foolishly, I opened it and started to read: I immediately found myself deep under water carrying a limpet mine. [. . .] There was no alternative but to go back to the beginning.' He hadn't been able to put it down, had been late for his surgery, and now had recurring images of a limpet mine kissing a hull. It was quite extraordinary because, 'I am such an inveterate non-reader before breakfast that I do not even take a daily newspaper.' Why had Cape sent him such an irritating book? Anyway, who was this so-called Ian Fleming? Was it a pen name? Or could he be related to a distinctly unbookish Fleming he had known at medical school?*

21st April, 1954

I was driving myself up from Dover yesterday morning and it took me more than half an hour to get through Maidstone. Unworthily I cursed the town little realising what a beneficent influence was at work there. Only an hour later I got to London to find your letter.

It really is extremely kind of you to have written so charmingly and I only wish the book had been sent to you by me. But it must have been some rival physician trying to sabotage your practice as I am no relation of any medical Fleming – not even of Sir Alexander.

If after finishing LIVE AND LET DIE you would still like to know more about the author and are prepared to lay out 10/6d for a copy of CASINO ROYALE, my previous book, you will find a potted biography of the author and an extremely moderate pencil drawing.

I flash through the town in a 2½ litre, black Riley, every Friday evening ten minutes either side of 7 p.m. and back again every Monday morning either side of 11 a.m. and if I ever hit anything in the process I shall come straight along to Loose Road to be mended.

Again with very many warm thanks for your really charming letter.

TO DAVID CAPE, 30, Bedford Square, W.C.1.

23rd June, 1954

Dear David,

Many thanks for your letter of June 21st and I must say that if you made a loss on CASINO ROYALE and are now making a loss on LIVE AND LET DIE I shudder to think what you must be suffering from some of the other books on your list.

I always understood that on a 10/6d novel the get-out figure was around three thousand copies and since you have sold about eight thousand of both my books you should be what is generally known as "comfortably situate".

But perhaps the secret lies in your mention of overheads which presumably include the salaries and expenses of the directors and staff of Cape's. But then it is very misleading to compare your net profit with my gross profit. I also have overheads and could show a comfortable net loss on both these books.

However, since in theory we are both agreed that the book would benefit by the advertising campaign you suggested and since your firm is clearly on the verge of bankruptcy, I will agree to go fifty-fifty and let us proceed forthwith on the lines of your proposed campaign.

If we are to do the book any good we should press on with this immediately and before everyone has left on their holidays.

But I do recommend on behalf of all Cape authors that you now abandon the "all prices are net" line at the end of your copy which is quite meaningless and not used by any other publishers. The space thus saved may even turn your losses into profits.

This is rather like the man who went to the Gillette Company saying that he had the secret of how to increase their profits gigantically. He refused to divulge his secret until a substantial payment had been made and he then said "put five blades into each packet instead of six".

The only difference is that I give you this brilliant idea for nothing.

TO A. J. JOSEY, ESQ., Evening Despatch, Corporation Street, Birmingham 4

Keen as always to encourage publicity, Fleming was delighted by the approach a Birmingham newspaper took to its serialisation of Live and Let Die.

25th August, 1954

I have just got back from America and I must hasten to thank you and congratulate you on the really fine show you gave to LIVE AND LET DIE.

Apart from the pleasure you gave me I do think that the whole treatment of the serial was quite brilliant. The competition was an excellent one but above all the editing and cutting, analysis of the characters and "The Story so Far" pieces were most expertly done by somebody who really knows what he was doing.

As an editor you really squeezed the utmost value out of the serial instead of, as did other papers who ran it, just slapping it on to the page with a "take it or leave it" attitude to your readers.

Your treatment was real salesmanship and I should be surprised if you don't find it easy to get the authors you want if you accord them this sort of handling.

I would be most interested to hear how the serial went and what sort of response you got to your competition, so please drop me a line if you have a moment.

My next book is with Cape's but will not be appearing until April. I think it will make a good serial although the "Saturday Evening Post" have turned it down on the grounds that "it is too dramatic".

For LIVE AND LET DIE Cape's sold the Group rights to the Provincial Press and I suppose it would be a question of getting your London office to have a look at it if you are interested.

Anyway many thanks and congratulations for your treatment of the last one and if you would like a letter from me on the results of your competition or any other promotion idea of this sort, please let me know and I will be delighted to help.

TO MRS. H. M. POLLEY, 3 Royal Crescent, Brighton

Hilda Polley, pointed out that Live and Let Die *was the title of the last comedy written by her husband Syd. 'It was a very ingenious title,' she wrote, 'and I remember Frank Cellier saying he'd like to play in it if only for the title.' How, she wondered, had Fleming come by it? Further, Mr Polley had nearly finished a novel when he died, and although Sir Osbert Sitwell had suggested an ending Mrs Polley felt he would be too busy to finish the book himself. Might Cape (or, by inference, Fleming) be interested in the manuscript? She enclosed an SAE for reply.*

25th August, 1954

Dear Madam,

Thank you very much for your letter of August 17th and I am sorry that owing to my absence abroad I did not reply earlier.

It is indeed a curious coincidence that I should have chosen the same title as your late husband but it did in fact simply come to me out of the blue one day when I was driving down the Dover Road.

Regarding your late husband's novel, I really think your best course would be to send it to a literary agent such as Curtis Brown Ltd who are good people and would advise you as to whether a publisher would be interested.

In return Mrs Polley said the Dover Road was a most romantic place to think of a title. 'Her husband's Live and Let Die *had been written for the Australian actress Marie Lohr, but the war had intervened. Syd, she continued, had a genius for arriving at titles – 'Firelight', 'Bridleway', 'Something Must Be Done', 'The Story Speaks', 'Portrait Of A Lady' and 'Quiet Please'. Should Fleming ever be at a loss he was welcome to use any of them.*

TO LORD BEAVERBROOK, Flat 95, Arlington House, London W.1.

Beaverbrook was a man whom Fleming admired. During the Second World War he had served as Minister of Supply and his newspapers were noted for their daring and ingenuity. (In tribute, Fleming made the Express *one of the few papers that Bond read on a regular basis.) When he enquired about serialisation rights, Fleming was enthusiastic. Nothing came of it, but the* Express *later ran a series of James Bond cartoon strips that would achieve iconic status.*

31st August, 1954

Ann's told me of your very kind message about LIVE AND LET DIE and I was certainly surprised and delighted by Malcolm Thompson's review,* which I am sure did the sales some good.

He is by far the best fiction reviewer and I wish we could steal him from you for the "Sunday Times".

As a matter of fact, before publication the "Evening Standard", according to Jonathan Cape's, were dickering with the idea of serializing LIVE AND LET DIE but I dare say it was decided that small adds [sic] made even better reading.

However, just in case any of your papers might be interested, the third book, which Cape's say is the best of the three, is now with Curtis Brown and EVERYBODY'S put in a first bid for it. In America the "Saturday Evening Post" were interested but came to the conclusion that it

* George Malcolm Thompson (1899–1996), Beaverbrook's personal secretary and critic for the *Evening Standard*. He described *Live and Let Die* as 'tense, ice-cold, sophisticated; Peter Cheyney for the carriage trade'.

was too dramatic! – a disadvantage which I imagine would not dismay your editors.

Anyway there it is and for countless reasons I would much prefer that it was sent to the Express Group, if you have any use for fiction these days.

Ann sends her love. She is just off to Northern Ireland for a few days to roast an ox in aid of her son's twenty-first birthday.

TO IAN MCKENZIE, "Nahariya", 33 Silsoe Street, Hamilton, New South Wales

Ian McKenzie was a lawyer practising in the Australian coal town of Newcastle. He had only written one fan letter before, to an actor in the touring Stratford Company – 'because so much good work goes unpraised' – and now felt he should write a second. He and his friends had admired Casino Royale *and* Live and Let Die *and were looking forward to the next. Fleming's reply gave an intriguing glimpse into his wartime service and hinted at a Bond adventure that, alas, never came to fruition. As often, when referring to Bond's armaments, Fleming meant Beretta the gun, rather than Biretta the ecclesiastical headgear.*

2nd September, 1954

It really was extremely kind of you to have written such a charming letter.

I only once wrote such a letter – to an Austrian novelist Leo Perutz* – and I remember what an effort it was.

But when you come to write your first book, even if it's upon an abstruse point of law, you will know what a warm glow it causes to hear from a reader.

My third book is just being printed and will appear next April. The publishers are pleased with it and I hope it will also satisfy you and your friends.

* Leo Perutz (1882–1957), Austrian mathematician and novelist. Fleming was probably referring to his *Between Nine and Nine* (1918), a tale of romance and intrigue set in Imperial Vienna, which was translated to widespread acclaim in the 1920s and possibly influenced Fleming's first short story, 'A Poor Man Escapes'.

I have wonderful memories of Australia as a result of having served briefly at our Pacific Fleet Headquarters in the "Daily Half Mile" in Sydney, and I hope one day I shall come back and bring James Bond and his Biretta with me in search of trouble and just that one, final, fatal Australian blonde.

TO WILLIAM HICKEY, ESQ., "Daily Express", Fleet Street, E.C.4.

William Hickey was a Regency memoirist whose name had been appropriated by the Daily Express *for its gossip column. In December 1954 'Hickey' ran a piece that concerned a Dublin grocer's remarks about* Live and Let Die. *Fleming, who wasn't above writing lightweight chatty columns himself, hastened to advise.*

2nd December, 1954

SO FRESH!

Your Dublin grocer reads thrillers.

On Lexington Avenue, New York, there is a restaurant called "Glory-fried Ham-N-Eggs" which boasts that "The Eggs we serve Tomorrow are still on the Farm".

This restaurant features briefly in a Secret Service thriller of mine entitled LIVE AND LET DIE, but I "improved" their slogan into "The Eggs we serve Tomorrow are still in the Hens".

On Monday I was in New York and my American publishers told me that, for the American edition, they were reverting to the original slogan in order to avoid letters of correction from New Yorkers. So I was all the more delighted to read on my return to London that my version has been rescued for posterity by a thriller-addicted grocer in Dublin!

TO MR. CHARLES BROWNHILL, 1 Warwick Avenue, Bedford

In very neat handwriting schoolboy Charles Brownhill wrote to say how much he had enjoyed Live and Let Die. *He had never written to an author (though he had once completed an Enid Blyton competition) and he was keen to get his hands on* Casino Royale *even if it meant disrupting his A levels.*

26th May, 1955

Thank you very much indeed for your letter of May 24th which gave me a great deal of pleasure.

Authors are always pleased to get such praise from one of their readers just as I expect you will be when you see your marks in the Advanced Level Certificate!

I have just published a new thriller called MOONRAKER, which I hope will give you as much fun as LIVE AND LET DIE.

Again with many thanks for your kind thought in writing.

TO RICHARD USBORNE,* "Firlands", Ellesmere Road, Weybridge, Surrey

To appease his obstreperous author, Cape made a lucrative deal with Foyle's bookshop for a Book Club edition whereby 20,000 copies of Live and Let Die *were to be published by their subsidiary World Books. Richard Usborne's review, which first appeared as a puff in 'World Books' Broadsheet', featured prominently on the dust jacket. It touched a chord with Fleming, who feared comparison with his literary contemporaries.*

6th July, 1956

I have just seen your very kindly review of "Live and Let Die" in the "World Books Broadsheet".

You have always understood that my object in writing these books is to entertain, and you are one of the few reviewers who seem to understand this lowly objective and you never tell me that I ought to be writing like somebody else, which is what depresses me about some critics.

I remember that, in a previous review, you wrote that you would like to hear more about Smersh. The message got through and you may be

* Richard Usborne (1910–2006), journalist and author who had served with SOE during the war. As befitted the eccentric recruitment policy of British Intelligence he spent the last forty-five years of his life studying the works of P. G. Wodehouse.

interested to know that the next volume in the collected works, provisionally entitled "From Russia with Love", deals with an attempt by Smersh to destroy Bond. In fact, the first half of the book takes the reader entirely into the Smersh camp.

I don't know how the book will do and many will certainly find the inner workings of Smersh rather slow-going, but at any rate I feel that I have made an attempt to pay off a debt of gratitude to one of James Bond's most kindly sustainers.

TO MISS JOAN HOARE, 33 Monkridge, Crouch End Hill, N.8

Miss Joan Hoare said she hadn't enjoyed a book so much since reading Bulldog Drummond at the age of fourteen. But, 'in a spirit of constructive criticism', she felt obliged to point out that it was Balmain, not Dior, who produced the perfume 'Vent Vert'.

'I venture to write because in the "Broadsheet" accompanying the book you say you take a real interest in avoiding such mistakes [. . .]. It can well be imagined that a modern thriller gains effect from references to the latest fashions in living & I would suggest that any lady of your acquaintance with the requisite "savoir vivre" would surely be only too delighted to help you check your slips in the feminine field.'

21st October, 1958

Thank you very much for your charming letter of October 17th and for all the kind things you have to say.

Of course you are quite right about the Vent Vert. This egregious slip was picked up by many sapient females at the time of its first publication and, through some oversight, my correction never got into the cheaper edition.

I suppose until I go to my grave sharp-eyed, sweet-scented women will continue to rap my bruised knuckles for this mistake, and I can only say that I rather enjoy the process!

Again with many thanks for taking the trouble to write.

3

Moonraker

A T THE OUTSET, 1954 boded well for Fleming. He had been awarded the post of Atticus, leading columnist for the *Sunday Times*, which gave him free rein to expatiate on anyone and anything that caught his fancy. It was an enviable position for a journalist and during his three-year tenure he made the most of it. Best of all, however, was a letter he received in January from film producer Alexander Korda* saying how much he had enjoyed a proof copy of *Live and Let Die* and asking Fleming if he would be interested in writing for films. Fleming replied that his forthcoming novel might be just what Korda was looking for. And with this glittering prospect in mind he departed London for Goldeneye.

There were good moments. During his two-month furlough he inveigled Ann into the sea and taught her how to catch and cook an octopus. 'I was sad about the octopus,' Ann wrote in a letter to Evelyn Waugh. All the same, it made a very good lunch, fried with conch and lobster, served on saffron rice. When she looked at Fleming's work she felt even sadder: 'The heroine is a policewoman called Gala, she has perfect measurements. I was hopelessly ignorant about such important facts . . .' Only when Noël Coward brought a corsetry saleswoman for drinks did she get her husband's drift.

And there were bad. Although Fleming worked with his habitual discipline, Ann's guests were more than he could stand – among them a honeymoon couple who stayed for 'twelve interminable days'. After a while he had had enough. 'Ian said I was to tell them that they must not

---

* Alexander Korda (1893–1956), a leading figure in the British film industry.

call "Lion" and "Bear" to each other while he was writing,' Ann recorded, 'but I could think of no tactful approach; finally Ian whose tact is notorious said at luncheon "We should love you to continue using the house but we are going away for three or four days." An appalling silence fell.' Ann mollified as best she could, with the result that the honeymooners stayed a little longer. Fleming called her a traitor.

Possibly the Flemings did decamp from Goldeneye because on 28 March, shortly after their return to Britain, Atticus condemned Jamaican hoteliers for ramped prices and bad service: 'Ten days ago, in one of these hotels, a visitor rang three times and telephoned for the maid, finally to be told that the maid could not come until the rain had stopped.' Furthermore, the same thinly disguised visitor was foolish enough to order a dry martini. 'The level of the glass fell half an inch when he had removed the jumbo olive. It cost him 5s. 8d. and the lights in the bar fused while he was drinking it.'

On their return from Jamaica, Ian and Ann visited the South of France where, at the Villa Mauresque, he persuaded Somerset Maugham to allow the *Sunday Times* to serialise a selection of his short stories. When published in June 1954, with gigantic posters and an invitation for readers to compare their ten favourite novels against Maugham's own selection, it added another 50,000 to the paper's already considerable circulation and prompted Kemsley to consider a separate entertainment section – which materialised eight years later as the ground-breaking *Sunday Times Magazine*.

Whether for reasons of disruption or the fact he was trying to write for film, Fleming wasn't happy with the manuscript. The plot was fine, and very much of its age: a millionaire industrialist, Sir Hugo Drax, had developed a missile that would serve as Britain's unique nuclear deterrent – the trouble being that he and his team were undercover German veterans who intended to drop an atom bomb on Britain itself. Bond's involvement stemmed from an invitation by M to investigate Drax's flukish run of luck at Blade's, London's premier gentleman's club. As he soon discovered, Drax was a card sharp. Having outcheated him at a game of bridge, Bond found himself assigned to guard duty at Drax's missile installation. Piece by piece he unearthed Drax's plans and, after several brushes with death, managed to alter the missile's course so that it landed in the North Sea. Its detonation killed several hundred innocent observers aboard a warship – also Drax, who had fled, gloatingly, in a submarine – but saved the millions that would have died had it hit London.

The action was set mainly in the county of Kent, where Fleming spent most weekends, and was researched with rigour. He sought advice from, among others, the Bowater Corporation, then the world's largest producer of newsprint, and the British Interplanetary Society (whose recent chairman, Arthur C. Clarke, was sadly unavailable for comment). Given a growing vogue for wartime literature, and Britain's technological advances in rocketry and nuclear physics, it was pitched perfectly at the domestic market.

Nevertheless, Fleming felt there was something missing. The title, for a start, eluded him. As did the gung-ho certainty of his previous two books. It was almost as if by putting 007 on home territory he had shorn him of his vigour: Bond did not get his girl, the policewoman Gala; he won the war but not the battle – Drax's missile missed its intended target, but still caused multiple casualties; and the plot went beyond (or perhaps beneath) the usual romantic escapism. To compound Fleming's uneasiness the film deal with Korda came to nothing. He fell prey briefly to pessimism and wondered if Bond had any future at all.

He quickly regained his self-confidence. One of his mantras was that if you didn't make your own way then nobody else was going to do it for you. On 4 April 1954, under the title *Spur to Fame*, Atticus included a verse by poet laureate John Masefield:

Sitting still and wishing
Makes no person great.
The good Lord sends the fishing.
But you must dig the bait.

Noting that it had inspired hundreds of people – 'mostly budding authors one suspects' – Fleming renewed his assault on Cape for higher royalties and better publicity. Remarkably, it worked.

There were other causes for optimism. Metro-Goldwyn-Mayer was interested in the book, as was Rank. Thus enthused, he flew to America in August to research his next novel. For once there would be no quibbles about the title. It was to be called, from the start, *Diamonds are Forever.*

FROM SIR ALEXANDER KORDA, London Film Productions, 146 Piccadilly, London, w.1.

In a letter dated 1 January 1954 Sir Alexander Korda waxed enthusiastic about Live and Let Die *– 'Your book is one of the most exciting [books] I have ever read. I really could not put it down…' – but didn't think it was one his company would take up. Nevertheless, he encouraged Fleming's future efforts in that direction: 'I feel that the best stories for films are always the stories that are written specially for films. Would you be interested in working on one?'*

TO SIR ALEXANDER KORDA

6th January, 1954

Thank you for your most exhilarating letter. I hope the public will share your views.

I think my next book, which I shall start to write on Sunday in Jamaica and finish around March 10th, may be more to your liking as it is an expansion of a film story I've had in my mind since the war – a straight thriller with particularly English but also general appeal, set in London and on the White Cliffs of Dover, and involving the destruction of London by a super V.2, allowing for some wonderful settings in the old Metropolis idiom.

I have never written a film synopsis as I haven't known what shape this sort of thing takes but if your office would care to send me along a specimen – as short as possible – I will dash it off and send it on to you from Jamaica.

I shall see Little Bill on my way through New York on Friday, and will pass messages.

TO WREN HOWARD

Replying to Howard's enquiry about an offer from Bonnier, a Scandinavian publisher, Fleming gave vent to an unusual display of despair and self-doubt.

12th March, 1954

Thank you very much for your letter of March 1st, which I held until my return here.

I quite see your point but I think that Bonnier's letter verges on blackmail!

They have now had CASINO ROYALE for a year without publishing it, and they now say they like the second book better than the first, but are not prepared to pay the same money for it.

All this seems odd and unbusinesslike.

At the same time I agree with you that Bonnier are the best publishers I could have, and I am perfectly happy to leave myself entirely in your hands in this whole matter.

But do you think it would be wise to wait a month or so and see how the second book goes? If, by any chance, it is a real success it would strengthen our hands.

I am terribly sorry to hear that Jonathan has been ill, although I am afraid this is a fate that none of us will escape at the age of 75.

Would you please send him my very warm regards when next you write.

I have written a third book of James Bond's adventures but I'm afraid it requires a great deal of work before it will warrant the eagle eyes of William Plomer and Daniel George.

It has been written too hastily – 70,000 words in six weeks – and I have a horrible feeling that I have begun to parody myself, which is obviously a great danger when one is writing of characters like James Bond in whom one doesn't believe.

Readers don't mind how fantastic one is but they must feel that the author believes in his fantasy.

As soon as I can I will try and put more flesh on the grisly bones and cut some of the clichés which are beginning to festoon my hero. And then it will come along for your judgement.

Incidentally, Curtis Brown have sold the serial rights of the second book to "Blue Book", which is a good American adventure magazine, and Macmillan have done a very good job on CASINO which appears on the 23rd in America.

But I can see that the future of James Bond is going to require far more thought than I have so far devoted to him and if your firm is likely to continue to be interested in him, I do think the future of the series and the development of Bond himself should be given some careful consideration by the brains of Messrs. Jonathan Cape.

At present I can see nothing but a vista of fantastic adventures on more or less the same pattern, but losing freshness with each volume.

Some words of encouragement and inspiration from you will help.

TO WREN HOWARD

While Howard's reply is lost, it seems to have given Fleming the encouragement he sought.

19th March, 1954

Thank you very much for your letter and please don't take my cri de coeur too seriously.

I think there are plenty of bullets left in Bond's gun. It is the freshness of the situations I put him into that are most important and for these there are no wits to rely upon except my own.

If I write more optimistically today it is because I am much impressed by the reception of booksellers, etc., to LIVE AND LET DIE. Some reviewers may lambast it but I have a feeling that it may conceivably sell, particularly as it will be coming out just in time for Easter.

That being so, I am going to be irritating and urge that you will be very kind and see that it doesn't go out of print.

Considering the dreadful muck in the thriller line that sells 10,000 copies, I really am rather worried, purely as a result of talking to booksellers and others, that there might be a run on it.

Whatever its merits or otherwise, people do seem to be quite incapable of putting it down once they have started it, and that is the sort of book that people want when in pain or train or 'plane.

An author is bound to get an inflated view from the talk of his own friends but, being myself in the newspaper and publishing business, I do think that in my case some of this false optimism can be discounted.

Would you consider putting another edition in hand without more ado or is that asking you to indulge in too great a hazard?

If you have any doubts on this score, I do hope that on this occasion you will take a gamble.

It does seem to me that in this thriller business a certain amount of barn-storming is desirable and I would be greatly encouraged if I felt that I had a publisher who was prepared to allow a wild light to creep into his eye when the omens appeared to be propitious.

TO W. SOMERSET MAUGHAM, ESQ., Villa Mauresque, St. Jean, Cap Ferrat, A.M., France

9th April, 1954

Forgive me for dictating this letter but since it is half business I want to be able to remember what I said.

First of all thank you for my wonderful day off in the sunshine and for my night out amongst the bright lights with dear Alan* who really is the most enchanting companion.

Even my two hours' wait at the airport was not wasted as I sat behind Mr. Orson Wells [sic] in the buffet and eavesdropped on his views on the wide screen cinema which, for your information, he says is a hopeless shape for an intelligent producer.

---

* Alan Searle (1904–85), Maugham's secretary and companion.

Annie hung on my words when I got home and she sends you her love in exchange for the Avocados which I insisted we should take down to the country tonight and eat by ourselves.

As for the "Big Project",* Kemsley continues to be vastly enthusiastic, and I went and had a talk with Frere† this morning who is equally so.

The only trouble is going to be the technical problem of finding space in the paper. We want to dress each extract up attractively and give it plenty of air and typographical embellishment, all of which eats into the page [. . .]

Having carried things so far I shall now bow gracefully out of the scene and leave the rest of the machinations and negotiations to the "Sunday Times".

And it only remains to thank you again for having received me so kindly and for having allowed yourself to be persuaded to cast a generally favourable eye over the project.

By the way, the Kemsleys are going down to Monte Carlo next Wednesday and they will be staying at the Hotel de Paris. Perhaps you might like to invite them to call on you.

FROM WILLIAM PLOMER

31st May, 1954

My dear Ian,

Have just finished and much enjoyed the new book, & shall send it over to Daniel on Wednesday. I have been through it with minute care and a pencil & have applied both to your punctuation and spelling. You don't have to accept my corrections but they are reasoned ones.

1. General impressions. You have a tendency, as the climax approaches, to increase the strain on the reader's credulity. This was evident in <u>Live and Let Die</u>, and is here evident again. I am not sure how important it is to <u>lessen</u> that strain. Ideally, you ought not to slacken the tension.

* The proposed serialisation of Maugham's short stories.
† Alexander Frere (1892–1984), Maugham's editor at William Heinemann.

2. First hundred pages particularly good I.F. Blades is excellent & the card-game <u>most</u> exciting.

3. I enjoyed the car-chase, all the stuff about racing cars and technical – or astronautical – details about the Moonraker set-up.

4. Much enjoyed local chalky colour, down to bee-orchids. Full marks for botany.

5. Not pleased with title. I should like HELL IS HERE.

6. It might be a good thing in the blurb to refer to Bond as "Commander James Bond, C.M.G." It would give a Buchanish flavour.

7. Joke about Loelia Ponsonby* more conspicuous than character-drawing of <u>this</u> L.P.

8. *I* cannot agree that moustaches are "obscene", even with short hair-cuts.

9. I don't think M. ought so often to speak "drily."

10. I think you should be careful about letting your characters grunt, bark, and snarl too freely.

11. <u>Whittaker's Almanac</u> is in fact <u>Whittaker's Almanack</u>, and a <u>murrain</u> is not the same as a <u>moraine</u> (examples of pedantic fine-tooth-combing by W.P.)

12. I don't know, in view of the current morality drive, whether the indecent insults in German are better left in or taken out or disguised.

13. I am uncertain of the propriety of committing the Queen & the D. of Edinburgh to such conspicuous patronage of Sir H. Drax.

14. I send you all these carpings, in case some of them are helpful when you give the typescript its final tuning-up for the printer. They don't prevent me from taking off my hat to you for another really exciting story which, in my opinion-for-what-it-is-worth, will quicken the metabolisms of your public, and enlarge it. Your readers will certainly not find the English setting any less sensational than the more exotic ones of your previous books.

15. You might consider a story in which Bond loses every battle but the last one.

* Bond's secretary, but in real life the aristocratic society figure Loelia Ponsonby (1902–93). Fleming often appropriated his friends' names for characters in his books.

16. I have said nothing about Gala, that super hour-glass or figure-of-eight. You might do worse than bring her back again in your next, even if she is Mrs Vivian by then, with a little Pygmalion (Pygma for short) at her apron-strings.

17. I wish you much luck with this book, and can hardly wait for the next.

18. You don't have to answer all this – just acknowledge it on a p.c.

FROM DANIEL GEORGE, Laurel Cottage, Hammers Lane, Mill Hill, N.W.7.

Daniel George, Plomer's fellow reader at Cape, sent him a brief critique, with the note: 'I.F. telephoned this afternoon & asked my opinion: so I read him this letter.'

4th June, 1954

My dear William,

I may be doing you wrong but I think you said that – for you – Ian's new book got away to a flying start but lost speed later. I feel almost the opposite. We've tooled along for fifty pages before we get really going. After that, we have to hold our hats – and personally I feel as though I'd broken through the sound-and-fury barrier and am still slowly descending to earth. In every way this seems to me an enormous advance on the other two bits of Bonderie. With the worst will in the world I can't find much wrong with it. However, one is not a critic for nothing (though almost), so here are some comments which you may pass on to the author if you feel it desirable to do so.

p. 55 Bond here talks as though he were Sherlock Holmes and M Dr Watson. Would M really need telling about peripheral vision? Boy Scouts are taught how to increase theirs.

p. 67 And would M or anyone else also need telling about the effects of Benzedrine? (As you know, it's my favourite breakfast food.) The 'business' of taking it as a white powder in champagne seems overdone.

p. 120 I'm rather dubious about the use of 'mild steel' for the engine. Why should mild steel (i.e. unhardened, ordinary, commercial steel) be used? If there's a technical reason for this strange choice it isn't made clear. Or if it is, I've stupidly missed it.

274 et seq. The long spiel by Drax needs close revision, I think. It sags here and there into "Well" and "However, to continue" and "God knows how long I lay in the ditch" and "It gradually became an obsession." Also "Faugh!" The whole piece, I suggest, must be much tighter. The author should try reading it aloud.

As for the rest, what I think will strike any reader is the absence of everybody else while Bond and Gala get to work . . . No, perhaps I'm wrong. The only readers who become sceptical may be those who, like me, wait until they've almost recovered their critical faculties before they think about it.

Perhaps it is too bad of me to add that I knew Drax would not survive the story as soon as I saw (on p. 71) that he turned on his heel and did it again on p. 86.

Apart from that and a bit of lipbiting and smiling or grinning ruefully or wryly, the book is comparatively free of clichés.

TO W. SOMERSET MAUGHAM

Fleming wrote to congratulate Maugham on the splendid, if not outlandish posters that were being used as part of the Sunday Times *promotional campaign.*

10th June, 1954

This is a great day for "les amis de Somerset Maugham". In honour of the Queen's birthday the town is being plastered with your face and the massed bands are playing for you both.

The Hallowe'en turnip [Maugham's portrait] being reproduced on the front page of the "Sunday Times" is nothing to the giant scraper-board mask which, on the top floor of this building, is gazing angrily up Gray's Inn Road towards King's Cross and down Gray's Inn Road towards Lincoln's Inn.

It reminds me of the "Black Widow" poster designed to "Keep Death Off the Roads", but in fact the whole campaign is having an electric effect on England and people can be seen in restaurants with scrubby bits of paper and pencil jotting down Hawthorn [sic], and Ulysses.

I will gather together a great bundle of our advertisements and ship them out to you but the twenty-foot square posters would be too much for the mails and I will have to try and send a photograph.

Incidentally, they would just about paper the outside walls of your villa and I like the idea of you and Alan emerging from between your lips. It would be a good scene in a Cocteau or Dali film, and I may steal it for my fourth thriller.* (The third is with Cape's and they say it is the best but it doesn't amuse me as much as the others.)

Anyway the whole venture has aroused interest all over the world and everybody is delighted.

As part of the ballyhoo I was requested to write a light piece on my visit to you and in some trepidation I did so.

But Lord K is so overwhelmed by the importance of the occasion and so loth, I think, to allow it to be thought that it was anybody's idea but his own that he told me he thought the piece was not sufficiently "dignified".

So I send it to you to see what you yourself think. It is difficult not to be vulgar in these sort of things but I feel I have avoided the major pitfalls.

Annie is in wonderful form and is delighted with the announcement in the "Times" this morning, although she says it isn't enough and hopes that you have at least precedence over Dame Sitwell.† She's spinning like a top through the Season and I am looking forward to enjoying her company again when she comes to rest at the end of July. She loved your letter and will, I expect, reply this week-end from St. Margaret's.

I must stop now as the chapel bells are ringing and this is too long by at least half.

FROM SOMERSET MAUGHAM

16th June, 1954

My dear Ian,

I have read your article with great amusement. I don't see that it is undignified. There is nothing I want less than to have anyone take me

---

* The idea was used in *From Russia with Love*.
† Maugham was awarded the Companion of Honour that year. He had, however, been hoping for the more prestigious Order of Merit.

for a stuffed shirt on a pedestal. The only objection I have to make is firstly you speak of my having a chef, whereas my simple, and even spartan needs are satisfied by a cook. Secondly, you speak of the poetess being offered soup at luncheon. That is something that I should be ashamed to offer any guest, drunk or sober. I look upon soup at luncheon as barbarous, detestable, uncivilized and conducive to promiscuous immorality.

If you have a moment to spare, and can tell me what sort of reaction the first article has had on the public at large, I shall be most grateful.

Yours always,
Willie

TO WREN HOWARD

29th June, 1954

Having brushed up the typescript a bit as the result of the comments of William and Daniel, I am sending it over to you.

There's one fairly long rewriting job on Chapter 22 which Daniel recommended, with which I agree, and I have simply not had time to get down to it and it doesn't in fact affect the book in any way.

I am not entirely happy with the title but nothing we have been able to think up is an improvement.

If any other readers have ideas I shall be most grateful to hear them.

TO J. B. REED, ESQ., The Bowater Paper Corporation Ltd., Bowater House, Stratton Street, W.1.

One of the dramatic set pieces in Moonraker *involved a car chase in which Bond's vehicle was thrown off the road when Drax's henchman, Krebs, unleashed a roll of newsprint from the lorry ahead. For advice, Fleming sought out Bowater, the world's biggest supplier of newsprint and an organisation of near Blofeldian stature, which not only operated paper mills but, to safeguard against strikes, owned its own forests and ran its own dedicated shipping line.*

30th June, 1954

Dear Sir,

I wonder if you would be kind enough to give me a little help in my capacity as a spare-time writer of thrillers.

In my next book a Bowater's newsprint carrier features briefly and dramatically, and I wonder if you would tell me if the following sentences are correct:

1) "One of Bowater's huge Foden Diesel carriers was just grinding into the first bend of the hairpin labouring under five tons of newsprint it was taking on a night run to one of the Ramsgate newspapers."

(Apart from correcting the facts, have you actually got a customer in Ramsgate or elsewhere on the Isle of Thanet?)

2) "His head lamps showed the long carrier with the eight gigantic rolls, each containing half a mile of newsprint."

If you would be kind enough to scribble in corrections or suggestions on this letter and return it to me, I would be most grateful.

Yours Faithfully,

He was advised that although Bowater had a client on the Isle of Thanet, they did not deliver at night. Their lorries were eight-wheeled AECs which typically carried twenty-one rolls, each containing five miles of newsprint. It was the very kind of detail that Fleming relished.

TO WREN HOWARD

9th July, 1954

Very many thanks for your letter of yesterday and I am delighted you are pleased with the book.

Your points of detail are all excellent and most valuable and they will all have attention. Any other similar comments, however harsh, will be very welcome.

Curiously enough the book was always called THE MOONRAKER until a week after I finalised it when Noël Coward reminded me that Tennyson Jesse* once used the same title.

Do you think it would matter using it again or that we ought to get clearance from somebody?

Alternatively perhaps we could call it "THE MOONRAKER SECRET" or "THE MOONRAKER PLOT" or at any rate tack on one other word.

I have the master typescript and I will tidy it up and give it to Michael at the end of the month so that it can go early to the printers.

My Autumn looks as if it's going to be rather busy and I would very much like to get the proofs corrected and off my chest as soon as possible.

I will also rough out a jacket for Michael to consider.

I will attack the contract next week.

TO WREN HOWARD

The search for a title continued . . .

15th July, 1954

What do you think of THE INFERNAL MACHINE as a title?

Or alternatively WIDE OF THE MARK or THE INHUMAN ELEMENT?

Personally, I think the first might be the one. It is an expression everyone knows but has long been out of fashion.

Despite Fleming's enthusiasm for The Infernal Machine, *none of his suggestions found favour. At the bottom of the letter Howard scribbled a list of alternatives:* Bond and the Moonraker, The Moonraker Scare *and* The Moonraker Plot. *All were later crossed out, leaving at the end just a single word. He circled it firmly:* Moonraker.

* F. Tennyson Jesse (1888–1958), English crime writer. Her book *Moonraker* was first published in 1927.

TO MICHAEL HOWARD

Fleming took particular pride in designing dust jackets for his novels. Casino Royale *and* Live and Let Die *had both been his and now with* Moonraker *he made a third attempt. An abstract design of pillars of flame, by Ken Lewis, it wasn't as successful as the previous two.*

28th October, 1954

I have now devised the enclosed and I think it's on the right lines. Robert Harling also very much approves which, in case you don't know him, is a considerable triumph.

What do you think?

I think the author's name could be a bit larger or alternatively in a different type, and I think the motif of the background might be a little bit bolder and not quite so niggly.

But it at any rate contains the red, yellow and black, which experts have always told me are the most striking for poster purposes, so it should show up well on the bookstalls.

I await your verdict and I also enclose an alternative design on which Harling has turned his thumbs down.

The colours are wrong but I still think something could be made of the idea if you don't like the flaming one.

TO E. B. STRAUSS, ESQ., 45 Wimpole Street, London, w.1.

Eric Strauss (1894–1961) was an eminent psychiatrist who treated both Graham Greene and Evelyn Waugh. Fleming had sought his advice on megalomania and discovered in Strauss's Men of Genius *that childhood thumb-sucking could have baneful consequences – hence the gap-toothed Drax.*

5th January, 1955

It is now exactly a year since I borrowed your "Men of Genius" and I have felt ashamed of myself for not having returned it to you before.

The Hemmung [psychological inhibition] was undoubtedly created by my desire to keep the book in my possession. It appears to be quite unobtainable and it has given me so much pleasure that even now I am loath to let it go.

However, please forgive me for the delay and thank you most warmly for your kindness in lending it to me, and in being so patient with the borrower.

A perfectly horrible man whose diabolical schemes for the destruction of this country stem, I have maintained, directly from a pronounced diastema of the centrals has resulted from your loan and will appear in my next thriller, THE MOONRAKER, of which I will send you a copy on its publication in April.

I hope you will then approve of the motivation I have provided for my villain.

Again with many apologies and my warmest thanks and very best wishes for 1955.

TO MICHAEL BODENHAM, ESQ., Director, Floris Ltd., 89 Jermyn Street, London, S.W.1.

Floris, *perfumiers and soap makers to the gentry, were 'most interested to read your kind mention of "Floris" in your new book "The Moonrakers"'. They sent their appreciation, plus a sample of their products and 'thanks to you for this association in a most excellent and entertaining novel'. Fleming was an enthusiastic endorser of the products used.*

23rd August, 1955

Having been a life-time consumer of your products the least I could do was to pay tribute to your firm in enumerating the luxurious appointments of Blades Club, and it was quite unnecessary though very nice of you to have sent me such a fragrant bouquet in return.

My books are spattered with branded products of one sort or another* as I think it is stupid to invent bogus names for products which are household words, and you may be interested to know that this is the first time that a name-firm has had the kindly thought of acknowledging the published tribute.

Again with many thanks.

TO GEOFFREY M. CUCKSON, ESQ., Nottingham

19th September, 1955

Thank you very much for your kind letter of September 7th which greeted me on my return from Istanbul.

I am so glad you like the adventures of James Bond. They also give me much pleasure but you are one of the few of my readers who has suggested that the background work does require a great deal of trouble.

All your comments are, as a matter of fact, very much to the point and I agree that perhaps Gala should have been gagged. On the other hand the effects of the bang behind the ear she got would not, I think, have worn off within the three-quarters of an hour drive left to Ebury Street. I think you can rely on the fact that Krebs made sure she was still more or less unconscious before he and Drax helped her cross the pavement into the house.

After Bond's rather frustrating holiday abroad he immediately got involved in some further hair-raising adventures which will appear in April under the title DIAMONDS ARE FOREVER, and I hope the book will bring another charming and perceptive letter from you.

---

* Here and elsewhere, Fleming was ahead of his time in the art of what is known today as product placement – though in his case it was for verisimilitude's sake rather than gain.

TO MISS JEAN GRAMAN, 109 Sheen Lane, East Sheen, S.W.14.

On a point of German etiquette, Jean Graman told Fleming he had got his honorifics wrong. 'While a creature like Krebs is only too possible, he would not dream of addressing his superior as "mein Kapitan".' She proposed several alternatives along a military line – i.e. Obergruppenführer – and concluded with the words, 'I hope this small hint will help to make your next book as authentic as possible.'

19th October, 1957

Thank you very much for your letter of October 9th and I am delighted that you enjoyed "Moonraker".

I see your point about 'mein Kapitan' and I had thought of various other possibilities, of which perhaps a better one was 'mein Chef'.

The point is that this was a peacetime organisation in which military titles would have been inappropriate. It was perhaps because I was myself in the Navy that I decided to use 'Kapitan' as being possible and also understandable to the many of my readers who do not know German nearly as well as you do.

Anyway, many thanks for having taken the trouble to write on a very legitimate point of criticism.

TO MISS SHIRLEY HILLYARD, 302 Chapel Lane, Cardington

Shirley Hillyard, who worked at the Bedford Public Library, was one of Fleming's most delightful correspondents. On behalf of her colleagues (but maybe just herself), she said, 'We would have written before but until a traveller told us that you were foreign correspondent to the Sunday Times, *we did not know who you were.' They were intrigued to know if he was anything like his hero, and having read that he had just returned from Istanbul on the Orient Express were certain that he must be. 'We all like James Bond,' she added, 'except the librarian who thinks he is very immoral but perhaps that doesn't matter when you are in the Secret Service.'*

5th October, 1955

Thank you very much for your charming letter of October 3rd and I am delighted to hear that you and your friends at the library are not disturbed by the passionate side of James Bond's nature.

I entirely agree with you that he should be allowed some relaxation in the midst of the perils he has to face, and if he were to marry and settle down he would be of little value to the Secret Service.

Another of his adventures will appear in April together with the daffodils. It will be called DIAMONDS ARE FOREVER and I hope you will enjoy it.

Kindest regards and best wishes.

TO MICHAEL HOWARD

6th June, 1958

We talked about a reprint of "Moonraker" the other day. Since then I have been in to Hatchards and they asked me when one was coming along as they are having many enquiries for it.

If you remember, it was in the same way that I finally persuaded you to reprint "Casino Royale" which appears to have gone well.

If you feel it necessary to make a similar arrangement over "Moonraker" as we did over "Casino Royale", by all means do so, but I think it is a pity not to catch the crest of this wave by keeping all the books in print until the wave has subsided.

Undoubtedly if you decide to do a reprint a new jacket would help. The one we had was, I am sure you will agree, the worst of the lot.

TO MRS. COLLINS, Battle House, Goring, Oxon

Regarding Bond's bridge game with Drax, Mrs Collins was disappointed. 'Surely,' she wrote, 'a good player as Drax was supposed to be would have taken out the re-double into 7 No Trumps – Doubled but not vulnerable 3 down (2 clubs & the Queen of Diamonds) the penalty would only have been 500!' Quite.

28th July, 1959

Thank you very much for your letter of July 23rd and of course you are perfectly right about the Bridge problem. A still better suggestion would have been that Drax should have bid 7 hearts, which he makes.

But the point was that, with that gigantic hand not knowing that his partner had support in hearts and void in clubs, it was natural for him to expect a gigantic penalty in the club bid.

Incidentally, he was not a particularly good player, but a very good cheat!

Thank you very much for having taken the trouble to write.

TO MAJOR V. P. TALLON, M.B.E., R.A.M.C., British Military Hospital, Hannover, BFPO33

Among the characters in Moonraker *was Major Tallon, Head of Security at Drax's missile base. It was too much of a coincidence for Major Tallon, Security Officer at the Hannover hospital for the British Army of the Rhine. Tallon was an uncommon name, and his was the only one to have featured on the Army List since the war. How had Fleming come by it?*

Tallon, a stickler for detail, had written to the Daily Express *in May to comment on various unlikely details to do with the ship featured in* Moonraker *and, the fictional Tallon having been killed in the book, wrote jokingly to deny the reports of his own demise. The* Express *apologised, saying they couldn't find him in any of their obituaries. 'Much amusement was got out of it – mainly at my expense.'*

18th August, 1959

Thank you very much for your letter of August 11th and it is indeed a remarkable coincidence that your name and duties should have featured in "Moonraker".

Unfortunately, this book was written some six years ago and I cannot for the life of me remember how I came to choose the name of Tallon. I might have seen it in a newspaper or, more likely, on a shop front. When I see a name that attracts me, I jot it down and use it for an appropriate character.

Oddly enough, you are the second person to have written recently on this subject. Two or three weeks ago I had a letter from Australia from a Miss Moneypenny asking me how I had come to choose her name for M.'s secretary.

Alas, I am afraid I had to give her an equally unhelpful reply.

At least both Major Tallon and Miss Moneypenny were excellent servants of the State!

TO S. PLEETH, ESQ., 18 West Parade, Rhyl, N. Wales

Seheer Pleeth, a Swiss national living in Wales, wrote that Fleming had mis-spelled Patek Philippe as Parek Phillippe. While on the subject of watches, and given that Fleming appeared to be a perfectionist, the most exclusive watch in the world was actually an Audemars Piguet – a Hispano-Suiza compared to the mere Rolls-Royce or Bentley of Patek Philippe. 'How about a tale involving Bond in a situation within the boundaries of my own rather spy infested country – Switzerland?'

29th June, 1960

Thank you very much for your letter of June 26th and for having taken the trouble to write to me.

Certainly a mis-print has crept into the edition of "Moonraker" you read, and I will take the matter up with the publishers.

I am very interested in what you have to say about Audemars Piguet which, on your recommendation, will feature in a subsequent book.

I have just come back from Switzerland and I daresay one of these days 'M' will send James Bond there in the course of his duties. In the meantime, I am actually to-day writing about Switzerland, and in particular Geneva as part of a Thrilling Cities Series which will appear in the Sunday Times in August. I hope it does not infuriate your country too much.

Again many thanks for your letter.

4

Notes from America

'IT SEEMS TO me that much of the factual reporting on Ian Fleming, however accurate, leaves undescribed much of the fellow I knew.

'I knew him better than most; in the classical sense we often tired the sun with talking and sent him down the sky, and for that matter, the moon, too.'

Ernest Cuneo Papers – Franklin D. Roosevelt Library, New York

In 1959 Fleming wrote an article describing his friendship with Raymond Chandler, at the time a Titan in the world of thrillerdom. He could never have suspected that he himself would be held in the same regard or that his long-time friend Ernest Cuneo* would write about him in the same way. What follows has been constructed from a series of notes that Cuneo wrote in the early 1980s.

It was in 1942, at the New York apartment of Sir William Stephenson, head of British Intelligence in the western hemisphere, that the two men encountered each other. Stephenson occupied a palatial penthouse suite at the Hotel Dorset on W54th Street, where every evening he hosted meetings to discuss the latest intelligence reports. As Cuneo recalled, 'The drawing room was two-storied, there was a huge fireplace in which logs always glowed, and the lighting was subdued. It was an elegant and spacious room of warm shadows, and this being war and I of a foreign service, was acutely aware of them. Here,

---

* Ernest Cuneo (1905–88), lawyer, newspaperman and intelligence operative. He supplied Fleming with the introductions he needed for the New York scenes in *Live and Let Die* and was later rewarded with a cameo role as Ernie Cureo, the cab driver who assisted Bond in *Diamonds are Forever*.

as the lights of the metropolis blinked on, visiting great and near-great of the British High Command gathered. It was here I met Ian Fleming.'

A straight-speaking ex-football player, lawyer and journalist, Cuneo was a new recruit to America's security service, the Office of Strategic Security (OSS), precursor to the Central Intelligence Agency. Fleming, meanwhile, was a faintly aloof member of Naval Intelligence, rather junior in rank to the officers who congregated at these meetings. When Cuneo remarked on this, Fleming said, 'Do you question my bona fides?' To which Cuneo replied, 'No, just your patently limited judgement.' They both laughed. And when Stephenson's meetings devolved, as they often did, to the 21 Club, they came to know each other better.

'Oddly,' *Cuneo wrote,* 'as I saw him, he was more easily classified, from a physical standpoint, as American rather than British. He had a fine head, a high forehead with a head of thick brown, curlyish hair, parted on the side and neatly combed over to the left. His eyes were piercing blue and he had a good, firm jaw. His nose, however, had been broken and unrepaired. This gave him the look of the Philadelphia light-heavyweights of the Tommy Loughran school. [...] Fleming carried himself like an American more than an Englishman. He did not rest his weight on his left leg; he distributed it, his left foot and shoulders slightly forward. This is a typical American athlete's stance, and contains more of a hint of the quick boxer's crush than the squared erect shoulders of the Sandhurst man.'

Fleming, he discovered, knew very little about wine but could tell good from bad. He did, however, seem to be an expert on caviar and had a keen sense of fantasy. 'He told me, for example, the old Russian boyars used to carry a small solid gold ball to test it. They dropped it from a few inches and it was supposed to imbed itself half-way. I asked him why the hell he didn't have one, and I relished a small sense of victory when he just sniffed.' *And then there were the martinis.* 'Of all the maddening trivia through which I have suffered, nothing quite matched Fleming's instructions on how his were to be made. [He] was painfully specific about both the vermouth and the gin and explained each step to the guy who was going to mix it as if it were a delicate brain operation. Several times I impatiently asked him why the hell he didn't go downstairs and mix it himself, but he ignored me as if he hadn't heard and continued right on with his instructions. Equally annoyingly, he always warmly congratulated the captain when he tasted it as if he had just completed a fleet manoeuvre at flank speed.

'All but tirelessly, we taxed and challenged each other over the years, each accusing each other for what he himself was. I fancied myself the realist and he the romantic. He fancied me as the romanticist and he the realist. [...] I explained to him after the manner of the cold-blooded Genoese of whom I am born, that the romantic was the reality, and in no case more than his. Unflaggingly, he on his part, declared that the harsh physical world was the reality and that romanticism was an escape. Immersed in the American school of Walter Winchell and Damon Runyan, to me the world was a vivid, magical, series of adventures, New York a Baghdad on the subway. Fleming vividly accepted this – as a fascinating fiction. He reminded me of a certain 19th Century boulevardier of Paris, who, it was said, would lapse into melancholy pensiveness, unable to reconcile himself to the death of Henry of Navarre, four centuries gone. Fleming, though he did not know it and would not accept it, was a knight who could not reconcile himself to the fact that women were not Elaines in ivory towers, and that the world was not one of black and white values.'

All the same, Cuneo admitted that Fleming was quite happy to ignore the ivory tower if it suited him. On a wartime visit to London he brought a selection of nylon stockings, at the time all but impossible to obtain in Britain. 'One day I dropped by Commander Fleming's desk and threw on it a half dozen pair. "Long, medium and short," I said. "I assume you're playing the field." "Actually, I'm not," he said, and feeling I might have invaded his sensibilities, I said, "Good, there are others who are," and reached for the packet. With a card-sharp's fleetness of hand he was stuffing them into his Navy jacket. "No," he said. "I'm not but some of my friends are." He assumed his attitude of thoughtfulness and added beatifically, "They'll be glad to have them."

'We roared with laughter. It seems to me we were always roaring with laughter and this is how I principally remember him. [...]

'We almost suffered emotional "bends" the day the war ended. Tension went out like a power line turned off. When I came into Bill's office the next day, he shoved at me a copy of the London Times and pointed a finger to a single line. It read, "The Home Secretary told the Commons last night that the emergency having ended, habeas corpus was restored". "I guess that's what it was all about," he said. "I guess it was," I said, and we both went over to "21".

'Like it or leave it, aside from its horrors, you miss the frightful challenge of war. I think Fleming missed it as much as most; he seemed both grumpy and disconsolate.'

Their friendship continued after the war and became even closer when Cuneo was appointed President of NANA, the North American Newspaper Alliance, a once-famous news agency in which Fleming and his friend Ivar Bryce became involved and which they hoped might still have legs.

TO ERNEST CUNEO, North American Newspaper Alliance, 229 West 43rd Street, New York 36

As Vice-President of NANA's European branch, and with Bryce as a roving Vice-Chairman, Fleming arranged for an office to be opened near his own, into which moved one Silvia Short who acted as both London Editor and Manager. While co-ordinating transmissions from Kemsley Newspapers he also embarked on a succession of deals to develop new outlets for NANA's services (the details of which are, alas, unrecorded), and to organise contributors. He sought, too, to clarify the rates that their correspondents received.

8th June, 1953

Dear Ernie,

In great haste.

1. Please see my letter of May 29th. The suggested payment to Manor was twenty *dollars*, not pounds. No wonder the collective hairs of N.A.N.A. rose on its global head. I will sort the matter out somehow.

2. Ivar and I have had a preliminary talk with [Paul] Gallico about a weekly or monthly column, and the omens are favourable, but he has now buried himself in Devonshire, and I think further progress will have to await my return.

Perhaps we could talk this over in New York and send him a joint letter.

3. Noel Barber* will resume his Paris column under the name of "Noel Anthony". I gather this will start up in two or three weeks time.

4. The Truman news is most exciting and I will throw an expensive fly over my proprietor before I leave.† This seems to me an extremely valuable property and, as I have told Ivar, my first reaction is that the whole syndication should be handled by the best agent on a 10% basis, thus you will squeeze dollars out of many tiny papers around the world, as well as out of the big ones.

I propose to suggest to K[emsley] a price of $300 per article for the "Sunday Times", which is about what a Sunday paper would bear. I will bring all my findings in this matter with me.

5. Please tell Mr. Wheeler‡ that the Carol series is now running in the "Sunday Empire News", of which he should examine the last two numbers. The remainder is not yet written, but I will try and bring over some more in draft form.

6. The Gallico series here was a resounding success. I am sending Schell [the editor] full cuttings, as they may assist the Pulitzer Prize project on the grounds of helping to further Anglo-American relations. I am delighted that the project was so supremely successful.

7. Miss Short and her secretary have moved into a neighbouring office to mine today, and they are very comfortable. We are having our first European N.A.N.A. meeting at 11.30 tomorrow with the Vice-President sitting on the Vice-Chairman's knee, the London Editor and Manager on the Vice-President's and a pretty secretary on the London Manager and Editor's. This is known in some circles as a "Turkish sandwich".

8. (Next day). K, as I cabled you, will play, but of course is most anxious to know when the series will start. I said in a few weeks time, and that I would try to learn some more in New York. You might have got a higher price elsewhere in London but Ivar was most keen that K should have first refusal, and this is the top price the "Sunday Times" will pay. More about this and other projects when I see you.

9. Ivar adds to my paragraph 2 that Gallico is much firmer than I suggest. He would write a weekly column on anything that caught his

---

* Noel Barber (1909–88), novelist and foreign correspondent.
† The memoirs of outgoing US President Truman.
‡ John Neville Wheeler, NANA's founder.

eye in the news, and he suggests that we try out some of the customers to see what the traffic will stand.

10. We had this arrangement with Gallico on the "Sunday Times" and also on the "Daily Graphic". His copy is always acceptable to the middle of a paper's readership, and it is always punctual. It won't set the Mississippi on fire, but it will always command space. I think we would do well on a fifty-fifty basis. Perhaps Mr. Wheeler would like to talk to some of his friends.

10 [sic]. I have looked into O.N.A.* and I attach the report of my very well-informed Berlin man. Without knowing all the facts, my impression of O.N.A. is that we might be buying a poke without even a pig in it.

11. Your splendid letters have delighted both Ivar and me – at any rate the front pages. I have noticed that it is a trick of very rich, powerful and important men to write letters with a ballpoint pen on both sides of airmail paper. We will both hear what you had to say on your second pages when we meet.

This is positively my last word before we meet in the flesh.

FROM ERNEST CUNEO

Among the items that NANA highlighted in 1953 were the Kinsey report on the sexual habits of Americans and, perhaps unsurprisingly, Fleming's own article for the Sunday Times *on the Pierre St Martin cave in the French Pyrenees.*

September 9th, 1953

Dear Ian,

I followed with avid interest your speleological expedition. I know there were high elements of disappointment attached to it: as Kinsey could have told you it is a hell of a lot more fun to take a girl to a hotel than to go off into a cave by yourself. All of this you will learn as you grow older.

I agree completely with your thesis on payment. Schell is on vacation and I shall call it to his attention when he returns. I find it aesthetically

---

* The Overseas News Agency, a wartime propaganda machine founded by British Intelligence, now trying to make its way in peacetime.

revolting to ask a man to do something, which perforce must be of excellent quality, and then ask him to accept shabby compensation which is as much a burden on your self-respect as it is on his.

On the same date Fleming sent Cuneo a long list of topics that might interest NANA that included the following: 'I have only one more thought and that is to do with "Scrabble", a word-making game which, I gather, is being a great success in the States. Is there any strip or pictorial representation that could be built out of this game with the same name?'

TO ERNEST CUNEO

In December 1953 Fleming paid a fleeting visit to New York, where he stayed in Cuneo's apartment. It was at the height of McCarthyism, and although Fleming may or may not at that time have met either Allen Dulles, head of the CIA, or the newly elected President Dwight Eisenhower, he appreciated that Senator McCarthy's persecution of perceived Communists was news-worthy and that advantage could be gained by interviewing two 'turned' spies, Elizabeth Bentley and Whittaker Chambers.

3rd December, 1953

Dear Ernie,

Life seems very quiet and humdrum without you, but without any effort I can hear a steady roar coming from your room in NANA punctu-ated by Ivar's racking cough.

As usual, it was heaven to stay in your apartment and renew acquain-tance with Caractacus, my favourite of all cockroaches, and be lulled by the sweet music of the house next door being pulled down, as I sipped your pre-McCarthy Bourbon.

I long for you to come over here so that I can provide you with a pale shadow of these delights. Perhaps one day you will condescend to leave your kingdom.

I spoke severely to the White House before leaving and I am glad to see that Dulles and the President have acted so promptly on my advice.

Last night I went into the whole situation with Rebecca West* and she would very much like to go over and have a look at it all. I suppose it won't be worth your while to have her do a series for NANA? She sees a Communist under every single bed and to have her interviewing Bentley and Chambers would surely be a great feather in your cap.

Also on business, I am trying to get an offer of the American rights of Ribbentrop's memoirs which are being published next week in Berlin, but there are so many vultures sitting round the carrion that I am not optimistic.

I don't think that we shall be coming through New York in January but flying direct to Jamaica to save money and days. Would you please tell Ivar this. But I shall be with you on my way back in March and perhaps I could pick up Ivar in Nassau and bring him along. [...]

I long to hear news of the book[†] and I hope you will drop me a line directly there is anything solid to tell.

I must go along to Scott's[‡] now and toy with some oysters and a roast grouse and discuss matters with a disreputable spy of my acquaintance.

Fleming later wrote to ask if Cuneo could lean on his legal client and journalist acquaintance Walter Winchell to review Live and Let Die.

TO ERNEST CUNEO (undated)

Your old friend James Bond would be vastly obliged if his sub-agent Cuneo could persuade that delicate source W.W. to give this volume of his autobiography nationwide publicity.

Pray fail me not!

---

* Cicely Isabel Fairfield (1892–1983), novelist, journalist and feminist who wrote under the pseudonym Rebecca West. Revolted equally by Fascism and Communism, she took a staunch anti-authoritarian stance.
† Cuneo was working on a biography of Fiorello La Guardia, Mayor of New York City, which would be published in 1955 as *Life with Fiorello*.
‡ Scott's, then located on Coventry Street, was Fleming's favourite London restaurant.

The next year Fleming was on his way to America to research Diamonds are Forever. *He sought Cuneo's company for a trans-continental rail trip that would take in Los Angeles, Las Vegas and Chicago.*

TO ERNEST CUNEO

29th September, 1954

My dear Ernie,

This has nothing to do with our various negotiations, but on a still more pleasant topic.

If you are still willing I would like to fly over on November 5th and after a few days with you in New York make our trek to the West for a week or ten days, getting back to New York in time for Ivar's arrival on November 23rd.

Then spend a couple of days with him and you and then fly home.

Do you like this idea?

I would love to see Las Vegas and then perhaps the Hollywood world very briefly if you can spare the time to chaperone me.

I would also very much like to make the trans-continental trip by train in the luxury to which you and I are accustomed and then perhaps fly back.

What do you think of all of this?

It would take you away from your desk for about ten days and I wonder if you can spare the time.

I do hope so, as my education is now only incomplete with respect to the West Coast of America.

Hope all goes well with Bill.* Play the game entirely your own way and forgive me if I have slightly overcooked the goose before presenting him to you.

---

* Bill Aitken, Lord Beaverbrook's nephew, whom Fleming had introduced as one of two possible investors in NANA.

Our warm encouraging thoughts will be with you next week but even if both deals end up by falling through it will be pleasant to think that if two such big fish were after the Corporation in one year, there will be others in the future.

Good luck.

From this and other visits, Cuneo discovered that Fleming had an insatiable capacity for physical exertion. He recalled in particular an occasion when Fleming visited his home, near Bryce's Black Hollow Farm in Vermont, and insisted they climb the 880-foot Goose Egg Mountain. By the time they had raced up and hurtled down, Cuneo was a wreck. But Fleming simply dived into the nearest pool of ice-cold water, splashed around for an hour or so, then casually walked the mile and a half back to Black Hollow Farm. 'His strenuous exercises I took to be the hair-shirt phase of his knighthood, akin to the Gotham monks who by starvation and self denial sought to exorcise by sweat and exertion the devils within all men. He would and did plunge into this everyday world; but at a pause, he became himself, a knight again.'

He also became alert to the diligence with which Fleming researched the facts that underpinned his novels. 'For the most part our conversations were animated, but they were subject to a peculiarly Flemingesque characteristic. Detail fascinated him, as it not only bored, but actually enraged me. If he ran across a trick of the trade, a nuance, a fillip, he would pursue it like a ferret, for example, how cowboys on the range made a barbecue sauce with sugar, ketchup and Worcestershire sauce. God, he'd pursue the detail like Sir Edward Carson cross-examining a murderer. The temperature and appearance of the fire, kind of wood burned, the size of the pan – all of these things he'd scribble down with the avidity of an explorer taking notes on the opening of Tutankhamen's tomb. Time and time again as these interrogations wore on, I'd say "Come on, Ian, the hell with it." For the most part he'd shoot me a reproachful glare and keep on scribbling. He explained this to me. He said that at the end of each day, he had compiled notes. These he amplified and typed out, no matter what the hour, at the rate of about 800 [words] a day. "Figure it out for yourself," he said. "At the end of a year, I have about 250 or 300 of these daily memos,* and when I go down to Jamaica, I weave them into a book."'

As they sped by rail across America, Cuneo was amazed by how this trait repeated itself. At every stop, even on the train itself, Fleming would talk to people, write in his notebook and formulate adventures in his mind. 'He conversed with the crew and made his usual notes. When we arrived in Chicago the next morning, he was all joy. I at once discerned that he had something in mind that would infuriate me, and I was right. "Off," he chortled, "Off we go to America's great shrine – the scene of the St. Valentine's Day Massacre." "Not me," I said. "You. But before you go, let's drop in at a little place they have here in Chicago. Nothing much but something I think you should see." I took him straightway to the Chicago Institute of Fine Arts, which in my view, is unmatched in all the world. Fleming was entranced, completely enveloped by the master-pieces. He commented in subdued tones; it was as near as I ever saw him come to reverence. He knew a great deal more about painting than I. I do not know enough about painting to say how much he knew about it, but expert or not, few I know have exhibited his deep feeling for it. He forgot St. Valentine's, I almost had to drag him out. Out in broad daylight, the enchantment evaporated. [. . .] He went off to the St. Valentine's scene – alone. They told him it was all changed, but he went anyway and scribbled away when he got back.

'We pulled out in the Super Chief. The great train was almost deserted then, quite a change from pre-war days when it was crowded and gay as a cruise ship. We were half way to Iowa before the Super Chief's stewards had fully absorbed their instructions on how to make his Martinis. [. . .] I had arranged for him to ride the cab with the engineers, which to my amazement, took quite some doing. I went with him. He was all over the engine, went back into the inferno of noise in the Diesel room – alone – and interrogated the engineer and his assistant on everything from the block signal system to the "dead man control". [. . .] Ian was delighted as he watched the great care with which they took the big train through the Raton Pass. He was off at every stop through New Mexico and Arizona,

---

* While it is true that Fleming was an assiduous note-taker, Cuneo's estimate may be a touch exaggerated.

talking to the men serving the train, walking briskly around the desert architecture stations, taking mental photographs by the score. [. . .]

'Fleming was at this time all but unknown. He was, in his own words, "waffling about" not even conceiving remotely of the fame to come.' *Yet he managed to gain access to the Los Angeles Police Headquarters, where he was absorbed by their methods and by their narcotics operation. The same magic worked at Las Vegas, where he and Cuneo were given first-hand instruction on how casinos were run*

During the journey they discussed matters of life. One topic was the hankering after fame. Cuneo having once been a promising professional footballer, he explained how glad he was to have rid himself of the desire for applause. Fleming disagreed.

'"Matter of fact," he said, "Know what I would consider the ideal existence? Know what I'd like if I could have anything I wanted? I'd like to be the absolute ruler of a country where everyone was crazy about me." Fitting it to the American scene for my benefit, he said, "Imagine yourself waking up in the White House. Instantly, the radio would announce to a breathless country, 'He's awake.' Bulletins would follow. 'He's shaving.' 'He's dressing.' 'He's breakfasting.' 'He's reading the papers in the garden.' Finally, at 10.30 'He's ordered the car!' And at 11 o'clock," said Ian, "I'd pass out through the gates, tossing medals to deliriously happy hundreds of thousands." "I'd like that," he said, and added, "And so would they. Too bad you don't like applause."

'"Ian," I said, "You miss the point. I shun applause because I like it too much. It might be like going back on dope."

'"That's good," he nodded. "Nothing like being aware of your defects of character. A sound approach. You don't usually admit them, you know."

'"Balls," I said.'

Another subject was the matter of Bond's extravagant sex life. 'Holy Smoke! Dragged over coral reefs, caught in steam pipes, sharks by the score, corpses all around – what came to Bond's mind, I assured him, would be the last to enter mine, or in fact, anyone I knew or had ever known. This amused Ian. I think Bond was a thing apart from him. Though created by him he seemed to be as detached from Bond as a scientist who has created a robot, and indeed, there were a considerable number of times when I thought Bond bored Fleming to tears. But the writing, the craftsmanship of detail, did not. I had the impression that Bond was the mere instrumentation of this craftsmanship, which is most excellent. Indeed, I think that some of Fleming's paragraphs are all but Keatsian, and that a good deal of his writing will survive James Bond. Fleming didn't. As a matter of fact, at that time, he was striving to get James Bond living and wasn't too sure he wouldn't die before.'

On the matter of sex, they both agreed that they had been brought up in puritanical societies. Cuneo said he had been educated to believe 'that evil "thoughts" were as bad as evil "deeds". The impossibility of this compounded the agony, it being as difficult as Tolstoy's condition of standing in a corner and not thinking of a polar bear. Fleming all but trembled with anger at the Established Hypocrisy, particularly of the Victorians. "Read the stuff," he said harshly, "Any of it and you can hardly believe it. In Jamaica I happened to pick up an old account of shooting. "'Ah," sighed the old planter, "To see these beautiful tropical birds, visions of beauty, and now dead through my fowling piece."' Suddenly he burst into sustained laughter until his face reddened – real laughter not bitter laughter. [. . .] Actually, he had had one terrifying experience which he remembered with horror, converted into laughter. I thought it was psychologically traumatic, and modified, it appears as one of the incidents in his books.'*

And then there was marriage and children. In the 1920s Cuneo had considered the future. 'My then view was that, given the allocated three score and ten years, I had fifty years to go – only 2,500 weeks, and I proposed to do what I pleased with them. [. . .] We were all aboard the Titanic and you might just as well have a hell of a time while the voyage lasted. It was the mood of the Roaring Twenties and roar we did, grinding out the juice of each day as if it were the last grape on the vine.' *But all this changed with marriage.* 'Men do not like to use the word "love". Fleming and I spoke often of our children, and neither used the term; but it was clear to me that Ian "loved" his son Caspar deeply, more deeply, possibly, than most fathers.'

On reaching Denver they took a quick whiff from the oxygen inhalers that were currently distributed throughout American airports, before catch-

---

* *The Spy Who Loved Me.*

ing a plane back to New York. It had been an epic, and revealing, journey.
'Ian used a lot of the material he gathered in his next book. He sent me
a first copy, as always, nicely inscribed. I was slightly chagrined to find
it contained a character called Ernie Cureo, a taxicab driver, and made
routine protest, well knowing I could do nothing about it, that he knew
I could do nothing about it and so what the hell. He sent me a plain
gold bill-clip inscribed, "To Ernie – my guide on a trip to the Angels
and back. 007" The word play, of course, was on Los Angeles.'

FROM ERNEST CUNEO

May 9th, 1956

Dear Ian:

Firstly, I was delighted with "Diamonds are Forever". It was action
packed, as anyone who considers the wrecking of a Lucius Beebe train
and the shooting down of a helicopter must readily admit. I did think
that the whole business was slightly overorganized for a paltry two million a year. But the descriptions of the train wreck and the queen at sea
[the *Queen Elizabeth* liner] were marvellously graphic writing. Suffice to
say that I picked it up and read it through without putting it down – and
all without a wet eye for poor Ernie Cureo, the lout. [. . .]

I may be over this summer on the new Mato Magazine.

Until then – Diamonds and Cuneo are forever.

FROM ERNEST CUNEO

Fleming often said that Cuneo had supplied most of the material for Diamonds are Forever, *and Cuneo was not short of incidents that he thought
Fleming might like to use in other books.*

April 12th, 1957

Dear Ian,

Thanks muchly for your book [*Dr No*]: I can hardly wait to read it,
but I hasten to express my appreciation.

Riding by Glen Echo Amusement Park, it occurred to me, as a lively scene, that Bond should fight a gun duel in the Hall of Mirrors, each man under blazing lights, and the myriad mirrors presenting exact likenesses to the other as target. A horrible lottery: 20 mirrors and 6 shots.

I couldn't get to Nassau, but I hear that Jo and Ivar had the best time ever and both are in the tan.

You, if you think it wise, might send a copy of your book to Stanley Meyer, Four Oaks Farm, Encino, California, who, in his new position as a director of MGM, might be in a position to get it direct attention.

Sorry we missed, but look forward to seeing you this summer.

TO ERNEST CUNEO

As a result of a successful takeover bid by a Canadian syndicate, Fleming found his career at NANA abruptly terminated.

23rd May, 1957

My dear Ernie,

I have never thought that Mr. Wheeler's strong point is tact, but I have just had a surprisingly abrupt letter from him terminating my position with the syndicates at ten days' notice.

This communication stung me to reply in similar vein and I enclose a copy of my letter to him.

At the same time I am writing at once to you to explain that if we are to engage in officialese ping-pong this is the choice of Mr. Wheeler and not of me.

Ivar and I had lunch together yesterday and I gather there has been a further change of ownership in the syndicates and that you have a tough job ahead of you sailing the ship more or less single-handedly, so naturally the last thing I want to do is rock the boat, even with the smallest ripple.

My friendship with you is far more important to me than my status with N.A.N.A. and now with the syndicates, and if you tell me there's no money in the till to pay out anything in compensation for loss of office I shall dry my tears and merely help myself rather more liberally to caviare when we meet at the "Twenty One" in August.

As the years progressed, and Britain gradually declined from being an imperial power to simply just a power, Cuneo felt that relations between Britain and the US were becoming frostier than before. 'Bill Stephenson was gone and much of the British American rapport evaporated with his departure. This affected deeply British-American friends. Fleming and I were no exception.' *When he teased Fleming about this he realised that he was, above all, a die-hard patriot.* 'That Fleming had his logic-tight compartments there can be no doubt. I discovered this when he was more or less savagely attacking the White House. I took on Buckingham Palace, deriding the monarchy as a fantastic anachronism.

'"No," said Fleming, "It's a ballet, say what you will, it's a ballet." I said that what was once the signature of empire was now a tourist attraction – and that the old adage that history repeats itself but only as a farce was never more apparent than in the trooping of the colors.

'He almost burst into tears. He said, "No, Ernie, it's a ballet, maybe, but a beautiful one." He was both sad and deeply moved. I hadn't the slightest doubt that ballet or not, he'd lay down his life for it.'

In 1961, by which time Britain's global presence had been all but dismantled, Fleming suffered a heart attack.

TO ERNEST CUNEO, ESQ., 784 Park Avenue, New York, 28

1st June, 1961

My Dear Ernie,

A thousand thanks for your splendid screed of May 16th which came as a powerful injection of mescalin in the midst of my ludicrous health problems.

These are now resolving themselves and I am more or less erect (in a respectable way). But I am afraid with an endless vista of twenty cigarettes and three ounces of liquor a day and, worst of all, no women, scrambled eggs or golf.

It's all quite ridiculous, and I am finding myself hard put to fill the vacua thus created.

It is no help to be told by Noël Coward that I must become "more spiritual", or by my ex Naval Intelligence Chief that I must write his life. Nor am I thrilled by the prospect of correspondence, chess or petit point, which are also offered.

Anyway I am definitely booked on the Queen Elizabeth on July 20th and, in the meantime, I look out of the window at the rain and eat food cooked in kosher margarine. What a life! [. . .]

Ivar moves from race course to race course watching his horses come in last. So far as McClory* is concerned I have a meeting with my Counsel next week on the copyright side, but my impression is that I will not have the satisfaction of seeing him shredded in the Courts since Jo [Bryce] thinks it would be vulgar for Ivar to go on the witness stand!

My immediate interest is trying to get hold of the Times' obituary which they had spruced up by a friend of mine when the tomb yawned!

With much affection,

TO ERNEST CUNEO

28th June, 1961

My dear Ernie,

I very greatly enjoyed the round tour of your innermost thoughts and though sometimes I find myself slightly airborne by the loftiness of your ratiocination, I think I have more or less got the photo.

By chance Bryce was sitting before me here yesterday afternoon and I allowed him a glimpse of your palimpsest. It entirely delighted him though, as in all great testaments, there were certain passages, notably

---

* Fleming was currently engaged in a court battle with Kevin McClory over copyright in his latest book, *Thunderball*.

those dealing with higher mathematics, which were too much for the common clay of his mind.

One thing is quite clear to both of us. The velocity of your thought, as also the velocity with which you cover the ground, betoken the constitution, physical and mental, of a giant, and we both feel, if you have not already done so, that you should add a codicil to your Will bequeathing your cadaver in toto to an appropriate medical or scientific institution. (Perhaps you might even spare a small piece for the Bryce Foundation!)

To get back to duller subjects, my health continues to improve and Ivar's horses continue to lose.

The rest we will discuss while the shadows gather round the skirts of Goose Egg and the ice of the emptying glasses rattles against our teeth.

With renewed and warm thanks for your positively stupendous letter.

'I saw Ian several times after his first heart attack. [. . .] Ian's aura showed he had been hit much more severely than he believed. He was annoyed more than alarmed, he smoked as much and drank and ate the same and stated emphatically that he intended to be bored by no regrets.

'He was in fullest faculty, of course, and if anything more effervescent than ever. He, however, lacked much of the aura, and when I saw him in London, I noted the crowsfeet around his eyes – born of heavy laughter – looked tired.[. . .]

'Actually, he was getting a bit sick of Bond before the Big Breeze Blew: he was contemplating killing him off in a final book. He had achieved a very considerable measure of success. He was required reading in Mayfair and on the North Shore. He had ignited a quite satisfactory and top-drawer readership. I think that when it exploded in a Vesuvius of popular consumption, it was as much a surprise to him as to anyone else.'

On reviewing Fleming's life, Cuneo returned to his Arthurian analogy: 'He felt no particular discontent with himself. He felt much discontent with the world in which he lived, for he was a knight out of phase, a knight errant searching for the lost Round Table and possibly the Holy Grail, and unable to reconcile himself that Camelot was gone and still less that it had probably never existed.'

5

Diamonds are Forever

IT WAS IN New York, on the way home from Goldeneye in March 1954, that Fleming noticed an advertisement in American *Vogue* – 'A Diamond Is Forever'. It caught his imagination, and for a short while Atticus ran items about these glittering treasures. On 20 June, he reported on the fifth largest diamond the world had ever seen. It came to 426½ carats and weighed 3.4 ounces in the rough – a splendour that was done little justice by being photographed alongside a box of matches. 'But,' he wrote, 'I suppose De Beers think of diamonds simply in terms of carbon burned into the form of crystals in which each atom is tetrahedrally linked to four others at distances of 1.54 Angstrom units, with a hardness of ten on Mohs's scale and a specific heat of 0.147, and that these crystals (perish the thought) burn at around 1,000 degrees Centigrade and produce carbon dioxide gas.' Angstrom, Moh and matchbox aside, the stone was still worth £100,000. So rare an item, so tormented its measure, so seductive its allure – here were the makings of a typically Flemingesque romance.

Diamonds are Forever drew Bond into the spectacular world of international diamond smuggling. The plot ranged from Sierra Leone, via Amsterdam to New York, Saratoga and Las Vegas and saw 007 working undercover to infiltrate a powerful criminal network – The Spangled Mob, run by brothers Jack and Seraffimo Spang whose employees included a pair of homosexual hitmen, Wint and Kidd. It involved horse racing, fast cars, mud baths, gambling and the freewheeling American go-between, Tiffany Case, with whom Bond fell in love. The climax came at Seraffimo Spang's ranch, Spectreville,* where Bond sent him to his death by diverting his private steam train into an abandoned mine. Returning to Britain with Tiffany on the *Queen Elizabeth* liner, Bond overcame an assassination attempt by Wint and Kidd and later went to Africa where he not only plugged the diamond pipeline but dealt fatally with Jack Spang. The book ended with Tiffany and Bond living together in his London flat and the prospect of marriage hanging in the air.

Fleming worked harder on this novel than he had for the previous three. He took advice from De Beers, who allowed him to watch the sorting and cutting of diamonds, and consulted Sir Percy Sillitoe, ex-head of MI5, who ran the International Diamond Security Organisation.† What inspired him most, however, were his own experiences.

In August 1954 he flew to America where he visited Ivar Bryce at his home in Black Hole Hollow, Vermont, and joined up with his old friend Ernie Cuneo to tour the nearby mud baths and race tracks of Saratoga. Ostensibly, his reason for meeting Bryce and Cuneo was to discuss the possible sale of NANA. But it also provided a rich source of material. Apart from Saratoga's famous attractions, he was fascinated by one of Bryce's friends, William 'Billy' Woodward Jnr, a millionaire who had inherited his father's banking fortune and feared that his showgirl wife was of the wrong social category. Fleming advised Woodward to divorce her – which she pre-empted shortly thereafter by shooting him. He noted him down as a character for his next book, under the pseudonym Willard White. But what really got Fleming going was Woodward's car, a Studillac, a hybrid that combined the power of a Studebaker with the luxury of a Cadillac. He enjoyed not only its energy but the imagination that underpinned its design. It was a specialist vehicle crafted precisely to its user's needs. The concept fitted Bond like a glove.

Fleming flew back to America in November, where he teamed up with Ernie Cuneo for a trans-continental train journey from New York

---

* Fleming would later adopt the word SPECTRE for a criminal organisation that appeared in several of his books.
† In 1957 Sillitoe assisted Fleming with his non-fiction book *The Diamond Smugglers*.

via Chicago to Los Angeles and then back to Las Vegas. Apart from the rich novelistic pickings which the journey provided, he had good reason to visit Los Angeles. Earlier that year he had sold the TV rights for *Casino Royale* to CBS* – it came out in October 1954 starring Barry Nelson as Jimmy Bond and Peter Lorre as Le Chiffre – and now, through his agent 'Swanee' Swanson, he did a lucrative deal for an option on *Moonraker.*

Then, in January 1955, he was off to Jamaica for the usual stint, returning in March to see the April publication of *Moonraker* and resume duties at the *Sunday Times.* By now his schedule was so busy that for his Atticus column he relied occasionally on his assistants – among them his future biographer John Pearson – to supply copy. But his hand was still in evidence. He always liked to end the column with a joke, and on 24 April he offered a wry take on what would become a Bond catchphrase, 'shaken, not stirred'.

"'A new recruit to the "Mounties" was being despatched to the wilds of the North-West on a lone and perilous mission.

Before he left, his commanding officer handed him a miniature cocktail shaker and two small bottles containing gin and vermouth.

"What am I to do with those sir? I don't drink."

"They're in case you get lost."

"I don't get you sir."

"If you think you're lost, empty those two bottles into the shaker, put in some hunks of ice and shake vigorously. Before you've shaken very long somebody's bound to appear out of the blue and say 'That's not the way to make a Martini'."

FLEMING TO ANN

After Ann had left Goldeneye for New York, Fleming described, along with gossip about his neighbours, an occasion that appealed to his sense of the

---

* It was to be the only time a Bond story was adapted for television.

romantic. The Killer's Net could have been taken from – and used as a title for – one of his novels. Daniel George, Cape's reader, would later criticise Fleming for his constant use of 'and', which he presumed was meant to give a sense of 'panting continuity'. He told him to stop it – but too late in this instance.

From Goldeneye, March 1955, Monday

My darling precious,

When I saw that the big bird had got you in its claws I went back to sunset and sat on the far groyne and swam and loved you for an hour and hated the idea of Edward [Molyneux] and Montego and Jamaica without you. Then I sat with Carmen [Pringle] for an hour and told her how wonderful you are and then I went to Edward's. At the bottom of his drive it was very exciting and all made for you, which made things worse. The night before a shoal of goggle-eyes (must look them up) had been seen and about fifty of the fishermen sewed their nets together and for the whole previous twenty-four hours they had been making a great sweep of the bay. And now the twenty canoes were in a circle and it was getting smaller all the time. So I found Edward and T.P. [Tony Pawson] and we stayed there until it was quite dark and the fishermen left men in two canoes with acetylene torches to keep the fish down and they all went home and I expect they all dreamed all night of the great circle of boiling fish. And the churchbells were ringing in Montego and it was madly romantic and like some great traditional fish festival in Italy. And they were due to come back to their boats at six in the morning and I told Edward that he had got to get up at five and be there and paint the whole thing. Then we had to leave it and go up to his airless and pretentious house and talk about you and Edward's servants and how much he was 'tiefed' and how Noël thought he was God. Then frozen New Zealand mutton for dinner and tomato soup and ice cream and after dinner Edward said What will you drink and I said Brandy and there was no brandy and T.P. played the House of Flowers record and I wanted to scoop you by hearing it first but Edward talked about Billy Rose wanting to buy his house at any price. Then bed, with the empty twin beside me and no air and no darling sniffs. As a result I woke up earlier than usual and cursed you for not being there and went down to the sea and they were all there and the ring of net was getting smaller, but still as big as a house, and the fish were boiling and jumping and they were all about a foot long and very silver with black eyes and the fishermen didn't want to hurry it, because the market knew all about the catch and all the hotels were waiting and the longer they had to wait the more they would have to pay because of lunch and not having bought any other fish. So I went back and it was cold and I bathed in the dull pool and thought of you being woken up in NY by the hot air crackling in the central heating, and had breakfast with bad scrambled eggs but lots of matching china and the toast wrapped up in a napkin. Then I went down again to the sea and Edward was there painting away and finally the circle was as big as a stage and they started hauling up parts of the nets and the fish waterfalled into the canoes and as soon as one canoe was full they started to fill another. I left after a bit and they had filled four canoes solid with fish. Nothing else but goggle-eyes. Then I finished correcting my book which seems terribly silly today and Edward's picture isn't bad, in fact I think the best he has done this year, and he was pleased I had made him (which shows there's something in the way I go on!) and agreed to call it 'The Killer's Net', which is what the blackamores call it when the circle gets small. And now I am getting tired and will shortcut the rest.

I love you
Ian

TO MISS CLAUDETTE COLBERT,* 615 North Faring Road, Los Angeles 24, Calif.

While in LA the previous year Fleming had met the actress Claudette Colbert and invited her to stay at Goldeneye.

28th April, 1955

I am very sad that you will not be in Goldeneye next winter, but you may change your mind and it is always there if you want it.

* Claudette Colbert (1903–96), French-born actress and Hollywood leading lady.

I hear there were great dramas after I left, with David Niven catching chickenpox and so on, and I fancy the general atmosphere was considerably disturbed. I shall hear all about it this week-end as Noël is coming over to have dinner with us before going back to America.

I have little hope of getting out to Los Angeles this year. I was there last November and I have absolutely no excuse for another holiday unless Hollywood suddenly decides to film one of my books. You would be the perfect heroine for any of them so if you see my Literary Agent on the Coast, Swanee Swanson, get him to tell you what you are missing.

TO MICHAEL HOWARD

1st September, 1955

Dear Michael,

Mark Bonham Carter [of the publishers William Collins] came to dinner last night and I quizzed him about his thriller authors.

I suppose everything he said has to be taken with a considerable grain of salt as he has been trying to prise me loose from you for the last three years, but even so his comments are interesting.

Of Hammond Innes he sells between 40–60,000 copies in hard backs and regularly prints a first edition of 40,000.

He said that if my fourth book was as good as the others he would guarantee to print a first edition of 20,000.

He says that around between 8–10,000 is the sound barrier in these sort of books and the only way to get through it is to make a large print run and simply shovel it down the retailers' mouths.

I told him that I thought that my readership was confined to the A-Class of reader and he said that that was completely disproved by the Pan Book sales of CASINO.*

He mentioned incidentally that he is doing a print of 125,000 of H.M.S. Ulysses,† the largest print that they have ever done of a first novel, but that Picture Post will be serialising it and that this will help.

---

* Following a deal with Pan Books the first Bond paperbacks had emerged that year.
† *HMS Ulysses* by Alistair MacLean.

He said that a pictorial jacket would certainly help my books, but that unless we made a great push to get through the sound barrier of 10,000 copies I would be permanently stuck there.

He said there were moments when a publisher had to beat the big drum about an author but that if all the stars were right when he did so it was the only way to get mass sales.

I am sure all this is not news to you but I wonder if we really shouldn't have a go with DIAMONDS ARE FOREVER and do a real operation on it.

If you would like me to come into financial partnership in any way on such a venture I should be happy to do so, but the main thing, I am sure, is the effort and drive put into the operation.

Mark mentioned incidentally that they have sold 15,000 copies of that Wedgwood book "The King's Peace", I think it was called, which I think he stole from you.

Of course Mark was shouting the odds a good deal but he knows that I have heard it all before from him and am wedded to you, but there is no doubt about it that Collins do go out on a limb from time to time and they appear to get away with it.

TO MICHAEL HOWARD

25th November, 1955

Dear Michael,

Various things.

First of all I'd be delighted to talk to your travellers on December 8th. Please let me know what time.

I have no idea how one "peps up" travellers. I should have thought the best thing for them to do would be to read the splendid puff in Smith's Trade News!

"John Bull" don't want to serialize. They say: "It's a bit too strong and spicy a dish for our readership".

I have had a letter from Curtis Brown which confirms that the nine months' option on the film rights of MOONRAKER has been sold in Hollywood for $1,000 with option to purchase for $10,000.

The purchaser is the actor John Payne about whom I know very little.*

I am asking Curtis Brown to forward the draft contract to you for approval before I sign it.

I shall almost certainly be in Jamaica by the time the contract appears and if you agree I would like to leave all arguments about it in the hands of you and your excellent solicitors.

Then when you are happy the contract will come back to me in Jamaica for signature and I will forward it back to Curtis Brown from there without giving it any thought whatsoever.

Now, as to the Hallman cover: I do most reluctantly feel that it won't particularly help the book. Some of the background faces are quite splendid but Bond in his white dinner jacket behind this pasty-faced doll, doesn't really come off, I think.†

What are we to do? Would you like to play around with the roughs from Ken Lewis I sent over? I am inclined to think this title is such a good one (forgive me!) that all it needs is first class typographical treatment on the lines of LIVE AND LET DIE.

The only trouble about Lewis is that he lacks a touch of imagination and I wonder if you would like to get one of your own artists to play about with the roughs, and see if he can get a bit more sparkle and some more exciting colours into them. Please let me know what you think. [...]

TO MICHAEL HOWARD

There were difficulties finding the correct jacket design. They were eventually resolved when Howard's wife, Pat Marriott, took on the job.

10th January, 1956

Dear Michael,

I am terribly sorry to hear you are having such pangs about the jacket.

* The option was not exercised and expired the following year.
† Adolf Hallman (1893–1968) had designed covers for several Scandinavian publications of Bond.

An idea might be to stylize Harling's idea – retaining the golden or yellow visiting card but spacing the diamonds evenly across a very dark blue or dark red background, and making the diamonds larger and more sparkling but each of the same, stylized, symmetrical design.

This would produce something of the same impact as the CASINO ROYALE cover. It would have rather a spotty effect at a distance but this would be minimized if you reduced the number of diamonds on the cover to about 8 or 10, and in any case the spots would be eye-catching.

I did the waffle for Smith's and sent it over to Troughton last week, so you might care to contact Burt and see that he publishes the stuff when you would like to have it, and also perhaps supply a photograph.

I enclose a rough copy and hope it pleases you.

TO MICHAEL HOWARD

Goldeneye, 14th February, 1956

Forgive this tropic scrawl. I am sitting in the <u>shade</u> gazing out across the Caribbean & it is heroic that I am writing at all. But I must congratulate you on the jacket. It's excellent, also text, & please thank your wife for her inspiration. I feel a soupcon of cleavage would have helped, but I know your politics on that – & there <u>must</u> be a credit line with "Diamond clip by Cartier".

You certainly knocked the breath out of Naomi [Burton] & I have also just fired her a snorter. The truth is of course that no agent wants to lose his name with even the meagrest Hollywood agent, whereas it couldn't matter less to the author or publisher. I daresay Naomi's in a bit of a spot but that's what she gets 10% for. Soft pedal her a bit now. She's a good girl.

Have done 52,000 of the next. Can't tell what it's like, but it goes fast & has been fun. Bit too much body hair & blood perhaps, but there are some chuckles for William whose poems I saw got a fine review in the New Yorker the other day. Give him my love. Must stop. There's a lobster to be speared & then as the sun sets & the fireflies come out a man called DARKO KERIM is going to shoot a man called TRILENCU with a SNIPERSCOPE.

FROM MICHAEL HOWARD

21st February, 1956

Dear Ian,

Many thanks for writing. I do appreciate your action and the effort it must have taken. Pat will be enormously relieved to know that you approve of the jacket. I am afraid, however, that the co-operation of Cartier must remain unacknowledged. I went into the point very carefully with my helpers in that House and they assured me that if such reference were made to the firm the whole proposition would have to go before old man Cartier and they told me that he, to put it mildly, is an unco-operative old gentleman and that he would insist upon the jacket being done his way. The stones I borrowed and the drawings and photographs they made for me were provided quite unofficially and several people's jobs might well depend on their help remaining anonymous.

I shall be glad not to have to pursue poor Naomi Burton further at the present time, and am glad that you have taken the ball for the moment, but I must tell you that Miss Briggs* is waxing hysterical and over this weekend has indicated pretty clearly that if Rank cannot buy the property now they are going to buy something else instead. It is driving us to distraction to see this splendid deal go down the drain and I do hope you will be able to cable us very quickly that the American negotiations are unscrambled and we can proceed with Rank.

I will give your messages to William when he comes in tomorrow.

TO GEOFFREY M. CUCKSON, ESQ., Nottingham

Mr Cuckson had written before, and now he did so again. Having read, and agreed with a review of Diamonds are Forever *by Raymond Chandler that criticised Fleming for not sticking to the action, he felt the book was fair enough but contained too much 'scenic description'. On a personal note he*

* Script editor at the Rank Organisation, who were still interested in the film rights to *Moonraker*.

added, 'You know my weakness for girls in bondage, and after the original
way you have handled it in previous books, notably Live and Let Die, *I was*
disappointed not to find any this time.' In a yet more specific postscript:
'Tiffany (or her equivalent) bound in a frogman's suit would be really
something!'

9th April, 1956

Thank you very much indeed for your long and most interesting letter
and for your kindly and sapient comments on my book.

I am inclined to agree with all your points but on the question of padding I have the excuse that I find technical details of a place like Las
Vegas so fascinating that I put them in over-generously. Those odds on
the various games, for instance, were hard to get hold of and would be of
vital importance to anyone visiting the place. So I quite admit to my
tendency towards overloading my books with Baedekerish information,
but Chandler was wrong in thinking this was "padding" which I abhor
in other writers.

But all your other comments are very much to the point and I value
them. You should definitely be a book reviewer, at least for your local
paper.

I will certainly see what I can do to find you a girl in a frogman's suit.

TO W. SOMERSET MAUGHAM, ESQ., Villa Mauresque, St. Jean, Cap Ferrat,
A.M., France

12th April, 1956

You shouldn't have bothered to write to me or at most it should have
been a typed letter in the third person. When I am as famous and as
patriarchal as you, I shan't be nearly so graceful about it, but more like
Evelyn Waugh who has various printed postcards, one of which reads:
"Mr. Evelyn Waugh regrets that he is unable to do what you so kindly
suggest", which seems to me to answer most of the problems that face
the famous.

However, of course I loved getting your letter and I am delighted you enjoyed the book. I thought it was great fun myself and I only wish that people would write more books of exotic and fantastic adventure instead of whining away in contrived prose about their happy childhood and their ghastly lives in corrugated iron universities.

Annie, of course, has made no comment whatsoever on the book as it is set in America whose existence she doesn't admit and I used words like "mirror" instead of looking glass. She doesn't realise how terribly vulgar it has become to talk about looking glasses ever since Nancy Mitford wrote about them.

In fact her character has greatly improved since she went to Enton Hall [a health farm in Surrey] and had nothing but an orange a day for a week. A lot of the Charteris bile was squeezed out of her and there have even been moments since I got back from Jamaica when she has even shown signs of cosiness – a terrifying manifestation which I must at all costs keep secret from her smart friends.

Annie wrote to me in Jamaica that you had not been well but I don't like the sound of these "bothers" you have been having. I suppose there are no small things in which I can be of help? Should you ever need un homme de confiance (and I mean "confiance") to do chores for you here or elsewhere you would, I hope, send me your instructions which would be executed faithfully and naturally without a word to anyone – least of all to the daily newspaper I have married.

But if you feel really deep despair, I will ship Annie down by Blue Train and accompany her myself if you wished. She loves you and would be a good tonic and I know she would hurry out if she felt she could make you happier.

Don't bother to answer this but don't forget that you have two slaves here in case there is anything you want.

TO MRS. SALLY REID, Oldfield Lodge Cottage, Bridge Road, Maidenhead, Berks.

When Diamonds are Forever *was serialised in the* Express *it was accompanied by a photograph of Fleming. 'Quite exceptionally for an author,' wrote Mrs Reid, 'your profile photograph in to-day's* Daily Express *reveals you as the type of man that could have written and experienced and imagined the thrillers mentioned in your article. The picture also revealed – in spite of the rugged planes of the face – a kindliness and self-analytical diffidence which does you credit and keeps your books human if tough.' She wasn't, however, at all keen on the business of serialising books – 'the frustrated suspense etc. diminishes interest'. It was the first time she had written a fan letter and did so in haste as she was shortly to embark on a three-week trip to Canada and the USA.*

30th April, 1956

How very kind of you to have written me such a charming letter about the serial in the "Daily Express". I'm afraid the book has been dreadfully cut about to fit it into the space they had, but even so I am glad you enjoyed it.

One day if you come to write a book you will realise what a delightful surprise it is to have a letter from an admirer out of the blue.

Again with many thanks and with best wishes for your trip to America and Canada.

TO MISS BETTY REESE, Vice President, Raymond Loewy Associates, 425 Park Avenue, New York, 22, U.S.A.

Betty Reese, PR operative for Raymond Loewy who had created the outline of the Studillac, wrote to thank Fleming for mentioning it in his latest book. 'You gave us a happy reference in fiction to a design of which Mr. Loewy is justifiably proud. If characters like "Studillacs" so must people.'

30th December, 1957

Your kind letter of December 10th was passed on to me by Macmillans, and I am delighted if my reference to Loewy design gave pleasure in the Palace of Loewy.

I may say that it was a sincere tribute to the prettiest and most practical design of any post-war American motor car.

TO WHITEFRIAR, c/o Smith's Trade News, Strand House, W.C.2.

In November 1955 Whitefriar had written a positive review of Diamonds are Forever. *'I'll stick my neck out here and now and say that this is the thrillingest yarn likely to reach the bookstands during 1956 ... To an armchair traveller like me, his evoking of the American scene, on land or in the air – or at sea – is quite superb.'*

12th April, 1956

I must write you a note to thank you most warmly for your kindness to DIAMONDS ARE FOREVER ever since you first read it, presumably in proof.

I am sure your praise has done as much as anything to make the book a success and in return I am at any rate pleased that the book entertained you. The life of a reviewer is a dreadful one and it is a real achievement to be able to raise the eyebrows of someone who has to read scores of books every week.

Anyway thank you very much for your encouragement.

TO JOHN G. RYAN, ESQ., Commercial Division Manager, Shannon Free Airport, Ireland

John Ryan wrote to say that a passage from Diamonds are Forever *had been read out at the latest meeting of the Co-Ordinating Committee of Shannon Airport. He cited the following: 'Steak and Champagne for dinner, and the wonderful goblet of hot coffee laced with Irish Whiskey and topped with half an inch of thick cream. A glance at the junk in the airport shop, the "Irish Horn Rosaries", the "Bog Oak Irish Harp" and the "Brass Leprechauns" all at $1.50 and the ghastly "Irish Musical Cottage" at $4.00, the* *furry unwearable tweeds and the dainty Irish Linen doilies and cocktail napkins. And then the Irish rigmarole coming over the loudspeakers in which only the words 'BOAC' were comprehensible . . .'*

Ryan wasn't having any of it. As the man responsible for Shannon's shops he was astonished to hear that Fleming considered their product "junk". 'As well as beautiful Irish linen, woollen goods and famous Irish tweeds, we also sell the best German Cameras, Swiss Watches and French Perfumes.' As for the Irish Coffee, it had been invented by Shannon's own chef and was praised highly by most transatlantic passengers.

29th May, 1956

Thank you very much for your letter of May 24th and I am greatly impressed that Shannon should have taken cognisance of my light-hearted thriller.

I often come through Shannon* and it will certainly be a great pleasure to meet you on my next visit and apologise in person for my happy-go-lucky references to the goods on offer in your shops.

Perhaps by then all the Bog Oak Irish Harps and Brass Leprechauns will have been bought up by the G.I.s!

TO MISS M. MARSHALL, 6 York Place, Edinburgh

In swirly script and on notepaper headed Palace Hotel, Milano (crossed out), Mildred Marshall wrote that her busy travel schedule made it hard to keep up with Fleming's books but she much enjoyed them. There was, however, a question about perfumes in Live and Let Die. *That aside, she would be very grateful if he could sign for her a copy of his latest – 'maybe "The Road from Moscow" (I hope that is right!)'. In a subsequent letter she stressed that her own lifestyle was extremely fascinating and she intended to write a book about it. The journalist Denzil Batchelor had promised to look at the manuscript.*

---

* Where flights between the UK and America stopped to refuel.

8th November, 1957

Thank you very much for your letter of November 3rd and I am delighted that you enjoy the adventures of James Bond.

Alas, attributing "Vent Vert" to Dior was nearly as bad as when, in one of my books, I made Bond eat asparagus with Sauce Bearnaise instead of Mousseline. I have also been severely reprimanded for having provided, in my last book, the Orient Express with hydraulic brakes instead of vacuum ones.

If I go on like this I shall one day find myself giving my heroine green hair.

Of course I will certainly autograph a book for you. The name of my last one was "From Russia, With Love".

Again with many thanks for your charming letter.

TO A. G. ALLEN, ESQ., 1 Upper Stone Street, Maidstone, Kent

Arthur Allen, a man of military stamp, complained that many of Fleming's so-called facts were 'a lot of rot'. First of all, it was impossible for two horses in the same race to be given odds of 6 to 4 on. Secondly, 'I should imagine it is quite a difficult feat to pick up a girl & lay her on the floor if you have an arm around her thighs, & why on the floor?' Thirdly, 'I have never yet seen a mobile Bofors where a Corporal, or any Other Rank, could turn the elevating & traversing cranks at the same time, &, to the best of my knowledge, there is only one firing pedal.' Unbristling his moustache to a slight degree, he admitted that his work as a 'pen pusher' didn't pay much so he couldn't afford Fleming's books or anyone else's. 'But I shall keep a watchful eye on the "Fs" in our local Public Library in the hope that they will purchase more of your books, at the moment they have only "Moonraker" & the one I have been criticising.'

11th March, 1958

Many thanks for your most interesting and expert letter of February 16th which I have just come back to find waiting for me.

The trouble about writing these books is that one cannot possibly satisfy all the various experts on their particular subjects, and all I can do when in doubt is to submit the passages concerned to somebody who should know.

In the case of the racing sequence in "Diamonds are Forever" the person in question was William Woodward Jr., the owner of Nashua, who was subsequently shot by his wife in very grisly circumstances, and you may notice that the book is dedicated in part to him.

However, I do not question your excellent reasoning and I only wish you had been within reach when I was writing the book!

As to your point about the girl, all I can suggest is that you should try making love to a girl on the Dunlopillo mattresses of the Queen Elizabeth. You would then know why I chose the floor.

On the other hand I must plead guilty to the Bofors passage but, although this was read for me by a gunnery expert from Hythe, I admit he was rather an elderly one and I dare say your points are legitimate.

I greatly enjoy these tough comments from my readers and hope you will stir up your librarian so that in due course I may receive some more sharp criticisms to help keep me up to the mark.

6

From Russia with Love

THE SUMMER OF 1955 was uncommonly hot in London. It was even hotter on the East Coast of America, where for a month the thermometer stood between 90 and 100 degrees Fahrenheit and office workers were beginning to strike for air-conditioning. 'After a flying visit to the United States, return to our "heat wave" is an indescribable relief,' wrote Fleming on 28 August. 'The wilting man in the street has no conception of the suffering in American cities . . . New York is a city almost on its knees and Washington, where the humidity is Amazonian, is prostrate.'

A week later, however, he was in Istanbul and it was here that the heat of 1955 reached tinder point. On 6 September, during a single night of violence, Muslim citizens turned against their Greek Orthodox neighbours in a display of ethnic hatred not seen since the great population exchange of 1923 that saw 1.5 million Greeks expelled from Turkey. So widespread and violent was the insurrection that it took an entire army division complete with cavalry and Sherman tanks to restore order. Fleming was at hand to witness it.

He had been invited to report on the 24th General Assembly of Interpol which was being held in the city as a nod to Turkey's recent acceptance as a member of NATO. The agenda was guaranteed to appeal, covering as it did drug smuggling, counterfeit cheques, forged fingerprints and a host of other nefarious activities. But fascinating though these subjects might be, they were of remote interest compared to the immediacy of the riot.

'Several times during that night,' Fleming wrote later in the *Sunday Times*, 'curiosity sucked me out of the safety of the Hilton Hotel and down into the city, where mobs went howling through the streets, each under its streaming red flag, with the white star and sickle moon. Occasional bursts of shouting rose out of the angry murmur of the crowds, then would come the crash of plate-glass and perhaps part of a scream.

'A car went out of control and charged the yelling crowd and the yells changed to screams and gesticulating hands showed briefly as the bodies went down before it. And over all there was the trill of the ambulances and the whistling howl of the new police cars imported from America.'

It was all very different from his usual journalistic fare. True, he could not resist frivolities such as the forthcoming 30th annual summit of the 'Association of Former Eunuchs' (membership twelve; down considerably since its foundation) and an apology from the Burmese Interpol delegate who regretted that his was a backward country which had no sex crimes though it hoped to catch up with the West next year. But for a moment Fleming was on the front line in a way he had not been since reporting from Moscow as a young recruit to Reuters in the 1930s.

The city fascinated him. Apart from its antiquity and aura of romantic decrepitude, it had long been a mecca for spies. While its espionage heyday had been in the Second World War, its situation on the fringe of the Eastern Bloc meant that it remained a centre of intrigue. He loved, too, the fact that it was still the final destination of that most evocative of trains, the Orient Express (on which he travelled). All things considered, it was an ideal place to set his next adventure.

From Russia with Love saw Bond being lured to Istanbul to meet a beautiful Soviet defector, Tatiana Romanova, who was willing to deliver a top-secret decoding device on condition she was escorted to safety by 007. Needless to say, it was a KGB honey-trap – orchestrated by the splendidly unappealing Colonel Rosa Klebb – whose aim was both to kill Bond and humiliate the Secret Service. To compound the disgrace, the agent of Bond's annihilation was to be the KGB's most prized operative, a psychopath from Ireland named Red Grant.

The writing seduced effortlessly. Every detail was vivid, whether it was the sweat that trickled down a KGB agent's face as he filmed Bond making love to Romanova, a man emerging from Marilyn Monroe's lips through a trapdoor set in a poster advertising her latest film, or the tunnel from which Bond raised a periscope to peer through a mouse hole in the Russian embassy's skirting board. The characters were no less colourful, ranging from the sinister, powdered Klebb to the menacing Red Grant and the larger than life Darko Kerim, head of Station T, who headquartered himself in a tobacco warehouse and whose staff comprised a multitude of sons by various mothers.

Unconventionally, Fleming started the book with a long description of Grant – who ranks as one of his most carefully imagined villains – and even less conventionally he ended it by killing his hero. After a tense battle on the Orient Express, during which he managed to despatch Grant, Bond tracked Rosa Klebb down to a hotel in Paris. But the apparently harmless old lady was equipped with poison-tipped knitting needles. When Bond tried to draw his Beretta it snagged on the waistband of his trousers, forcing him to fend her off with a chair. Her needles clattered harmlessly to one side. Her shoes, however, were equipped with poisoned blades and when 007 was on the cusp of victory she gave him a sharp kick in the leg. As the venom made its way through his system he collapsed. This, it seemed, was the end of Bond.

'I took great trouble over this book,' Fleming wrote on the flyleaf of his own copy. He had, too, and it showed. But if he had been hoping to use *From Russia with Love* to step off the Bond treadmill he had chosen the wrong moment. Enthusiasm for 007 was gathering apace and, as letters flowed in from a disappointed readership, it seemed that he had little option but to continue.

All this, however, was to come and as the summer of 1955 slid gradually into the cold British winter of 1956 he flew to Goldeneye where he stacked a ream of foolscap on his desk and, during the months of January and February, set his typewriter ringing.

TO C. D. HAMILTON

Life at the Sunday Times *was becoming increasingly stressful, as an ageing Lord Kemsley began to lose interest, and its overworked staff began to feel the strain. Kemsley would eventually sell the paper in 1958, an event which Fleming perhaps anticipated in a letter to his friend and colleague Denis 'C. D.' Hamilton, who was currently recovering from an illness.*

25th August, 1955

I have just got back from New York where I sweated it out for three weeks to find your splendidly cheerful and ebullient letter.

It is wonderful that you are gradually clambering out of the valley but you simply must make staying out of it your first priority by ruthlessly delegating work in all directions and by taking real rests at week ends.

It is absolutely fatal to go home each night with a brief-case loaded with bumpf. This ruins your health and your private life and leads, in case you didn't know it, to a dread disability known as "Barristers' Impotence" which I am sure you will wish to avoid.

So far as the office is concerned things will have to get worse before they get better and it would be much preferable to reserve your energies for the day when new policies are forced upon us by events rather than exhausting yourself with frustrating efforts to try and arrest the slide.

Dinner last night alone with K[emsley] and Lionel made me more than ever aware that there is absolutely no hope of our revitalising the machine at the present time or altering its inevitable progress towards the edge of the abyss.

For the future the main danger is that we may be so exhausted or frustrated that when the time comes to take a new view the zeal and the enthusiasm may no longer be in us.

But as I have said it is for that day that you should wait and meanwhile put your feet up on the desk and whistle for a wind.

Meanwhile hurry up and get well and reduce your handicap and make love to Olive, who must be wishing poor girl, that you had stayed in the army which is a far less hazardous career than the appropriately situated w.c.1.

TO ANN

In a letter that seems to have been written during the course of five consecutive gin and tonics, but was in fact spread over several days, two countries

and different bottles, Fleming sent Ann a heartfelt and gossipy message of
love, in which he also announced he had started work on his next book. She
declined to come to Goldeneye that year. Ostensibly the reason was her fear
of flying, but in reality the marriage was beginning to fray.

                                    Goldeneye, Jamaica, January 1956

My love,
    How different my writing looks from the others you get – from Peter
[Quennell] and Evelyn [Waugh] and Hugo [Charteris].* That is the sort
of thing one thinks about after 3 gins and tonics and 3 thousand miles
of thinking about you. It was horrible leaving the square. I said goodbye
3 times to your room and stole the photograph of you and Caspar. It's
now behind a bottle of Aqua Velva in *our* bedroom so as not to be blown
down by the wind. Things blown down by the wind worry me. For what
it's worth, which, at this writing – as they say in America – is not very
much to me, Jakie Astor flew with me to America.† Vacuum in New
York. It's a dead, dreadful place and I loathe it more and more. The Bry-
ces were very suspicious about your absence. What had happened? Jo
[Bryce] said you were the only woman I had ever loved and ever would.
Good? Bad? I said, as I say to everyone, that you are coming later. NANA
has changed. It doesn't belong to them any more. I took some money
out. Do you want a fur coat? What shape? What fur? I might get thin to
smuggle it. Draw a picture. Give your measurements. Spent the night
with the Bs. I <u>love</u> Ivar. I can't help it. He <u>needs</u> me (4 gins and tonics!)
Second night alone in Grand Central Station Oyster Bar. What do you
think I do when I'm abroad? Well I don't. I sit alone. In fact, I believe
you'd rather I didn't. Any person rather than no person. (I'm beginning
to write like Hugo. It's an obsession.) T. Capote was on the <u>Avianca</u>. Just

* Hugo Charteris (1922–70), Ann's novelist brother. He and Fleming did not always
see eye to eye.
† For his part, the Conservative MP John Jacob Astor recalled that Fleming 'sat on
the forward right-hand side of the first class and was wearing a light Burberry (and
looked like a Graham Greene character who was clearly a secret agent)'.

arrived from Moscow. Suitcase full of caviare for the Paleys* who have built a house beyond Round Hill. V. sweet and nice, loves you. Fascinating about Russia. Met the real jet set there who loved him. Found beautiful powder blue Austin on arrival. Drove through dark. Beach miraculous after 4 weeks. Norther ½ moon. Very sad without you. Today started book. Got two conches but no fun as you weren't there and sea <u>crawling</u> with lobsters. Also no fun. V. nice new gardener called Felix. It's a wonderful place and I can't sell it but you <u>must</u> be here. It belongs to you and you're stupid not to come here. You <u>must</u> get rid of your fears of things. Your fears of things are as bad as my fears of people.

(5th gin and tonic and goodnight my darling love and come if you possibly can) I love you only in the world.

TO ANN

Goldeneye, Jamaica, Saturday [11 February 1956]

My darling Treasure,

Truman Capote has come to stay. Can you imagine a more incongruous playmate for me? On the heels of a telegram he came bustling and twittering along with his tiny face crushed under a Russian Commissar's uniform hat. I told you he had just arrived from Moscow. Anyway it appears he couldn't stand the Round Hill life with the Paleys and Minnie and Co and just came to me to be saved and write his articles for the <u>New Yorker</u>. Anyway here he is till Tuesday and of course he's a fascinating character and we really get on very well though when I gave him a lobster without a head to carry this morning I thought we were going to have another Rosamund act.[†] But he was brave and went off with it at arm's length. It has poured with rain since he arrived on Thursday and is

---

* Barbara ('Babe') Paley (1915–78), American socialite, married to the philanthropist William S. Paley (1901–90), the founder of CBS.

[†] Rosamond Lehmann (1901–90), British novelist. On an earlier visit to Goldeneye there had been a small altercation when Fleming left a dead squid in her bedroom.

still crashing down. Just taking him off to Noël for drinks and dinner. Ah me. Anyway the book is half done and buzzing along merrily in the rain. It is now Sunday and I'm in the garden between showers and spells of hot sun. The Noël evening was typical. His Firefly house is a near-disaster and anyway the rain pours into it from every angle and even through the stone walls so that the rooms are running with damp. He is by way of living alone up there and Coley* has to spend half his time running up and down in the car with ice and hot dishes of quiche Lorraine! A crazy set-up. N. is going to sell Goldenhurst and Gerald Street and become a Bermuda citizen! So as to save up money for his old age. I can see the point but I expect the papers will say some harsh things.

Write again quickly. Your letters are wonderful and long.

I love you,

Ian

Truman and everyone send their love.

FROM WILLIAM PLOMER

Sunday 1st July, 56

My dear Ian,

I've just finished <u>From R. with L.</u>, and hasten to say that I've greatly enjoyed it & all your verbal inventiveness. V.g. beginning, & Red Grant & Rosa Klebb are <u>outstanding</u> in your lengthening gallery of monsters. I thought the planning in Moscow more thorough than suspenseful, but with a nicely knowledgeable air. All the Istanbul part & return journey <u>the greatest fun</u>. A fight "to the death" between two naked gipsy girls very Ianesque: I felt a mixture of relief & disappointment that it wasn't <u>quite</u> to the death. The periscope a great lark, but not <u>madly</u> credible. <u>Excellent</u> use made of Orient express & I particularly like the conclusion, with its to-be-continued-in-our-next air. A master-stroke to leave Bond not cock-a-hoop but wounded & unconscious & the reader in

---

* Cole Lesley (1911–80), Coward's secretary and later biographer.

suspense. I thought Tatiana very well & quickly trained, & was struck by the contrast between her early nervousness & diffidence and her self-possession when on the job.

I have gone through the typescript with a fine-toothed lead pencil & corrected or queried a good many points of spelling, punctuation, mis-typing, &c. And I enclose a list of details, some of which may be helpful.

This letter comes

From William,

With congratulations

also with thanks for the pleasure of reading the story & all best wishes for its success. Klebb is in the basket, & I hope Success is in the bag!

[PS] I thought the mouth of Marilyn Monroe business v.g. & v. cinematic.

[PPS] "J'aime les sensations fortes" would make just the right epigraph to your collected works!

FROM DANIEL GEORGE, ESQ., 18 East Heath Road, Hampstead, N.W.5.

6.7.56

Dear Ian,

I took your typescript home last night but as I'd had to attend a dinner of the Society of Bookmen I wasn't able to spend much time with it – enough, though, to be delighted by your opening chapter and the promised developments. The PEN Congress will make me almost incommunicado during next week, but in the week beginning July 16th I shall be available to discuss the book with you. Meanwhile I'd like to know how much you can stand in the way of minute criticism of your style. In a story of this kind pace and sharpness of impression are essential; every word must count; every statement must be direct; no simile must be distracting. I went over the first chapter again early this morning and have indicated in pencil the points I suggest you ought to consider. For some examples: too many of your sentences begin with or include the words 'there was'. Now it is always better to say 'A man was at the door' than 'There was a man at the door.' Similarly, it is desirable to avoid, wherever possible, 'the,' 'after that,' 'but.' Similes should be used only when they are helpful. I haven't the typescript before me, but in the first chapter, I think, you say the man's eyelids twitched suddenly like the ears of a horse. Up to that moment I'd visualised the scene perfectly. You destroyed my illusion by bringing in a horse . . . Can you bear it if I go on in this strain?

I hope to finish reading the story tonight.

FROM DANIEL GEORGE

8.7.56

Dear Ian,

Wm looked in at B Sq for a moment on Friday to say goodbye. As I hadn't then finished reading your book I wasn't able to discuss it with him properly – only to share his approval of it. He said something about an anti-climax, but I haven't discovered what he means. My own criticisms follow. You'd better brace up: I've given it the A-Z treatment.

CHAP 1. A superb opening – just the job for your lady readers. <u>Queries</u>. p. 8. ". . . in the house the telephone started ringing loudly." (Parenthesis. Things throughout the book always 'start' – never 'begin'. Why can't they just happen? What's wrong with 'the telephone in the house rang loudly'? Granted that out in the garden the ring of the telephone could be heard, would the answerer's voice be audible? Why (3rd line from bottom of this page) should the girl be afraid of being caught listening? Perhaps you're right, though, about this: she was scared of exhibiting any kind of curiosity. We don't, by the way, hear any more about her. No reason why we should, of course.

"There was" occurs seven times in this chapter, and "there were" once. An excess of "and", "but", "then", and "that" is noticeable.

CHAP 2. This must, or should have been, the most difficult chapter for you to write, especially from p. 14 onwards. In some respects, no doubt you are aware, Grant's career is paralleled by Kerim's (p. 147). I am not quite sure whether your style here is dead-pan enough. Anyhow, some cluttering words could be weeded out.

"There was" occurs at least 6 times; "there were" four.

CHAP 3. Don't you think that on p. 26 you have made Grant a little too stupid? He seems sharp enough – almost out of character – when he meets Bond.

Not so many examples here of "there were" and "there are".

CHAP 4. An excellent chapter – and since it begins in the present tense we have a change from "there was" and "there were" to "there are" and "there is".

CHAP 5. Also v.g. The usual 'therewasery' occurs.

CHAP 6&7. Ditto. Here, as throughout the book, I have made pencilled notes drawing attention to odd or repeated words and phrases. (When you see them you'll want to order me Rosa Klebb's No. 36)

You will be right in assuming that, subject to my infuriating pedantries, I have nothing but praise for everything until we get to Chapter 11 (p. 99). Here I think there is a flaw – fortunately one that can be removed by simple elimination.

Why should May ask a door-to-door salesman for his 'union card'? A person of her status would not have heard of such a thing. If she had, she would surely know enough not to ask a salesman for one. To what union could he possibly belong? It's weak to say that the man's card indicated he belonged to the Electrician's Union. If he were a member of that union he wouldn't be selling TV sets in his own time . . . No, this business is all nonsense, and must go. There's no point in it anyway. Nothing develops from it.

p. 104, last lines. Couldn't Paymaster Captain Troop have been just as objectionable if he had not been a Ranker? It looks like a gratuitous piece of snobbery to mention his lowly origin.

All the rest commanded my unqualified admiration. I think this is your best book, the most tightly and ingeniously constructed, the most original. It's so good that it deserves serious surface re-consideration. I mean, you can afford not to use worn-out phrases. If you must go in for mannerisms, let them be new mannerisms. On some pages the sentences all begin with 'And'. I can't see the point of this. Presumably you are aiming at producing an effect of panting continuity. Take out all the 'Ands' and see if it makes any difference.

I once wrote that while for ordinary novelists 'Far off a dog barked' or 'Somewhere in the house a tap dripped' was good enough, Galsworthy had to have 'In the distance a peacock shrieked'. You, I see, have 'Somewhere a horse neighed' (p. 144) and 'Somewhere a cock crowed' on p. 195. Congratulations! Congratulations also on having only one instance of knuckle-whitening. Shoulder-shrugging, I regret to say, is too much in evidence. There's no lip-biting, though.

I shall be away from B Sq all this week. Shall I keep the typescript here or post it back to you?

Bond could see Fleming's face as he read this letter. There was a sudden snapping together of his jaws, and his brows shot up into a corrugation. Then he threw the letter from him. 'Man must be mad,' he muttered under his breath.

Yours ever,

P.S. All your action & horror scenes are as good as anything I have ever read in this genre.

TO DANIEL GEORGE, ESQ., 18 East Heath Road, Hampstead, N.W.5.

9th July, 1956

What a wonderful letter to get on a Monday morning.

My best book? Do you really mean it? One gets so blind about one's own scribblings and I feared the whole Bond joke might be getting a bit stale.

I agree with all your points and will bend my mind to them directly I get the manuscript back. Do you think you could post it to

16 Victoria Square, s.w.1. or perhaps drop it in on the way to one of your lunches.

You are mad to think that I am thin-skinned about criticisms. One longs for them and the only place one gets them from is this publisher's reader.

The only point you make that I would query is your most vehement one about the TV salesman. I felt I had to make him sound rather a suspicious character and give him something of a Communist smear via the E.T.U., otherwise why should Bond prick his ears.

However, this and many other points I would love to discuss with you and I wonder if you would care to have lunch one day next week except Wednesday. I should think Hommany Grits and Branch water are about all you will be able to stand after this week's junketing.

Anyway, my very warmest thanks for your kind words and, above all, for having taken the trouble to read the rather messy typescript so quickly and thoroughly [. . .].

I badly needed a heartening letter and, above all, one from a real expert.

TO MICHAEL HOWARD

To Fleming's dismay Michael Howard (who always harboured a vague disquiet about Bond) took a very different tack from William Plomer and Daniel George. There was one incident in particular that raised his hackles: a fight between two naked gypsy women for the affections of their man.

17th July, 1956

Dear Michael,

Many thanks for reading the book so promptly and also for the truthful opinions.

Personally, I don't know what to think – Daniel says it is my best book and appears to mean it, and William was also very congratulatory. I am sure I know them too well for them to have written me something they didn't mean, so perhaps the answer is that the book has merits in a different sphere from the usual Bond formula.

I won't bother you with Daniel's and William's views because, presumably, they will be put down in an unvarnished form in their reports, but I am certainly depressed that you appear to have seen no merits whatsoever in the book.

My own comments on what you say are:

(a) I think the Russians seem dull because Russians are dull people and I intended to paint a picture of rather drab grimness, which is what Russia is like. SMERSH is, after all, a machine, whereas Drax was an individual. One of the troubles about the book is that so much of my description of SMERSH is absolutely true. Moreover, one simply can't go on inventing good villains. They are far more difficult to come by than heroes or heroines.

(b) the point about Bond is that he makes a fool of himself and falls headlong into the trap. This is a change from making him the cardboard hero and I cannot help thinking it is a healthy change. There is so much danger of these books being all alike and my main satisfaction (such as it is) with the book is that a Formula which was getting stale has been broken.

(c) I cannot say anything on the score of suspense because the book obviously has no suspense for me. Surely there was some suspense in wondering how far Bond was going to fall into the trap which we had seen laid.

(d) I don't see your point about the masseuse in what Daniel describes as "a superb opening", and what other use could have been made of her? It is intended to be a rather quiet opening with the "surprise" at the end, of finding that one is in Russia while, at the same time, introducing an unpleasant man.

(e) if Bond had stopped those women fighting there would have been no chapter. And the same applies to the break-in of the Faceless Ones. It would have been out of character for Bond to have stopped the fighting and so I had to stop it for him.

(f) I agree about the plans and the nightgown.

Subject to what Daniel and William say in their reports, my own view is that, while this may not be the perfect dish for the registered Bond reader, it will be considered by the more thoughtful ones a welcome departure from routine and I think there are enough nasty individual scenes to placate the Bond addict.

So far as the end is concerned, both Daniel and William are very much in favour.

Personally, I think I shall get a good deal of reader criticism such as yours, but I do think it is a good thing to produce a Bond book which is out of the ordinary and which has, in my opinion, an ingenious and interesting plot. There is also the point that one simply can't go on writing the simple bang-bang, kiss-kiss, type of book. However hard one works at it, you automatically become staler and staler and very quickly the staleness shows through to the reader and then all is indeed lost.

However, these are just my thoughts and I perfectly respect your point of view, though I admit to being depressed that there was no single aspect of the book which seems to have tickled your fancy.

Incidentally, I am off to America on the 26th and propose to polish the book up while I am away, so I would be grateful to hear in the next few days if you intend to publish it or not and, if you publish it, what your timetable is likely to be. It will be ready for the printer at the end of August and it is very important for me to get the page proofs and <u>finish with them</u> so as quickly to clear my mind for the next one.

The main joke about this letter is that it has caused me to tear up one I dictated last night which suggested that, on the basis of Daniel's and William's comments, you should put the book in for the Evening Standard £5,000 prize!

TO MICHAEL HOWARD

Howard sent an emollient note but still queried the necessity for a topless masseuse in the first chapter.

24th July, 1956

Dear Michael,

Many thanks for your charming letter, and I can assure you that I was only fussed by your criticisms in so far as they represented the first of what I expect to get from some of my readers who would really prefer to have the mixture as before.

I shall certainly try and deal with one or two of your factual points on my way through the book at the end of this week. The point about the masseuse stripping is that they do in the Crimea, and I meant the reader, at the end of the chapter, to realise that he might have known where he was. But I think the point is too obscure and needs cleaning up. I will also try and clarify the fighting women though, as a matter of fact, Bond did not stop the fight.

If I let you have the final typescript at the end of August, could I have the proofs by the beginning of October or thereabouts? If I can get them done fairly quickly it leaves me a couple of months before I go to Jamaica to start worrying about the next one, which one really can't do until this one is finally out of the way.

If anything comes up while I am away, cables addressed to KEMNEWS NEWYORK and beginning PROFLEMING will be passed on to me wherever I am.

Meanwhile, many thanks again for reading the book so quickly and thoroughly. My swift riposte would not have been sent off if I hadn't had a ghastly fear that not a single chapter of the book appeared to have excited you. I am afraid all authors are sensitive and require that the pill shall be wrapped up with at least one grain of sugar!

TO JOHN CARTER, ESQ., C.B.E., 16 Bedford Gardens, London, w.8.

Having bought The Book Collector *outright from Lord Kemsley the previous year, Fleming soon found himself at odds with the more pernickety members of the editorial board. On 19 November he had received a tart note from John Carter about a proposed advertising campaign – 'We ivory-tower dwellers (as I realise we are assumed to be) are sometimes puzzled by the ways of business men. Frankly, I'm puzzled now. Pray (as W.S.C. [Winston Churchill] used to minute) enlighten me on half a sheet of paper.' Fleming's reply went to a page and a half.*

20th November, 1956

Many thanks for your splendidly acidulated letter, but was it really necessary to be quite so crushing?

None of us are "businessmen" and we all have to rely on the bits of each other's time and talents that are made available – John [Hayward] doing all the editorial work, Percy [Muir] writing a serial for us, me looking after the business side and Robert [Harling] lending a hand on lay-outs and promotion.

Eleven months ago, as you mention, we were all most grateful for your American promotion ideas and agreed with them. A leaflet was produced and it needed a guiding hand to get it run off and sent across the Atlantic into the right hands.

I believe John did ask if you would be willing to mother this little child of yours, but got the answer that you hadn't the necessary secretarial help. I offered to provide this, but the offer was not taken up.

Then you went to America, and the original impetus was lost.

As you saw last Tuesday, we were all chagrined that this American promotion scheme, in its two parts – to booksellers, and to the possible new subscribers, such as Friends of the Morgan Library, which were mentioned – has not got under way.

Bending us over your knee, though possibly justified, is not the answer.

The position at the moment is that Robert has undertaken to re-make-up the text, John has agreed to marry up a list of possible subscribers with you and James Shand [the printer] has agreed to help choose an illustration and get the thing run off.

All that is needed is a keen Man of Affairs with an intimate knowledge of the market we are trying to penetrate. Could that man possibly be you? And would you be very kind and take the fragments of this problem and co-ordinate them with that gift for symmetry we all admire in you.

We would all be deeply grateful if you would do this.

The alternative, I am sure, would be five still more hang-dog faces at our next luncheon.

To which Carter replied with further sharp comments: 'In short, my dear Ian, your manful attempt to saddle me with the responsibility for first delaying, then smothering, and finally jettisoning my own promotion scheme does more credit to your ingenuity than to your memory.' Fleming just couldn't be bothered with this nonsense.

29th November, 1956

You really must not waste any more of your valuable time writing me abrasive letters about the promotional leaflet for The Book Collector.

One telephone call to Robert – God forbid that you should have made it – confirms that the leaflet is on its way to James Shand to be proofed. James will choose a couple of illustrations (Robert suggests the dirtiest and I agree) and the final proof will shortly reach you and John Hayward for approval. Any further circulation seems unnecessary.

A mailing list will be, or could be, immediately co-ordinated by you and John, and off the leaflet will go.

Robert agrees with alacrity to accept full responsibility for the delay and, if it will add to your satisfaction, I will accept full over-riding responsibility for Robert's irresponsibility.

And now let's get our feet back on the ground and our noses back to our many and more pressing grindstones.

TO MICHAEL HOWARD

One of the grindstones to which Fleming referred in his letter to Carter (above) was the prospect of writing a new book.

27th November, 1956

Dear Michael,

I shall be very interested to hear if sales go up but I doubt if there will be any effect, except to increase the rentable value of my property!

I'm afraid I certainly shan't be able to clean up another book by April and I shall be very relieved if I am able to write one at all, as the fountain of my genius is running pretty dry.

On the other hand, Al Hart writes as follows:

"You have surpassed yourself! The new one is far and away your best, from the very first page right through to that altogether admirable cliff-hanger of an ending. Pearl White* was never more effective.

"Seriously, I mean it: 'From Russia with Love' is a real wowser, a lulu, a dilly and a smasheroo. It is also a clever and above all <u>sustained</u> piece of legitimate craftsmanship. My chapeau is not only off to you, it is over the windmill."

This may cheer you up.

Moreover, your Mr. Williams seemed quite honestly to put it his number three favourite.

I think if you put aside your misgivings and decide it is going to be a smashing success, it will be, and I sincerely hope you aren't thinking of reducing your print below 15. I am sure, irrespective of the book's merits, that would be a mistake.

Howard, however, was not letting his author off the hook. As Fleming wrote on 12 December, presumably in reply to a dispiriting note about trade opinion, 'What are you trying to do, break my nerve? If you can find some obscure bookseller who is prepared to say a kind word about the book, I shall be delighted to have it. [Hatchards] tell me that your chief traveller likes it very much. If so, this welcome piece of information has been withheld from me!'

TO WREN HOWARD

Fleming had written on 28 December 1956 to clarify the terms of a serialisation in the Daily Express, *to thank Daniel George fulsomely for his comments – 'I think the book has been greatly improved as a result' – and to assure Howard that he had no intention of changing publisher. But he cast a warning note: 'Incidentally, when you talk airily of future books, I do beg you to believe that the vein of my inventiveness is running extremely dry and I seriously doubt if I shall be able to complete a book in Jamaica this year. There are many reasons for this, which I need not go into, but I am finding it increasingly difficult to work up enthusiasm for Bond and his unlikely adventures.'*

* Pearl White (1889–1938), US stage and film actress who specialised in serials.

2nd January, 1957

Dear Bob,

And a very happy New Year to you.

I was greatly heartened by your letter and by your judgement on the new book. Personally I agree with you and I think it has been still further improved by re-writing. I am quite certain that you will sell 20,000 copies if only because, thanks to World Books and Express serialisation, etc., my name is much better known.

I think some people will find it tough but then Russians are very tough people and I wanted to make them so. I think the plot is a good one and there's no harm in letting Bond make a fool of himself for a change.

I am also encouraged by your last paragraph and certainly intend to keep Bond spinning through his paces as long as possible. The trouble is that I take great pains with the factual background to these stories and my source material is running rather dry. It is also very difficult to find new ways of killing and chasing people and new shapes and names for the heroines. However these are my problems and I will try and cope with them, though perhaps not with the same monotonous regularity as I have achieved so far.

Thank you for being so understanding about the royalty position. I can assure you that I am very happy with Jonathan Cape and I have no desire at all that the partnership should be an unbalanced one. It is mostly for that reason that I have eschewed agents* and left subsidiary rights to you.

Many thanks for the contracts and I am returning your copy which you seem to have sent me inadvertently.

I now depart, weighed down by my secretary with about two hundred pages of blank foolscap and a new typewriter ribbon!

TO 'IAN FLEMING "ESQ" and/or his secretary' from an unknown ill-wisher

14th February, 1957

Somebody once said of Albert Schweitzer words to the effect that, in our poor world, there (meaning A.S.) went a truly great man. A man who has added something to the sum of love, dignity and beauty among us.

---

* Though he would later appoint a UK agent.

Having read a few pages of your revolting (and boring) writing, I see you as the exact antithesis of – for instance – a man like Schweitzer. You are doing your bit to make the world a beastlier place.

May I add this appeal to any others you may be receiving, and ask you, for the sake of anything decent and lovely you can think of, to stop.

I must also add that, if I myself ever had the chance (and if a much more exhaustive investigation confirmed: a) the dangerous beastliness of your writings; b) the width of their distribution) – I think I should try to kill you.

TO JONATHAN CAPE, from the above

I have never before in my life felt moved to write such a letter.

I imagine that many people feel on this subject as I do.

As his editors, you are co-responsible with Ian Fleming. And if you do not stop publishing his ghastly filth, I think pressure should be brought to bear on you (I suppose via your outlets and the distribution of your other publications).

TO THE EDITOR, The New Statesman & Nation, 10 Great Turnstile, High Holborn, W.C.1.

Following a piece in the New Statesman *that bemoaned the apparent death of Bond, Fleming despatched what would become his standard reply to the many fans who expressed similar regrets.*

29th April, 1957

Dear Sir,

<u>The Late James Bond</u>

As a result of Mr. John Raymond's poignant but premature obituary notice of Commander James Bond, R.N.V.S.R. there has been a flood of anxious enquiry.

May I therefore, as Commander Bond's official biographer, ask you to publish the following bulletin which, according to a delicate but sure source, was recently placed on the canteen notice board of the headquarters of the Secret Service near Regent's Park:

"After a period of anxiety the condition of No. 007 shows definite improvement. It has been confirmed that 007 was suffering from severe Fugu poisoning (a particularly virulent member of the curare group obtained from the sex glands of Japanese Globe fish). This diagnosis, for which the Research Department of the School of Tropical Medicine was responsible, has determined a course of treatment which is proving successful.

No further bulletins will be issued.

(Signed) Sir James Molony,

Department of Neurology,

St. Mary's Hospital,

London, w.2."

In view of the above I am hoping that, despite the cautionary note sounded by Mr. Raymond and subject, of course, to the Official Secrets Act, further biographical material will in due course be available to the public.

Yours faithfully,

Following the publication of which he wrote again on 3 May 1957 to point out a spelling error.

The Late James Bond

In the last paragraph of my letter I said "biographical" not "biological". The science of James Bond's physical life is after all only part of the story.

TO MISS GLADYS GALLIVEN, 1 Midhurst Drive, Goring-By-Sea, Worthing, Sussex

14th March, 1957

Thank you very much for your letter of February 7th and I am so sorry I have not answered it before. I have been away in Jamaica writing another James Bond adventure and your letter was waiting for me when I got back.

It is very kind of you to take the trouble to write and I am glad you like my books.

Why, I wonder? And, also, what do you dislike about them?

An author is always interested in learning these things from his readers and, if it would amuse you to put down in two or three hundred words the things you like and dislike about my books, in exchange I will send you an autographed copy of the latest one, "From Russia with Love", which will be coming out in about three weeks' time.

Again with many thanks for having taken the trouble to write.

TO MISS RENÉE HELLMAN, 2 Acacia Road, London, N.W.8.

Renée Hellman (Miss) wrote joyfully on hearing that Bond was only suffering from Fugu poisoning. She'd been hoping to save From Russia with Love *for a beach holiday in Santa Margharita but the temptation had been too much.*

30th April, 1957

Thank you for your charming letter and I am delighted you enjoyed the latest volume of James Bond's biography.

I am sorry you did not save the book up to read on the sands at Santa Margharita. That is just the sort of place he would wish to be read – particularly by a girl. You must try and be more continent next Spring!

Again with very many thanks for your delightful letter.

TO MAJOR W. MACLAGAN, Trinity College, Oxford

In the guise of a station officer in the Secret Service, the Senior Tutor of Trinity College pointed out several mistakes in Fleming's recent 'briefing'. Apart from misspelling the name of Grant's birthplace, he had also mentioned National Service – to which Grant, as an Irish citizen, would not have been subject. Furthermore, setting aside various elementary mistakes about the geography of Istanbul, Fleming had described the Mosque of Sultan Ahmed as containing Byzantine frescoes. 'It is well known, even among the comparatively ill-informed inhabitants of Istanbul, that this building was only erected between 1609 and 1617 by the architect Sedefkar Mehmet Aga, and contains no earlier work.' But he was relieved to hear that Bond's health seemed to be 'no worse than that of the former agent S. Holmes after his reported death at Reichenbach'.

30th April, 1957

Dear Sir,

Your minute of April 25th has been referred to the Department concerned. It is unlikely that it will find its way to the already over-burdened desk of M. but I have no doubt that appropriate action will be taken.

As the biographer of James Bond, I am very gratified to know that, in what amounts to a secret report of some 70,000 words, more errors should not have been noted by the sharp eyes and expert brains of the Trinity Station. On the other hand, I must, for my part, express astonishment that an error much more gross than those you detailed is to be found in line 1 of page 18.

Here a printer's error has written "asexuality" that appeared in the manuscript as "sexuality", thus rendering impossible a true appreciation of the psychology of the agent Grant.

The necessary erratum slip will appear in future editions of this volume but not thanks to the research work, in other respects meticulous, of Station Trinity.

On this occasion "reasons in writing" will not be called for but you, as commanding officer, will no doubt call for a general tightening up in the personnel of the research section.

So far as the welfare of James Bond is concerned, a bulletin from his medical advisors has been issued to the public press and will, I hope, appear this week in the correspondence columns of the "New Statesman and Nation" and "The Times Literary Supplement".

Yours Faithfully.

TO GEOFFREY M. CUCKSON, ESQ., Nottingham

With some regret as to the lack of bondage, Fleming's steadfast correspondent felt he could say little to match his critique of Diamonds are Forever.

30th April, 1957

Many thanks for your letter of April 26th and I am delighted that you enjoyed "From Russia, With Love".

At the same time I am very sorry not to have had something along the lines of your admirable criticism of my last book – far more positive than my reviewers.

Bond is, in fact, suffering from Fugu poisoning (a particularly virulent member of the curare group obtained from the sex glands of the Japanese Globe fish), so I am afraid it is unlikely that a further volume of his biography will appear before next April.

Again with many thanks for your letter.

TO WREN HOWARD

14th May, 1957

Dear Bob,

"From Russia with Love"

I am delighted with your progress with the book clubs and your success in screwing them all up.

I cannot remember how we split the profits from these book club deals before but please follow previous proportions.

Incidentally, you will be interested to know that the Express are desperately anxious to turn James Bond into a strip-cartoon. I have grave doubts about the desirability of this. A certain cachet attaches to the present operation and there is a danger that if stripped we shall descend into the Peter Cheyney class* which, while superficially attractive from your point of view, has, I think, disadvantages for both of us. Unless the standard of these books is maintained they will lose their point and I think there is a grave danger that inflation would not only spoil the readership, but also become something of a death-watch beetle inside the author. A tendency to write still further down might result. The author would see this happening and disgust with the operation might creep in.

On the other hand, the Editor of the Express, who sees these points, says that they would only do it if they could achieve a Rolls Royce job and he is preparing some roughs for my inspection and I will let you know how things go.

As my literary chaperone, the whole problem is one upon which I would like to have William's view in due course and perhaps you could give him the rag to chew over.

If I was a bit more hard-boiled it would be easy to guy the whole Bond operation in a great splurge of promotion and sales, but somehow it all goes against the grain a bit and I dare say much the same problem faces authors whose books are made into a lot of films.

Perhaps I have an abnormal affection for privacy and antipathy for display!

Anyway, I would welcome and abide by William's decision.

TO RONALD NATHAN, ESQ., Reservations Controller, Elal Israel Airlines, 295 Regent Street, London, W.1.

El Al noticed that of the many flights Bond could have caught from Istanbul, there had been no mention of their own. They sent a detailed brochure to illustrate the connections available. Fleming's reply skirted tactfully round the idea of Bond visiting the Middle East – the region seems never to have caught his fancy.

* To which Fleming had earlier aspired to rise.

1st July, 1957

What busy bees you all are to be sure at Elal Airlines and I shall certainly amend the paragraph to include Elal when the book is reprinted.

I am delighted that you enjoyed it and I hope one day James Bond may find himself being borne to adventure on your wings.

TO F. ENGALL, ESQ., 4/28 St. John's Park, London, S.E.3.

A traveller who knew his trains said that Fleming had got Bond's route on the Orient Express wrong. On leaving Turkey the train split south through Greece and north through Bulgaria. Bond, who was on the northern part, would have entered the Eastern Bloc via Svilengrad, rather than Dragoman, which was on the border between Greece and Yugoslavia.

19th July, 1957

Thank you very much for your letter of yesterday's date and I do see that I have slipped up badly over Dragoman. I can't think how this happened. I must have muddled the inward frontier town with the outward one, and I will correct to Svilengrad in future editions.

But I think you are mistaken about the two halves of the train. Certainly when I made the journey a couple of years ago the back portion of the train was detached at the Turkish frontier and took the route through Bulgaria. I happen to be fairly certain about this because Cooks issued me a ticket via the Bulgaria section instead of the Greek, although I had no Bulgarian visa, and in consequence I had quite a lot of trouble on the train.

Your quick eye has missed one grievous error pointed out by another train enthusiast. I gave the Orient Express hydraulic brakes instead of vacuum!

Again with many thanks for your helpful criticism.

TO JAMES KEDDIE, JR., ESQ., 28 Laurel Avenue, Wellesley Hills 81, Massachusetts, U.S.A.

On behalf of the Boston Chapter of the Baker Street Irregulars, his notepaper headed The Speckled Band (Office of the Cheetah), James Keddie wanted to know if Jimmie Bond was still alive and kicking as reported by the Herald Tribune.

24th September, 1957

How very kind of you to have written – and on such very exciting note-paper.

I am delighted that you are enjoying the adventures of James Bond but I am perturbed to learn that, through some slip-up in Security, a notice on the bulletin Board in the Secret Service should have reached the public in America.

However, for your confidential information, the details of the leakage published in the <u>Herald Tribune</u> are correct and James Bond has returned to duty.

The next chapter of his biography will appear in England, under the title "Doctor No", in March of next year – to coincide with the daffodil season.

TO DAVID WOOD, ESQ., 75 Kensington Gardens Square, London, w.2.

From Russia with Love included a great deal of information about the Soviet Union that Fleming knew would be of interest to his Cold War readers. Unfortunately, Mr Wood wrote to say that he had got Moscow quite wrong. A street he described as wide and dreary was in fact narrow and more fun than most, containing as it did two of the city's best cinemas. And no. 14, which Fleming mentioned as being opposite KGB headquarters, was in fact a baker's. As an aside, and with reference to a remark Fleming had made in a recent article, he recalled meeting the spy Alexander Foote, possibly by this time dead, whom he remembered as a bluff-spoken Yorkshireman who distributed Communist leaflets.

24th September, 1957

Thank you very much for your extremely interesting letter, which I was delighted to have.

I was very interested to read what you have to say about Sretenka Ulitsa. My own information came from a Russian spy who came over to our side and if I ever see him again I shall raise your points with him. For the time being, I can only suppose that the inoffensive baker has been installed as a "front"!

If Alexander Foote is dead it is news to me and, here again, your remarks are most interesting. He was certainly a first-class spy and I was glad to have an opportunity to raise my hat to him.

Again with many thanks for your helpful and factual letter and I am delighted that I have such a perceptive observer amongst my readers.

TO MISS A. D. STEWART, 24 Eglinton Crescent, Edinburgh

25th September, 1957

Thank you very much indeed for taking the trouble to write to me and I am glad that some of the James Bond stories have given you pleasure.

I appreciate what you say about the last book and I agree that Bond made a fool of himself. The trouble is that people do make fools of themselves in real life and unless Bond were some kind of cardboard hero, which he is not, my serious accounts of his adventures must contain the whole portrait – warts and all.

I think you will find, if you have not cast him aside completely, that in the next chapter of his life story, which will be published next March under the title of "Doctor No", James Bond will have benefited by the sharp lesson he learned on his previous case.

Again with many thanks for having taken the trouble to rebuke me so charmingly.

TO DOCTOR G. R. C. D. GIBSON, Chapel Road, Wisbech, Cambs.

Dr Gibson, with whom Fleming had previously discussed cars, announced that, 'Being a Scot, I retain a certain disapproval, probably Calvinistic, of authors and books and such works of the devil'. Nevertheless, he was disappointed that his local library had banned From Russia with Love *as being pornographic and hoped to see Bond back on the shelves soon. He had one motoring complaint, though: 'vintage Bentleys are really a bit vieux jeu these days', and if Bond was to be resurrected maybe it could be with an Aston Martin? As to a literary means of restoring Bond to health, 'how about "with one mighty leap he threw off the effects of the poison?"'.*

26th September, 1957

Dear Doctor Gibson,

How very kind of you to have written. [. . .] As to James Bond's motor car, he is in fact in the process of being re-equipped, and the body-builders are now at work on the chassis. For security reasons I'm sure you will appreciate that neither the make of the car nor its speed can at this date be revealed.

To which Gibson replied, 'obviously the fellow can't be making a large salary, which rules out the exotic stuff like Uhlenhaut's special Merc on a 300 SLR chassis – what about an Aston Martin DB 2 with a 3 litre engine.' Two books later Bond would indeed be driving an Aston.

TO DAVID CHIPP, ESQ., Reuters' Representative in Peking, c/o Reuters, 85 Fleet Street, E.C.4.

David Chipp, a journalist based in China, wanted to know why Fleming had killed Bond. Also, how did the Soviet cameramen know that JB would leave the lights on while making love to Romanova? 'Not everyone does!'

10th December, 1957

How faithless my readers are. Surely they should assume that if James Bond must one day die it will not be as a result of a kick on the shin. [. . .]

As for your very perceptive P.S., the voyeurs did not expect such rich pictorial fruit. The best they hoped for were one or two pre-prandial, so to speak, snaps which would have been sufficient for their purpose. They could not know, but could conceivably have guessed, that Bond would never be so unwise as to embrace a confessed Russian spy in the dark.

No, the cardinal error in this book was to furnish the Orient-Express with hydraulic instead of vacuum brakes – a gross mistake which the Black Belt grade amongst James Bond's audience have been quick to seize upon.

Incidentally, some of my happiest years were spent in Reuters and I only resigned when I was offered an appointment as Chief Representative in the Far East on a salary, with expenses, of £800 a year – barely enough to cover my opium consumption.

TO H. B. KLUGMAN, 23 Clovelly Road, Greenside, Johannesburg, South Africa

A South African fan felt that James Bond should not have suffered such an ignominious end. These things might happen in real life, but surely a fiction writer could ensure that justice prevailed? That's what most people wanted.

28th October, 1958

Dear Mr., or possibly Miss, Klugman,

Thank you very much for taking the trouble to write to me about "From Russia, With Love" and I entirely see your point.

The trouble is that James Bond has had it all too easy in his previous four adventures and it was time for him to suffer a rebuff and even a rather ignominious one. Even more so as he was altogether too cock-a-hoop about his victory over Red Grant and it was criminally foolish of him to have gone alone to the Ritz.

However, if you would care to read his next adventure, "Doctor No", you will see that he managed, but only just, to survive Rosa Klebb's poison, though incurring the wrath of M.

It is most encouraging when readers take the trouble to write, as you have done, even if on a mildly critical note, and I greatly enjoyed getting your letter.

TO W. ROSS NAPIER, ESQ., Findhorn, Gladney Road, Ceres, Cupar, Fife

Having fielded one criticism about his description of Moscow, Fleming hit a more serious obstacle when a Scottish fan provided pictures of No. 13 Sretenka Ulitsa, where the headquarters of SMERSH were meant to be placed. It looked perfectly ordinary, not at all as Fleming had described it, and definitely not the headquarters of anything.

11th October, 1961

Thank you very much for your fascinating letter of September 30th which has just reached me.

It was wonderfully zealous of you to do this detective work, and I am fascinated by your account, from which it is quite clear, and from your photograph, that no such building as I described could have existed at No. 13.

This upsets me very much.

The position is that Smersh, as an organisation, did very much exist and for the purposes I described, but I am under the impression that it has been closed down by Khrushchev, though obviously, vide the Khoklov* case, some department of M.W.D. [Ministry for the Interior] still carries on its duties.

When I was writing "From Russia with Love" I was fortunate enough to be in touch with a Colonel of the M.W.D. As a result of his description of the headquarters of Smersh I boldly put in the authentication note at the beginning of the book, and I can only hope he didn't also misinform me regarding the individuals whose real names I used, though the interior of the department doesn't matter so much.

So, all I can plead in view of your evidence, is that I was not being intentionally misleading.

Anyway, thank you very much indeed for your fascinating letter and for the photograph, both of which I shall keep in my files.

---

* Nicholai Khoklov, a Soviet defector, had recently survived an attempt by Russian agents to assassinate him with thallium – a colourless, odourless, radioactive element known as 'the poisoner's poison'.

7

Conversations with the Armourer

'SOME REVIEWERS OF my books about James Bond have been generous in commending the accuracy of the expertise which forms a considerable part of the furniture of these books. I may say that correspondents from all over the world have been equally enthusiastic in writing to point out errors in this expertise, and the mistakes I have made, approximately one per volume, will no doubt forever continue to haunt my In-basket.'

Ian Fleming: 'The Guns of James Bond', 1962.

From out of the blue in May 1956 a letter arrived from Geoffrey Boothroyd, a gun expert living in Glasgow. It contained a critique of James Bond's side-arms that caused Fleming a small amount of alarm. Hitherto, he had armed Bond with a .25 Beretta, a slim weapon little larger than a man's hand, which he wore in a chamois leather holster under his left armpit. Given a clear eye and a steady hand it could send a nugget of lead to deadly effect. The concept was stylish but, as Boothroyd pointed out, completely impractical. Nobody with any sense – not to mention a licence to kill – would use such a puny thing. And he went on to explain why. From holster to grip, chamber to bullet, he parsed the mechanics of short-range death.

It was disheartening for Fleming, who prided himself on the accuracy of his research, to have such a hole blown in his credibility. All the same, he was fascinated by Boothroyd's lore. He himself had handled a number of guns in his time and for a journalist owned a surprisingly large arsenal. He had a .25 Browning automatic, left over from his time in Naval Intelligence, plus a .38

Police Special Colt revolver given to him as a memento by General Bill Donovan, head of the American Secret Service. In a cupboard somewhere he kept a pair of Holland & Holland 12-bore shotguns, as well as a .275 Rigby for larger game. In addition he used a .22 Browning rifle for pest control at Goldeneye. But he was a novice compared to Boothroyd.

Their correspondence started in 1956 while Fleming was correcting the manuscript of From Russia with Love, and continued intermittently until his death. It was an unusual relationship. Boothroyd kept Fleming informed about his personal circumstances, while advising him on a variety of weapons that Bond might find useful. Fleming, meanwhile, anointed Boothroyd as Bond's fictional armourer and charged him, in real life, with answering the many queries that came in about his guns. Strangely, they did not meet until March 1961, when a public relations event brought them together in Glasgow.

In 1962, when their letters were published under the title 'The Guns of James Bond', it caused a minor sensation. Nowadays it is de rigueur for writers to specify a particular agent of mayhem: Glock, Sig Sauer, Ithaca – the names resound to anyone familiar with the formulaics of thrillerdom. In the 1950s, however, the world was more innocent. When British policemen chased a suspect they blew whistles or, more dashingly, rang a little bell at the front of their car. Guns were uncommon currency and if they were fired in anger it was a major event. All of this has changed, and the transition – at least in literary terms – can perhaps be traced to, or at least mirrored by, the correspondence between Ian Fleming and Geoffrey Boothroyd.

FROM G. BOOTHROYD, 17 Regent Park Sq., Glasgow, s.1.

May 23rd, 1956

I have, by now, got rather fond of Mr. James Bond. I like most of the things about him, with the exception of his rather deplorable taste in firearms. In particular I dislike a man who comes into contact with all sorts of formidable people using a .25 Beretta. This sort of gun is really a lady's gun, and not a really nice lady at that. If Mr. Bond has to use a light gun he would be better off with a .22 rim fire and the lead bullet would cause more shocking effect than the jacketed type of the .25.

May I suggest that Mr. Bond is armed with a revolver? This has many advantages for the type of shooting that he is called upon to perform and I am certain that Mr. Leiter would agree with this recommendation. The Beretta will weigh, after it has been doctored, somewhere under one pound. If Mr. Bond gets himself an S. & W. .38 Special Centennial Airweight he will have a real man-stopper weighing only 13 ozs. The gun is hammerless so that it can be drawn without catching in the clothing and has an overall length of 6½". Barrel length is 2", note that it is not 'sawn off.' No one who can buy his pistols in the States will go to the trouble of sawing off pistol barrels as they can be purchased with short 2" barrels from the manufacturer. In order to keep down the bulk, the cylinder holds 5 cartridges, and these are standard .38 S&W Special. It is an extremely accurate cartridge and when fired from a 2" barrel has, in standard loading, a muzzle velocity of almost 860 ft./sec. and muzzle energy of almost 260 ft./lbs. This is against the .25 with M.V. of 758 ft./sec. but only 67 ft./lbs. muzzle energy. So much for his personal gun. Now he must have a real man stopper to carry in the car. For this purpose the S. & W. .357 Magnum has no equal except the .44 Magnum. However with the .357, Bond can still use his .38 S.W. Special cartridges in the Magnum but not vice versa. This can be obtained in barrel lengths as follows: 3½", 5", 6", 6½" and 8¾" long. With a 6½" barrel and adjustable sights Bond could do some really effective shooting. The .357 Magnum has a MV of 1515 ft/sec. and a ME of 807 ft./lbs. Figures like these give an effective range of 300 yards, and it's very accurate, too, 1" groups at 20 yards on a machine rest.

With these two guns our friend would be able to cope with really quick draw work and long range effective shooting.

Now to gun harness, rigs or what have you. First of all, not a shoulder holster for general wear, please. I suggest that the gun is carried in a Berns Martin Triple Draw holster. This type of holster holds the gun in by means of a spring and can be worn on the belt or as a shoulder holster. I have played about with various types of holster for quite a time now and this one is the best. I took some pictures of the holster some time ago and at present can only find the proofs but I send them to you to illustrate how it works. I have numbered the prints and give a description of each print below.

'A' Series. Holster worn on belt at right side. Pistol drawn with right hand.

1. Ready position. Note that the gun is not noticeable.
2. First movement. Weight moves to left foot. Hand draws back coat and sweeps forward to catch butt of pistol. Finger outside holster.
3. Gun coming out of holster through the split front.
4. In business.

This draw can be done in 3/5ths of a second by me. With practice and lots of it you could hit a figure at 20 feet in that time.

'B' Series. Shoulder holster. Gun upside down on left side. Held in by spring. Drawn with right hand.

1. First position.
2. Coat drawn back by left hand, gun butt grasped by right hand, finger outside holster.
3. Gun coming out of holster.
4. Bang! You're dead.

'C' Series. Holster worn as in A, but gun drawn with left hand.

1. Draw commences. Butt held by first two fingers of left hand. Third finger and little finger ready to grasp trigger.
2. Ready to shoot. Trigger being pulled by third and little finger, thumb curled round stock, gun upside down.

This really works but you need a cut away trigger guard.

'D' Series. Holster worn on shoulder, as in 'B' Series, but gun drawn with left hand.

1. Coat swept back with left hand and gun grasped.
2. Gun is pushed to the right to clear holster and is ready for action.

I'm sorry that I couldn't find the better series of photographs but these should illustrate what I mean. The gun used is a .38 S.W. with a sawn off barrel to 2¾". (I know this contradicts what I said over the page but I can't afford the 64 dollars needed so I had to make my own.) It has target sights, ramp front sights, adjustable rear sight, rounded butt, special stocks and a cut away trigger guard.

If you have managed to read this far I hope that you will accept the above in the spirit that it is offered. I have enjoyed your four books immensely and will say right now that I have no criticism of the women in them, except that I've never met any like them and would doubtless get into trouble if I did.

FLEMING TO BOOTHROYD

31st May, 1956

I really am most grateful for your splendid letter of May 23rd.

You have entirely convinced me, and I propose, perhaps not in the next volume of James Bond's memoirs but in the subsequent one, to change his weapons in accordance with your instructions.

Since I am not in the habit of stealing another man's expertise, I shall ask you in due course to accept remuneration for your most valuable technical aid.

Incidentally, can you suggest where I can see a .38 Airweight in London? Who would have one?

As a matter of interest, how do you come to know so much about these things? I was delighted with the photographs and greatly impressed by them. If ever there is talk of making films of some of James Bond's adventures in due course, I shall suggest to the company concerned that they might like to consult you on some technical aspects. But they may not take my advice, so please do not set too much store by this suggestion.

From the style of your writing it occurs to me that you may have written books or articles on these subjects. Is that so?

Bond has always admitted to me that the .25 Beretta was not a stopping gun, and he places much more reliance on his accuracy with it than in any particular qualities of the gun itself. As you know, one gets used to a gun and it may take some time for him to settle down with the Smith & Wesson. But I think M. should advise him to make a change; as also in the case of the .357 Magnum.

He also agrees to give a fair trial to the Berns Martin holster, but he is inclined to favour something a little more casual and less bulky. The well-worn chamois leather pouch under his left arm has become almost part of his clothes, and he will be loath to make a change, though, here again, M. may intervene.

At the present moment Bond is particularly anxious for expertise on the weapons likely to be carried by Russian agents, and I wonder if you have any information on this.

As Bond's biographer I am most anxious to see that he lives as long as possible and I shall be most grateful for any further technical advices you might like to pass on to him.

Again, with very sincere thanks for your extremely helpful and workmanlike letter.

BOOTHROYD TO FLEMING

1st June, 1956

I was truly delighted to receive your charming letter. This is the first time I have had either the inclination or the temerity to write to the author of any books that pass through my hands; quite frankly in many cases the rest of the material is not worth backing up by correct and authentic 'gun dope.' You have, incidentally, enslaved the rest of my household, people staying up to all hours of the night in an endeavour to finish a book before some other interested party swipes it.

If I am to be considered for the post of Bond's ballistic man I should give you my terms of reference. Age 31, English, unmarried. Employed by I.C.I. Ltd. as Technical Rep in Scotland. Member of the following Rifle Clubs: N.R.A., Gt. Britain, English Twenty Club, National Rifle Association of America, non-resident member. St. Rollox Rifle Club, West of Scotland Rifle Club, Muzzle Loading Association of Gt. Britain. I shoot with shotgun and rifle, target, clay pigeon, deer, but, to my deep regret, no big game. (I cherish a dream that one day a large tiger or lion will escape from the zoo or a travelling circus and I can bag it in Argyle St., or Princes St., Edinburgh.) I do both muzzle loading and breech loading shooting, load my own shotgun and pistol ammunition. Shoot with pistol mainly target and collect arms of various sorts. My present collection numbers about 45, not as many as some collections go but all of mine go off and have been fired by me. Shooting and gun lore is a jolly queer thing, most people stick to their own field, rather like stamp collectors who specialise in British Colonials. Such people shoot only with the rifle and often only .303 or only .22. There are certain rather odd types like myself who have a go at the lot, including Archery. It's a most fascinating study if one has the time, and before long it's given up and you collect old Bentleys or it becomes an obsession. We all have a pet aspect of our hobby, and mine is this business of 'draw and shoot', or the gun lore of close-combat weapons. On reflection it is pretty stupid as it's most unlikely that I shall ever do this sort of thing in earnest but it has the pleasant advantage of not having very many fish in the pond and however you look at it you are an authority. In Scotland I have the space to do this sort of thing, and have two friends who are not 150 miles away to talk to. I seem to have taken up a lot of space on this, must want to impress you!

I have written one thing on Scottish pistols, but tore it up after reading a really superb effort by an American. He had access to a lot more weapons and anyway, no use kidding myself, he knew how to write or the magazine re-wrote it for him. Since then I've found a new thing for an article which will be written before the end of the year and sent to America. This will be on the firm of Dickson in Edinburgh, who are old established gun makers. Lots of pictures of ye olde craftsmen at the bench, the more pictures the less writing. I have also given one or two lectures on firearms to the T.A., Home Guard and the Police. Occasionally we are able to give demonstrations of some of the things we talk about but as some of the tricks require an expenditure of about 10,000 rounds of ammunition one cannot afford to become an expert trick shot.

Now to the work. I doubt very much if you will be able to see a S. & W. Airweight model in England, at least in a shop. I therefore enclose S. & W. latest catalog, which shows current models. Perhaps you would let me have this back, as I have to send it off to another chap who is going to S. America and he wants to buy a gun when he gets there. The only people in London who may have S. & W. new-model pistols will be

Thomas Bland and Sons, William IVth St., Strand. Current demand for pistols in this country is restricted to folks going off to Kenya, Malaya, etc. The few that know anything about pistols for close up work will probably buy modified guns from Cogswell and Harrison. This type is a cut-down S. & W. .38 Military & Police Model generally similar to the photo enclosed. You have seen this gun of mine and were quite interested. You may retain this print if you wish. (I had to learn photography as well, this is an improvement over earlier work.) I'm sorry I can't help regarding an actual inspection of a new-model S. & W. The only people who may have one are Americans in this country or James Bond.

Re holsters. A letter to S.D. Myres Saddle Co., 5030 Alameda Blvd., P.O. Box 1501, El Paso, Texas, will bring you their current holster catalog. The Berns Martin people live in Calhoun City, Mississippi, and a note to Jack Martin, who is a first-class chap and a true gunslinger, will bring you illustrations of his work. Bond's chamois leather pouch will be ideal for <u>carrying</u> a gun, but God help him if he has to get it out in a hurry. The soft leather will snag and foul on the projecting parts of the gun and he will still be struggling to get the gun out when the other fellow is counting the holes in Bond's tummy. Bond has a good point when he mentions accuracy. It's no good shooting at a man with the biggest gun one can hold – if you miss him. The thing about the larger calibres is, however, that when you hit someone with a man stopping bullet they are out of the game and won't lie on the floor still popping off at you.

Regarding weapons carried by Russian agents. I have had little experience of using weapons from behind the Iron Curtain or of meeting people who use them. I did once meet a Polish officer who was some sort of undercover man and cloak-and-dagger merchant and he used an American Colt Automatic in .38 cal. I would suggest that a member of SMERSH would in all probability make his choice from the following and use for preference either a Luger with an 8", 10", 12" or 16" barrel with detachable shoulder stock for assassination work from a medium distance, say across a street. A short-barrel 9mm. Luger (Model 08), 4" barrel, might be carried for personal protection, although it is rather large to carry about. In the same class as the Luger and having equal availability to someone employed by SMERSH would be the Polish

Radon P.35. This takes the standard Luger cartridge and also the more powerful black bulleted machine pistol 9mm round. It closely resembles the Colt Model 1911, or perhaps more so the Colt 9mm Commander. Another choice would be the Swedish 9mm Lahti. This is a strong and very well-made pistol strongly reminiscent of the Luger. It weighs 42 ozs loaded as compared with 32 ozs for the short barrel Luger.

The Russian Tokarev pistol Model 30 appears to be the standard side arm of the Soviets, and once again is a close copy of John Browning's basic pistol, calibre 7.62 Russian or 7.63 Mauser and designed in the 1930s. This pistol looks like the Belgian Browning auto pistol made by Fabrique Nationale, Liege, except that it has an external hammer. There is no manual safety, and if the gun is carried loaded at full cock, obvious safety hazards exist. Carried at half-cock the gun undoubtedly would be safer, but the hammer design is such that cocking the hammer is not an easy job and the first shot would be a slow one from the draw.

In this same general class would be the Walther P.38, which was used by the German army as a replacement for the Luger. Evidence is that the pistol is not quite as good as it might be, this being probably due to production difficulties met with during the war. This also takes the 9mm cartridge. One of the advantages of the Walther is that it can be used double action, i.e., there is no need to cock the hammer for the first shot provided the barrel has a cartridge 'up the spout'. After the first shot the gun operates as does the normal auto pistol.

For carrying on the person the following arms could be chosen: Walther PPK 7.65 mm, Mauser HSc 7.65 mm or the Walther PPK in 7.65 mm cal., Sauer Model 35 in 7.65-mm calibre.

The above represent a class of weapons similar to the Beretta but of rather better quality.

All of the above were tested for accuracy, endurance, by the US Army Ordnance Corps in 1948. Also included were the Jap. Nambu and the American Colt 1911 A1 Auto. In accuracy the Nambu came first, followed by the Russian Tokarev, the Sauer being third. Colonel F.S. Allen, USAF, who wrote an article on the findings of the O.C. tests, concluded by saying that for an emergency defence weapon he would have a .38 Special lightweight S.W., a decision which I heartily agree with.

I hope that when the SMERSH operative, armed perhaps with one of the guns mentioned above, meets Bond, your friend will be able to demonstrate the effectiveness of Anglo-American cooperation, a competent English pistol man behind a truly lethal .38 Special.

The above should give some idea of the type of weapon likely to be carried by SMERSH men, the Russians being rather similar to ourselves where firearms are concerned, they do not hesitate to use foreign weapons if they are better than those produced by themselves. An instance of this was their use of the Finnish Suomi light machine gun during the last war. In brief, one could be safe in arming an agent of SMERSH with the Tokarev, Radon, or Luger in that order. Pocket weapons would be either German Mauser or Walthers.

Please convey warmest regards to Mr. Bond and assure him of my closest interest in his activities and very willing cooperation in his 'gun needs' for as long as he wishes. Instead of remuneration, an introduction to Solitaire would more than adequately compensate me for the little trouble I have taken. Between you and me, I quite enjoy it.

FLEMING TO BOOTHROYD

22nd June, 1956

I have been away in Vienna, and seeing a man about a flying saucer in Paris, and I have only just had your letter of June 1st with enclosures.

Thank you again most sincerely for taking all this trouble, and also for sending me the very interesting information on your own career and hobbies. You certainly seem to lead a full life!

I am intrigued by your mention of archery. I have long thought Bond could do a lot of damage with a short steel bow and the appropriate arrows. What do you think of this suggestion, and do you know someone who would instruct me on weapons, ranges and so forth?

I am returning the Smith & Wesson catalogue and, since I am off to New York at the end of July, I propose to purchase a Centennial Airweight.

Would this not, in any case, be the best weapon for Bond? There is no hammer to catch in his clothes.

I am vastly intrigued by your own M. & P. model and by the way you have beautified it. Bond will certainly adopt your two-thirds trigger guard. I don't intend to go too deeply into the holster problem and I intend to accept your expertise in the matter of the Berns Martin holster.

Only one basic problem remains in changing Bond's weapon, and that is the matter of a silencer. It would have to be an extremely bulky affair to silence a .38 of any make and I simply can't see one fitted to the Centennial. Have you any views?

As a matter of fact, a change of Bond's weapons is very appropriate. In his next adventure, which deals with an intricate plot by SMERSH to kill Bond, he finally gets into really bad trouble through the Beretta, with silencer, sticking in his waistband.

It is too late now to save him from the consequences of ill-equipment, but in the book that follows, if I have the energy and ingenuity to write one, I shall start off with a chapter devoted entirely to his re-equipment along all the lines you suggest.

But in this chapter the matter of a silencer will have to be overcome and, in fact, in his latest adventure which I mention above he could hardly have used an unsilenced .38 in the room at the Ritz Hotel in Paris where he wrestles fruitlessly with his snarled gun.

Turning to foreign weapons, have you by any chance got the article by Colonel Allen on the findings of the O.C. tests, or could you tell me where it appeared? It sounds most useful to my purposes.

Once again, please accept my very warm thanks for your kindness in taking Bond's armoury in hand and sorting it out. As a small recompense for your trouble I am sending you a shiny and rather expensive book on Odd Weapons which has just appeared and which perhaps you do not possess. It is not exactly on your beat, but it may entertain.

As requested, Boothroyd supplied Fleming with Colonel Allen's analysis of handguns but without the last page, which he had lost and summarised thus: 'He concludes by giving his personal choice of side arms as being for

*lethality a handloaded .44 Special, target shooting a .22 Colt Auto Woods-
man and for an emergency defence weapon a lightweight .38 Special, either
Colt or Smith & Wesson.'*

*As to killing people with a bow and arrow, Boothroyd's choice of consul-
tant was Slazenger.* When Fleming went to America, Boothroyd was happy
to recommend several gun merchants but if time was short he should visit a
New York store called Abercrombie and Fitch.*

BOOTHROYD TO FLEMING

29th June, 1956

Your letter of the 22nd June and a most satisfactory package were waiting
for me on my return to Glasgow last Monday. The promised book 'Firearms Curiosa' arrived safely and I am most delighted with it. I have a
similar book called 'Hand Cannon to Automatic' which was given to me
some years ago dealing with the rather more exotic type of firearm. Your
gift is far more comprehensive and gives actual photographs of the various pieces instead of the line drawings which illustrate my other book.
Incidentally, it arrived just in time, a chap turning up the day after it
arrived with a small 'squeeze' pistol that he wished identifying and I was
able to retain my 'expert' rating by giving him all the details on what
turned out to be a Gaulois pistol, very rare, very strange.

I do not feel competent to give authoritative information on hunting
bows and arrows, I have had a go at rabbits with them and hope one day
to kill a stag in the approved manner. [. . .] I understand that some Commando units were issued with bows and arrows during the late War and
from my own experience I should not like to be in the way of a hunting
arrow propelled by a bow of more than moderate weight. [. . .]

Silencers. These I do not like. The only excuse for using one is on a .22
rifle using low-velocity ammunition, i.e., below the speed of sound.
With apologies, I think you will find that silencers are more often found

---

* Fleming did, in fact, equip a female assassin with a bow and arrow in his 1960 collection of short stories *For Your Eyes Only*.

in fiction than in real life. An effective silencer on an auto pistol would be very ponderous and would spoil the balance of the gun, and to silence a revolver would be even more difficult due to the gas escape between the cylinder and the barrel. Personally I can't at this stage see how one would fit a silencer to a Beretta unless a special barrel were made for it, as the silencer has to be screwed on to the barrel projecting in front of the slide on the Beretta.

This business of using guns in houses or hotels is a very strange one. So few people are familiar with what a gun sounds like that I would have very little hesitation in firing one in any well constructed building. This remark is only regarding the noise or nuisance value. I would not fire a pistol in a room without some thoughts on the matter, as bullets have a bad habit of bouncing off things and coming home to roost. I have fired .455 blanks at home on several occasions even in the middle of the night without any enquiries being made, the last time was at Christmas when I blew out the candles on the Christmas cake with a pistol and blanks. To conclude, if possible don't have anything to do with silencers.

FLEMING TO BOOTHROYD

12th July, 1956

Thank you very much indeed for the two magazine articles. These are extremely informative and valuable and I can see a splendid chapter of stolen expertese [sic] coming out of all your help.

I shall be almost ashamed of writing the chapter without saying that this comes to you by courtesy of Mr. Boothroyd.

I sympathise with you about not liking silencers, but the trouble is that there are occasions when they are essential to Bond's work. But they are clumsy things and only partially effective, though our Secret Services developed some very good ones during the war, in which the bullet passed through rubber baffles. I have tried a Sten silenced with one of these and all one could hear was the click of the machinery.

I rather like the picture of you going through life firing bullets "in any well-constructed building"! But I agree with you that one could probably get away with a single shot in a hotel bedroom. Your Christmas trick would, of course, be helped by its association in a listener's mind with cracker-pulling.

By the way, the jacket of my present book is going to be a trompe l'oeil, painted by the only English master in the art, called Chopping,* who really paints things so that you can pick them straight off the canvas. The picture will consist of a revolver crossed with a rose and it should be a very handsome affair. I have looked in vain for a Beretta .25 which would obviously be to the point but, if I fail to find one, would you care to have your own Smith & Wesson made forever famous?

It is such a very handsome gun that, although it has nothing to do with the story, it would look so splendid on the jacket that that would not matter.

You might care to turn the matter over in your mind and let me know at your leisure.

I suppose the artist would probably need the gun for around a month – possibly for the month of September. You send me a bill for the amount. Chopping is an extremely reliable and sensible man and you would not have to fear for its safety while in his keeping and, as the Deputy Commissioner of Scotland Yard is a close personal friend, we would have no complications over fire-arms certificates.

This is only an idea and I may be able to find a Beretta in New York. But you might care to let me know what you think in principle of the suggestion.

By the way, have you ever heard of that extraordinary Frenchman who appears in "Firearms Curiosa" with the breastplate covered with pistols? He sounds an intriguing character and I would be very interested in any line on him from you or your friends.

Again, with warm thanks for this most profitable correspondence.

On 31 August, Boothroyd commiserated with Fleming for having been unable to buy a gun in New York. 'From what I gather from correspondents in N.Y.

---

* Richard Chopping (1917–2008), famous for his realistic style, would later illustrate numerous Bond jackets.

it is more difficult to obtain permission to own a hand gun unless one is a politician or prepared to pay the customary graft to the local Precinct police than it is anywhere in Britain.'

He added, too, some notes about life in his new home (just a few steps from his last in Regent Park Square, Glasgow). 'Since my last letter to you I have been married and the time has been fully occupied by painting and finding a home for all my guns. My wife has allowed me the use of a very large room and several pieces of peculiar furniture at the local sale rooms ensures that all ammunition and hand guns are under lock and key together with my ammunition specimens.'

FLEMING TO BOOTHROYD

4th September, 1956

Very many thanks for your most helpful letter and let me at once congratulate you warmly on your marriage. It is wonderful news and, from what you tell me, she must indeed be the ideal wife if she is prepared to be married to your guns as well as yourself.

I got a letter from Richard Chopping by the same post as yours and he is coming up on the 7th, and says that the picture will not take him more than a fortnight. On the strength of this estimate, to which I will keep him, I can guarantee that the gun will be back with you at the latest by the 26th, even if it means interrupting the painting.

I will see that you get a reproduction of the original, signed if you wish by me, and I dare say it will make an acceptable decoration for your gun room.

Chopping's work is really remarkable. His trompe l'oeil really does deceive the eye. You feel that you could pick the object up out of the canvas. Jonathan Cape's are most enthusiastic and I think, with your co-operation, we shall achieve a really fine book jacket.

I am sorry I shall not be seeing you on your next visit to London but, if you are anywhere in the neighbourhood of Gray's Inn Road, I shall take it amiss if you don't find 10 minutes to drop in and have a talk.

With best wishes to you both for a very happy life together, and again with my warm thanks for putting your shoulder so staunchly behind James Bond's problems.

The following day Boothroyd wrote to say he was happy for Chopping to borrow the gun provided it was back by 26 September. He reassured Fleming, too, that the marriage was going swimmingly: not only had his wife no objection to his turning their ground floor into a shooting range but one evening she had helped him blast off 174 rounds. The neighbours heard nothing (or at least were polite enough not to mention it) and she put up 'a most creditable performance despite that disadvantage of a high noise level which often causes flinching'.

Understanding of her husband's obsession though she may have been, Mrs Boothroyd probably flinched ten days later when the police came knocking at her door. On the night of 15 September, in what would become infamous to Glaswegians as the 'Burnside Murders', three women – mother, daughter and sister-in-law – were shot dead with a .38 calibre pistol. Boothroyd, who lived in the vicinity and had just such a weapon, was high on the list of suspects.

BOOTHROYD TO FLEMING

18th September, 1956

I have just had a visit from our local CID who wanted to know where my .38 pistol was. The reason for this uncalled for interest in my collection is due to a very misguided character who slew two ladies and a girl on the outskirts of Glasgow on Sunday night using a .38 pistol.

Believing that honesty is the best policy I told the two CID chaps that the pistol was not in my possession but was in London in your possession. They saw my receipt which showed them when the pistol was posted and your telegram confirming safe arrival.

The chaps that called are unknown to me and it is possible that the wheels of the Law may (a) call upon you in London to make sure that the pistol is where I said it was, and (b) if they are bloody minded, ask you if you have a Firearms Certificate which allows you or your agent to have the pistol in your possession. A further possibility is that the Police may come to me and ask why I let the pistol out of my possession not knowing that you did hold a permit.

The section of the act which applies states that anyone not having in his possession a firearms certificate is liable to three months in clink or a fine of £50 or, worse still, both. I am liable to the above imprisonment but only a fine of £20.

I am assuming that our local gendarmes are fully engaged in tracking down the murderer, however, I never trust Policemen to do the sensible thing so it is possible that some chap with knowledge of the Firearms Act might wish to get himself some promotion by unmasking my villainy so I am letting you know what has transpired so that you can take the appropriate action should you think this necessary.

It is a funny world, the most unlikely events cause repercussions all over the place and our gunman friend would have to choose this time to go shooting people and he would have to use a .38. Incidentally, no one heard the sound of the shots which goes to prove my point about firing off guns.

Sorry this should have happened but I thought the best plan would be to let you know in case anything untoward happens. Perhaps you will be able to get a special dispensation from your friend the Deputy Commissioner, I to my regret only know Inspectors and Sergeants.*

FLEMING TO BOOTHROYD

20th September, 1956

Well, well, I am so sorry that the shadow of James Bond has fallen across your path so decisively.

But have no fear. I have a valid Firearms Certificate, number 109950, and an alibi for Sunday night.

* Fleming's friend in the police force was Deputy Commissioner Sir Ronald Howe, who featured as Sir Ronald Vallance in *Moonraker*.

Of course the long arm of the law may now take a swipe at the unfortunate Richard Chopping, but the gun will be back in my possession on Monday and I think I will be able to stall them without involving our distinguished artist.

Anyway, have no fear. The gun will be back in your possession by the 26th and this sticky passage in your life will have ended.

Incidentally, Chopping is very happy with the way the picture is going, though the finer points of the gun have been causing him pictorial agony.

FLEMING TO BOOTHROYD

1st October, 1956

Many thanks for your letter of the 25th and I am glad that everything has now calmed down.

The final chapter was really splendid. Chopping had arrived in this office and delivered the picture and I was just telling him the story of our little case of murder when the telephone rang and there was Chief Inspector Blake of Scotland Yard very full of "ums" and "ahs" and "on the 16th instants". Fortunately I was able to give him the number of my revolver licence which also covers a .38 colt Police Positive, and I explained at length that you were very much an innocent party to what was, in any case, quite within the law, and he retired satisfied.

I naturally never mentioned Chopping's name. He assumed that the pistol had been in my possession throughout.

Meantime Chopping sat wide-eyed and obviously expecting to find the Black Maria on its way for him.

However, now all is quiet again and I enclose a photograph of Chopping's picture which I am sure you will agree is superb. The rose, incidentally, is red.

You might care to tack this to your wall pending the production of a coloured lithograph from the original which will probably take some months. But you will also receive a copy of this in due course.

Incidentally, would you please send me a note of your expenses in connection with all this. Please don't be obstinate about this matter as, in any case, they will be deductible from my expenses in connection with the book.

Again with my warmest thanks for your help in all this.

By now Fleming was in the final stage of editing From Russia with Love, *in which Bond's trouble extricating his silenced Beretta nearly proved his downfall. In the next book,* Dr No, *all was put straight when the service's Armourer, one Major Boothroyd, confiscated his 'lady's gun' and gave him a proper weapon. Following publication in 1958, Boothroyd wrote to thank Fleming for his fictional promotion but felt obliged to point out a few mistakes. The M.1. carbine used in* Dr No, *should have been a Winchester not a Remington. And although Bond had been equipped with a Berns Martin holster it could only be used with a revolver, not the Walther automatic with which he had been issued.*

He suggested an alternative holster for the Smith and Wesson: the Tom Threepersons model. 'Tom Threepersons,' he explained, 'was a full blooded Cherokee Indian who had quite an adventurous life. His father was shot down in cold blood, Tom avenging the killing when the killer came out of jail. Tom went to Canada and served with the R.C.M.P. [Royal Canadian Mounted Police]. He then returned to Texas and served with the Pershing expeditionary force against Pancho Villa. He put in several years with the Border Guards and the El Paso police. How many gunfights he had and how many people he killed no one knows.'

Boothroyd clearly knew his man, but despite this intriguing snippet Fleming's reply gave a faint indication that he had had enough of gun lore for the moment.

FLEMING TO BOOTHROYD

2nd April, 1958

Thank you very much for your splendid letter of March 23rd and I am glad that you are pleased with your second personality.

I am very much put out that I have made further technical errors in your realm of knowledge and I shall try to correct them in subsequent work in line with your most interesting and informative recommendations.

Thank you very much for the Smith & Wesson catalogue which I shall be delighted to keep, and I now return the Myers catalogue which has been most informative. Tom Threepersons must have been a remarkable man and we must try and keep his fame alive.

I am surprised to find you still in Glasgow instead of having been promoted Chairman of I.C.I. by now. It is time we brought pressure to bear on London headquarters.

With kind regards and again many thanks for your various advices.

In March 1961, Fleming travelled to Glasgow, where he and Boothroyd were scheduled to appear on Scottish Television. It wasn't Fleming's standard bill of fare, and to compound his unease he had 'the baffling experience of being interviewed by a young man who had never read any of my books'. Afterwards the Scottish Daily Express *held a party in which he and Boothroyd posed for the photographer shooting at each other with revolvers.*

'Boothroyd, the expert, escaped unmarked from this duel,' Fleming later wrote. 'The thriller writer, less tough and rustier on the draw, was doomed, a very few days later, to suffer a heart attack which laid him temporarily as low as a real stopper from the Smith and Wesson.*

'Mark you, I am not actually nominating Boothroyd as mine own executioner, but it certainly was a curious sequel to an already bizarre relationship!'

It was less a sequel than the beginning of a new chapter. Encouraged by their correspondence, Boothroyd had embarked on a book, A Guide to Gun Collecting, *to which Fleming, when they met in Glasgow, had agreed to provide an introduction. At the time, Fleming had been enthusiastic about the project. But when Boothroyd wrote again in April 1961,*

* Boothroyd pointed out that he had in fact been photographed holding a Ruger.

reminding him of the offer and wondering if he would like to see the manuscript, he learned from Fleming's secretary, the redoubtable Beryl Griffie-Williams, that 'Mr. Fleming is away at present as he is suffering from slight tension due to overwork, and the doctor has insisted that he has complete rest for at least two weeks.' The slight tension was a heart attack.

When Fleming mustered the strength to reply, it was in polite yet under-standably weary terms – even so he couldn't resist suggesting ways to make the book more sensational.

FLEMING TO BOOTHROYD

1st May, 1961

As from The Clinic

I have now seen your correspondence with my secretary and you are quite right, the last thing I want to do is to read through the manuscript which would be double Dutch to me. I will simply write an entertaining account of our relationship.

If the publishers don't accept the book immediately please send it on to Jonathan Cape, my own publishers, saying that I shall be writing the introduction and I am sure they will be interested. In fact I think your agent might be wise to do that straight away.

I should certainly change the title, which is a bit dull. Why not call it "A Love of Guns"? And add a chapter, if you haven't already done so, explaining your particular passion as best you can!

I will get around to the introduction in a few weeks' time and make it as interesting and entertaining as I know how.

Please don't bother to answer this until you have finally settled with a publisher, but I do suggest you take my advice and try Capes.

A couple of months later Fleming was back in the saddle and discovered that his introduction was longer and more detailed than expected. So much so, that he felt it had the makings of a full-length article.

FLEMING TO BOOTHROYD

12th July, 1961

Many thanks for your letter of July 5th, but I do so hope you will dig out the brief details of the murder case so that I can include them simply as a matter of record.

All the other brief references in my piece to this occurrence show the police in nothing but an extremely complimentary light, and I am sure you shouldn't worry about them.

I have had a word with your publishers and I realise that your book is part of an instructional series, which sounds an excellent idea.

But, as you will see when you receive the draft, my introduction is a pretty heavyweight affair entitled "The Guns of James Bond", and is really more of a feature article than an introduction.

Accordingly, I have had a word with the Sunday Times and though they haven't seen the typescript they would, in theory, very much like to publish it as a piece of Bondiana, and it is probable that I may also be able to place it in the United States.

Now, this new idea would be infinitely more beneficial to your book and your general fame, I am sure it would delight countless readers, and properly timed publication in the Sunday Times would give your book a tremendous send off.

I shall be sending you a copy next week for you to add to as appropriate from your files, and then I would like to send it back for final typing and also, I hope, to agree with my suggested treatment of this business which seems to have grown rather larger than you may have expected.

Since the article is largely based on the expertise contained in your letters, I would pay you a fee proportionate to what I am able to extract from publication here and abroad, and it is quite possible that in the end you may make more money out of your contribution to this article than out of the book itself!

And then, of course, the article with some concluding phrases commending your book, could be used as a foreword by Arco [Boothroyd's publisher] when they publish as they plan to do approximately in January or February.

I do hope the whole tale as I have written it will amuse you as much as it has entertained me. I have written to the Editor of the Daily Express, Glasgow, for copies of the various photographs which were taken of both of us, and it would be embellished with a suitable one together with a photograph of the Chopping picture.

Please don't bother to reply to this until you have read the piece, but please try and dig out brief facts about that murder case so that we can round off the story appropriately.

I will have a word with your agent to tell him what I have in mind, but since this is an entirely friendly arrangement directly between you and me I don't see why he should have a commission from you on the profits I hope you will make from this article.

The murder details that Boothroyd unearthed were indeed brief. Although rounding off Fleming's article perfectly, they failed to mention that the culprit, Peter Manuel, was one of the decade's most infamous serial killers. Born in 1927 in New York to Scottish parents, he had been in and out of prison for rape and sexual offences since the age of sixteen, and in 1956 embarked on a spree of bloodshed that earned him the name 'The Beast of Birkenshaw'. He eventually confessed to eighteen murders before being hanged at Barlinnie Prison, Glasgow, on 11 July 1958.

'The Guns of James Bond' appeared in the American magazine Sports Illustrated *in March 1962 and in November of the same year the* Sunday Times *(who had initially turned it down) ran it under the title "James Bond's Hardware". It sold well in America, too. In fact, so established had James Bond now become that the piece earned Fleming considerably more than the first UK paperback edition of* Live and Let Die. *'I have greatly enjoyed it,' he wrote to Boothroyd, 'and looking back on it all what fun we had!'*

By this time the first Bond film, Dr No, was underway, and on Fleming's recommendation the producers Albert 'Cubby' Broccoli and Harry Saltzman had hired Boothroyd as firearms consultant. For the launch party in Pinewood Studios there was talk of Boothroyd, Fleming, Sean Connery and, strangely, the entertainer Michael Bentine, erstwhile member of The Goon Show, staging a gunfight. Boothroyd offered to supply the weapons and (live) ammunition but, come the day, wiser counsel prevailed.

Not that Fleming had much strength for that kind of shenanigans anyway. His health was deteriorating and his enthusiasm for Bond, once so energetic, was beginning to flag. The two men kept up an intermittent exchange, the chatty role being sustained by Boothroyd who informed Fleming of details such as his purchase of a 'Queen Anne bureau with all the usual secret hidey holes. This piece of quite delightful furniture will always serve as a most pleasant reminder of our friendship.' Fleming's letters, on the other hand became terser and increasingly it was Beryl Griffie-Williams who took the strain. She had been privy to much of the conversation and had become as fascinated with Boothroyd's expertise as her employer. When Fleming died in 1964 the letters stopped. Boothroyd outlived him by two decades.

8

Dr No

IN APRIL 1956 Fleming wrote a series of travel articles for the *Sunday Times*, one of which opened with a typically *carpe diem* sentiment: 'After the age of forty, time begins to become important, and one is inclined to say, "Yes" to every experience.' The experience he had in mind was an expedition to the Bahamian island of Inagua, organised by Ivar Bryce, to study the world's largest population of flamingos. The birds were dramatic enough, but what really caught Fleming's imagination was the 100-square-mile lake in which they lived – a shallow, mangrove-fringed expanse 'the colour of a corpse', which exuded a miasma of rotten-egg decay – and the secluded, semi-feudal life of Inagua's 1,000-strong population. The only source of employment was a salt works, overseen by a European family who guarded their fiefdom with vigour. 'It is a hideous island,' he wrote, 'and nobody in his senses ever goes near the place.' The last time Inagua had been surveyed was 1916, since when it had dropped off the bureaucratic map. Could there be a better villain's lair?

Initially, he used the setting as a basis for a TV script, *James Gunn – Secret Agent*, which he submitted to American producer Henry Morgenthau III in September 1956. When Morgenthau turned the script down, he reworked it as a novel. The plot centred on a remote, swampy Caribbean island owned by Dr Julius No, a secretive man of German/ Chinese extraction who owned a guano-exporting business. Visitors were discouraged, and local fishermen returned ashen-faced, with tales of a fire-breathing dragon. Ornithologists, however, were concerned that Dr No's activities were destroying native bird colonies. Complaints from the Audubon Society prompted an investigation, and when several members of the Secret Service's Jamaican office were subsequently murdered, Bond was put on the job.

It was Fleming's most fantastical offering to date – also one of the most exciting. Dr No was an over-the-top villain in the pay of the Soviets who wore glass contact lenses (then something of a rarity), had his heart on the wrong side of his body (even more so) and was equipped with steel claws instead of hands. Behind his cover as a guano magnate, he ran a luxuriously appointed underground bunker that doubled as a jamming station to bring down American test missiles. Bond and his cohorts – Quarrel, a stout-hearted Cayman Islander; and Honeychile Rider, the abused, broken-nosed orphan of a plantation family – faced perils ranging from poisonous centipedes to flame-throwing marsh buggies. It culminated in a series of dramatic scenes in which Honeychile was pinned to a beach to be eaten by crabs, while Bond faced a sadistic obstacle course that involved crawling through a metal tube filled with tarantulas before being vented into a lagoon containing a giant squid. Having survived all of which, 007 smothered Dr No under a pile of guano.

When Fleming flew to Jamaica in January 1957, he did so with a feeling of satisfaction. Not only did he have a solid outline for his book, but he had by now achieved such a degree of fame that in December 1956, when Prime Minister Sir Anthony Eden, whose wife Clarissa was a friend of Ann, sought somewhere to recuperate after the Suez Crisis, it was Goldeneye that came to mind. Ever the patriot, Fleming accepted without demur.

Ann, however, was beginning to find Jamaica awkward. She disliked flying and travelled separately with Caspar by ship. The journey took eleven days, eight of which were spent in a gale. 'We were tilted at the most acute angle,' she wrote, 'and my curtains were horizontal with the ceiling.' As for the lower decks, they were, 'awash with waves and broken glass and blood'. When she finally docked it didn't help to find that Fleming was having (or attempting to have) an affair with a neighbour,

Blanche Blackwell.* Ann left early, after a show of discordance which imprinted itself so forcibly on Noël Coward's mind that he wrote a play about it.†

Dismayed but undeterred, Fleming continued his research. In March he visited the Cayman Islands, primarily to hunt for seashells, which he collected in an enjoyably amateur fashion, but also to see first hand the home of Quarrel. All this he used for another series of *Sunday Times* articles, which included a fascinating digression on the history of the giant squid. Apparently, one such specimen had been engaged in mid-Atlantic combat by the French battleship *Alecton* in 1869. The ship fired at it repeatedly, 'but her cannon-balls traversed the glutinous mass without causing vital injury'. When the crew looped it with a line, the creature fell in two. From the chunk they managed to haul aboard they estimated its total weight at two tons.

Barely had he returned home than in April he was off again, this time to Tangier, having committed himself to a series of articles on diamond smuggling for the *Sunday Times*. It was a subject dear to his heart and he took to it enthusiastically. He had the backing of Sir Percy Sillitoe, formerly head of MI5 but now advising De Beers, and was working with a South African agent, John Collard, to whom he assigned the pseudonym John Blaize. He wasn't impressed by Tangier: it was raining when he arrived and continued to do so throughout his two-week stay. Nor did he think much of either the locals or the expat community whom he described in a letter to Ann as mostly, 'buggers [who] do absolutely nothing all day long but complain about each other and arrange flowers'. Whereupon, having complained about them a bit more, he arranged three dozen roses in his bedroom and made the best he could of this famously louche destination.

Between 1923 and 1956 Tangier had been an International City, outside the jurisdiction of any particular state, and as such had become a byword for every shade of murky dealing and home to Europe's escapists and drifters. He caught up with David Herbert, a footloose socialite who had

---

* Blanche Blackwell (b. 1912), a member of one of Jamaica's prominent trading families, became a close confidante of Fleming towards the end of his life.
† Coward tactfully forbore to stage it. Titled *Volcano*, the play was finally performed in 2013.

worked as a spy in Morocco during World War Two, and met Gavin Young, orientalist and sometime member of MI6, whom he later steered towards a successful career in journalism and travel writing. He also consorted with the columnist Alistair Forbes, whose career with the *Sunday Despatch* was coming to a premature close. But what drew him most was the thieves' kitchen of Socco Chico, '[where] crooks and smugglers and dope peddlers congregate, and a pretty villainous bunch they are too'. He was impressed, too, by a visit with Collard to the Atlantic coast where he encountered a forest of radio masts – one of the world's great communication hubs – where he 'could imagine the air above us filled with whispering voices' and where, bizarrely, the beach was carpeted with a shoal of Portuguese men o' war blown ashore by a gale.

Fleming's high hopes did not survive the gauntlet of officialdom. By the time Collard, De Beers and Sir Percy had wielded their blue pencils his manuscript had lost much of its vim. *The Diamond Smugglers* was published by Cape in November 1957, to considerable acclaim (and an offer of £12,500 from Rank for the film rights) but Fleming was disappointed. In his privately bound copy of the book he wrote, 'It is adequate journalism but a poor book and necessarily rather "contrived" though the facts are true', adding gloomily, 'It was a good story until all the possible libel was cut out.'

Nevertheless, it had been an extraordinary year. In June he had been invited to play in a golf tournament that paired professionals with celebrity amateurs. It was the first of its kind and to his astonishment he played with that year's British Open winner, Peter Thomson, and acquitted himself admirably. The triumph was exquisite. Describing the occasion for the *Sunday Times*, he wrote: 'Those treacherous crocodiles, my friends, who had come to laugh at my discomfiture, changed their tune. Now they edged up and whispered that my handicap would have to be reduced at Sandwich. I brushed them aside. The sun was shining, the course was beautiful. What fun it was playing with the Open Champion!'

Then, in November, he sat alongside his mother during a remarkable court action that saw the ageing but still beautiful Eve being sued by an only slightly younger Parsi lady, Bapsy Pavry, over the affections of the decrepit Marquis of Winchester. The judge thought both of them silly but ruled in Eve's favour. Press photographers were on hand to capture the defendant and her famous son as they emerged from the Royal Courts of Justice.

In the same month he was invited by the *Sunday Times* to produce a series of articles about the world's exciting places. It was right up his street and he accepted at once, thus laying the foundations for his future travel book *Thrilling Cities*. Marital difficulties aside, the sun was indeed shining on him and, as far as his writing career was concerned, the course seemed beautiful. Furthermore, he had an idea for his next novel. It involved gold.

TO MICHAEL HOWARD

Replying to Howard from Goldeneye on Richard Chopping's final dust jacket for From Russia with Love, *Fleming was impressed.*

Feb 4 – perhaps [sic]

My dear Michael,

I think the jacket's really splendid. Many thanks & congratulations. We ought to win some sort of a prize.

Have done nearly 40,000 of No 6. No idea what it's like. Set near Jamaica, called DOCTOR NO, I think. A simple tale. It shouldn't be longer than 60, you'll be glad to hear.

The policemen stationed round the property for the Edens have carved "WELCOME SIR ANTHONY" on all my trees. Who do I sue?

Greetings to all I'm working for in Bed. Sq.

Any news of anything?

TO MICHAEL HOWARD

Howard did indeed have news – to whit, Fleming's books had sold more than a million copies worldwide.

20th Feb, 1957

Dear Michael,

Many thanks for your advices.

For your ads, how about:-

"IAN FLEMING has written 4 books in 4 years. They have sold over one million copies in the English language. They have been translated into a dozen languages, including Chinese & URDU.

No. 5 is called FROM RUSSIA WITH LOVE (It will probably not be translated into Russian). Jonathan Cape etc."

Just my ego at work! Al Hart has sold the Chinese, Thai & Urdu rights! With his & paperback figures & yours & world books & Pan – well over the mill!

However.

Back about March 14. One more chapter of No to go!

Forgive scrawl.

TO ANN, from the Hotel El Minzah, Tangier

In a gossip-strewn missive Fleming gave his wife the lowdown on Tangier and his progress on The Diamond Smugglers. *The emphasis on 'pansies' and 'buggers' possibly reflects more the milieu in which Ann moved – as did Fleming to a lesser extent – rather than any specific homophobia.*

Saturday [Easter 1957]

My precious,

Your letters have been lovely and have sustained me here. I simply couldn't write before because my brains have been boiling over with writing about five thousand words a day – a terrific job. But it has been very exciting and the story is sensational – at least I think so. Please don't say a word about it or we may be stopped publishing.

This is a pretty dreadful place and the weather has been ghastly, freezing cold and constant wind. The paint is peeling off the town and the streets are running with spit and pee and worse. The Arabs are filthy people and hate all Europeans. My life has revolved around a place called Dean's Bar, a sort of mixture between Wiltons and the porter's lodge at Whites. There's nothing but pansies and I have been fresh meat for them. David [Herbert] is a sort of Queen Mum. He calls himself Lord Herbert and has that in the telephone book. Says he can't get them to change it as they don't understand 'honourable'. He's been very sweet to me but I'm fed up with buggers. Jimmy Smith has arrived with Diana Campbell-Gray and they are staying with David and getting thoroughly depressed by the weather and the stagnation. Francis Bacon is due next week to live with his pansy pianist friend who plays at a bogus Russian restaurant. Otherwise there is Ali [Forbes] who lives secretively with his girl and is rarely seen. He has been a solace to me and we have had meals and walks. He knows he can't write and asks me how to. Rather pathetic. He is very frank about his disabilities but desperately lazy and the only hope for him is to marry a rich woman. He knows he is unemployable. He's now being recalled to London for 'consultations' and fears the worst. There's a new editor and Eade has resigned. He's going next Tuesday. He's really got a sort of death wish about his job. The girl is very beautiful – a softer Barbara [Skelton] and calls him 'Papa'. [. . .] They have a very nice modern flat looking over the harbour and I was very privileged to be invited there for drinks. He's an endearing but hopeless character. I suggested he should put an advertisement in <u>The Times</u>: 'Experienced nest-fowler offers services. Can make jokes and drive car into walls.'

My Zulu [Collard] is an exceedingly nice man and a great boon. The town is madly intrigued by us and we have laid a false trail about a coelacanth. We even thought of carrying around a mysterious tin canister into which he would drop worms from time to time. Even my secretary, a good girl with a drunken nose, is besieged with enquiries about us. We go for immense walks along the wet windy beaches and I collect shells while he stamps on the Portuguese men of war that litter the beaches. They make a loud bang.* Some nice shells including small Venus Ears . . . [remainder lost].

---

* In his book Fleming described their conversation as being 'punctuated by what sounded like small-calibre revolver shots.'

14th March, 1957

I am now back having completed a further stint on the behalf of English literature. It will require a great deal of tidying up before it is in adequate shape for your glazing eyes, but I will keep you informed of progress so that you can set aside the necessary two or three hours in the early summer.

Meanwhile, I came across this book in America and, as it comes from an obscure publisher, it occurred to me that it might have been missed over here.

The stories have a nice macabre touch in many cases but some suffer from the naivete which you will know so well from your Japanese existence.

On the other hand, it might get by as a curiosity and I told Michael Howard I would send you my copy, which herewith.

Please let us have lunch almost immediately.

Having warned Plomer that Dr No *would shortly be upon him, he now handed in the MS for* The Diamond Smugglers, *which he provisionally titled* The Diamond Spy.

29th April, 1957

As I promised you in Lewes, here is another book for you to read.

It isn't very long – only about 40,000 words – but it will be bolstered up with plenty of dramatic photographs, maps, photostatic documents, etc.

There is no hurry for this so far as Capes are concerned, but what I really want, of course, is your view of the stuff.

It hasn't been read here yet but will be this week, and the plan is that we should serialise it in September.

This would allow Capes, if they were interested, to bring it out in time for Christmas, though probably not till early November as we would be wanting a clear run with it. Perhaps, in the circumstances, Capes would rather hold it over until later.

Anyway, please send me one of your enchanting judgments as soon as you can.

Incidentally, it is all absolutely true with the exception of the man's name, and it is very important that we should say nothing about it until September as we don't want to have an injunction slapped on us by De Beers or anyone else, so could you please ask the others also to keep the whole project under their hats whether they decide to publish it or not.

See you soon I hope.

TO WILLIAM PLOMER

7th May, 1957

A thousand thanks for the fat and cheering bulletin. How extraordinary about the Fugu. I must go to my Plomer shelf and look up the reference. Presumably you did not consume the sex glands.

All your comments on *The Diamond Spy* are noted and particularly the libel points which, of course, we will go into very carefully. I have already marked two passages for libel and I discussed them yesterday with Blaize [Collard] who is now reading the typescript with his old friend and booby, Sillitoe.

Incidentally, Blaize had a very unfortunate time at Monte Carlo. I gave him an infallible system which nearly broke him and when he did get a number "en plein" a French tart pinched his stake and he practically started a riot.

But curiously enough he is exactly as I have described him and an extraordinarily nice man.

I will keep your factory informed of progress with the series but you might ask them to let me have the typescript back as soon as possible as I shall need it to work on pretty thoroughly from now on.

My other opusculum will be coming to you around the end of this month – I hope not too soon to build up an allergy.

TO H. W. VALLANCE LODGE, ESQ., 4, Bloomsbury Square, W.C.1.

Having transferred his literary rights to Glidrose, Fleming sought to offload as many expenses as possible on to the company. In a letter to his accountant he tried, rather wildly, to explain why his latest sports car should qualify as a tax-deductible item.

12th June, 1957

Many thanks for your message and here is some ammunition which you may or may not care to use in reply to the Inspector of Taxes.

"It might be thought extravagant that the Company should have purchased a rather expensive sports car for Mr. Fleming in preference to a modest family saloon were it not for the nature of Mr. Fleming's highly successful books. These are Secret Service thrillers in which the hero and other characters make frequent use of fast cars and live in what might be described as "the fast car life".

This may seem a far-fetched explanation but, in fact, the success of Mr. Fleming's books has depended in considerable measure on their verisimilitude and extracts from reviews, from The Times Literary Supplement downwards, and evidence of this literary virtue can be produced in quantity.

In order to write credibly about these things (and not incredibly as do some authors) Mr. Fleming's need of this sort of car has been accepted on condition that the Company bears only a proportion of its cost.

Apart from its use in England, Mr. Fleming has used the car on one Continental trip through Germany to the International Police Conference at Vienna in June 1956 and the circumstances of this journey will form the basis of one of his stories. [. . .]

In conclusion I might perhaps remark in regard to all Mr. Fleming's literary work that, although imagination plays a great part in the characters and plots, accurate reportage of things seen and experienced is the quintessence of their success and if the Company which owns his manuscripts is to prosper, it will be necessary to foster the acquisition by Mr. Fleming of the necessary backgrounds and first-hand experiences with which to write his books, of which he has so far written six in six years, each with an entirely different setting for his plot."

FROM WILLIAM PLOMER

18th June, 1957

My dear Ian,

I've greatly enjoyed <u>Doctor No</u> – and so will, I hope, millions of other readers. A good brisk start, tension well maintained, Caribbean local colour most acceptable, wishful-erotic element, "physical exertion, mystery, & a ruthless enemy" all well up to standard – and <u>fresh</u>. In short, congratulations. I think my favourite moment is when Dr No taps his contact-lenses with his steel claws. (I've been practising with my Biro on my spectacles but it doesn't ring true.) <u>All</u> the detail is immensely enjoyable, & the trouble you take with it is <u>essential</u>. I can't nag at you enough about the collection of fresh and precise & unusual detail when you are using what is, to some extent, a sort of plot-formula. But you know its importance & effectiveness as well as I do.

I got so fond of Dr No I was quite sorry to see him vanish under a mound of excreta. All that trouble of his for that! What a shower!

Very few adverse criticisms. I wondered if the dragon wasn't a bit pantomime-like, tending to produce hilarity instead of a frisson? Why wasn't the seizure of the table-knife & the lighter noticed? Why weren't they quickly missed? Wouldn't the wire spear in the trouser-leg be a bit inhibiting in the tube-climbing? And isn't the tube-climbing a bit reminiscent of <u>Moonraker</u>? Honeychile' (a spelling of which I disapprove) I regard as your Rima,* & the most attractive of your

---

* Rima the Jungle Girl, heroine of a novel by W. H. Hudson, *Green Mansions: A Romance of the Tropical Forest* (1904).

leading ladies so far. I much regret the shrivelling up of the faithful Quarrel.

I enclose a list of small points. I notice there are more in the first half of the book than in the second, but I don't know whether this is because I read on in more & more excitement, or whether there are really fewer minutiae for me to carp at in the latter part of the book.

I now propose to hand over the typescript to Daniel. There is a smell of guano everywhere . . .

All best wishes for the greatest possible success of the book.

[PS] Isn't there some local slang word for a cross between a Chinese & a Negro? Or why not <u>invent</u> one? "Chinese Negro" doesn't sound quite right, somehow. What I shd. like wd. be some word like <u>dago</u> or <u>mestizo</u> – <u>chigro</u>, perhaps . . .?

TO WILLIAM PLOMER

19th June, 1957

I carefully weighed the envelope in my hand. If thin, it would mean two pages of exquisitely kind "not quite up to scratch". If fat, then at least qualified approval plus the usual pages of corrections.

It was fat. With self denial I finished my breakfast and lit the first cigarette and then unfolded the green sheets, still with many qualms.

Now I am as sated as the wart hogs I visited at Whipsnade last night after their evening meal and the only hurdle that matters to me with these books has been scrambled over.

Of course I agree with all your comments and, in particular, chigro has entered the language.

I will attend to all the points you make but I think I am all right with the tarantulas whom I have carefully read up. I think we can assume that these are the South American variety, more puissant than your South African pets.

I had thought of a map of Crab Key and I'm sure it's a good idea if the Bedfordians agree.

I am ashamed to say I had forgotten the tube climbing in <u>Moonraker</u> and I will think of a way of altering at any rate the first lap.

I'm glad you liked Honeychild and relieved that you seem to have swallowed Doctor No. It is so difficult to make these villains frighten, like Fu Manchu and the other classical Schweinerei, but one is ashamed to over-write them, though that is probably what the public would like.

I have various questions to ask you in due course but the main thing is that you seem to have rattled fairly quickly through the book, which was the main object of the exercise.

I got the words and title of "Marion" in Jamaica, where it has long been my favourite, but it has now been put on records and cleaned up and I dare say it is now called "Mary Ann". My version is the original Jamaican but I dare say there will be much writing in about it and I will have to decide what to do.*

I note the ghastly clichés. How awful it is that so many slip by when one is making little effort to write "well". I will attend to them.

Anyway, here come my warmest thanks for the uplift and for the immense pains you have once again taken with my annual stint.

TO WILLIAM PLOMER

Aware that he was battering Bond beyond the point of endurance, Fleming suggested to Plomer that the book might be titled 'The Wound Man'. To which end he supplied an illustration that was first published in Venice 1492 as a guide for surgeons. It depicted every type of injury a man could expect to receive in the course of medieval combat.

26th June, 1957

I have always had a great affection for the picture you will find on page 3 of the enclosed stuffer† for my house magazine and I insisted on it being included in this pamphlet.

---

* Fleming had included a slightly risqué song in his original manuscript.
† A leaflet advertising *The Book Collector*.

Do you think we should re-title "Doctor No" "The Wound Man" and use it as a frontispiece? I could bring out the point in the text when M. is discussing Man's ills with Sir James Molony.

Or do you think the idea is a bit far fetched?

Perhaps you would like to mull it over with the other Capians and instruct me?

There may be an "amusing" piece in this Sunday's <u>Sunday Times</u> on the most dreadful experience since the Dieppe raid, so eschew the Saturday lollipop and set aside your fourpence for a copy.*

FROM WILLIAM PLOMER

28th June, 1957

My dear Ian,

I was v. pleased with your letter about my letter to you about Dr No. And now I have your suggestion & the picture of The Wound Man. It's a <u>striking & poignant</u> picture.

My immediate reaction is that your idea is a bit far-fetched.

I don't like the idea of <u>The Wound Man</u> as a title, for various reasons:

i) I prefer <u>Dr No</u>;

ii) "Wound" can be pronounced in two ways;

iii) I don't think it particularly apposite;

iv) The picture has a mediaeval character; &

v) Might convey a touch of parody, or self-parody;

vi) & draw attention to Bond & away from Dr No, who ought perhaps to <u>loom</u> in this book.

But I will convey the picture & your suggestion to the other Capians for mulling over next Wednesday. By which time I hope I shall also be able to hear about the effect of the book upon some of them.

---

* Fleming was referring to his celebrity golf tournament, which he described in an article titled 'Nightmare among the Mighty'.

Stimulated, it might almost appear, by your exemplary diligence & perseverance, I've finished my own oeuvre & sent it off to the typists.*

FROM MICHAEL HOWARD

1st July, 1957

Dear Ian,

Last week I managed to lay my hands on the manuscript of DOCTOR NO by jumping the queue and stealing my turn before Daniel got down to his detailed overhaul. I, of course, am delighted to find that you have stuck strictly to the rules this time and produced a first-rate formula model for the fans! Congratulations on having done so, so well.

It is a relief to find Bond back in circulation again, but the neurologist's warnings are ominous – that battered body can only bear so much more beating, and back it goes at once to be burned and bruised all over again. One hopes that what Bond tells himself while undergoing it is true – that the strains and stresses in this adventure are purely superficial ones, and, uncomfortable though they are, they will not draw deeply on his diminishing reserves of courage and endurance. In other words, you can keep him in good enough shape to last out several more books to come, I trust.

Daniel tells me that he has made a list of points for your attention. I find it impossible to maintain enough detachment while sharing Bond's adventures to take note of stylistic details – I think the only point which struck me was the rather recurrent smell of bacon and coffee, which was, perhaps, already familiar from the earlier books.

With an eye to your ever growing readership, I wonder whether it would not be wise to remove that reference to the club priding itself that "no Negroes, Jews or dogs are allowed"?

Is it not a little obscure why Bond does not climb over the wire fence instead of draping himself on it within reach of the octopus? And are the local negroes really as ignorant as Doctor No about the habits of those crabs which the girl knows perfectly well will not harm her? Finally, if every visitor to the island is tracked down with radar, machine

---

* William Plomer's memoir, *At Home*, was published by Cape in 1958.

guns and flame-throwers and exterminated on sight, was it worthwhile to construct the elaborate hospital front, and how often did those twittering nurses have any patients to practise on?

But mostly these aren't the sort of questions one should ask oneself after gratefully accepting the adventure as a whole, and for my money this book proves that whatever murderous intentions you have harboured temporarily against Bond when you set SMERSH on to him last time, you still can find plenty of excitement and out-of-the-way background interest to keep him going for a long while to come.

I should like to allow time for William to read this manuscript before it goes to the printer so that you can dispose of any points which he may raise then, and avoid corrections in the proof. Presumably you'll be going off as usual about Christmas time, and will want to get your proofs in November and have them out of your way before you leave. Easter is early next year, and I would like to publish on March 31st, which is the Monday before Good Friday.

Have you a ready-made jacket this time, or will you leave this one to me?

TO MICHAEL HOWARD

Writing to thank Michael Howard for a copy of Norman Lewis's latest novel, The Volcanoes Above Us, *Fleming hazarded a few ideas about the jacket for* Dr No. *Despite the excellence of Chopping's design for* From Russia with Love, *the artwork for* Dr No *was to be by Howard's wife, Pat Marriott, who had done the jacket for* Diamonds are Forever.

1st July, 1957

My dear Michael,

Many thanks for the new Norman Lewis.* I have always meant to read his books but have always somehow missed them. But I shall read this and give you my views.

Incidentally, since I gather that <u>Doctor No</u> has passed through the eye of your needle, perhaps we should start thinking of a jacket.

* Norman Lewis (1908–2003), journalist, author and travel writer.

Of course we could make a splendid typographical one but it also occurs to me that we might do something with Botticelli's Venus, of which I enclose a copy.

In the book Bond finds that Honeychild reminds him of Botticelli's Venus seen from behind. How would it be to essay the idea with her standing on a Venus Elegans shell, of which I have some examples?

The other symbols in this picture would also have to be different but the idea might come off if it was done with elegance.

I attach the make-up I have in mind.

Incidentally, I fancy you might have somewhere the original type-scripts of three or four of my books and I wonder if they could be dug out at leisure as I would rather like to have them.

Let us have lunch soon and I would like to No what you think about the Doctor.

TO MRS. MICHAEL HOWARD, Dippenhall Cottage, Nr. Farnham, Surrey

Fleming discussed the jacket further with Pat Marriott. Her first draft was good but, for all their collaborative hopes, it did not work. In the end she produced an entirely different design.

10th July, 1957

How very sweet of you to have written in such glowing terms. It is a great relief to have survived not only the X-ray eyes of all the Capians but even of one of the vivandières of Bedford Square!

I love the very feminine point you make and which had escaped me about Honeychile digging out the family silver. I see that unwittingly I have touched the funny bone of the feminine mystique.

Now about the jacket. I would love you to do one for me and you have immediately put your finger on the point of the idea. Chirico with a touch of Dali is just what I was thinking of, plus your points about precision and reality.

The dark brown beach with the pink shells leading off to the distant river mouth is straightforward and I will send you a specimen of the Venus shell in which Honeychile can stand.

I think we shouldn't give her the diving mask or the belt as these would take away from the Botticelli point.

But what are you going to do about the emblems in the top corner of the picture? Black crabs suspended in the air don't seem right, but a dragon's snout belching flame might do for one corner and a smoking machine gun barrel in the other.

On the whole perhaps it would be better just to have the figure standing on the shell on the sea shore. Anything else might be too much of a caricature and in any case would interfere with Michael's lettering.

Anyway, I'm sure the idea is worth trying and I do hope it comes off. See if you can't do an idea of a rough before I leave on the 30th.

I would love to come and see you both soon in your nest but I can't see any hope for the time being. I am already away far too often at weekends and I'm afraid a visit will have to wait until I can free myself of some London chores.

Best of luck with the jacket.

TO JOHN HAYWARD, ESQ., C.B.E., 19 Carlyle Mansions, Cheyne Walk, SW.3.

13th September, 1957

Having clashed the previous year with John Carter over The Book Collector, *Fleming soon found himself at odds with its learned editor John Hayward. His attempts to rejuvenate the magazine, however, fell on stony ground.*

I have now digested, as far as my tracts are capable, the latest number of The Book Collector, and my first reaction is that this is surely the most leaden in content we have ever produced.

It seems to me that, even in the case of Dave Randall, the piety of his memorial to Mr. Lilly has squeezed out the occasional lightness of touch with which he has written for us before, and Mr. Downs' style, full of "notable assemblages", "concomitant with" and "pertaining to", is really splendidly banal. I particularly like his description of William Shakespeare as "another great early figure".

I sincerely feel that the eyes of even our most maniacal bibliomanes will glaze if we continue to serve them such very suety fare. Not only that, is there not also a danger that all our authors will start writing down to this supremely drab level? Once one adopts a particular literary formula, as we have found on the Sunday Times, authors, however lively, are apt to adapt their style to that formula assuming it is what we want.

Only in the Commentary is there humour and a forthright and pleasantly critical viewpoint.

We have been over this subject ad nauseam during our lunches and I thought we were all agreed that we would endeavour to lighten without vulgarising The Book Collector by obstinately including in every issue, even at the cost of some pages of finest and weightiest scholarship, an article which would appeal to the intelligent amateur book collector. And I do hope that we can adhere to this principle in future. Various suggestions were made, including a piece by Desmond Flower on Churchill's manuscripts. We all know Desmond Flower.* Could this not be commissioned? Then at our next meeting we could all have other suggestions.

One other small point. I have a nagging fear that, as has happened in other realms of scholarship, the dead hand of the American "expert" may strangle The Book Collector if we don't ration its content of American prose. I dare say one of the reasons for this heartfelt cry of mine is that just about half of the Autumn issue is written by Americans.

I must now get back to Diamond Smuggling.

TO MICHAEL HOWARD

Replying to Howard about various copy editing details, Fleming hinted that a different kind of Fleming adventure might be on the cards. His grand design eventually dwindled to a series of three articles about the Seychelles, 'Treasure Hunt in Eden', which featured in the Sunday Times *in 1958. But*

---

* Desmond Flower (1907–97), bibliophile and publisher. As director of Cassell & Co. he had secured a major coup with the acquisition of Winston Churchill's six-volume history of the Second World War.

the impulse behind it would resurface in 1962 as his globe-spanning travel-ogue Thrilling Cities.

26th November, 1957

My dear Michael,

Herewith the corrected "Doctor No", and I hope I have cut out enough "ands" to satisfy your father. The passage he sent me was certainly horrible and I hope I haven't missed others.

You will see that in the list of previous works I have separated "The Diamond Smugglers" from the rest with a sub-heading of "documentary" and I hope you agree.

Would it be a good promotional idea to put the number and dates of reprints opposite each previous book?

I notice that "doctor" is spelt at the top of the pages and I had at first queried this but I am sure it should stet, apart from the bother of making the change.

Any news of the jacket? I should love to see a late version before I go off.

Incidentally, apart from whatever opusculum I am able to produce in Jamaica, it looks as if you will have another bonus Fleming on your hands next year if you want it.

The Sunday Times have gone on urging me to suggest another series and I have turned down so many of their ideas that I finally proposed to do a series called "Round The World In Eight Adventures" and they are ecstatic.

I have the adventures more or less mapped out – a real treasure hunt that is going on in the Seychelles, the Great Cave of Niah in North Borneo, gold-smuggling in Macao, and so forth, and I shall take a Leica.

I can't say how the project will turn out, nor whether I shall have enough energy to play Red Indians when the time comes, but that is the idea at the moment.

The connecting theme is that the world is still a very exciting place in spite of aeroplanes and suchlike and that just because some types of adventure are old-fashioned that doesn't make them any less exciting.

The idea is that I should go off at the end of April and take two to three months over it. Anyway we will see, and I only mention the project now as I am writing to you.

Whatever you think of it, please keep entirely to yourselves – even more so than the 'Diamond Smugglers' because (a) I don't know whether I shall do it yet and (b) it may not come off.

TO C. E. MAISEY, ESQ., The City Bookshop, 164 High Street, Guildford, Surrey

13th March, 1958

How very kind indeed of you to have written to me about "Doctor No".

It is quite remarkable that a busy man like yourself, who receives thousands of books every year, should find the time to write to an author of one of them.

As a matter of fact, your charming letter couldn't have arrived at a more opportune time as I have been soundly laid across the barrel in this month's issue of The Twentieth Century* and my ego was mildly dented.

Since, by the same post as your last letter, I received news that Raymond Chandler wants to review "Doctor No" in the Sunday Times, this double windfall has completely restored the crack in the veneer.

Thank you very much indeed and the next time I am in Guildford I shall make a point of calling on you and thanking you in person.

TO THE EDITOR of the *Manchester Guardian*

Fleming had suffered a rebuke at the hands of Bernard Bergonzi in Twentieth Century *for 'a diet of unrestricted sadism and satyriasis'. This was followed by an article in the* Guardian *condemning him for 'the cult of luxury for its own sake'. It was a sinister development, the paper intoned, and a sign of moral decay: 'This is an advertising agency world, where the man of*

---

* A monthly literary magazine.

© 2012 Brad Frank

Ian Fleming's 1962 portrait by Amherst Villiers. 'The crankshaft designer […] is making me look like a mixture between Nehru and Somerset Maugham.'

© The Cecil Beaton Studio Archive at Sotheby's

Ian and Ann with their son Caspar who was born in August 1952.

Rob Melville

Fay Godwin

Daniel George, one of the editorial team whom Fleming dubbed the 'Capians'.

Cape's main editor, Michael Howard. At first doubtful about the Bond novels he later conceded they were all that kept Jonathan Cape in business.

William Plomer,
the South African-
born poet who was
Fleming's friend and
literary mentor.

Fleming at his
Sunday Times
desk in 1958.

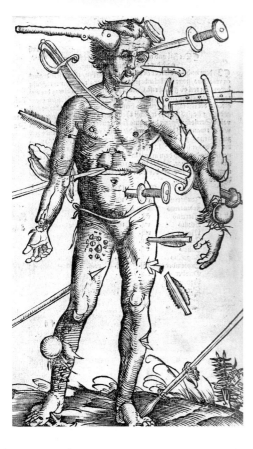

A fifteenth-century surgeon's guide to
battle injuries that caught Fleming's
fancy. 'Do you think we should re-title
"Doctor No" "The Wound Man" and use
it as a frontispiece?' he asked Plomer.

Evening Standard / Hulton Archive / Getty Images

Gamma-Keystone via Getty Images

Fleming and his mother Eve outside the Law Courts during her 1957 battle for the affections of Monty, Marquis of Winchester.

Back at court, this time with Ann in 1963, for the *Thunderball* dispute – 'a maddening copyright case which […] is going to be a stupendous nuisance'.

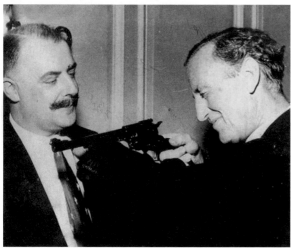

With firearms expert Geoffrey Boothroyd – aka Major Boothroyd, 007's Armourer – in March 1961.

Ralph Crane / LIFE Images / Getty Images

© The Ian Fleming Bibliographical Archive

Raymond Chandler in his heyday. By the time Fleming met him in 1955 alcohol and depression had taken their toll.

Fleming described No.13 Sretlanka Ulitsa in Moscow as the headquarters of SMERSH. But as a fan pointed out (with pictorial evidence), it clearly wasn't.

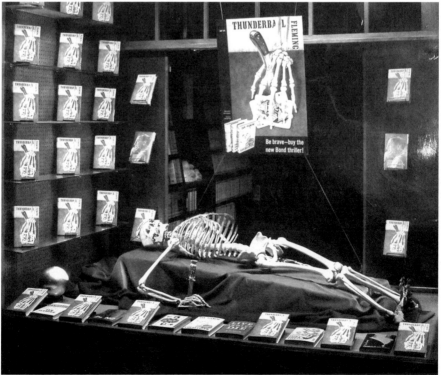

Bookshops vied to produce the best Bond window display. This one went the extra mile for *Thunderball*.

* I don't believe an American has said this since the recent death
of A. Lincoln

Thunderball

Page/Line

	For	Read
123/15	sponge bag	Dressing case or toilet kit
" / 33	cashiered	fired
124/2	sounded	pulled
" /6	trunks	suit
124/6	spade and bucket	pail and shovel
" /9	unbuttoned	let their hair down
" /13	in the pot	delete
125/7	posted	mailed
" /15	angry	sore
" /17	rubbed	rubbed out
" /20	lain	laid
" /27	got	gotten
128/2	phosphorus	radium
" /6	appointment	date
" /10	close up	up close
" /26	sixpenny sick	?
134/5	Mr. H.C.	Mr. C or H.C.
136/10	damnably	damn
137/7	stack	pile
" / 18	sniff	smell
"/20	we've got damn-all	we have damn little
"/24	shareholders	stockholders
145/20	bottle	fifth or quart
" "	measures	shots
146/26	muck	garbage
147/5	true bill	god-damn, first class, gold-plated, net-no-discount, etc.et
147/6	riles me	bugs me, burns me up, makes me sore
" /"	Arse-end	ass-hole
148/9	at readiness	on call, on deck
149/29	eggs and bacon	bacon and eggs
175/21	lot	gang, bunch
179/2	backsides	ass, behind
184/19	webbing	delete
204/32	commander	skipper
207/9	full out	all out
" /14	Chief of the Navy	no such office
208/14	to ransom	for ransom
211/2	we're looking fools	we look enough like fools
	enough a	some
224/9	bit of a	some
" /13	trick cyclists	head shrinkers
225/19	aloft	above
226/26	going to do	having, holding
227/28	gammy	game
228/1	speaker system	squawk box, loudspeaker
234/6	by gum *	bejesus
" / 19	with	delete
245/12	chap	guy

Herman W. Liebert of Yale University was so appalled by the 'Americanese' in *Thunderball* that he supplied a list of corrections. Fleming later asked him to consult on *The Spy Who Loved Me*.

Fleming loved air travel. Here he strides in style through a nascent Heathrow en route to Jamaica.

Express / Getty Images

Ursula Andress, Sean Connery and Ian Fleming on the set of *Dr No.*

Times Newspapers

An aficionado of fast cars, Fleming was among the first people in Britain to own a supercharged Studebaker Avanti.

Harry Benson / Express / Getty Images

The desk at Goldeneye in 1964. Fleming had just completed his last 007 adventure, *The Man with the Golden Gun.*

*distinction sits secure in the knowledge that his is the very best butter. And
since the reader is plainly expected to identify himself with Bond, these works
are symptomatic of a decline in taste.' In a soul-searching trump of despair:
'If one of the most bourgeois and peaceable people of the world decide that a
diet of sex and violence is to its liking, is it not because it can thereby subli-
mate its more anti-social instincts?' Fleming was goaded to reply.*

5th April, 1958

Sir, – I am most grateful for the scholarly examination of my James Bond
stories in your leader columns on Monday but, since this follows close upon
a nine-page inquest in "The Twentieth Century," I hope you will forgive a
squeak from the butterfly before any more big wheels roll down upon it.

It is true that sex plays an important part in James Bond's life and that
his profession requires him to be more or less constantly involved in violent action. It is also true that, as in any real spy-life, when the villain gets
hold of Bond, Bond is made to suffer painfully. What other punishment
for failure would be appropriate – that Bond should receive an extra heavy
demand note from the Inland Revenue, or that he should be reduced in
his Civil Service rank from principal officer to acting principal?

But, as you, sir, put it "What is more sinister is the cult of luxury for
its own sake – and the kind of luxury held up for the reader's emulation.
The idea that anyone should smoke a brand of cigarette not because they
enjoy them but because they are 'exclusive' (that is, because they cost
more) is pernicious and it is implicit in all Mr Fleming's glib descriptions of food, drink and clothes."

I accept the rebuke, but more on the score of vulgarity than on the
counts you recite. I have this to say in my extenuation: One of the reasons
why I chose the pseudonym of James Bond for my hero rather than, say,
Peregrine Maltravers was that I wished him to be unobtrusive. Exotic
things would happen to and around him but he would be a neutral figure –
an anonymous blunt instrument wielded by a Government Department.

But to create an illusion of depth I had to fit Bond out with some theatrical props and, while I kept his wardrobe as discreet as his personality, I did
equip him with a distinctive gun and, though they are a security hazard,

with distinctive cigarettes. This latter touch of display unfortunately went to my head. I proceeded to invent a cocktail for Bond (which I sampled several months later and found unpalatable), and a rather precious though basically simple meal ordered by Bond proved so popular with my readers, still suffering from wartime restrictions, that expensive, though I think not ostentatious, meals have been eaten in subsequent books.

The gimmickry grew like bindweed and now, while it still amuses me, it has become an unfortunate trade-mark. I myself abhor Wine-and-Foodmanship. My own favourite food is scrambled eggs (in "Live and Let Die" a proof-reader pointed out that Bond's addiction to scrambled eggs was becoming a security risk and I had to go through the book changing menus) and I smoke your own, Mancunian, brand of Virginia tobacco.

However, now that Bond is irretrievably saddled with these vulgar foibles, I can only plead that his Morland cigarettes are less expensive than the Balkan Sobranies of countless other heroes, that he eats far less and far less well than Nero Wolfe, and that his battered Bentley is no Hirondelle.

Perhaps these are superficial excuses. Perhaps Bond's blatant heterosexuality is a subconscious protest against the current fashion for sexual confusion. Perhaps the violence springs from a psychosomatic rejection of Welfare wigs, teeth, and spectacles and Bond's luxury meals are simply saying "no" to toad-in-the-hole and tele-bickies.

Who can say? Who can say whether or not Dr Fu Manchu was a traumatic image of Sax Rohmer's father? Who, for the matter of that, cares?

Yours &c.

IAN FLEMING

FROM NOËL COWARD, Firefly Hill, Port Maria, Jamaica, B.W.I.

6th May, 1958

Dearest Beast,

This is just to inform you that I have read 'Dr No' from cover to cover and thoroughly enjoyed every moment of it. Your descriptive passages, as usual, are really very good indeed, but, as the gentleman in Oklahoma sings about Kansas City, 'You've gone about as fur as you ken go.' I am willing to accept the centipede, the tarantulas, the land crabs, the giant squid (except on that beastly table at Goldeneye). I am even willing to forgive your reckless use of invented verbs – 'I inch, Thou inches – He snakes, I snake, We palp, They palp, etc; but what I will neither accept nor forgive is the highly inaccurate statement that when it is eleven A.M. in Jamaica, it is six A.M. in dear old England. This dear boy, not to put too fine a point on it, is a fucking lie. When it is eleven A.M. in Jamaica, it is four <u>P.M.</u> in dear old England and it is carelessness of this kind that makes my eyes steel slits of blue. I was also slightly shocked by the lascivious announcement that Honey-chile's bottom was like a boy's! I know that we are all becoming progressively more broadminded nowadays but really old chap what could you have been thinking of?

I am snaking off to New York on Thursday where I shall be for two weeks and then I inch to Cannes, or rather Biot, where I shall be for June and July.

I have been very sad without you although Blanche [Blackwell] takes me to Goldeneye every so often to have a swim and a good cry. Violet [Fleming's housekeeper], I fear, is rapidly losing her looks, what with childbearing and one thing and another, but I <u>think</u> it is really one thing and another.

I must weedle this letter to a close now and clank into my shower as Cargill* of The Gleaner is coming to dinner.

Love and kisses to Annie and my Godson [Caspar]† and the usual slavering hero worship for yourself.

---

* Morris Cargill (1914–2000), lawyer, businessman, politician, writer and, from 1953 until his death, columnist for the Jamaican *Gleaner*. In 1965 he published a book, *Ian Fleming's Jamaica*, with an introduction by Fleming.
† Caspar's other godparents were Cecil Beaton, Clarissa Eden, Peter Fleming and Ian's golfing friend Duff Dunbar.

TO B. W. GOODEN, ESQ., 10 Old Broad Street, London, E.C.2.

Although Mr Gooden's original letter is lost, he clearly had a point to raise about Bond's choice of watch.

5th June, 1958

I have just got back from abroad to find your sapient rebuke of 007's time-keeping equipment.

I have discussed this with him and he points out that the Rolex Oyster Perpetual weighs about six ounces and would appreciably slow up the use of his left hand in combat. His practice, in fact, is to use fairly cheap, expendable wrist watches on expanding metal bracelets which can be slipped forward over the thumb and used in the form of a knuckle-duster, either on the outside or the inside of the hand.

In passing on his comments to you, I would add that James Bond has trained himself to tell the time by the sun in either hemisphere within a few minutes.

Thank you, nevertheless, for raising the point and 007 wishes to assure you that when an appropriate time-piece is available he will wear it.

TO F. N. GARDNER, ESQ., F.L.A., Highcroft, Woodbury Hill Path, Luton, Beds.

24th June, 1958

Jonathan Cape have been kind enough to let me see the stern and well spirited thousand-word rebuke you have addressed to "Now And Then".*

I can find no fault with your well argued statement. Doctor No was certainly the hero of the book and James Bond the villain. It is high time Bond stopped poking his nose into the lives of these soft-living and, on the whole, harmless monsters.

* Cape's house journal.

On the further points you make I should, however, mention that Bond, as a member of the Civil Servant's Union, would have had plenty of high level Union protection if it had come to an argument with other Whitehall authorities.

One small point. It is quite clear that, living in land-girt Luton, your acquaintanceship with octopuses is small. They are, in fact, timorous creatures of great charm and positive kittens compared with the giant squid with which Bond had to wrestle for his life.

Anyway, my warmest thanks for your scholarly interest in my opuscula and I look forward greatly to seeing your essay reprinted in "Now And Then".

TO W. SPEID, ESQ., P.B. 164 R., Bulawayo, S. Rhodesia

W. Speid (of what is now Zimbabwe) thought that 'Bond's adventures are starting to verge on the fantastic'. Unlike From Russia with Love, *none of the characters seemed real and he particularly didn't believe in Dr No, who was merely a 'puppet invented to put Bond through the hoops'. In terms of authenticity, Speid recommended John Marquand's* Stopover: Tokyo *(1957). He also suggested Bond should go to Austria, or maybe Venice, and do some real spying.*

14th October, 1958

Thank you very much for your most perceptive letter of September 14th and, as a matter of fact, I entirely agree with you. "Doctor No" was very cardboardy and need not have been.

But I do not agree with you over Marquand's "Stopover Tokyo". I much preferred his earlier books about Mr. Moto.

The trouble is that it is much more fun to think up fantastic situations and mix Bond up in them. The ordinary spy world is, in fact, a very drab one and, while a great book waits to be written about it, I am not the one to write it.

I am glad to say that my next book "Goldfinger", which will come out in March, does not touch on the Caribbean, but I dare say you will find this book also somewhat air-borne and I am only sorry that I am in danger of losing such a sensible and humorous-minded reader.

Again with many thanks for having taken the trouble to write to me.

TO TERRY WING, ESQ., Sentry Hill, Marlow, Bucks.

A teenage pupil wrote to settle a bet he had made with a classmate as to whether or not Fleming came from the vicinity of their school.

21st June, 1962

Thank you very much for your letter of June 15th and you are right in thinking that Dr. No is the sequel to From Russia with Love.

I think you ought to call off the bet with Macfie as in fact I used to live at Nettlebed and my brother [Peter] lives there. So he was nearly right.

Certainly I do a lot of travelling as one can't really write truthfully about a place one hasn't seen for one's self, and having been in Naval Intelligence during the war, I do know something about spies and spying.

I am at present driving a Ford Thunderbird which I have had for two years, but I am in the process of changing to a very new model, the Studebaker Avanti, with a top speed of 174 and acceleration from 0 to 60 in 6.5 seconds.*

So far as your future is concerned I shouldn't bother to try and emulate James Bond. You are already an adventurous chap with plenty of guts or you wouldn't be writing to authors out of the blue at the age of 12 and a bit!

As a prize for your enterprise (bad English that!) I am sending you an autographed copy of my last but one book, which you don't seem to have read.

Best of luck for the future.

---

* The Avanti had only been introduced in America that April, making it quite likely that Fleming was the first person in Britain to own a model. His customised version, which he owned until his death in 1964, boasted black leather upholstery and crimson-numbered dials on the dashboard. Its numberplate was 8 EYR.

9

Goldfinger

IN 1958, FLEMING wrote a review of *The Spy's Bedside Book*, an anthology of spy stories edited by Graham and Hugh Greene, to which he himself was a contributor. The first sentence read: 'I cannot understand why the great spy novel has never been written.' He had, in fact, just completed a rather good one himself.

Among the items that piqued his imagination during the 1955 Interpol conference in Istanbul had been a report by the Indian representative on the magnitude of gold smuggling and the ingenuity of its practitioners. It was the second most smuggled commodity after heroin, the man said. In 1954 alone his country had intercepted more than six million pounds of contraband bullion, and this was barely the tip of the iceberg. So long a financial shadow had the war cast on the world's currencies that everyone wanted gold, and there seemed no end to the means they would use to get their hands on it. As always, the combination of treasure and intrigue proved irresistible.

Fleming began his research in the summer of 1957 and by the time he arrived in Goldeneye the following January he had a plot mapped out. *Goldfinger* centred, as with *Moonraker*, on a millionaire villain who liked to cheat at cards (also, in this case, golf). Unlike Drax, however, who planned to destroy Britain with a missile, Auric Goldfinger wanted to control the world's gold supply – his ultimate goal being to seize the contents of Fort Knox. When his activities threatened to destabilise Britain's economy, Bond was put on the case. Goldfinger was a splendidly unpleasant man, with a deft touch in torture and revenge: when one of his employees betrayed him he suffocated her by coating her entire body in gold paint; and when he caught Bond spying on him he splayed him across a saw table and waited patiently for him to talk as the circular blade moved slowly towards his groin. Almost as sinister as Goldfinger was his Korean henchman, Oddjob, who had a cleft palate, was a karate expert, ate cats and wore a steel-rimmed bowler hat that doubled as a deadly Frisbee.

On the plus side, Bond was aided by his old friend Felix Leiter and a lesbian aviatrix named Pussy Galore who started in the employ of Goldfinger but was successfully turned (in more senses than one) by 007. The climax came when the combined efforts of Bond, Leiter and Galore succeeded in thwarting Goldfinger's attempted assault on Fort Knox. But this was just a false horizon. As with *Diamonds are Forever*, further sensation awaited. This included not only the death of Goldfinger but the satisfactory outcome of Oddjob being extruded at high altitude through an aeroplane window.

Fleming was at the top of his game. *Goldfinger* was full of energy and the longest of his novels. But his personal life was becoming ragged, his relationship with Ann having reached a state that could kindly be described as one of mutual bewilderment. Increasingly they went their separate ways, which in Fleming's case took the form of a prolonged trip to the Seychelles in April 1958.

He was travelling on journalistic business for the *Sunday Times*, the object being to report on a treasure hunt – not just a haphazard quest like his metal-detecting efforts at Creake Abbey in 1953 but the genuine, cop-per-bottomed article supported by maps, historical research and a share issue with a potential return of £120 million. That the prospector (an ex-officer at Buckingham Palace) genuinely believed he was on to something, and did so with a fervour that by most standards would classify him as mildly insane, made it all the more enticing. The shareholders alone were of interest. As Fleming wrote of one: 'In 1938 an elephant knelt on his left leg while a tigress chewed off his right. But that is how it is in this story. Even the smallest walk-on parts have a touch of the bizarre.'

Getting to the Seychelles was itself an adventure, involving a twenty-four-hour flight to Bombay followed by a four-day journey by ship.

Fleming was delighted by the fact that as they neared shore they were greeted not by seagulls but a large bat. And when filling out the customs declaration, 'Instead of the usual warning about importing alcohol, agricultural machinery and parrots, I was cautioned that "Passengers must specifically state if they have in their possession OPIATES, ARMS AND AMMUNITION, BASE OR COUNTERFEIT COINS.' The treasure hunt fitted perfectly into this scenario, carrying as it did a whiff of skulduggery, piracy and subterfuge. But it was the Seychelles themselves that took centre stage. Fleming was absorbed by their colourful history and the eccentric lives of their inhabitants. He noted that the cathedral clock struck twice in case people hadn't heard it the first time, that it was an offence to carry more than one coconut, and that a local paper had just recorded the case of Regina v Archange Michel (indecent assault). 'What do you make of that?' he wrote.

The flora and fauna were equally theatrical, including sang-dragon trees that oozed red sap when cut, cowries twice the size of golf balls that glittered like aquatic jewels, emerald lizards with blood-red toenails, and white terns that flew out to sea in pairs, seemingly with locked arms 'like perfect skaters on a giant rink of blue ice'. Best of all was the 'Vallai de Mai' – which no less an authority than Gordon of Khartoum had located as the Garden of Eden – whose trees bore fruit and flowers that were, as Fleming explained, of 'grotesque impudicity [. . .] When it is dark, they say that the trees march down to the sea and bathe and then march back up the valley and make massive love under the moon. I can well believe it.'

The result was published in three consecutive issues of the *Sunday Times* under the title 'Treasure Hunt in Eden'. Part travelogue, part mystery story and part paean to a romantic outpost on the rim of the British Empire, every paragraph shone with enthusiasm. It was one of his finest pieces of journalism, yet one that for all its energy carried a wistful coda. 'I could convey no picture of these treasure islands,' he wrote, 'without explaining that the bizarre is the norm of a visitor's life and the vivid highlights of the Seychelles are in extraordinary contrast to the creeping drabness, the lowest-common-denominator atmosphere that is rapidly engulfing us in Britain.'

Determined to keep drabness to a minimum, he embarked on an Italian holiday with Ann, followed by a trip to Monte Carlo where he had arranged a meeting with shipping magnate Aristotle Onassis to discuss scripting a film about the casino. Although they reached a verbal agreement Fleming had to turn it down because he was shortly afterwards invited by CBS to write a series of Bond adventures for television. That June he flew to America to discuss matters, but for one reason and another the deal fell through. It was a disappointment but not too much because a further opportunity arrived in November when he was introduced to film producer Kevin McClory who was keen to develop Bond for the big screen.

All in all, life was looking good, and the year had supplied so much novelistic material that it was hard to distil it into a single volume. Accordingly, he decided that Bond's next outing would best be served by a collection of short stories.

TO GRAHAM HUGHES, ESQ., Goldsmith's Hall, Foster Lane, Cheapside, E.C.2.

In the course of his research Fleming approached several experts, some of whom found his queries too dubious for their normal course of business. Mr Hughes was among them, and directed Fleming towards a more accommodating firm, Johnson Mattheys.

30th August, 1957

I really am most grateful for the trouble you have taken over my questions, and would you please thank Mr. J. S. Forbes for having provided many of the answers.

I realised that a lot of my queries were most improper ones to address to The Worshipful Company and I confess that your maidenly question marks in answer to some of my murkier questions made me smile.

I do apologise again for all the trouble I have caused you and for the many raised eyebrows there must have been at Goldsmith's Hall in the past few weeks.

I will now proceed to pester Mr. Roberts of Johnson Mattheys and I hope he will be as indulgent as you have been.

TO S. C. ROBERTS, ESQ., Messrs. Johnson Mattheys, Hatton Garden, w.c.1.

30th August, 1957

Your name has been given to me by Mr. Graham Hughes of Goldsmith's Hall and I wonder if you would be kind enough to help me. I am writing a novel of suspense in which Gold plays a conspicuous part and I am most anxious to document myself on some out-of-the-way aspects of the metal.

Mr. Hughes has helped me over many of my questions and he suggests that you might be kind enough to educate me on some other aspects of the subject.

I would also greatly appreciate being allowed to watch the actual process of melting miscellaneous gold objects at your refinery. May I call upon you at any time when you have half an hour to spare?

Please forgive me for enlisting your help in these author's problems but experts in gold are very few and far between.

TO ANN, Goldeneye

Ann refused to come to Jamaica that year. It wasn't her fear of flying, or the prospect of a stormy crossing by sea, that put her off. Rather, it was the slow disintegration of their marriage. The past few months had been hard for both of them and Ann saw Goldeneye as one source of their woes.

Sunday [early January, 1958]

My darling,

It is all just the same except that everything is bigger and more. The flight was perfect, only five minutes late at Mo Bay. Mrs D'Erlanger was on board with her daughter, which may have helped.* She seemed quite pleasant and was very queenly with the ground staffs at all the stops. I arrived in a tempest and it has stormed more or less ever since – torrential winds and rains which are going on now and look as if they would go on for ever. Thank God for the book at which I

---

* Sir Gerard D'Erlanger was chairman of BOAC, whose planes served Jamaica.

hammer away in between bathing in the rain and sweating around the garden in a macintosh [. . .] The sofas were covered with [stains] as it appears the servants have used the house as their own since I left. Paint peeling off the eaves, chips and cracks all over the floor and not one bottle of marmalade or preserves. So I have had to set to and get in the painters etc. who are still banging away after a week. Noël and company aren't coming out till April. The <u>Nude</u> is to have a season at San Francisco. Apparently Noël wears a crew cut in it which must look horrible.

Well, that's what Flemings call a Sitrep, just to show you I'm alive. I can't write about other things. My nerves are still jangling like church bells and I am completely demoralised by the past month. I think silence will do us both good and let things heal. Please put your health before anything else. Try and put a good face on the house* and don't let your hate of it spread to the others or we shall indeed end up a miserable crew, which would be quite ridiculous to say the least of it.

Take endless care of yourself.

XXX

Ian

TO ANN, Goldeneye

The tribulations of Goldeneye aside, Ann resented having to spend time in Kent, where she knew nobody and languished alone while Ian went off happily to play golf. She wanted them to find a new home, away from his old stamping grounds. Fleming was uncertain – Ann had recently spent time in a clinic and was taking a variety of anti-depressants – but he went along anyway. They eventually settled on a house in Sevenhampton, near Swindon, which, after extensions and several years' building work, had all the attributes they required but managed at the same time to suit neither of them very well.

---

* They had just moved from White Cliffs to The Old Palace, in Bekesbourne, Kent, which was not as grand as it sounded and where Ann was particularly unhappy.

20th January, 1958

My love,

At last a letter from you after more than two weeks. They both arrived together – a left and right hook! Well, if life somewhere else will make you happy we must move, as anyway living with an unhappy you is impossible. But do remember that one cannot live by whim alone and chaos is the most expensive as well as the most wearying luxury in the world. And for heaven's sake don't hurry. Do let's take real backbreaking trouble before we spend all this fresh money and have to spend more keeping up the sort of house I suppose you are looking for. And I beg you to have a stream or river in the grounds, I shall simply pine away if we go to live in the middle of a lot of plough with deadly little walks down lanes and dons every weekend.* But anything, anything to make you smile again and find you somewhere where you will rest and not tear yourself to pieces. I'm terribly worried about your health and I pray that Enton's prison walls have mended your darling heart and somehow got you off this tragic switchback of pills which I implore you to stop. They have nothing to do with the [Bekesbourne] Palace but are a way of life which is killing you, and me with you because it horrifies me so much. You've no idea how they change you – first the febrile, almost hysterical gaiety and then those terrible snores that seem to come from the tomb! Darling, forgive me, but it is so and all I get is the fag end of a person at the end of the day or at weekends. If a new house will help all that let us move as soon as we can and I will have to invent a new kind of life for myself instead of golf which I shall want to play neither with Michael Astor nor Hughie. I'm fed up with other people's neuroses. I have enough of my own. But don't pretend that I am always travelling or am always going to travel. One changes and gets older and anyway by next summer I will have seen the world once and for all. Here is different because it is peace and there is that wonderful vacuum of days that makes one work. And do count the cost. Your pot is down to about 70,000 and two more years at 10,000 a year will reduce it to your iron ration of 50 after which we shall just have to live on income. Mama can easily live another ten or twenty

* Ann's coterie included several Oxford academics.

years.* Living on our combined incomes means that we shall not have more than 5000 a year which is as rich as one can be. One can live well on that in one house but not in two. These facts have got to be faced just as it had to be faced that we should leave St Margaret's quickly.

My darlingest darlingest love get well and write me a happy letter. I would give anything for one. Bless you and hugs and kisses.

TO ANN, Goldeneye

Tuesday [undated]

My sweetheart,

A vulture is sitting on top of the roof above my head. It is squatting on its stomach across the gable like a hen roosting and looks too ridiculous. When I walked out into the garden just now away from my bondage I thought this would be a bad omen and that there would still be no letter from you. I have spent a whole week getting up and peering towards the tray to see if something has arrived. But the funny vulture was a good omen and there was a nice fat packet from you which I have now devoured. I think you manage to write very sweet letters in answer to my vehement ones most of which I always regret when they have gone, and I promise I understand every bit of your point of view. If I FIGHT my case it is just for the same reason as you FIGHT yours. We both feel the other is getting too much of the cake when in fact there's plenty for both if only we'd sit down peacefully and share it instead of grabbing. I envy you your life of parties and 'the mind' and you envy I suppose my life of action and the fun I get from my books. The answer is that compared to most people we are both enviable and lead enviable lives. I perfectly see your point about the house and I only beg that where we finally settle will have something that appeases my savage breast – some outlet for activity, because I am hopeless and like a caged beast in drawing- and dining-rooms and there is nothing I can do about it. It's instinctive. You used to sympathise with

* Fleming was counting on some funds when his mother died. In the end she predeceased him in 1964 by 16 days, by which time the matter had become irrelevant.

it and in a way I admire it in me, but I realise it must be hell to live with and I can only say that if it has an outlet I can keep it under some sort of control.

I must now go and bathe in the grey sea and then go for a long walk up a mountain to sweat the gloom away. I shall be home in a minute my love. Kisses and kisses and kisses.

FROM WILLIAM PLOMER

28 June, 1958

My dear Ian,

I have just finished <u>Goldfinger,</u> & have found that it stuck to me like a limpet, or limpet-mine. I think it well up to your best Bond level, full of ingenious invention, & fantasy, & interesting or curious or unfamiliar detail. You certainly needn't have warned me about the golf. I found the tension of the game tremendous. In fact, I believe you could create extreme anxiety out of a cake-judging competition at a Women's Institute – one of the cakes would probably be a product of nuclear fission, or of bacterial warfare at least.

I was quite sorry to see the last – and what an exit! – of Oddjob: one had got so used to having him around. I particularly liked the conversation with the gangsters – and <u>of</u> the gangsters – at the conference table. Pussy is a real wit – I should like to read a whole book about her.

I don't much like the circular saw business. I think it too like a caricature of your previous torture-scenes. It doesn't (for me) create alarm or suspense – it is too wildly unreal. Surely a circular saw makes far too much noise for any simultaneous talk to be heard? And anatomically I am a little worried. Whizz goes a fly-button – but didn't other objects get in the way first, or does Bond have undescended testicles?

Couldn't you dispense with this sort of torture-scene here, and make use instead of the zillionaire's <u>hypnotic</u> powers? Couldn't he use them on Bond and silly Tilly, in order to get a hold over them, & get then aboard the westward-bound aircraft? Yes?

I don't feel that the circular saw produces any frisson in the reader – merely a guffaw. Am I wrong?

Also, p. 111, Colonel Smithers is a fearful bore. Do we need him at all? And if so, could we have his lecturette shortened or omitted? It is terribly unreal to me. Bond had surely only to consult an encyclopedia if he wanted to know about gold. I should be inclined to cut the visit to the Bank altogether.

I enclose a list of notes & queries. I expect Daniel will be sending you more, when he has read the story.

I have corrected your spelling of cabochon, carrosserie, bagagiste, & Alsatian.

Is there any particular reason for writing "Mister" out in full instead of "Mr"?

And what happened to the Claddagh ring? I did hope it would turn up again. I expect Goldfinger melted it down & sent it off to India . . .

Now I fear this letter will look like a picking of holes, or attempted picking of holes, in the stout & brilliant fabric you have woven. Not at all, of course. I only wish it to be as well armoured as possible against the digs of envious reviewers & readers. Speaking for myself, I must say I have enjoyed the proceedings immensely – more, in some ways, than ever before. And, as you know, I send you every possible wish for the utmost success.

I shall look out for the Home Service on 10 July,* & shall hope to see Q. of S. in the <u>Sunday Times</u>,† & to see you when you come back, with gold on your fingers, from N.Y.

TO MISS JENNIFER ARMOUR, Messrs. Jonathan Cape, Ltd., 30 Bedford Square, W.C.1.

Jennifer Armour, Cape's marketing director, wrote enclosing the proofs of advertisements due to appear in The Bookseller, *and also requesting Fleming's signature in a copy of* Goldfinger. *It was a present for her*

---

* A live radio interview with Fleming and Raymond Chandler.
† 'Quantum of Solace', a short story Fleming had written on return from the Seychelles was first published by the *Sunday Times*.

brother, who was shortly to turn twenty-one 'and whose literary educa-
tion (and consequent behaviour) has been almost entirely confined and
influenced by James Bond'. She explained that he had been expelled from
both school and the Navy and was 'a generally Bad Lot, all on account of
Bond'.

11th March, 1959

This seems to be a pretty poor 21st Birthday present for what sounds like
an expensive young man, but anyway here is the autographed copy. Tell
him that both Winston Churchill and I were black sheep once and that, as
long as he doesn't make it a habit, it isn't a bad way of life up to around the
age of 21, which is approximately when my own shade of black dwindled
to its present elephant's breath grey.

Many thanks for the pulls of the advertisements. The long one is very
saucy indeed and perhaps you noticed that the News Chronicle also
commented on it.

TO BERNARD DARWIN, ESQ., Dormy House Club, Rye, Sussex

In one of his finer authorial moments Fleming managed to dedicate three
whole chapters to a game of golf without once losing the reader's interest. The
match, between Bond and Goldfinger, ended in the latter's defeat despite his
having cheated. However, as many golfers pointed out, Goldfinger had theo-
retically won. It concerned a matter of balls.

8th April, 1959

Thank you very much for your kindly letter and I will now confess that a
lot of my cronies at the Royal St. Marks, such as Beck and Hill, say they
would have given the match to Goldfinger because he ended the match
with the ball he had started with. It is clearly a matter for the Rules of Golf
committee and the matter must, of course, be raised officially with Gerald
Micklem.

TO THE HON. ANTHONY BERRY

Fleming's friend Anthony Berry (son of his employer, Lord Kemsley) wrote to say that the journalist Jack Jones would mention Goldfinger *in the* Western Mail *– for which service he, Berry, expected to be rewarded in gold bullion. He had, however, one small criticism concerning wine: 'But should not Goldfinger have known that Piesporter Goldtropfchen is a Moselle and not a Hock?'*

8th April, 1959

I shuddered when I got your note and hastily reached for the book. Within an hour I was talking to Ian Gilmour* and he also made the point.

It is maddening and I have hastily put in a correction for the next edition they are printing. I had asked my invaluable secretary, Una Trueblood, to check on one or two facts in the manuscript and, in particular, to ring up my wine merchant and ask him for the name of the finest hock he had. When he produced this one I put it in without question. Obviously I must change my wine merchant.

I hope Jack Jones will give it the works in his series and, when he does, an old gold filling from one of my teeth will reach you in return.

When can I come down and visit you both to discuss Kemsley Newspapers and canasta?

TO LEONARD RUSSELL, ESQ., 14 Albion Street, Hyde Park, London, w.2.

Leonard Russell was Literary Editor of the Sunday Times, *as well as being a friend of Fleming and a fellow golfer.*

9th April, 1959

It really is shameful that you haven't yet finished "Goldfinger". I suppose you're lounging around on a tiger-skin sofa eating a big box of chocs and reading Diana Cooper!

---

* Sir Ian Gilmour (1926–2007), later a Member of Parliament but from 1954–59 owner and editor of the *Spectator* magazine for which Fleming was motoring correspondent.

I'm very proud of your performance on the golf course since my lesson. The Royal St. Georges is blushing with pleasure at their newly acquired fame. But there is talk that, in fact, Goldfinger won the match because he began and ended the 18th hole with the same ball and I am being strongly urged to submit the whole matter to the Rules of Golf committee. This I am doing today.

You are missing nothing here and if I was you I should stick to the chocs and the tiger skin.

Love to Dilys and see you both soon I hope.

TO MISS R. N. RENDLE, 48 Hammond Road, Fareham, Hampshire

27th April, 1959

How very kind of you to have written and I am delighted that you are such a firm fan of James Bond. Some of his critics don't like him because he enjoys himself too much!

I suppose one day James Bond will come to a sticky end but, at the present moment, he is in excellent health and quite able to look after himself. I know he will be encouraged to stay alive in view of your interest in him!

I enclose a dreadful photograph of myself which you have my permission to put on the fire.

TO JACK JONES, ESQ., The Western Mail, Cardiff

29th April, 1959

I have been away for ten days, but I must write immediately to thank you sincerely for the extremely kind things you wrote about "Goldfinger" in the *Western Mail*. It was wonderfully encouraging appreciation by somebody who would not normally stoop to my kind of book, and I am most grateful.

I quite see your point that the book should have ended before the last two chapters but I'm afraid I had no further plans for Mr. Goldfinger and I am a devotee of the corny ending where the villain dies and the hero gets his girl – though in this case it wasn't really more than half a girl! But, in the end, I was sorry to see Goldfinger go. He was a so much nicer man than James Bond!

Again with my warmest thanks for your most kindly critique.

TO THE HON. ANTHONY BERRY

29th April, 1959

I must say you and Mr. Jack Jones did me proud and I have written today to thank him.

Thank you, too, for wasting so much space on me. Unfortunately I have looked in vain for the gold filling and I can't trace it. I fear it must have been melted down to make my wedding ring for Anne.

However, I'm sure you will agree that gratitude is worth far more than gold bullion, so here it comes.

TO SIR FREDERICK HOYER MILLAR, G.C.M.G., C.V.O., Permanent Under Secretary, The Foreign Office, Downing Street, S.W.1.

Anticipating problems with prospective film or television deals, Fleming had written to the Foreign Office requesting assurance that his books did not breach security guidelines: 'My books are fantastic and, having had experience in these things, I have taken pains to see that they would not give offence to my old friends in the Intelligence world. I also know from senior members of that world that, far from causing offence, the adventures are followed with affectionate interest tinged with hilarity by members of "The Firm".' On receiving clearance he gave fulsome thanks.

3rd June, 1959

Forgive me for not having written before, but I only got back from abroad yesterday.

First of all, thank you very much indeed for your swift and kindly response to my rather bizarre request, but I am horrified to hear that you are one of my "ardent readers". I shall have to put up my sights a bit higher in future!

I think your suggested formula is very reasonable and goes as far as could be expected. It should be perfectly adequate for the film and television people and of course you can take it for obvious reasons – not least of which is that I am still a member of the special branch of the R.N.V.S.R . [Royal Navy Volunteer Supplementary Reserve] – that I shall keep a sharp eye on any film or television production which may eventuate.

It would be very kind if you could send me a formal note on the lines you suggest.

When next we meet I will invite you to seal this pact in James Bond's latest stimulant. This, on the lines of pink gin, is pink Steinhager – a tough Austrian schnapps that definitely quickens the trigger finger!

TO J. H. DOVE, ESQ., 12 Selborne Terrace, Heaton, Bradford 9

4th June, 1959

Thank you very much for your letter of May 12th and, in theory, I entirely agree with you.

In fact, I tried hard to cut out these "he saids" and "she saids", leaving in only those which are necessary for sense and continuity.

A matter of taste comes in here and I do not like dialogue to be as curt and bald as it often is in modern writing and I prefer "he said" to "Bond said" unless it is necessary to indicate the identity of the speaker.

However, as I write my next book, my knuckles will smart from your cane and I will see if I can do better.

TO STANLEY BOWLER, ESQ., F.R.P.S., F.R.S.A., 37 Burton Road, London, S.W.9.

While replying to Mr Bowler on a matter of photography, Fleming's mention of Norman Lewis may well have stemmed from the fact that he had recently asked him to report on Cuba where, despite official reports to the contrary, he was certain trouble was brewing.

4th June, 1959

Very many thanks for your extremely perceptive and interesting letter of May 17th.

Of course you are quite right and I will confess that, although I discussed the matter at some length with my friend who is a distinguished practitioner of your craft, Mr. Norman Lewis, the result was very much of a fudge about which I had many qualms.

Now that you mention your alternative, it is a maddeningly obvious solution to the problem and one of which I had sufficient knowledge to make use after consulting with an expert such as yourself.

Should I have cause to dabble again in photography, I shall certainly take advantage of your kind invitation to consult you.

In conclusion, I am most grateful for your valuable letter and I apologise for insulting the intelligence of yourself and countless other experts in your field.

TO DR G. R. C. D. GIBSON, 1 The Green, Anstey, Leicester

Dr Gibson, one of Fleming's most diligent motoring correspondents, was delighted to see that Bond had graduated to an Aston Martin and enclosed a card for the Aston Martin Owners Club: 'I'm sure he would enjoy being a member of the A.M.O.C. although I'm not so sure that we would feel comfortable at having him around!' He had much enjoyed Goldfinger *but 'although not a psycho-pathologist, I think it is slightly naughty of you to change a criminal Lesbian into a clinging honey-bun (to be bottled by Bond) in the last chapter.' Incidentally, why didn't Fleming try an adventure about Formula 1 racing? 'Nobody has yet written a good novel on the subject.'*

23rd June, 1959

Thank you very much for your splendid letter of June 17th and for your kind invitation for James Bond to join the A.M.O.C.

Since neither Bond nor his biographer are owners of an Aston Martin, I can do no more than pass your invitation on to the head of Admin. at the Secret Service from whose transport pool the DB III was drawn.

Incidentally, I don't agree that the car should be described as the "Mark III". That reads a bit too stuffily!

I also disagree with your penultimate paragraph, couched though it is in such graphic language. Pussy only needed the right man to come along and perform the laying on of hands in order to cure her psycho-pathological malady.

I have in mind a story with motor racing as its background, but it isn't quite along the lines you helpfully suggest. I will try and get around to it in due course and shall not be surprised if I then receive a sheaf of acid complaints from experts such as yourself.*

Again with many thanks for cheering up my morning at the office.

TO WREN HOWARD

The architect Erno Goldfinger, whose modernist structures were making their mark on London's skyline, was unhappy that Fleming had used his name. Fleming did not know him personally, but his record working for the Daily Worker *and the British Communist Party ensured a vigorous response.*

Goldeneye, Oracabessa, Jamaica, B.W.I.

Tuesday [undated]

Dear Bob,

Many thanks for your letter and first of all may I send warm congratulations to you all and particularly Michael [Howard] for the splendid production of <u>Goldfinger</u> which has just reached me? Michael has done wonderfully by all my books but this is by far his best and the cover is a

---

* Fleming did indeed use motor racing in an episode for an abortive Bond TV series. His outline was adapted in 2015 by Anthony Horowitz for the novel *Trigger Mortis*.

stroke of genius. By the same token please pay ten guineas from my account as a present to the individual who bowled out the Canasta mistake. This would have cost me dear and I am most grateful to whoever it was. Please tell him so.

Okay for Foyles and many thank for the success.

Don't stand any nonsense from this Golden-Finger. There may be few in the UK telephone directory but get your sec to ring up the US information people at the embassy and count the number in the New York directory. Ditto the German embassy with their telephone books. And sue his solicitors for the price of the copy you sent him. Tell him that if there's any more nonsense I'll put an erratum slip and change the name throughout to GOLDPRICK and give the reason why.

Hope you do well with the book and I'll be back around the tenth to lend a hand. I have sent William a note about progress on my next.

Regards to Jonathan and all.

The exact nature of Goldfinger's complaint remains uncertain, but Michael Howard thought it worthy of serious consideration, given that the Daily Express *was about to serialise the book. As he replied on 13 March, 'I hated like mad giving way to Mr Goldfinger but in your absence and time being so short I was disinclined to take the responsibility of standing firm and perhaps having trouble with the serialisation. If anything had been done to cause the* Express *to delay publication they might easily have cancelled the deal which would have cost you too much money. We had discovered quite a bit about the gentleman in question. None of it was very pleasant and all of it made us unusually wary.' Goldfinger was placated with an apology and six free copies of the offending tome.*

10

For Your Eyes Only

WHEN FLEMING FLEW to Jamaica in 1959 he had already made a head start on his forthcoming portfolio of short stories. Among the host of peculiarities that had caught his mind during his trip to the Seychelles the previous year was the stingray – or more specifically its tail. Possession of these fearsome items was strictly regulated: citizens were forbidden to own a specimen more than three feet long, it had to be bound at each end and could only be used as a walking stick. As Fleming pointed out, in the wrong hands they could be vicious weapons: 'A single lash with the five foot tail can maim for life.'

Fleming used it to dramatic effect in 'The Hildebrand Rarity', which he wrote shortly after his return to Britain in 1958. Here, Bond is on leave in the Seychelles when he encounters an American millionaire, Milton Krest, cruising the islands in search of rare specimens for his tax-dodge charity, the Krest Foundation. The object of his attentions when Bond meets him is a pink-striped fish – the Hildebrand Rarity – to acquire which he is happy to poison great stretches of ocean. A brash, brutal man, he has a trophy wife named Liz whom he likes to keep in order with the aid of 'the Corrector,' a three-foot stingray tail (unbound) that hangs on the bedroom wall. When one day he is found dead with the Rarity thrust down his throat it is clear that his wife was the culprit but the incident is hushed up as an accident.

The expat community of the Seychelles also provided a source of inspiration. 'There are innumerable wafer-thin "Colonels" living on five hundred a year [who] are uninteresting people, the flotsam and jetsam of our receding Empire,' Fleming wrote, 'who put nothing, not even a touch of the authentic beach-comber back into the haven they have chosen to whine out their lives in.' He gave a milder but no less scathing portrait of the claustrophobic nature of colonial life in 'Quantum of Solace', a cautionary tale in the Somerset Maugham style* that describes the fate of a glamorous air stewardess who marries a shy diplomat stationed in Bermuda, only to find after she embarks on an adulterous affair that her seemingly unworldly spouse has a fine line in revenge. The quantum of solace to which the title refers is the measure of love that allows a marriage to survive; when it reaches zero there is no hope. Perhaps this was a reflection on the state of Fleming's own relationship, but more likely it showed his increasing despondency with Bond and life in general. Having listened to the tale, as recounted by the Governor of the Bahamas, Bond leaves for his next task – a meeting with the FBI and US coastguards – in anticipation of an event 'edged with boredom and futility'.

Like 'The Hildebrand Rarity', 'Quantum of Solace' had also been written the previous year, so with these two stories in his pocket he only had to come up with a few more. But even then little ingenuity was required: he simply plundered some of the ideas he had submitted to CBS for a potential television series. Not that they were any the worse for that. They included 'From A View To A Kill,' concerning a Soviet assassin, based in a forest outside Paris, who targets motorcycle couriers working for SHAPE (Supreme Headquarters Allied Powers Europe); 'Risico', a drug-running tale set in Italy, with a spectacular chase around Venice's Lido that involves one of Bond's pursuers stepping on an unexploded mine; and 'Man's Work', the story of a female archer who seeks to assassinate an ex-Nazi who has killed her parents for the sake of their Caribbean estate. It did not matter that they were old material. Each of them was vivid, heartfelt, well researched – for 'Man's Work' Fleming consulted his weapons expert Geoffrey Boothroyd about bows and arrows† – and above all they had his natural feel for place and atmosphere.

---

* Based on a true story related to Fleming by Blanche Blackwell.
† See 'Conversations with the Armourer'.

Yet Fleming wasn't sure about them. In a letter to Ann he said that at least one of the stories wasn't worth publishing. Later, the polite yet perspicacious William Plomer also had some thoughts about the direction Fleming was taking. Of one line in 'Man's Work' he commented: 'These "random thoughts" are diverting. Something new. One never supposed that Bond's thoughts were ever "random". It makes him almost human.' And there were, as so often, doubts about the title. Fleming's first suggestion was *The Rough with the Smooth*, which eventually transmuted into *For Your Eyes Only*, from one of the stories that itself had started life as 'Man's Work'.

When Fleming returned from Goldeneye that spring he was faced with a variety of tasks. The first was to write an account of his friendship with Raymond Chandler, who had died earlier in the year. After several rejections it was eventually published by *London Magazine* in April 1959. The second priority was to reorganise his position with the *Sunday Times*. Lord Kemsley had sold the paper to Roy Thomson in June the previous year, thus terminating Fleming's advantageous arrangement. Thanks to his numerous contacts, among them the editor C. D. Hamilton, he was paid a fee of £1,000 for a set number of articles per annum, and even retained a seat on the editorial board. Less comfortable was his situation with *The Book Collector*. Ever since he had assumed outright ownership in 1955 there had been squabbles between himself and Robert Harling, the modernisers, and John Hayward and John Carter, the traditionalists, with Percy Muir hovering uncertainly in the middle. As was becoming clear, a compromise between the two sides was unlikely, and their correspondence was full of petty misunderstandings accompanied by petulant threats to resign.

These, though, were run-of-the-mill matters compared to a sudden wave of interest in Bond's screen potential. An American producer, Maurice Winnick, who had links to Metro-Goldwyn-Mayer, contacted Fleming on his return from Goldeneye with a view to adapting 007 for television. Then there was Fleming's old friend Ivar Bryce who, in a casual, millionaire-ish manner, had decided to become a film producer. By chance he struck lucky with his first offering *The Boy and the Bridge*, directed by

Kevin McClory, which came out in July. With a view to expanding his career he proposed to found a film studio, Xanadu, and wrote Fleming a personal cheque for $50,000 worth of shares in the company in return for rights to a Bond story. His attorney, Ernie Cuneo, visited London in April – 'charging round like a bull in a china shop knocking down the Wardour Street and Elstree inmates like ninepins', Fleming wrote fondly to William Stephenson – and later dashed off a draft plot.

None of the approaches were solid. Winnick's television schemes fell away, as did Bryce's plan for a Xanadu studio – Fleming never cashed the cheque, knowing Bryce's undependable ways – but a deal with McClory remained on the cards, and hope alone was enough to raise his spirits. So much so that in October he wrote an article for *The Spectator* headed immodestly 'If I were Prime Minister'.

Fleming's prescription for Britain – 'I am a totally non-political animal' – was a hefty dose of whimsy into which had been stirred a surprising amount of good sense. He recommended that the Isle of Wight be turned into a vast pleasuredrome of casinos and *maisons de tolérance*. He would pass laws to 'stop people being ashamed of themselves', would abolish overtime, appoint a Minister of Leisure to ensure the population enjoyed itself, and would reform men's clothing, 'which I regard as out-of-date, unhygienic and rather ridiculous'. He would also introduce a minimum wage, abolish expense accounts 'and other forms of financial chicanery', promote the crafts and apprenticeships, reform the Press, encourage a constant flow of emigration within the Commonwealth and replace petrol cars with electric ones. His government's banner publication would be a quarterly called *Hazard* that provided unvarnished statistics on the dangers of processed food, alcohol, tobacco and shoddy car manufacture, as well as providing the correct odds for football pools and Premium Bonds. This, he said, would allow him to face with a clear conscience the fact that, 'from the Exchequer's point of view, the most valuable citizen is the man who drinks or smokes himself to death'.

All of these, he admitted, were small things. The big things were time-wasting, 'too vast and confused for one man's brain'. Atomic weapons, for example, were just one of the matters he would leave to be decided by his Ministers and 'the wave of common sense which, it seems to me, by a process of osmosis between peoples rather than politicians, is taking rapid and healthy control of the world'.

Nuclear warfare, of course, was one of the great fears that underpinned British life during the Cold War. Nevertheless, Fleming was disingenuous in his claim that atomic weapons were too big for the consideration of just one man. He was considering them quite thoroughly for his next book, *Thunderball*.

TO JOHN HAYWARD, ESQ., C.B.E., 19 Carlyle Mansions, London, S.W.3.

As part of his ongoing wrangle over The Book Collector *Fleming raised a point about payment of a bill.*

17th December, 1958

I was rather surprised at your suggestion this morning that I should pay out of my own pocket £42 for the auditors' fee for The Book Collector and, on thinking it over, I am really not quite clear what your argument is. The company paid its own auditors' fee last year – £63. Why should there now be a change?

You say that the company is running at a loss and that I should do something to reduce this loss on the grounds that you and Percy both give services to the company without remuneration.

Let us be clear about this. There is no reason why you and Percy should give services to The Book Collector without remuneration. We have some £2,000 in the bank and there is no reason why you and Percy should not be paid appropriate fees like any other contributors.

As to the periodical running at a loss, the object of our decision last week to increase our advertising rates was to correct this situation.

My contribution to The Book Collector was to save it from extinction and pay the costs of its foundation as a company and I have never pretended to be of more use to the company than as an occasional host.

You say that Percy also agrees that I should pay the auditors' fee. If that is so, which I have yet to hear from him, I shall at once reconsider my position vis-à-vis The Book Collector and arrange by one means or another to sever any connection with it.

But these are strong words and I hope you will agree that the periodical can continue on its way in its previous cheerful, if rather happy-go-lucky, fashion.

To which Hayward replied, 'You say that you were "rather surprised" – you bet I was rather surprised too! I innocently supposed that you would jump at the opportunity of lending a hand.' He also pointed out that contributors were never paid, except when they were in the direst of financial positions. And so it all went on.

FROM WILLIAM PLOMER

12th April, 1959

Dear I,

I've greatly enjoyed The Hildebrand Rarity. "Whacko!"* seems the best comment. I found Liz a little underdone at first, but she certainly redeemed herself in the end. A few stray comments: [. . .]

The ending is excellent – tantalizing. I hope Bond got the Corrector as a souvenir – and managed to remember to collect the tail of the sting-ray he killed before embarking for Chagrin. (I'm not quite happy about the single palm tree – I feel it would have collapsed under so many boobies, &c. Could there perhaps be a ruined "installation" of some sort left over from the War? It would lend atmosphere. Otherwise Chagrin suggests slightly one of those comic desert islands so hackneyed of caricaturists. Or do I fuss & quibble too much?) The story has been <u>much</u> enjoyed by your g.r. (gentle reader).

   i)   Shall I keep the manuscript until further notice?

   ii)   pass it on to anybody else at 30 Bedford Square?

---

* A reference to *Whack-O!*, a TV series that ran in the late 1950s and early 1960s, and involved a cane-swishing teacher administering corporal punishment to any pupil within reach.

iii) try & post it or have it posted to you, in spite of the 3-inch bolts
     that hold it together?
iv) or what

TO WILLIAM PLOMER

14th April, 1959

Thank you a thousand times for the encouraging and hilarious examination of "The Hildebrand Rarity". You really are marvellously prompt at
doing my homework for me and I shall, of course, slavishly obey your
instructions and amend accordingly.

Michael Howard wants to read it, so could you please pass it on to
him and I will, in due course, send a lorry to collect it.

The <u>Spectator</u> has sent back my piece about Chandler saying it is too
long for them. I dare say Shakespeare used to run into this sort of trouble, but I shall now send it on to <u>Encounter</u> as quick as I can before the
whole subject goes stale.

I am in the grips of the most ghastly series of tele-folk and I have two
meetings at Capes with these people this afternoon. I suppose one day I
shall have to accept the basket of golden coconuts they persist in offering me, or at any rate saying that perhaps they might offer me in certain
circumstances. Ah me!

FROM WILLIAM PLOMER

Next came 'From a View to a Kill'.

18th April, 1959

My dear I,

Terribly exciting! How <u>do</u> you do it? Brilliant opening – excellent
Bond's-eye-view of Paris (which was overdue) – a nice plain name for
the girl for a change – tension well maintained – Excellent climax. Very
few quibbles but . . . [Amongst Plomer's points, which mostly concerned

Fleming's erroneous descriptions of flowers was: 'Brown squirrels are generally, I think, called red squirrels.']

I take off my crash-helmet to you. I can't wait for the next story – at least, I can – I must – because I'm about to make a little sortie to Bavaria, & expect to be back by mid-May. By then you will have written several more, I hope.

Unless told to the contrary I'll pass the typescript on to Michael Howard before I go.

TO WILLIAM PLOMER

'Risico', which was perhaps the story with which Fleming felt least happy, followed.

12th May, 1959

Following the straight left I delivered about two weeks ago and which will be waiting for you on your return, here comes a nasty right hook in the shape of the fourth short story of the bunch of five.

My suggestion is that we should put these four together in a book with the fifth, "Quantum of Solace", in the middle of them, and call it:

THE ROUGH WITH THE SMOOTH.
Five Secret Exploits
of
James Bond.

I suggest starting with "From A View To A Kill" then "Man's Work", then "Quantum of Solace", "Risiko"[sic] and finishing with "The Hildebrand Rarity".

I have heard nothing from Michael on the first two you shunted on to him but you might care to suggest to him that we could discuss the whole project when I get back from Venice, where I am taking Anne on Thursday, around June 1st.

Sorry to shovel these two heavy spadefuls on to the old beetle's back but that definitely completes your stint for this year.

13th May, 1959

My dear I,

I placed "Risico" on the top of the mounds of typescript awaiting me, & read it with my usual keen curiosity to see what you have written. The Italian setting makes a nice change & the sandy purlieus of the Lido are nicely touched in. The business of the Grundig chair is adroit – I think Bond ought to have noticed it, & smelt a rat if not a grundig. A nice moment when the pursuer is blown up – another when the central harpooner is seen to be Colombo. Perhaps because Colombo turns out to be so cosy & cordial, the tension is much relaxed, and the climax is (to me) less exciting than it ought to be. In fact, I think it the least exciting of the collection of short stories so far. Would it perhaps be possible to keep the reader in suspense a bit longer by making Colombo keep Bond in suspense a bit longer? But I don't suppose you want to alter or revise what you have written, & perhaps I am being too fussy. But in spite of the new setting (which I'm all in favour of) I feel that <u>perhaps</u> this story is a little too close to formula and not quite rich enough in those little sardonic or mondain inventions or details you use so well.

I'll pass the typescript on to Michael Howard. [...]

I enclose a little bunch of quibbles wh. I hope will be useful.

p. 6, l. 4 up – "wry sense of humour"? The word "wry" is terribly overworked by fictionists at present, & is commonly attached to a smile, laugh, or grin. I don't like it any better attached to a sense of humour. I think what you mean is that M. was ironically conscious of his obsessions, or that he could regard them with a half-humoured detachment. Yes? Please not "wry" [...]

p. 54, l. 4–6 "sickening thud." The most worn of all trite expressions. Even "horrible thump" would be better. "Spread-eagled" seems also a bit worn, antique and heraldic. Why not say "and lay in a grotesque heap, with one dislocated leg protruding"? Or something of that sort.

Now I think you must check your Italian spelling [...]

FROM WILLIAM PLOMER

17th May, 1959

My dear Ian,

Man's Work is most exciting, & I've much enjoyed it. I enclose a few comments.

I am passing the story on to Michael together with your plan for the book & your suggestion about discussing the project when you return. I like the order in which you have arranged the contents. The title is not, I think, electrifying.

I hope you're both enjoying yourselves very much. Don't step on any land-mines in the purlieus of the Lido, and if you <u>can</u> think of a better title . . . You could perhaps use Man's Work as the title, keeping the sub-title about Five Secret Exploits.

TO MISS NOELA MONEYPENNY, 83 Strong Avenue, Graceville, Brisbane

25th June, 1959

Your letter has finally caught up with me here and I am very amused by your query.

I really can't remember how I came to give M.'s secretary your name. It seemed to me a pretty and unusual one and I expect that was the only reason.

I have just had a look in the London telephone directory where I find there are three Moneypenny's, all apparently male. I expect, if you looked into the matter, you would find that it is a very old Anglo-Saxon name.

Anyway, thank you for your charming letter and I am sorry I can't give you any more interesting or romantic reason for borrowing your name.

TO WREN HOWARD

In the hope of giving the firm a much-needed injection of vigour, Cape's board had appointed an American editor named Robert Knittel. His tenure was short-lived, but he lasted long enough to persuade Fleming to put his film interests in the hands of a professional agent, rather than relying on his own haphazard efforts.

2nd July, 1959

Dear Bob,

Encouraged by Robert Knittel and pestiferated by conflicting inter-ests and bids, I have now placed all my film, television and dramatic rights in the hands of M.C.A. Mr. Laurence Evans of their office here is the man who has taken me under his wing and if and when you get any of these maddening letters from independent producers and other fly-by-nights, would you please pass them straight on to him.

Bob Knittel said that if I got married to M.C.A. he would write a letter to Jules Stein requesting a red, or at least a pale pink carpet treatment for me, and it would be very kind indeed of Bob if he could do this so that M.C.A. from the top to bottom knows that I have powerful friends and that they have acquired a potential dia-mond mine!

Sorry to bother you with all this shilly-shallying but it is a great relief to me to have rid myself of this mink-coated incubus.

If Mr. Winnick re-appears on the scene, which I think improbable, would you please refer him also to Mr. Evans.

TO WREN HOWARD

As early as July 1959 Fleming was getting himself in a tangle over film rights, the question being whether or not in a previous agreement with the Rank Organisation he had signed away Bond in his entirety along with the rights to Moonraker. *On 1 July he wrote to Wren Howard, 'It does seem to me that there is a nasty delayed action bomb ticking away beneath my chair so far as future film and television rights in "James Bond" are concerned'. The matter was eventually clarified, but not before Fleming sent a sharp note to Cape.*

15th July, 1959

Dear Bob,

I am rather appalled by the contents of your letter of July 14th and I am very surprised that the strongly adverse opinion of [law firm] Rubinstein Nash about the "Moonraker" contract was not reported to me way back in April and May.

It was quite by chance that I myself checked on the "Moonraker" contract and raised just the points of Rubinstein Nash in my letter of July 1st.

In the meantime, and before signing up with M.C.A., I have sold a one-time television spectacular in "From Russia With Love" to Hubbell Robinson Associates [an offshoot of CBS] and I have also sold the rights to a full length feature film of James Bond of which I am now doing the script. This was sold to Xanadu Productions, an independent producer belonging to a friend of mine.

I regard this as a very serious matter indeed unless we can find some way out of the mess. What do you advise?

There seems to me to be two possibilities:

a) Either go ahead and hope that Rank won't notice but, in this case, am I being fair to the two recent purchasers and shall I not be placing myself as well as them in a position of considerable jeopardy?

b) Would it be best to write a nonchalant letter to Miss Joyce Briggs along the lines of the enclosed?

I must say that, with the best will in the world, I am surprised that this contract with Ranks was not more carefully negotiated by Jonathan Capes and that I was not informed earlier of the serious situation revealed in April and May of this year, despite the fact that we had considerable correspondence about similar doubts in the case of the "Casino Royale" contract.

TO M. HOWARD

1st October, 1959

Dear Michael,

I have thought over the question of a title and I rather like 'FOR YOUR EYES ONLY'. This used to be stamped on secret papers in the early days of the war and is still occasionally in use.

If you like this, it could perhaps go on the jacket above a really splendid colour photograph extended to the borders of a fine rule human eye (with a grey iris – this is James Bond's). The pinkish surround could then be bled upwards and downwards into, say, a pale grey, on which the lettering could be superimposed.

I think this could be made handsome and startling.

If you like this idea, perhaps we could re-title 'Man's Work' accordingly and start the book with it. If you could let me have that story back I could write in an appropriate sentence or two embodying the title.

TO M. HOWARD

26th October, 1959

Dear Michael,

Here is Dicky Chopping's proof which I discussed with you on the telephone. Personally, I think it is absolutely splendid and I'm so glad you are inclined to agree, even without seeing it.

I also enclose Dicky Chopping's comments for your professional eye. Will you please take it all on from here with Dicky, as I have got to be away for the whole of November?

My only immediate comments, with which I think Dicky agrees, are that the colours should be as bold as he can possibly make them and I'm prepared to sacrifice the grey-blue of James Bond's eyes for a brighter blue if Dicky would prefer it.

I explained to Dicky that logically "For Your Eyes Only" should be stamped on a portion of a document – at the top of it and not interfering with the text – and I enclose a draft of how this might look on a real document and with words which would, in fact, be appropriate to my story. The title should be red and perhaps, if it amused Dicky, rather fuzzy as if it really were a rubber stamp.

I really do think Dicky is a most ingenious chap. If he were wise he would put himself entirely in our hands and we could keep him constantly supplied with exciting work.

Over to you.

P.S. Having dictated a draft scrap for Dicky, I think I had better leave it to you and him how and where it, or part of it, is used in his design.

TO D. N. DAVIES, ESQ., Messrs. Lentheric, 17 Old Bond Street, w.1.

D. N. Davies, of the toiletry specialists Lentheric, wrote to congratulate Fleming for mentioning his firm's products and enclosed a sample for his delectation. En passant, he mentioned that his wife had worked with Fleming in Naval Intelligence during the war.

10th December, 1959

Thank you very much indeed for your kind letter of December 2nd and for the fine Lentheric travelling kit you were kind enough to send me. I am glad to see that the case leaves plenty of room for a Beretta!

As a matter of fact, it is not James Bond who uses your, or any other, shaving lotions. I am ashamed to say that it is very often a subsidiary character or occasionally a villain. But we must assume that, even with Lentheric, all your customers can't be heroes!

I do indeed remember your wife. Patricia Trehearne was by far the prettiest girl in the whole of Naval Intelligence and she brought a light of varying intensity into all our eyes. It is only right that she should have entered into such a fragrant union with the head man at Lentheric. Please give her my warmest regards.

Again with many thanks for your kindly inspiration.

11

The Chandler Letters

'NOT MANY PEOPLE knew Chandler, so I will not apologise for the triviality of our correspondence. It fitted in with our relationship – the half-amused, ragging relationship of two writers working the same thin, almost-extinct literary seam, who like each other's work.'

Ian Fleming, *London Magazine*, December 1959

When Raymond Chandler published his first story in 1933 it was a defining moment in his career. 'After that,' he wrote, 'I never looked back, although I had a good many uneasy periods looking forward.' Much the same could have been said of Fleming, and indeed their lives followed strangely parallel courses. Born in Chicago, 1888, Chandler was educated in Britain at Dulwich College – even took British citizenship – and worked in a variety of jobs that included journalism and a spell at the Admiralty, before finding his true metier. By the time the two men met, in 1955, Chandler was famous for his punchy crime books starring private eye Philip Marlowe, the most recent of which (appropriately titled The Long Goodbye*) had come out in 1953. But, at the age of sixty-six, he was in decline. Plagued throughout his life by alcoholism and depression, he reached a nadir following the death of his wife in December 1954. After a botched suicide attempt in February 1955 he sold his home in La Jolla, California, and returned to Britain.*

It was in May 1955, at a lunch given by the poet Stephen Spender and his wife Natasha, that the two authors' paths crossed. Fleming admired Chandler for his naked display of bereavement but at the same time was fascinated by the picture of decaying genius that he presented. 'He must have been a very good-looking man,' he recorded, 'but the good, square face was puffy and unkempt with drink. In talking he never ceased making ugly, Hapsburg lip grimaces while his head stretched away from you, looking along his right or left shoulder as if you had bad breath. When he did look at you he saw everything and remembered days later to criticise the tie or shirt you had been wearing. Everything he said had authority . . .'

They had much in common: they enjoyed the same writers, patronised the same bookseller, Mr Francis of Prince's Arcade, and were prone to the same moments of self-doubt. When Fleming lent him a copy of Moonraker *Chandler rang a few days later to say how much he had liked it and to ask if a few words of praise would help. For Fleming, who was undergoing a crisis of confidence, it was just the boost he needed. 'Rather unattractively', he wrote, 'I took him up on this suggestion . . .'*

TO CHANDLER

26th May, 1955

Your elegant writing paper makes you sound very much at home, and I shall call you up next week and see if you would like to walk round the corner and pay us a visit.

Incidentally a good restaurant in your neighbourhood is Overton's, directly opposite Victoria station. Book a table and go upstairs where you will find an enchanting Victorian interior and the best pâté maison in London.

I wouldn't think of asking you to write to me about Moonraker but if you happen to feel in a mood of quixotic generosity, a word from you which I could pass on to my publishers would make me the fortune which has so far eluded me.

Incidentally, The Spectator is almost girlishly thrilled that you will do The Riddle of the Sands for them and the things you said to me and I published about Prince's Bookshop have brought Francis a flood of new business. So the impact you are having on London is that of Father Christmas in Springtime.

FROM CHANDLER

4th June, 1955

I cannot imagine what I can say to you about your books that will excite your publisher. What I do say in all sincerity is that you are probably the most forceful and driving writer, of what I suppose still must be called 'thrillers' in England.

Peter Cheyney wrote one good book, I thought, called <u>Dark Duet</u>, and another fairly good one, but his pseudo-American tough guy stories always bored me. There was also James Hadley Chase, and I think the less said of him the better. Also, in spite of the fact that you have been everywhere and seen everything, I cannot help admiring your courage in tackling the American scene . . . Some of your stuff on Harlem in <u>Live and Let Die</u>, and everything on St Petersburg, Florida, seems to be quite amazing for a foreigner to accomplish.

If this is any good to you would you like me to have it engraved on a gold slab?

It was not only good but excellent, and the imprimatur of such an established author gave the Bond novels the impetus they needed. Fleming appreciated it wholeheartedly.

TO CHANDLER

6th June, 1955

These are words of such gold that no supporting slab is needed and I am passing the first sentence on to Macmillan's in New York and Cape's here, and will write my appreciation in caviar when the extra royalties come in.

Seriously, it was extraordinarily kind of you to have written as you did and you have managed to make me feel thoroughly ashamed of my next book [*Diamonds are Forever*] which is also set in America, but in an America of much more fantasy than I allowed myself in <u>Live and Let Die</u>.

There's a moratorium at home at the moment as the Duke of West-minster* (whom may God preserve) has ordered us to paint the outside of our house and the whole thing is hung with cradles and sounds of occasional toil.

But they will be gone in a few days' time and I hope you will be one of the first to darken our now gleaming doorway.

TO CHANDLER

29th June, 1955

Just to remind you that you are having lunch with us on Thursday, 30th June, at one o'clock.

Victoria Square is about three hundred yards away from you, quite close to Victoria Station – or to Buckingham Palace, whichever way you look at it.

Apart from my wife Anne, there will be a friend of mine, Duff Dunbar a brilliant lawyer and one of your fans; Rupert Hart-Davis, the best young publisher in England who does the crime reviews for "Time and Tide" in his spare time. If anyone else comes along I will warn you but it is certainly no heavy-weight affair and nobody will say: "How do you think up those wonderful plots Mr. Chandler?"

Despite living in nearby Eaton Square, Chandler proved an elusive guest. When at last he accepted an invitation to lunch, the occasion was not a success. 'Our small dining room was over-crowded. Chandler was a man who was shy of houses and "entertaining" and our conversation was noisy and about people he did not know. His own diffident and rather halting manner of speech made no impact. He was not made a fuss of and I am pretty sure he hated the whole affair.'

That Chandler attended at all was probably because Natasha Spender was present. Since the death of his wife he had embarked on a path of semi-platonic promiscuity, transferring his affections from one hopeless object of

---

* Who owned the freehold to Victoria Square.

desire to another. He seemed lost without women, and Natasha was one of many at whom he cast his eye. As Fleming wrote, 'In the few years I knew him, he was never without some good-looking companion to mother him and try and curb his drinking. These were affectionate and warm-hearted relationships and probably nothing more. Though I do not know this, I suspect that each woman was, in the end, rather glad to get away from the ghost of the other woman who always walked at his side and from the tired man who made sense for so little of the day.'

Chandler left Britain shortly afterwards to begin the process of reapplying for US citizenship, but he returned in 1956. One of his first tasks was to review Diamonds are Forever *at the invitation of Leonard Russell, Literary Editor of the* Sunday Times. *He was ambivalent in his praise and concluded with the words: 'Let me plead with Mr. Fleming not to allow himself to become a stunt writer, or he will end up no better than the rest of us.'*

When Fleming wrote to thank him, Chandler replied:

FROM CHANDLER

11th April, 1956

Dear Ian,

Thank you so much for your letter of Wednesday and if the payment for my outstanding review had been received a little earlier I should have been able to eat three meals a day.

I thought my review was no more than you deserved considering your position on the SUNDAY TIMES and I tried to write it in such a way that the good part could be quoted and the bad parts left out. After all, old boy, there had to be some bad parts. I think you will have to make up your mind what kind of a writer you are going to be. You could be almost anything except that I think you are a bit of a sadist!

I am not in any Hampstead hospital. I am at home and if they ever put me in a hospital again I shall walk out leaving corpses strewn behind me, except pretty nurses.

As for having lunch with you, with or without butler, I can't do it yet –
because even if I were much better than I am I should be having lunch
with ladies.

TO CHANDLER

27th April, 1956

Dear Ray,

Many thanks for the splendid Chandleresque letter. Personally I
loved your review and thought it was excellent as did my publishers, and
as I say it was really wonderful of you to have taken the trouble.

Probably the fault about my books is that I don't take them seriously
enough and meekly accept having my head ragged off about them in the
family circle. If one has a grain of intelligence it is difficult to go on
being serious about a character like James Bond. You after all write 'novels of suspense' – if not sociological studies – whereas my books are
straight pillow fantasies of the bang-bang, kiss-kiss variety.

But I have taken your advice to heart and will see if I can't order my
life so as to put more feeling into my typewriter.

Incidentally, have you read <u>A Most Contagious Game</u>, by Samuel
Grafton, published by Rupert Hart-Davis?

Sorry about lunch even without a butler. I also know some girls and
will dangle one in front of you one of these days.

I had no idea you were ill. If you are, please get well immediately. I am
extremely ill with sciatica.

FROM CHANDLER

1st May, 1956

Dear Ian,

I am leaving London on May 11th and should very much like to see
you before I go. I suggest that we have lunch together at one of your

better Clubs if you can arrange it. I don't think you do yourself justice about James Bond and I did not think that I did quite do you justice in my review of your book, because anyone who writes as dashingly as you do, ought, I think, to try for a little higher grade. I have just re-read <u>Casino Royale</u> and it seems to me that you have disimproved with each book.

I read several books by Samuel Grafton, but the one you mention I don't know; I will order it.

I don't want any girls dangling in front of me, because my girls do their own dangling and they would be extremely bitter to have you interfere.

You know what you can do with your sciatica don't you?

FROM CHANDLER

9th June, 1956

I didn't like leaving England without saying good-bye to the few friends I knew well enough to care about, but then I don't like saying good-bye at all, especially when it might be quite a long time before I come back. As you probably know, I long overstayed the six months allowed, but I had a compelling reason, even if I get hooked for British income tax. I am also likely to lose half my European royalties, which isn't funny. It's all a little obscure to me, but there it is. And it doesn't matter whether your stay in England is broken half a dozen times. If the time adds up to over six months within the fiscal year, you are it.

I am looking forward to your next book. I am also looking forward to my next book.

I rather liked New York this time, having heretofore loathed its harshness and rudeness. For one thing the weather has been wonderful, only one hot day so far and that not unbearable. I have friends here, but not many. Come to think of it I haven't many anywhere. Monday night I am flying back to California and this time I hope to stick it out and make some kind of a modest but convenient home there.

I am wondering what happened to all the chic pretty women who are supposed to be typical of New York. Damned if I've seen any of them. Perhaps I've looked in the wrong places, but I do have a feeling that New York is being slowly downgraded.

Please remember me to Mrs. Fleming if you see her and if she remembers me (doubtful). And how is His Grace the Duke of Westminster these days? Painting lots of houses, I hope?

TO CHANDLER

22nd June, 1956

Dear Ray,

How fine to get not one but two letters from you – and one of them legible at that.* I hope you have left a forwarding address with the Grosvenor or otherwise you will think me even more churlish than you already do.

I cannot understand your tax position and I certainly do not believe that we will try and squeeze your European royalties out of you for overstaying your time a little. If it looks like something fierce of that kind, please let me know and I will make an impassioned appeal on your behalf.

Eric Ambler has a new thriller coming out next week, which no doubt Prince's Bookshop will send you. If not, I will. It is better than the last two but still not quite the good old stuff we remember. I have done a review for the <u>Sunday Times</u> headed 'Forever Ambler' which struck me as a good joke.

My own muse is in a bad way. Despite your doubts, I really rather liked <u>Diamonds are Forever</u> . . . It has been very difficult to make Bond go through his tricks in <u>From Russia, With Love</u>, which is just going to the publishers.

Shall be in and around New York and Vermont for the first fortnight in August and, in the unlikely event that you should happen to be in

---

* Chandler had also sent a near-indecipherable scrawl about *Live and Let Die*.

reach of the area, please let me or Macmillans, New York, know and we will share a Coke in which the contents of a Benzedrine inhaler have been soaked overnight. Which, I understand, is the fashionable drink in your country at the moment.

FROM CHANDLER

4th July, 1956

Dear Ian,

I have already ordered Eric Ambler's new thriller since he told me about it some time before it came out. I think the title of your review, 'Forever Ambler' is a pretty good joke in the third class division.

Of course I liked <u>Diamonds are Forever</u> and I enjoyed reading it, but I simply don't think it is worthy of your talents.

It is unlikely that I shall be in New York or Vermont in August. It is much more likely that I shall be in Paris. Frankly a Coke in which the contents of a Benzedrine inhaler has been soaked overnight hasn't reached La Jolla. What does it do to you? The fashionable drink in this country is still Scotch.

TO CHANDLER

11th July, 1956

Dear Ray,

I cannot believe that you will end up by having trouble over your tax problems here. Our tax gatherers do not come down hard on the foreign visitor, and I am sure they will accept your medical alibi. I strongly advise you not to worry about the problem until faced with some kind of a demand.

As for my opera, you are clearly living under a grave misapprehension. My talents are extended to their absolute limits in writing books like <u>Diamonds are Forever</u>. I am not short-weighting anybody and I have absolutely nothing more up my sleeve. The way you talk, anybody would think I was a lazy Shakespeare or Raymond Chandler. Not so.

My only information to help you on your Paris visit is that on Thursdays, in the night club below the Moulin Rouge, there is an amateur strip-tease which might bring a flicker even to your worldly eyes. But I have not sampled it, so this information is not guaranteed.

Now get on with writing your book and stop picking your nose and staring out of the window.

By now Chandler was in a bad way, drinking heavily and making heavy weather of what would be his last novel, Playback. *When Fleming looked at it he saw 'a formless jumble of sub-plots, at the end of which Marlowe was obviously going to marry a rich American woman living in Paris'. Gloomily, they discussed Marlowe's future. Chandler thought it would be the end of him: his wife would sack his secretary, redecorate his office and make him change his friends. Then, because she was so rich there would be no point Marlowe working and he would eventually drink himself to death. Fleming tried to cheer him up: 'I said that this would make an excellent plot and that perhaps he could save Marlowe by making Mrs. Marlowe drink herself to death first.' But Chandler couldn't muster the enthusiasm: 'The truth was that it had nearly all gone out of him and that he simply could not be bothered.'*

Back in the United States, towards the end of 1957, Chandler sent Fleming an oversized panoramic postcard 'From the World-famous Palm Canyon' in Colorado. This was followed shortly afterwards by another in which he chastised Fleming for teasing his latest female companion about their relationship.

TO CHANDLER

29th November, 1957

Why do they think that Palm Canyon is 'world-famous'? What world do these people frequent?

It was fine to see your gusty script again and to know that you are still alive, and I heartily approve your plan to move over here. Perhaps you will get so bored here that you will be forced to get on with that long-overdue book.

Naturally I never rag O. about you. She's been telling tales. She is a wonderful girl and I guess you are very good for each other.

Hurry up and come along.

When Chandler returned to London in 1958 he was on a downward slope. Fleming gave him an introduction to the Italian gangster Lucky Luciano in the hope that he would do an article for the Sunday Times.

TO CHANDLER

19th March, 1958

Dear Ray,

Please see page 11 of the enclosed Sunday Graphic. As you see, your bird looks in good health and spirits but that spaghetti looks a trifle under-cooked.

Henry Thody, who writes this story, is the Sunday Times and Sunday Graphic representative in Rome and I could arrange for him to meet you and chaperone you down to Naples, make all arrangements, and see you off.

He is a splendidly eccentric chap with huge black handle-bar moustaches and you will like him.

Now all you need is your tickets.

So far as Capri is concerned, I should start off for a day or two at the Qui Si Sana, which is in the village of Capri in the middle of the island. But then I should explore a bit and perhaps move to one of the hotels down at Piccolo Marina, which is right on the sea.

I enclose the ten shillings which you kindly loaned me and, although the bank rate is 7%, I have not added interest because I think you are rich enough without it.

See you on Monday at one o'clock at the Boulestin.

Ha Ha! about catching you at the Etoile with that pretty girl. You'd better get yourself organised!

The Luciano initiative was a failure, culminating in a lengthy screed that Fleming damned as 'sheer bad writing'. On 10 July, they held a conversation in a twenty-minute BBC radio broadcast, The Art of Writing Thrillers. *Chandler was already drunk by the time Fleming collected him at 11.00 in the morning, and much of what he said had to be deleted. When he apologised for mentioning masturbation a BBC woman consoled him: 'It's quite all right Mr. Chandler, we hear much worse things than that.'*

Afterwards they had lunch at Boulestin's, where the conversation took a reflective turn. What did the future hold? How would their careers end? Taxation, they agreed, had killed the wealthy writer and films were the only salvation. Chandler said that Dashiell Hammett 'had never let his work decline. He had just written himself out like an expended firework . . . [In the end] as one grew older, one grew out of gangsters and blondes and guns and, since they were the chief ingredients of thrillers, short of space fiction, that was that.' Pertinently, given the anxiety Fleming would face over this very question, they discussed how authors like themselves could get rid of the albatross they had slung around their necks. Chandler shrugged and said he could never kill Marlowe, 'because he liked him and other people seemed to like him and it would be unkind to them'.

They never saw or heard from each other again. Chandler decamped to America, and although Fleming sent him a copy of his latest book he received no reply. Rumours came in early 1959 that Chandler had delirium tremens and was unwell. On enquiring at Prince's Arcade Bookshop, which had a standing order to send Chandler anything they thought he might like, Fleming learned that this year they had not been asked to. Mr Francis agreed that this was very bad news indeed. Chandler died a week later on 26 March 1959.

Fleming wrote an account of their friendship for the London Magazine *but regretted not having produced the glowing obituary that appeared in* The Times. *He never forgot how much he owed Chandler for that first, favourable review. 'I wish I had been the author,' he wrote, 'so that I could have repaid him for the wonderful tribute he had written out of the kindness of his heart for me and my publishers.' Perhaps, too, he felt a sense of loneliness at the departure of yet another of his literary heroes. They had begun to vanish with alarming rapidity over the past decade and with them had gone the context in which he had established himself. No longer was he the brave new writer of* Casino Royale *but a man whose time, like Chandler's, was running its course.*

When he sent the article for approval to Chandler's agent, Helga Greene, she agreed sorrowfully that he had captured the man: "Don't correct anything please: the mistakes are hardly important enough and the overall picture is correct, only a little bleaker, thank God, than the reality". Contradictorially, though, she later wrote, "I was so furious that it was difficult to write at all. I wonder if the sarcasm will get through Fleming's thick skin?" She attached a note to Chandler's file in UCLA saying "that the executrix of the estate wishes to point out that this article is quite inaccurate and should not be used as a basis for any studies on how Raymond Chandler worked or wrote".

12

Thunderball

DURING THE LAST half of 1959 Bond's future on the silver screen quavered uncertainly. Inspired by Ernie Cuneo's first draft for a screenplay, Fleming had produced a sixty-seven-page treatment, with substantial alterations and additions, which he then passed on to Ivar Bryce and the producer Kevin McClory. In turn, McClory made his own suggestions and amendments to which were added the attentions of a professional screen writer, Jack Whittingham. By the end of the year, however, Bryce's interest had waned, leaving McClory still enthusiastic but with no certainty of a backer. Meanwhile, Fleming had other things on his mind.

Lord Kemsley having sold the paper to a new magnate, Roy Thomson, Fleming's easy-going arrangement with the *Sunday Times* was coming to an end. In November 1959 he was sent on a trans-global expedition from which sprang a series of articles that would eventually form the first half of his travelogue *Thrilling Cities*. The journey took him to Hong Kong, Macao, Tokyo, Honolulu, Los Angeles, Las Vegas, Chicago and New York. Each destination had its own charm, but in an age when any flight was an adventure his description of air travel was almost as thrilling as the cities themselves. Few readers could resist the exoticism of a sentence that read, 'An hour or more of slow, spectacular sunset and blue-black night and then Beirut showed up ahead – a sprawl of twinkling hundreds-and-thousands under an Arabian Nights new moon that dived down into the oil lands as the Comet banked to make her landing.'

It was to be one of his last assignments as a *Sunday Times* employee. As the Kemsley apparatus adjusted itself to Thomson's regime, Fleming looked for a new office and a new secretary. For the former he settled on a room in Mitre Court, off Fleet Street, and for a secretary he chose Beryl Griffie-Williams, who would prove a dedicated, efficient, fiercely loyal guardian and one on whom Fleming would increasingly rely. Then, in January 1960, he was off to Goldeneye for another Bond novel.

Given that McClory's project seemed to be in a state of flux, Fleming saw no reason not to use elements from the outline as a basis for his next novel, *Thunderball*. The book starts with Bond being sent for a detox at the Shrublands health retreat where, after a contretemps with one Count Lippe, whom he scalds to immobility in a steam bath, he learns that an American plane containing atom bombs has been hijacked from its base in Britain, and the two countries are being ransomed to the tune of £100 million. Behind the demand is a group called SPECTRE, 'The Special Executive for Counterintelligence, Terrorism, Revenge and Extortion' – of which, it transpires, Count Lippe was a member. SPECTRE is a perfect storm of evil, combining veterans from every violent organisation in the world – the Gestapo, Triads, SMERSH and the Mafia – under the overall control of Ernst Stavro Blofeld.

Born in the Polish port of Gdynia, to a German father and a Greek mother, Blofeld is an overweight, asexual, power maniac who, like most Bond villains, has a physical peculiarity: the pupils of his eyes, like Mussolini's, are completely surrounded by the whites. But while Blofeld is the spider in the web, it is one of his subordinates whom Bond must face: Emilio Largo, ex-member of an elite Italian naval unit, whose luxury yacht, the *Disco Volante*, supposedly involved in a hunt for sunken treasure, is anchored off Nassau.

Flying to the Bahamas, Bond teams up with his old friend Felix Leiter to locate the hijacked plane, now camouflaged in shallow water. Having enlisted the support of Largo's mistress Domino, whose brother had been the pilot, Bond launches an underwater assault with the aid of American frogmen to retrieve the bombs. When cornered by Largo in an undersea cave he is saved by Domino, who fires a spear gun into

Largo's chest. On both sides of the Atlantic the operation is known by the code name Thunderball.

Fleming wasn't happy with the manuscript, which he thought not up to his usual standard. Perhaps this was because he had lived with the idea for so long that it had lost its freshness, or maybe that having a ready-made outline to hand he dashed it off too fast. In January he warned Wren Howard to, 'Tell Wm. P. I'm half way through a long and very dull Bond & to sharpen his red pencil as never before.' He was, however, fond of his latest villain, Blofeld – so much so that he gave him his own birth-date, 28 May 1908 – and would feature him in another two adventures.

If Fleming wasn't happy with the book then McClory and Whittingham certainly weren't either. As far as they were concerned Fleming had simply stolen their material. He replied that he was writing a book of the film, should it ever materialise. Differences of opinion led to lawyerly exchanges and a 1963 court case that was settled with Fleming's admission that his novel was based on a treatment by himself, McClory and Whittingham.*

Even as the idea of a *Thunderball* film began to disintegrate, Fleming worked the broadcast seam. In March 1960 he met a glamorous agent named Ann Marlow, at Sardi's in New York, and later that year, over champagne and scrambled eggs, he assigned her agency rights for TV and radio. Tearing a piece off the menu he scrawled boldly, 'To MCA – I would like Ann Marlow to be my exclusive radio and television repre-sentative – worldwide'. To which he added his signature and address.

Later, he followed the success of his first 'Thrilling Cities' articles with a second instalment that saw him driving across Europe to report on Hamburg, Berlin, Vienna, Geneva, Naples and Monte Carlo. He examined everything with his usual eye for the unconventional, and in Naples was delighted to secure an interview with 'Lucky' Luciano, the Mafia boss who had helped the Allies during their occupation of Italy in the Second World War.

Then, in November 1960, he was back in Beirut for a connecting flight to Kuwait, whose rulers (under the auspices of the Kuwait Oil

---

* The matter did not end there. Court cases continued after Fleming's death and the dispute was not fully resolved until 2012.

Company) had invited him to write a book about its emergence as an oil-rich, modern state. He wasn't the first to be enlisted as a Gulf propagandist – Dylan Thomas had written pungently about the region for Anglo-Persian Oil in 1952 – but although Fleming managed to uncover a tale of missing treasure, and described an extraordinary battle between a scorpion and a tarantula, he struggled to muster any enthusiasm for the place. When the Kuwait Oil Company received his manuscript, titled *State of Excitement*, they were not happy with it, and in the end it was never published.

Throughout 1961 Fleming continued to pursue Ann Marlow as an avenue to Bond's televisual success. But then came a firm offer from film producers Cubby Broccoli and Harry Saltzman.* Faced, at last, with the chance of achieving what he had always hoped for, Fleming struggled to extricate himself from his deal with Marlow. In the end she conceded gracefully.

Thunderball being a contentious topic, Broccoli and Saltzman decided to start with a different novel: *Dr No*. Their arrangement with Fleming involved one or two legal hesitations but by 1962 filming was underway.

TO A. L. HART JR., ESQ., The Macmillan Company, 60, Fifth Avenue, New York 11, U.S.A.

Before leaving for Jamaica, Fleming sent his friend and publisher Al Hart a note to say that he was quitting Macmillan in favour of a different US publisher, Viking.

2nd December, 1959

We spoke and I still have blood on my hands from the meeting but this is now the formal letter which I suppose is necessary.

Briefly, I would be very grateful if the Macmillan Company would release me from my contract with them so that I can try my hand with the Viking Press.

As you know, several publishers have tried to persuade me to leave Macmillans and I have always resisted them on the grounds of my general satisfaction with Macmillans and in particular because of

* Albert R. Broccoli (1909–96), Harry Saltzman (1915–94).

the very happy personal relationship you and I have always had together.

On the other hand, I have always felt slightly lost in the huge firm of Macmillans and I would like to try my hand at a smaller house to whom I would perhaps be more important. Several of my friends, including Graham Greene and Peter Quennell, are published by Vikings and it is they who have recommended the firm to me.

I have spoken with Vikings and I believe they will consider inviting Macmillans to sell them the old James Bond titles as and when they go out of print with you. I hope this may be possible.

Finally please believe that I am most grateful to Macmillans for having given me shelter for so long and so rewardingly. As for yourself, I will not offend you with any clichés. All I can say is that I expect we shall both miss each others letters.

I am sending a copy of this to Phyllis Jackson at M.C.A. who are now, after the departure of Naomi Burton from Curtis Brown, my North American agents and I expect she will be getting in touch with you about the details of all this. I am also sending a copy to Jonathan Capes to keep them informed.

TO RICHARD CHOPPING

22nd March, 1960

It was very nice to hear from you, although the subject is rather a grisly one about which Michael Howard had already written to me in Jamaica.

I entirely agree with you that all your work ought to be much more highly paid, but I am thinking much more of squeezing the millionaires.

The position regarding the wonderful jackets you have done for me – and the last one is just as splendid as the others – is that Jonathan Capes pay their standard fee of 25 guineas and I pay the rest. I have always been very happy to do this, since your work is so marvellous that I am left with a picture that both Annie and I love to have, but I have not really bargained – though I am sure I ought to have – for more than double the usual price.

How would 100 guineas suit you?

If you feel this is a miserable recompense, please add on what you think would be a fair compromise and I shall naturally agree, but only on condition that you continue to do my jackets every year.

The main thing is that it was marvellous of you to take on the job so readily and so quickly and so brilliantly, and I assure you I shall not argue if you think a higher price would be right.

See you very soon I hope.

TO WILLIAM PLOMER

29th March, 1960

I was delighted with your brother's joke from Jamaica, and so was Annie. I am sorry I missed him.

Fragrantise is one of my own words for 1959, and I apply it lavishly.

I have finished a giant Bond, provisionally called "Thunderball" (which the critics will know what to do with).

For all I know it is just about that, and I am wondering if it is worth doing a fresh typescript before you have seen it.

You may say that it needs drastic re-writing. I certainly got thoroughly bored with it after a bit, and I have not even been able to re-read it, though I have just begun correcting the first chapters. They are not too bad – it is the last twenty chapters that glaze my eyes.

Would it be a good idea, however mucky and totally uncorrected the type, if you were to give it a piercing glance before I start hacking around?

If you think it will get by, that will be all right, but if you think it definitely won't I would go down to Swanage or somewhere and try and do some re-writing – much as I should hate it.

I do not know if you will think this is a good idea or not – probably not. Anyway, please let me know and I will bring the stuff, or not, with me when we have lunch together.

Would Wednesday, the lucky 13th April, suit you? I am longing to see you and hear all the gossip.

TO MRS. JEAN FRAMPTON, Mayfield, Bockhampton, Christchurch, Hants.

Jean Frampton was the typist who turned Fleming's messy manuscripts into something fit for the typesetters. She often had useful comments to make, and for this book Fleming implored her to spare no efforts.

31st March, 1960

Dear Mrs. Frampton,

I hope you will now clear your desk for a further chore on my behalf.

I have written a full-length James Bond story, provisionally called "Thunderball", and I am correcting my original manuscript bit by bit. I now enclose the first four chapters which I would be most grateful if you would type, one original plus four or five copies, whichever is easier for your machine.

I am afraid this is not a good typescript and I would be deeply obliged if you would apply your usual keen mind to any points – <u>absolutely any</u> – that might help the book get into shape.

Naturally this kind of editing would earn an extra fee and I only ask you to undertake it because your occasional comments on the work you have done for me have been so helpful.

Anything that your quick eye and mind falls upon, <u>however critical</u> and in whatever aspect of the writing, would be endlessly welcome.

I am sorry to have to pass on to you a rather half-baked job, but I have so much work pressing in on me from all sides that in this particular instance a little help from an intelligent person like yourself would be most valuable.

I shall be sending you further chapters as I go through them for obvious errors.

TO RICHARD CHOPPING

20th July, 1960

I gather Michael Howard has had a talk to you about a possible jacket for a new book, and I also gather that you are waiting on me to hear further details of the picture I suggested to you when last we met.

Briefly, I would now very much like you to do a picture for me, whether it will be a jacket or not, for a fee of 200 guineas, if you think that reasonable.

The picture would consist of the skeleton of a man's hand with the fingers resting on the queen of hearts. Through the back of the hand a dagger is plunged into the table top.

Michael and I will assemble the props and send them down to you if you feel you would like to do this picture, and a tentative deadline would be early September if you can possibly manage that.

Please do this Dickie as it would be a really wonderful subject for your macabre vein.

FROM MICHAEL HOWARD

As Fleming continued to worry about the quality of Thunderball, *Michael Howard wrote to reassure him.*

18th August, 1960

I suppose it is because you present such an urbane and sturdy front to the world that one tends to forget the quivering sensibilities of the artist which lie behind it. But they must account for those acute pangs of doubt and dissatisfaction which you have repeatedly expressed to William and to me, for which neither of us can see any real justification.

Let me say first of all – since sometimes I have been inclined to let this be taken for granted – that we want to publish THUNDERBALL: but more than that, may I assure you that I have the fullest confidence that we can take your sales a great stride forward with it. I mean to sell just twice as many as before and I shall not rest until we do. And what's more I mean to sell them at 16s. so there will be even more in it for you. [. . .]

The only criticism of any substance which I would make is at the end, where I really feel that some explanation is needed for Domino's sudden reappearance on the seabed, having apparently escaped 'with one mighty bound' from her captivity and torture aboard the

'Disco' and furnished herself with a bikini and aqualung despite her state of shock. That, however, is one of the points you are already polishing.

For the rest, I am inclined to believe that the rather more realistic approach and absence of excruciating incidents is an advantage. So is the length which is not, by any means, excessive and I did not find my interest flagging anywhere. The underwater scenes, the little bit of gambling, the sidelights on catering arrangements are all excellently done and exactly what is expected of you. Really you have done it again quite superbly and you need have no qualms at all. Congratulations!

TO MICHAEL HOWARD

22nd August, 1960

A thousand thanks for your cheering letter and I will now get down to the corrections I hadn't already done. The final draft should be with you this week and I will also do a blurb very shortly.

So far as the oil story is concerned do you think you could procrastinate for a few more weeks until I can clear my desk of other commitments and get around to having a talk with them. Surely there is no great hurry. I don't go out there until November and I won't have written the piece before Christmas. Couldn't we let the whole project stay where it is for a few more weeks?

Again with a thousand thanks for your encouraging letter. Apparently Viking are also very pleased with the book, so at least some of my fears were unjustified, and naturally I am pleased with your plans to give it a real shove this time.

I have had two or three talks with Dickie Chopping who seems to be getting on splendidly with the jacket having found a really splendid knife in Colchester. He has accepted my idea of green baize for the background and this should make something a bit more striking.

TO MRS. R. J. FREWIN, Apartment 305, Toronto 12, Ontario, Canada

Mrs Frewin of Toronto, a sharp-witted and observant fan, took Fleming to task over several inconsistencies in his novels. Among other things she wanted to know why: a) the light above M's door seemed to be green in one book and red in another; b) Bond gained his oo qualification for killing a man in cold blood yet later said he had never done such a thing; c) the method for contacting head office seemed to vary; d) Bond took his coffee now black, now white; e) M's office was variously on the ninth floor and the eighth; and f) some of Fleming's dates didn't work.

Additionally, she bemoaned the incapacitation of Leiter in Live and Let Die, *begged Fleming to resurrect Mathis, and told him not to write any more short stories: 'They don't do him justice and your female fans may not have husbands who read* Playboy. *(So maybe the money is quicker, but since when has Bond cared about money).'* To assist him in future endeavours she supplied a plot featuring Bond, his old secretary Miss Ponsonby, and Mathis.*

'I look forward with great anticipation to the next installment.'

13th October, 1960

Dear Mrs. Frewin,

Thank you for your really wonderful letter. In searching for even the meagrest riposte, may I point out that 'instalment', the last line of your letter, is spelt with only one l.

Now, let me say at once that all your points are extremely well made though you slipped up badly in not noticing that Vent Vert is made by Balmain and not by Dior, and that the brakes on the Orient Express are not hydraulic but vacuum.

Here are the answers to your specific points:

a) Miss Moneypenny, for obvious reasons, objected to having a red light in her room, and insisted on the more appropriate pastel shade bulbs, until the day the Office of Works repainted her room in green. The day

---

* 'The Hildeband Rarity' had appeared in *Playboy* earlier in the year.

after the painting was completed, and not noticing the green light against the green paint, she went into M's room with some signals to find him fast asleep at his desk. She tiptoed out, but at once rang up the works department and had a red light fitted, which is still there.

b) Forgetfulness.

c) For security reasons the regulations for contacting headquarters are changed from time to time.

d) Bond only takes cream with his coffee at breakfast time.

e) The floors were re-numbered when two floors were concertinaed into one to accommodate very large and bulky equipment for a new communications centre. The top floor is now the eighth.

f) Yours also truly puzzled and I must talk to Bond about this.

You will realise, of course, that in writing James Bond's biography I am entirely dependent on what he tells me, and if he is occasionally equivocal, particularly in the matter of dates, I assume that he has some sound security reason for confusing me.

So far as your general comments are concerned, I should mention that Felix Leiter is by no means incapacitated, as you will have seen from 'Diamonds are Forever'. He reappears in excellent health in the next volume of the biography entitled 'Thunderball', which will be published here next April.

Mathis is in good health and spirits and Bond tells me he is almost certain to run into him again in the near future.

Thank you also very much for the suggested plot (Bentley please, not Bently!) but I am not sure that Bond is as keen as all that on Miss Ponsonby. She has recently shown signs of withering through over long protection of her virginity, and even Bond has complained to me that she is becoming neurotic.

Finally, in exchange for a letter which has given me a vast amount of pleasure and entertainment, I am sending you a copy of my last book which, it appears from your letter, you have not yet read. I am sorry it consists of short stories, but I can only write what Bond tells me. These were fragmentary adventures between his longer assignments.

Again with my warmest thanks for your deep analysis of my opuscula.

'It's "me" again', Mrs Frewin replied. While thanking him for the copy of For Your Eyes Only, *she felt it wouldn't go amiss if she said that he had a poor grasp of Canadian idiom, knew little about Quebec's linguistic niceties, had obviously never visited Canada in October and on her side of the Atlantic 'installment' was spelled with two 'l's.*

TO MICHAEL HOWARD

31st August, 1960

Dear Michael,

"Thunderball"

One or two points while I remember them.

I think readers, and certainly reviewers, must be getting rather fed up with our paeans of reviewing praise, on the back of the jacket. Can you think of any new way to say what a splendid chap I am without all these quotations? Anyway, the reviews of "For Your Eyes Only" weren't all that hot though there is a good one in the <u>New Yorker</u> which my secretary has if you want it.

The other suggestion is that this book should have a very good sale in the whole of the Caribbean area* and particularly Nassau, where it should arrive at the height of the season. Would you like to consider taking the trouble to have one of those paper bands, or whatever they are called, across the jacket of your consignment to those parts, saying, for instance, "<u>The</u> thriller set in the Bahamas"?

TO MICHAEL HOWARD

Howard had enquired about a detail in Thunderball *where the hijacker released cyanide gas to kill the plane's crew. Also about Fleming's possible promotion of Booth's gin.*

---

* To which Michael Howard appended the caustic note: 'both shops? – MH'.

5th December, 1960

My Dear Michael,

Many thanks for your letter and for the proof of the jacket which I think is quite excellent although the cards look a bit dirty and frayed at the edges. I suppose we can't brighten them up a little.

I agree that the re-write of my blurb is no great improvement. I have amended the one in the proof copy you sent me and you may even think that this is better.

I have corrected my proof to date but have had one or two suggestions from Vikings which I shall incorporate.

I am not quite sure what you mean about the film "North by North West", but anyway I am checking whether it was released on the Odeon circuit. I think the Cyanide capsule was far enough away from the murderer not to have affected him. 100% oxygen is essential, as if the air bleed was left on he would suck in some of the cyanide gas. The distinguished Wing Commander from the Air Ministry, who briefed me in all this, seemed quite happy about Pettachi breathing it in, and if 25 minutes is bad for him I am afraid we must just fudge it.

I don't know how the gin thing is going, but I couldn't bear shirts. I don't mind James Bond's name being used but I'm afraid I don't want my name to appear in promotional stuff.

I am getting on with the Kuwait book, and will get in touch with you as soon as I surface.

Heaven knows how I am going to get around to having a bash at the Thrilling Cities book, and I am afraid we must postpone any more work on it until the spring, I simply cannot squash it in.

By the way, please congratulate your printers on their proofs [of *Thunderball*] – very clean indeed with only a very few of the tiniest of literals etc.

I shall be sending you my corrected proof in a day or two. Could you please marry it up with your own corrections to save me time and worry, and if there are differences of opinion perhaps we can settle them over the telephone.

Kuwait was hell!

TO ADMIRAL J. H. GODFREY, Florence Ward, St. Thomas' Hospital, London, S.E.1.

Fleming's old boss at Naval Intelligence, Admiral Godfrey, was in poor health and had sent his now-famous assistant a note from hospital.

6th December, 1960

Sorry for the delay but I am completely submerged in Kuwait.

I saw the soothsayer during the last week of October, but, alas, I haven't kept a note of the exact date. He held my wrist watch and after discussing various other problems he said, more or less, "I see a naval officer friend of yours, he is in some kind of parental position towards you and you are friends. I can quite clearly see a naval cap badge. This friend of yours is not well and I think he would appreciate a letter from you. I advise you to write to him."

I'm afraid that is all I can remember, but you can imagine that your postcard came as something of a shock!

I do hope you are getting along all right. I shall do my best to come in and see you again this week or next, but this blasted book is making a terrible turmoil out of my life. And, just at this moment, another close friend of mine, Duff Dunbar, whom I think I have talked to you about, has had some kind of a stroke and is getting near the danger list, so that is also piling on the pressure.

Anyway get well as soon as you can, and then take it easy – useless piece of advice for someone with your lively mind!

TO MISS ANN MARLOW, Apartment 15C, 1160 Park Avenue, New York 28, N.Y.

In March 1961 Fleming suffered a heart attack. While recuperating he wrote to assure Marlow that he would soon be up and about.

1st May, 1961

My dear Ann,

A thousand thanks for your fragrant good wishes, but I can assure you that I shall be firing on all cylinders in a very short while indeed. I have spent the last three weeks in this prison writing a children's book, so the time has not been wasted.*

My arrangement with M.C.A. is simply that they are my agents for television, film and radio, and also, in America only, for books and magazine articles etc.

Here is a copy of my agreement with them which please return in due course as it is my only one.

I only met Sandford once but he seemed to me quite bright. I expect all they are worrying about is getting their 10% and this, if anything happens, I suppose they will do.

Thunderball is going great guns over here and I see that Boucher in the New York Times was fairly kind to me the other day after insulting me for many years.

It was lovely to hear from you and I pray you won't also burn too many candles at too many ends.

TO JACK WHITTINGHAM, The White House, Oxshott, Surrey

Whittingham, the scriptwriter for McClory's project, suffered a heart attack at much the same time as Fleming and wrote to exchange news.

10th May, 1961

Dear Jack,

I am horrified to hear that you have been on morphine and not only that, but that you are already contemplating your next stint at Whitsun. Is this really wise, or can you take the new thing on in a fairly leisurely fashion? It seems to me that you are getting back into your professional stride a bit quickly!

* Marlow replied, 'A children's book! Oh, those poor kids – you'll frighten them to death with James Bond Jr.'

I am so glad that your legal advisor is now in touch with my solicitor. I don't wish to sound ominous or to pre-judge anything, but I do think from what I hear from the legal cohorts on our side, that a graceful composure of such differences as you and I may have between us might be wisdom.

However, as I say, this is all on the "Old Boy" wave and the main thing is that we should both be in good heart (!) again as soon as possible.

Again, with warm thanks for your kindly letter

TO ANN MARLOW

1st June, 1961

My dear Ann,

I am now back in business and this is just to thank you very much for your letter of May 12th and to hope that you do in fact come over to London during June.

I have had a sharp squawk out of Phyllis Jackson about your and my financailles, but she arrives here on Sunday and when I see her next week I shall calm her down.

The point, as I see it, is that our arrangement is that you would like to have a shot at seeing if you can get a James Bond series going in much the same way as you dealt with Willie Maugham.

This option will obviously not be in perpetuity and the scribble I gave you over the scrambled eggs was simply to give you freedom of action with sponsors, agents, etc., for a reasonable time to test the market.

If you see no prospect of getting the property off the ground presumably you will tell me so and the responsibility will then revert to M.C.A, and you will return the engagement ring!

Personally, of course, I am hoping very much that it will be you and not some Mr. Finkelstein who becomes commère of James Bond on television, and I hope, when you have time, to hear if you have had any result, positive or negative, from your preliminary sniffing around.

But the main object of this letter is simply so that I can tell M.C.A. with a clear conscience that the James Bond properties are not in escrow to Marlow in Perpetuity, which is, in their legal minds, what they seem to think, under the spell of your beauty, has happened.

In American show-biz, and indeed in all show-biz, it seems to be just no good saying "she is just not that kind of person" or that you and I and Bill happen to be friends, this is not the language of show-biz.

So will you be an angel and write me a note covering these points in some fair and sensible way, so that I can tell M.C.A to shut-up and stop interfering in our "affaire".

Willie Maugham passed through here while I was in the London Clinic during siesta hour and was not allowed in! I wrote to tell him that at my age one needed rest after lunch and that he really ought to follow my example and not go traipsing around London at three o'clock in the afternoon! It was a shame as I had greatly looked forward to talking to him about you.

Forgive this letter which seems to have got dreadfully long and verbose.

TO ANN MARLOW

14th June, 1961

My dear Ann,

You really are an angel to have been so swift and kind with your cable and letter.

The position is that a large and worthwhile producer wishes to make a full feature film of James Bond with an option on the rest of the books. The condition, of course, is that I will not dispose of the radio and television rights during the continuance of this agreement.

In fact my scribble to you over the scrambled eggs was I now see from reading my contract with M.C.A. as you will have seen, a definite transgression on my relationship with M.C.A. which has always been pleasant and fruitful.

So what I would now like to ask you is to send me back that paper and in exchange I will ask M.C.A. to grant you on my behalf some sensible option rights as and if this present deal peters out as I have found so often happens in show biz.

I do hope that you will think this sensible and reasonable and, above all, friendly and fair.

If and when you agree I can tell you that if this present rather major project comes off and the property gets rolling, I shall do my best to see that you get a seat on the bandwagon – if any!

I will tell you more about all this when I see you in New York and in the meantime thank you again for being such a darling.

TO ANN MARLOW

3rd July, 1961

You really are an angel and I am not in the least surprised that you should feel rather 'miffed' by the way things have worked out. But the point is, as I told you, that there is a considerable film deal pending which, greatly depends, of course, on absolute cleanliness of copyright which, according to M.C.A., could not be achieved while my blank cheque to you was outstanding.

All I can do at the moment is to order you a small memento from Cartiers in token of my esteem and affection, and I shall bring this over in the Queen Elizabeth leaving on the 20th. So please keep some minutes for me for delivery and further explanations.

Mark you, all this film business may be just talk in which case our financailles can go forward undisturbed. But in all this I have simply had to be guided by M.C.A. and when I hold your hand again it will simply have to be M.C.A. who slips on the ring, as this property is now so extensive and has so many facets that if I am to milk it successfully the campaign will have to be pretty masterly.

But, as you say, we have the rest of our lives and I now once again assure you that if and when television comes into the picture your interests will be paramount with me.

Meanwhile, of course, I am longing to see you again, though by doctor's orders it can't be scrambled eggs this time!

TO ANN MARLOW

12th July, 1961

Alas, the medical brains of Britain have forbidden me to visit America next week, so those minutes I was going to steal from you will have to go to somebody else.

The small token from Cartier will have to reach you by other means and anonymously, but when it turns up you will know it is from me, it is 'From London with Love'.

It's all very maddening and I pray that fate and the doctors will be kinder later in the year.

TO ANN MARLOW

15th August, 1961

Your re-addressed letter of July 18th nearly brought about a divorce as it found its way into my wife's mail, and although I had explained to her my deep admiration and affection for you when I got back from America, quite a lot of explaining had to be explained.

(I refrain from vulgarly suggesting to you, "you've got the name let's have the game"!)

First of all, I am terribly sorry that this MM business had gone awry.* It is really very silly of her as this was a wonderful piece of casting that

---

* Marlow had failed to secure Marilyn Monroe for one of her deals.

would have vastly added to her prestige. I do hope you scramble out all right with some equally splendid girl.

I haven't seen Saltzman's announcement in the <u>New York Times</u>, but in fact, as is usual with show biz, nothing has yet been signed, and anyway if they go ahead with their film programme it will be many years before television comes into the picture.

When and if it does, I shall press your suit, if you see what I mean, with vigour.

But I am sure you will agree that if Saltzman makes a success of the films the value of any television series will be vastly enhanced.

Meanwhile I am pestiferated by doctors and lawyers and am rapidly becoming a shadow of the scrambled eggs man you know.

Have just had a cable from Bill Stephenson, please explain the situation to him as sympathetically as you can.

TO HARRY SALTZMAN, ESQ., 16, South Audley Street, London, w.1.

Producers Harry Saltzman and Cubby Broccoli soon discovered, as Cape had before them, that Fleming liked to become involved in the minutiae of production.

31st August, 1961

Dear Harry,

While I remember it, I met last night an extremely intelligent and attractive coloured man called Paul Dankwa,* who is studying law here but has been very much taken up by the bohemian set, and I have met him on and off for several years.

He told me he had just finished appearing in the film 'A Taste of Honey'.

I think it would be worthwhile you tracking him down and having a look at him for the role of Quarrel in Dr. No. His address is,

* Paul Danquah (b. 1925), actor and lawyer, starred in several films during the 1960s and became the first black presenter of a children's programme on British TV in 1966. Despite Fleming's intervention he did not get the part.

9 Overstrand Mansions, Prince of Wales's Drive, Battersea, telephone Macaulay 5212.

I told him I would mention his name to you and he was very excited at the prospect.

He has all the qualities this role demands and, in particular, a most pleasing personality and good looks.

TO MRS. BLACKWELL, Bolt, Port Maria, Jamaica

Apart from suggesting possible cast members, Fleming decided to organise accommodation in Jamaica for the film crew of 'Doctor No,' and to arrange a recording studio for the soundtrack. Writing to his neighbour (and mistress) Blanche Blackwell he wondered if her musically inclined son Christopher might like the job.*

25th October, 1961

Forgive the typing but a lot of this is going to be boring stuff for you to pass on to Christopher.

The Company has written to Christopher giving him most of the dope and asking him to be their local contact and production assistant on 'Dr. No'.

They will probably want him to do such miscellaneous jobs as recommending hotel accommodation and beating down the proprietor, for 60 or 70 people. He will also have to dig out and suggest local actors and actresses for small parts and keep an eye on the labour to see that it keeps working happily during the six or eight weeks they will be shooting.

The suggested location is the Morant Lighthouse area with those swamps behind and the beach you and I know.

I have suggested that they put the team up at Anthony Jenkinson's hotel, but I am not sure if he has enough rooms. Christopher might like to have a word with him about it. But of course they may decide it is too far from Morant and prefer one or other of those hotels up behind Kingston.

---

* Chris Blackwell (b. 1937) had founded Island Records in 1959. Fleming's intervention was a boost to his career. In short order Blackwell became a major record producer and later introduced Bob Marley to the world.

They also want to do all their musical score for the picture in Jamaica, and this should be a real chance for Christopher to seek out talent and lease them his recording studio.

I have no idea what fee to recommend Christopher to ask for, but I should think £100 a week for his general services and extra for studio and sound recording, etc. But perhaps he had better wait and see what they offer when Saltzman, the producer, and the rest of them arrive around January 11th.

I am sure Christopher will do this job splendidly and I think he will find it enormous fun.

The producer, Terence Young,* seems very nice and the man they have chosen for Bond, Sean Connery, is a real charmer – fairly unknown but a good actor with the right looks and physique.

If Christopher does well on this assignment it can easily lead to others in Jamaica and elsewhere and an exciting sideline for him.

All your news about the hedge and the flowers is very exciting. You are an angel to have taken so much trouble and I am longing to see it all.

But this is dreadful news about the car. I have always feared you would run into trouble with it and it's a blessing that you survived. For heaven's sake get something smaller and more manageable for those twisty roads, and stop driving so fast, there's absolutely no hurry!

My Jamaica plans are now changed after many stormy sessions [with Ann] and we come out together around January 20th and have much the same programme as last year.[...]

No other news for now, but it certainly looks as if we are all going to have great fun with this film business in January.

TO SIR WILLIAM STEPHENSON, 450 East 52nd Street, New York

Stephenson cabled to berate Fleming for not making enough of his publicity – 'appears to me that you are haughtily sniffing the end of a Smith and Wesson forty five'.

---

* Terence Young (1915–94) directed three of the first Bond films.

7th November, 1961

Many thanks for your chastening cable which actually fetched up at the right address. Please use it frequently.

Not much news from here. My host of medical advisers seem to be delighted with my recovery and, as you can imagine, I am losing no time in loosening up on their counsels of moderation in all things.

The film deal with United Artists is going ahead and they are going to film "DR NO" in Jamaica in January and February, and the advance party has already gone out to prospect for location. But, as usual with show business, no actual money has actually changed hands yet.

I shall be coming out to Jamaica around January 18th and will be paying you my usual visit around the middle of March. So please warn The Pierre to lay in plenty of oysters.

TO HARRY SALTZMAN,

Fleming had already received several offers to promote products, all of which he treated with a casual shrug. Whether or not the film company wanted to consider 'product placement' he left to their own decision. The brand in question remains unknown.

7th December, 1961

My dear Harry,

I have acknowledged the attached but told them to get in direct touch with your Company.

Incidentally, I expect you will be getting similar approaches from other branded products used by James Bond.

I don't know what your policy in this matter will be, but I have personally found that the use of branded names in my stories helps the verisimilitude, so long as the products are quality products.

Admittedly one is giving free publicity to these people, but I don't think it matters so long as their products are in fact really good.

Anyway, over to you.

TO DAVID NIVEN, ESQ., White's Club, 37, St. James's Street, London, S.W.1.

The actor David Niven,* whose TV company had recently failed in its bid to acquire rights to James Bond, wrote on 23 October 1962 to ask if Fleming could think of a suitable character – 'a high-class crook, à la "Raffles" or a super-modern "Sherlock Holmes" – for him to play in forthcoming four-part series. 'Will you, dear chum, look back through your files and come up with something a little off-beat that would suit me?' Despite a proposed fee of £1,000, Fleming turned the offer down.

7th November, 1962

My dear David,

I have just this minute come back from New York working on just such a project as you suggest but for an entire television series, and the copyright situation would be terribly snarled up if I went into business with you, and I think I should gracefully decline.

However, why don't we eat a few pounds' worth of Colchesters together (at your expense) some time after you arrive? And if I have had enough baths by then I may have dreamt up a bright idea in one or another of them.

But I should warn you that my brains are boiling with the effort of keeping James Bond on the move, and I confess that my chief reason for Operation Colchester would be to see your endearing mug again.

I have to be in Tokyo from the 14th to 21st and if I eat their deadly blow fish on the wrong day of the month I may not show up, but at any rate I shall depart this life with

Affectionate regards to yourself.

Niven tried again the following year, suggesting that he could write under the pseudonym Charlie Hopkins 'and thereby not involve your valuable name in anything as tawdry as television!! In any event, don't forget I really

---

* David Niven (1910–83), Oscar-winning actor who subsequently appeared as a high-class crook in *The Pink Panther* (1963) and later starred as James Bond in a 1967 film adaptation of *Casino Royale*.

am highly experienced in this line of country and whether you ever do any-thing with us or not, do not hesitate to pick my microscopic brain.' As fur-ther inducement he added that, 'I suppose you have become my favourite writer next to Chaucer.' Again, Fleming declined.

TO RAYMOND HAWKEY, ESQ., 50 Campden Hill Towers, London, W.11

Raymond Hawkey* had produced a ground-breaking cover for the Pan paper-back edition of Thunderball. *His design, which included two bullet holes, was so striking that it inspired thriller writers for years to come.*

9th April, 1963

Dear Raymond Hawkey,

Thank you very much for the pulls of the really brilliant cover you have designed. I think it is quite splendid and I don't think the filthy lit-tle Pan sign spoils it too much.

But what happens to the skin in subsequent books? Will it change colour?

Thank you also for the amusing photograph of me and Len Deighton. I am sorry to say I thought Evans' piece was pretty skimpy, but don't tell him I said so!

TO ANN MARLOW

Marlow, ever optimistic, wondered if Fleming would be interested in a TV series about incidents in his life.

15th October, 1963

My dear Ann,

It was lovely to hear from you and your television idea sounds very interesting.[†]

---

[*] Raymond Hawkey (1930–2010), inspirational designer employed by Pan who was given free rein to produce covers for the entire Bond opus.

[†] Fleming had earlier that year relinquished rights to a TV proposal featuring his cre-ation, 'Napoleon Solo'. The character would later become a mainstay of *The Man from U.N.C.L.E.* series.

The trouble is of course that I have no control over these television series on which Eon Productions have the option after the completion of three full length James Bond feature films.

So I'm afraid the only course is for you to put your ideas to Harry Saltzman and see if he will wear them.

Naturally I would love to be involved with you over all this, but, as Terence Young should have told you, I have absolutely no say in the matter.

The Simenon interview wasn't bad, but it wasn't very cleverly edited and put together, but I expect it will appear somewhere in the States before long.

Please give my best love to Bill and Mary when you see them next.

With much affection.

TO ANN MARLOW

Despairing, Marlow suggested a programme devoid of Bond called Here's Fleming!

29th October, 1963

My dear Ann,

At last I have got the picture clear, but I am sorry to say that I simply hate the idea.

I have far too much to do anyway and I also greatly dislike projecting my image any further than I can throw it.

I am terribly sorry, but there it is and you must forgive me once again.

Much love.

13

The Spy Who Loved Me

B Y 1961 FLEMING's life had become more complicated than he would have wished. Apart from the stress of writing, which was beginning to wear him down, he and Ann were drifting apart. She was conducting a thinly disguised affair with Hugh Gaitskell, a high-ranking Labour politician, while Fleming was consorting openly with Blanche Blackwell, who owned a nearby house in Jamaica. It was all rather sad.

The turmoil seemed to have had no effect on his output, however. Perhaps it even jolted his imagination, for when he returned from Jamaica he delivered a manuscript that departed radically from the norm. Instead of the standard Bond saga, he had written a pseudo-autobiographical interlude in the life of a young woman named Vivienne Michel. Fleeing disappointment in love, Canadian-born 'Viv' leaves Europe to travel solo through the Adirondacks on a Vespa scooter. When she becomes involved in an insurance scam at the isolated Dreamy Pines Motor Court, James Bond arrives to rescue her from certain death. It contained some excruciating details that were obviously based on Fleming's early sexual experiences. And the language used by Viv to describe her saviour slipped into the farthest corners of Cartland. But it had its charms, and for the time (and for the author) it was a brave stab at reinventing Bond. At Bedford Square they thought it was just the ticket.

Fleming was on full charge when he handed it in. He had always been accused of writing beneath his abilities and now he had produced something that if not exactly literature was at least new. There was also his latest book, *Thunderball*, which had just been released and was selling well, and he had delivered the manuscript for *State of Excitement*, his book about Kuwait. Also, as a nod to his status as proprietor of *The Book Collector*, he had been invited to address the Antiquarian Booksellers Association's gathering in late July. He was full of confidence, and riding high on his success.

But his health was failing. For a long time he had had problems with his heart, to which had recently been added difficulties with his kidneys and back. He was uncertain about Bond's prospects and the legal difficulty over *Thunderball* had taken its toll. In early April, while at a *Sunday Times* meeting, he suffered a major heart attack. His friend Denis Hamilton ushered him out of the room and helped him to hospital.

Outwardly, Fleming treated it as no more than a setback. 'Being ill is heaven!' he wrote on a postcard to his half-sister Amaryllis. On the other side, in a typically wry touch, was a picture of an Aztec crystal skull. Jokingly, he drew a skull and crossbones on the back of the envelopes he sent to his friends. To Percy Muir he wrote that 'years of under work and over indulgence' had caught up with him. Behind the façade, however, he realised that life would never be the same again.

During his convalescence at the London Clinic and later at the Dudley Hotel, Hove, he was forbidden a typewriter lest he strain himself by writing a new Bond. Undeterred, he ordered pen and paper and embarked on a children's story based on the bedtime stories he told his son Caspar. It was about a magical car called 'Chitty-Chitty-Bang-Bang'.

A famous racing car, long since abandoned in a scrapyard, Chitty is rebuilt by the indefatigable tinkerer and inventor Commander Caractacus Pott. When Pott takes his family on an outing to the Kent coast, Chitty reveals hidden secrets. She not only flies, but swims and drives under her own command if the Potts are in danger. When the Potts uncover a secret cache of weapons in France, they blow it up. And when gangsters take the Pott children hostage, meanwhile pondering a heist on a famous Parisian sweet shop, it is Chitty that saves the day. Underpinning the book was Fleming's favourite mantra: 'Never say "no" to adventures. Always say "yes" otherwise you'll lead a very dull life.'

His initial suggestion for an illustrator was Wally Fawkes, whose cartoons appeared in the *Daily Mail* under the nom de plume Trog. But the *Mail* refused to allow their star cartoonist to work for an author whose books were serialised regularly in strip form by the rival *Daily Express*. As an alternative, Cape approached the illustrator Haro Hodson, but after a few trials Fleming thought his sketches were not quite right. Finally, they appointed the acclaimed artist John Burningham, whose *Borka: The Adventures of a Goose With No Feathers* had won the Kate Greenaway Medal in 1963.

But this was in the future, and in the meantime he found himself with another bit of Bonderie on his hands. To help launch the *Sunday Times'* new colour supplement, due out in 1962, C. D. Hamilton asked him to write a short story featuring 007. 'The Living Daylights', which Fleming dashed off that October, saw Bond in Berlin, providing cover for a defector who was being pursued by a Russian assassin, codenamed Trigger. The assassin, it transpires, is a woman whose cover is as a cellist in an all-female orchestra. 'There was something almost indecent in the idea of that bulbous, ungainly instrument splayed between her thighs,' Bond reflects. 'Of course Suggia had managed to look elegant, as did that girl Amaryllis somebody.* But they should invent a way for women to play the damned thing side-saddle.' When the moment comes, Bond fires not to kill but to disarm.

By late 1961 the film deal he had signed the previous year was catching fire, with an extraordinary amount of pre-production publicity that included far-fetched plans for new editions of *Dr No* put forward by Harry Saltzman. And his US sales had received a massive boost when, earlier that year, an article in *Life* magazine had listed *From Russia with Love* as one of President J. F. Kennedy's ten favourite books. By any standards it had been an extraordinary time. And yet, there was his health.

In 1961 *Queen* magazine published an article titled 'Six Questions'. The first was: 'What do you expect to achieve in the sixties? Are you

---

* His half-sister Amaryllis was by now a highly regarded cellist. When Fleming was at the height of his fame she gleefully recounted how somebody, on being introduced to him at a party, had no idea who he was and wanted to know if he was related to her.

aiming at any particular quality or quantity of work?' Fleming, one of several contributors, replied: 'One can never expect to achieve any-thing – even less if one is in the fifties and living in the sixties.

Since I am a writer of thrillers I would like to leave behind me one classic in this genre – a mixture of Tolstoy, Simenon, Ambler and Koestler, with a pinch of ground Fleming. Unfortunately I have become the slave of a serial character and I suppose, in fact, since it amuses me to write about James Bond, I shall go on doing so for the fun of it.'

TO WILLIAM PLOMER

From Goldeneye, February 1961, 'Friday, perhaps'

My dear Wm,

Thank you a thousand times for your sparkling & hilarious letter which had both of us rolling in the Bougainvillea. I am much relieved that you could stomach Kuwait. I felt almost ashamed at asking that you should read it & sub it. But I was so fed up & overstuffed with the subject that the M.S. had come to nauseate me. My main con-cern was to make it look as little as possible a P.R.O. job & from what you say I may at least have been successful in that. Of course it will get a majestic pasting from the Arabists who will get it for review but to hell with them! I'm tired of their snobbish coterie & have been for years.

The new Bond is very odd & heaven knows what you will think. I am a 23 year old French Canadian girl & writing rather breathlessly which comes, deceptively I suspect, easy. Bond is just today about to rescue her from an ugly predicament!

Good misprint in the Gleaner – about a wedding "Not to be sar-torially outdone, the bridegroom wore an orchid in his bottom-hole".

A. sends much love in which I join.

TO MICHAEL HOWARD

From Goldeneye, dated 'Saturday'

Dear Michael,

Thank you very much for your newsy letter & your father's splendid puff in the S.T. Good news about the subscription but it still leaves you with the well-packed shelves in the warehouse! If you get some early copies, would you send me one. My secretary has my movements – Nassau & then N.Y.

Bad news about Graham Greene particularly as he is a friend & stayed in this house the whole of Nov. I'm afraid we must come clean and apologise.* Would you ask Anthony Colwell† to do this, <u>at my request</u>, enclosing brochure & quote from cutting? I'm rather upset as I think I raised this point in my first letter about his draft blurb.

Got a very nice letter from Wm. & he seems to have been able to stomach the book. About a blurb – I v. much doubt if I can manage this before I get back as my mind is too much elsewhere. But why the hurry? It has only just gone to the Sheikhs!

Rather surprised about Courtaulds. What are the arrangements & what the reward?‡ I was asking Booths £5,000 for the privilege – not that they were willing to pay it – but Courtaulds is a £50,000,000 company. They should definitely not trade on my handiwork what-ever publicity my books get. And I shall also want many dozen shirts made to measure from their stuff! Would you ask Elaine Greene of M.C.A. to get in touch with them and screw them good and proper. And please rush me copies of their copy. I won't alter unless it is too ghastly – but no point making a fool of the chap. I do

---

* Fleming had hoped Greene would write an introduction to an American omnibus, *Gilt Edged Bonds*. Greene demurred at the last moment, by which time Fleming's publishers had already produced publicity material.

† Cape's new marketing director.

‡ Courtaulds, one of Britain's largest textile companies, manufactured a range of synthetic clothing. By means unknown, they managed to use James Bond to promote their products. Fleming was not happy.

wish I had been consulted about all this. You know I was very much against the project.

Paul Gallico will be too long for N&T [*Now and Then*] but we may put it to some other good use.

OK for 29th in Scotia.

Don't at all like the idea of Face to Face.* I am no good at that sort of thing & dislike being eviscerated.

Just finishing The Spy who loved me. It will be about 55,000. Absolutely no idea what it's like but it wrote rather easily which is a bad sign I expect.

TO C. D. HAMILTON, ESQ., Thomson House, 200 Gray's Inn Road, London, W.C.1

19th April, 1961

My dear C.D.,

Although neither of us knew it I am afraid I was in the middle of a rather major heart attack this time last week. One never believes these things so I sat stupidly on trying to make intelligent comments about the thrilling new project [the colour supplement] about which I long to hear more. However, a thousand thanks for noticing my trouble so quickly and for shepherding me away when the time came.

Alas, this is going to mean at least another month in the Clinic without moving and then two or three more behaving like an old man. But after that I hope I shall be quite all right again, though I shall never be able to pack quite so much into my existence as I have foolishly been trying to do.

Anyway all is well and I am splendidly looked after, and in a week or two when I am allowed to see people I do hope you will come by and tell me more of these exciting plans.

As I am not supposed to be writing I will ask my secretary to sign this and send it off. In the meantime thank you again for taking me firmly by the hand!

* A BBC TV series of probing and often psychologically revealing interviews.

TO WILLIAM PLOMER

From 'Shrublands', April 1961, Sunday

My dear Wm,

I have been here for nearly a week, condemned to four more, & then 5 months inactivity. Heart! I think telling all those funny stories in Glasgow* was the last straw!

Now, forgive me for adding one more pat on the poor dung-beetle's back but this is going to stop me doing much work on "the S who L'd me" and as I have grave doubts about it would you be an angel & read it in its present, not bad, typescript – but entirely privately – & then tell me what you think. You see, there is an excellent opportunity to kill off Bond, appropriately & gracefully, & though when it came to the point in the story I forbore, I feel, and have felt before this address, that the time has come.

If you would read it, would you be an angel & call here on Wed a.m. if you can manage (sleep in p.m.) & I will explain more & give you the shovelful to take away.

Forgive this whiff of miscellaneous grapeshot & fear not for my health which in fact is quite excellent & will become far better for this very necessary little jog in the ribs from the Holy Man.

P.S. No primroses from Bob Howard, please!

TO MRS. VALENTINE FLEMING, Grosvenor House, Park Lane, London W.1.

24th April, 1961

Darling Mama,

Forgive me dictating this but they still refuse to let me do any writing.

I adore the splendid anthurium and its buds are already showing a fine form. It was a terribly clever idea as it's such fun seeing how it changes every day and thank heaven it will outlast my three or four more weeks in this dump.

* Where Fleming had been interviewed by Geoffrey Boothroyd.

As for caviar and smoked salmon, they just about keep me alive!

Next week I shall be allowed to have an occasional visitor, so please come in and tell me that you have found yourself a good expensive maid to look after you.

With stacks of love.

TO THE RT. HON. CHRISTOPHER SOAMES, C.B.E., M.P., Ministry of Agriculture, Fisheries and Food, Whitehall Place, London, S.W.1.

24th April, 1961

My dear Christopher,

You may have seen from the public prints an exaggerated account of a mild malaise that is keeping me away from the bridge tables. (By the way poor old Dovercourt passed on in the next room last Saturday!)

Now the point is that I am condemned for the rest of my life to three ounces of hard liquor per day, and since I have to be really rather careful about it I wish to concentrate on the purest and finest liquor obtainable in England. This vital piece of information will be known in your Ministry – i.e. which is the finest refined spirit, gin whisky or brandy on the market at any price.

Do you think you could possibly extract this vital piece of information on the absolute understanding that this is for my private information only?

I am so sorry to bother you with this picayune enquiry, but it is just conceivable that you also may be interested in the reply.

TO MICHAEL HOWARD

To keep Fleming's mind busy Michael Howard sent him one of Cape's latest – Mad Shadows, *a tale of dysfunctional family life by the twenty-year-old Canadian author Marie-Claire Blais.*

24th April, 1961

Thank you very much for the charming note and I can assure you that I shall be firing on all cylinders again before too long. Meanwhile I am writing a children's book, so you will see that there is never a moment, even on the edge of the tomb, when I am not slaving for you.

I read the Canadian prodigy last night and was macabrely fascinated. I suppose this is the sort of best fairy story our children will all be reading in the future.

As always a beautifully produced and jacketed book, again the jacket so good it deserved an author to it!

Hope you are not getting too stuck with Thunderball. Do please let my secretary know from time to time how you are getting on with it.

TO HUGO PITMAN, ESQ.,* Willmount, Ballingarry, Thurles, Co. Tipperary

25th April, 1961

Dearest Hugo,

Thank you for your lovely letter which was just the glass of champagne I needed.

My doctors are delighted with me and I think I only have another two or three weeks here before being allowed to go down to Brighton to sit in one of those blasted shelters and look at the yellow sea.

After that I shall gradually get back into commission and the only difference in my life will be that you and I have to have lunch on the ground floor of Scotts instead of the first!

With much love to you and kisses for any women who may be around you!

---

* Hugo Pitman, an old friend, was connected to the stockbrokers Rowe and Pitman, for whom Fleming had worked in the 1930s.

TO THE REVEREND LESLIE PAXTON, Great George Street Congregational
Church, Liverpool

*In between letters to family, friends and editors, Fleming found time to rebuke
a vicar in Liverpool, who had recently lambasted Bond as the epitome of
worldly vice.*

25th April, 1961

Dear Mr. Paxton,

I see from the public prints that the Sunday before last you preached
a sermon against the leading character in my books, James Bond, and,
presumably by association against myself.

Now, having had a Scottish nonconformist upbringing and considering myself at least some kind of sub-species of a Christian, I am naturally very upset if it is thought that I am seriously doing harm to the
world with my James Bond thrillers.

Would you be very kind and let me have a copy, if you have one, of
your sermon, so that I may see the burden of your criticisms and perhaps find means of mending my ways if I feel that your arguments have
real weight behind them.

I can, of course, myself see what you might mean about my books,
but it occurs to me that you may have put forward profounder arguments than those which are already known to me.

Forgive me for troubling you in this way, but I am sure you will agree that
the prisoner in the dock should at least know the burden of the charge.

FROM WILLIAM PLOMER

28th April, 61

My dear Ian,

I am in the middle of being <u>absorbed</u> by the results of your collaboration
with Mademoiselle Viv (Bimbo) Michel – your best she-character up to
now – and am annoyed at having to break off the process of absorption

to write a letter. But I do want to say that I think the book full of your usual brio and Schlauheit & to let you know that I am <u>much</u> enjoying as well as absorbing it.

If you like, I would like to look in on you next Wednesday morning at about 11.30. I could bring with me a very few notes & queries, & could tell you by then how the book strikes me as a whole. Send me two words to say

a) if I may come & see you then;
b) if I may hand the typescript over to Michael Howard on Wednesday;
c) if there is anything else I can bring you.

When I do come, I will try not to exhaust you by prolonged loquacity.

I hope you are feeling as free as possible from anxieties & fatigue.

Your old chum Bob Howard asked me to give you his best messages & to say that he hadn't written to you only because he doesn't want to badger you with correspondence.

TO WILLIAM PLOMER

From Clinholm, 30th April, 1961

My dear William,

As you can imagine, your first reactions to the book were a shot of mescalin, but don't feel you have to be gracious about the second chunk for fear of plunging me beneath the sod. From you I need no placebos. Only the true verdict will do & I can assure you that my E.C.G. can stand anything now. Let us decide about Michael when we have spoken at 11.30 on Wed. If you feel there is much to be done, I would rather do the tidying up before it gets into the pipeline.

I am of course longing to see you & please bring nothing but your face! Your last visit was more beneficial than you can imagine – apart from other considerations, to hear other peoples' tales of woe greatly reduces the perspective of one's own.

Coming to Metropole, Brighton, on Monday, fortnight until Friday. With Annie. It would be lovely to fix a 'déjeuner sur l'herbe', or 'sur les sables couvertes de capotes anglaises',* somewhere between us. Please consider & deliver your instructions on Wed.

Am receiving the most extraordinary advices from various genii. "Be more spiritual" (Noël Coward), "write the story of Admiral Godfrey" (Admiral Godfrey), "Be sucked off gently every day" (Evelyn Waugh).

Over to you!

TO MICHAEL HOWARD

31st May, 1961

My dear Michael,

Many thanks for your letter of May 26th and also for the book which I liked very much at first sight. If I go on liking it I will certainly write you a short review for "Now and Then".

I am now sending you the first two "volumes" of Chitty-Chitty-Bang-Bang. Heaven knows what your children's book readers will think of them, but they are in fact designed for a readership of around seven to ten.

If you decide that you like them much will depend on the illustrator and I wonder if we couldn't get Trog. He is by way of being a friend of mine since he did the John Bind series in Fluke. I only fear that he might be too expensive.

Anyway please let me know what you think of the whole gambit and we will then decide what to do about it.

M.C.A, New York, liked the SWLM, but I haven't yet heard from Vikings whom I had asked for plenty of suggested corrections and I will wait for them before going over the ms again.

But I would be very interested to hear the reactions of your readers if and when you get any.

* Brighton's shingle beach.

I am now gradually reactivating myself and I hope to be up in London for about two days each week. Though much will depend on a gigantic medical conference this afternoon.

Yours ever.

TO MRS. VALENTINE FLEMING, Hotel Mirabeau, Monte Carlo, Monaco

Fleming's mother, who since the war had flitted between various grand addresses, smart hotels and exotic destinations, had come temporarily to rest in Monte Carlo with her ancient beau, the ninety-eight-year-old 'Monty', Marquis of Winchester.

1st June, 1961

Darling Mama,

I am now up and about again but still not supposed to write much so please forgive the dictation.

It was lovely to get your birthday present and I shall have great fun buying myself something to relieve the boredom of convalescence.

Brighton for a fortnight was a great tonic, and at a giant meeting of the various doctors yesterday they seemed satisfied. Though it does sound as if convalescence from one of these things is, in fact, more or less endless and that I shall have to "take care" for ever more, which is very much against my nature.

However, as everyone says, it might have been much worse and you will be amused to know that The Times had actually written my obituary when it seemed that the tomb was about to yawn! I am doing everything I can to see if I can't get hold of a copy.

Please don't worry too much about the house [Sevenhampton]. I am not happy about it myself but it's quite impossible being married unless you are prepared to compromise, and I shall just help Anne as much as I can with it and go fifty/fifty on the cost. At least it will be a good solid base in the country, and I expect fairly soon after it is finished we will forsake Victoria Square, and I shall take to planting lupins, or some other elderly and responsible pursuit, as it seems that strenuous golf is now out for always.

It sounds as if you have at last got your Monte Carlo life more or less straight, and I am delighted that the Rolls is being a success, and I do hope that the maid will be a real help. As for Monty, I do beg you to leave all the grisly nursing to nurses and not wear yourself out carrying bowls of soup (and other hospital ware!) around.

It is sweet of you to offer the Villa Mary, but it doesn't look as if we shall be able to get away for some time. Why don't you move into it yourself, or are you really happier in that small cell in the Mirabeau?

Caspar is getting on very well at [his school] Summer Fields and curiously enough being pushed rapidly up the school. He has even been made head of his dormitory, from which I can only guess that the other inhabitants must be the most appalling collection of little monsters. Anyway he is looking wonderful and one of the factors that decided us on Warneford was that he simply adores having a place to run about in, and it will be close by both for Summer Fields and Eton, and it has the Thames nearby for expeditions.

Please don't worry any more about me. I shall just have to adjust myself to "growing old gracefully", which will be a most entertaining spectacle for my family and friends!

TO MICHAEL HOWARD

Howard replied on 5 June to Fleming's letter of 31 May: 'CHITTY CHITTY BANG BANG's adventures have me enthralled. She is truly an invention of genius, and I trust that you can reel off at least ten more episodes with no trouble at all.' He was less certain about an idea that Fleming put forward in the interim, that they should be published under the pseudonym 'Ian Lancaster'.

6th June, 1961

My dear Michael

Very many thanks for your letter of yesterday and I am delighted that you like the first two CHITTY-CHITTY-BANG-BANGS. I must confess that

I have no idea what to do with her next, but I suppose it would be possible to keep up to a book a year.

So far as the illustrator goes, if Trog were interested I am not sure it wouldn't be desirable to enter into some kind of partnership with him by which he would be assured of, let us say, a third of the royalties. This would give him enthusiasm in the project and make the thing a joint effort, which such books should really be. If you think well of the idea and you see no objection, I would not be worried if you were to have a talk with him on this basis. Perhaps the best idea would be to have a triangular lunch together if you can fix that. He is an extremely nice man and great fun, and from the quality of his cartoons in the Spectator I am quite sure he has the graphic qualities we need, though he would have to bend his mind rather carefully to the original drawing of the car which must, I think, not look <u>too</u> funny.

I doubt if you will get much reaction out of William. I mentioned the project to him but he can't bear children's books and it will be much more important I think to get the judgement of your regular children's books advisor.

One small point while it crosses my mind. I find that in these children's series the parents very often can't remember if little Billy has had just this particular adventure. So might I suggest that each volume should be in a distinctive colour and that the number of the adventure should be emphasised?

Of course I have no objection to being linked with the books in a vague way, but I am not sure that that will necessarily help their sales!

I will press on with correcting TSWLM and will hope to have it with you by the end of the month, though of course Vikings may come in with a shower of suggestions and criticisms.

By the way, although it is something of a trade secret which you should keep to yourself, The Sunday Times is going to break out into a shiny paper colour supplement instead of its magazine section towards the end of the year, and it is quite possible that they would like to serialise these CHITTY-BANG-BANG stories. Although this would gobble up a lot of your readership, not everybody in England reads The Sunday

Times, but you might bear the possibility in mind from the point of view of timing the illustrators' work.

I only mention this now as C. D. Hamilton has just been on the telephone about something else and I mentioned our new venture and he was enthusiastic.

You may be amused to see what Macmillans have done with your jacket. Pretty good for them!

Yours Ever.

TO THOMAS H. GUINZBURG, ESQ., The Viking Press Inc., 625 Madison Avenue, New York 22

Guinzburg, head of the American publishing house Viking, was uneasy about Fleming's latest. He wrote on airmail paper (Fidelity Onion Skin) that, 'the various readers feel this draft, while it is certainly acceptable Fleming, is not quite top-grade Fleming'. He suggested he put the manuscript aside for a while and write a couple of other books first. Cape, he pointed out, had already established a market for Bond but, 'We, on the other hand, are only just beginning to establish the elements of the specific apparatus that surrounds and enhances the image of Bond, and we are afraid that this story, at least in its present form, does a disservice to that kind of emphasis.'

20th June, 1961

Dear Tom,

Many thanks for your piece of Fidelity Onion Skin of June 9th but I am indeed horrified to hear of poor Harold's troubles. Please give him my warmest wishes for a rapid recovery and urge him to take a decent and non-business holiday and not to hurry back to work.

Now, about "The Spy Who Loved Me", oddly enough the very reasons for your doubts about it are those put forward by Capes for any special virtues it possesses.

All at Capes think the breakaway from the routine Bond both healthy and desirable and in his most recent letter Michael Howard expects to do even better with it than <u>Thunderball</u>, which is now just over 40,000.

As for your idea of holding up its publication until I have written a couple more conventional full length thrillers, you seem to think that I am a Rex Stout!* I have scraps of ideas for future books but nothing in the least firm. And heaven knows when these two imaginary thrillers will, in fact, get written.

Accordingly, I am afraid I must put the ball back in your court. Bond is after all the hero of this book and though he is seen through the looking glass so to speak, Capes are sure that the new gimmick is an excellent idea.

Meanwhile you have had a note from me about Mr. Liebert from the Yale Library, and, unilaterally, I have taken advantage of his offer and he is at the moment correcting the American lingo and the American background to the story with a delighted and very sharp pen. He has undertaken to return the corrected manuscript to me by July 6th, since Capes want to get it into page proof during August.

Perhaps it would be as well for you to put away the uncorrected typescript I sent you and wait to see Cape's page proofs before you decide what you want to do.

My own recommendation is for you to take the rough with the smooth and drown your doubts in strong liquor.

Incidentally, would you please activate your publicity people and ask them to send me some reviews of T'ball. I have had nothing from Vikings except a few meagre scraps early on, nor any news of how the book is going.

Macmillans, as you know, are producing their Omnibus on July 24th, and no doubt this will also activate your sales of <u>Thunderball</u>.

TO MRS. JAMES BOND, 721, Davidson Road, Chestnut Hill, Philadelphia 18, Pasadena

'It was inevitable we should catch up with you . . .' On which ominous note Mrs James Bond began her letter of 1 February 1961. Fleming had never made any secret of the fact that he had borrowed his hero's name from one

---

* Rex Stout (1876–1975), prolific American thriller writer, creator of Nero Wolfe.

of his favourite books, Birds of the West Indies, *by the American orni-thologist James Bond. But now, almost ten years after he had written* Casino Royale, *news reached the Bonds that* 'you had brazenly picked up the name of a real human being for your rascal'. *They didn't really mind, as the real Bond had led an adventurous life, his colourful exploits being not too far, in the ornithological scale of things, from those of his fic-tional equivalent. 'I told MY JB he could sue you for defamation of charac-ter,' Mrs Bond concluded cheerfully. 'But JBBA [James Bond British Agent] is too much fun for that and JB authenticus regards the whole thing as "a joke".'*

20th June, 1961

Dear Mrs James Bond,

I don't know where to begin to ask your forgiveness for my very tardy acknowledgement to your letter of February 1st.

I received it in Jamaica and since I was almost on the way to Nassau I decided to telephone the Chaplins on arrival and get in touch with you and your husband.

Unfortunately I could get no reply from their telephone number and I again put your letter aside. Then, when I got back to England in March, I proceeded to have a swift heart attack which laid me out until now, and it is only today that your letter is again before me and blackest of consciences is sitting on my shoulder.

I will confess at once that your husband has every reason to sue me in every possible position and for practically every kind of libel in the book, for I will now confess the damnable truth.

I have a small house which I built in Oracabessa in Jamaica just after the war and, some ten years ago a confirmed bachelor on the eve of mar-riage, I decided to take my mind off the dreadful prospect by writing a thriller.

I was determined that my secret agent should be as anonymous a personality as possible, even his name should be the very reverse of the kind of "Peregrine Carruthers" whom one meets in this type of fiction.

At that time one of my bibles was, and still is, "Birds of the West Indies" by James Bond, and it struck me that this name, brief, unromantic and yet very masculine, was just what I needed and so James Bond II was born, and started off on the career that, I must confess, has been meteoric culminating with his choice by your President as his favourite thriller hero (see Life of March 17th).

So there is my dreadful confession together with limitless apologies and thanks for the fun and fame I have had from the most extraordinary chance choice of so many years ago.

In return I can only offer your James Bond unlimited use of the name Ian Fleming for any purposes he may think fit. Perhaps one day he will discover some particularly horrible species of bird which he would like to christen in an insulting fashion that might be a way of getting his own back.

Anyway I send you both my most affectionate regards and good wishes, and should you ever return to Jamaica I would be very happy indeed to lend you my house for a week or so, so that you may inspect in comfort the shrine where the second James Bond was born.

TO R. CHOPPING, ESQ., The Store House, The Quay, Wivenhoe, Essex

22nd June, 1961

The jacket season has come round once again and I and Cape do pray that you will once again be the artist for the same fee of two hundred guineas, if you still think that reasonable recompense.

If, as I desperately hope, you agree we are in rather a quandary this time to suggest a suitable motif, and it occurred to me that you might have some brilliant idea for there are no emblems in the book which would be in any way suitable.

The title of the book is "The Spy Who Loved Me" and so what suggests itself of course is a juxtaposition between a dagger or a gun and an emblem representing love, rather on the lines of your gun with the rose.

But what can we use now?

How about one of those frilly heart shaped Valentines with a dagger thrust through it?

Or there might be young ivy leaves entwined in a gun, or forget-me-nots.

But none of these ideas thrill me with the possible exception of the Valentine with a splendid red heart pierced by a dagger.

But it crossed my mind that you have painted many keepsakes for people and that something might conceivably suggest itself to you.

Anyway, first of all, will you please do the jacket and, secondly, will you please have a brilliant idea?

I am back on all fours again and any time you are in London we could meet perhaps here and rub our two brains together.

I will now ring up Heywood Hill and see if they have any Valentines.

TO MICHAEL HOWARD

22nd June, 1961

Very many thanks for your letter of yesterday and I am delighted, but mildly astonished, that your Children's Book department has swallowed CCBB with so much gusto.

As to the points, they are all perfectly legitimate, except that CCBB in fact does a hundred in top gear, though I may have written this in a muddled fashion.

Now you are extremely kind to suggest that someone in Capes might do the editorial polishing and correct the little bits and pieces that have been brought up. I really can hardly bear to look at these stories again and anyway I am knee deep in "The Spy" and other bits and pieces.

So could I now leave the text to you and merely have a final look through the finished product?

I think I have very good news about Trog, whose real name and address is W.E. Fawkes, 24A Eton Avenue, N.W.3.

He is, in theory, delighted with the whole idea and has taken the stories off to read. He has been longing to illustrate a book and is not in any way tied up. So it is possible that you will have another valuable property on your hands as he really is a household name, which will vastly help to sell the series.

He very much likes the idea of a partnership with two thirds of the royalties to me and one third to him.

When he has given his final decision I think I will ask him to get in direct touch with you so that you can talk over the number of illustrations, the use of colour, etc.

I told him that as far as I knew you had no suggested date for publication and that you weren't contemplating trying to rush this out in time for Christmas, but, in fact, he is a very fast worker and I think would fit in with any plans you may have.

I see the point about trying to have three or four stories to start off with, but I think there is a snag in this.

You will presumably have to market the books at around ten or twelve shillings, and while the average parent might go to two volumes I rather doubt if they would spread themselves to all four.

Moreover, there is the snag that at this moment I haven't got two more adventures in mind, though I dare say I could conjure another couple up fairly quickly if you were very insistent.

Anyway I will let you know directly Trog gives his decision and then we can get the machinery into action.

As far as "The Spy" is concerned I have nearly finished my own corrections, but in the meantime a remarkable chap has sprung to life in the Library at Yale University with some very sharp comments on the Americanese in "Thunderball". I was so impressed with his correspondence that I have now engaged him to go through "The Spy" with the sharpest possible pen to smarten up all the gangsterese and other American angles. He has agreed with alacrity, and has undertaken to air mail the text back by July 6th.

Since I fancy he may be very drastic this is going to involve me probably in a great deal of rewriting, but I hope a much improved book.

So I can't really give you a firm date for delivery of the text until I see how much has got to be done.

Anyway I shall do my very best to get it all finished by the end of July and I hope this will be all right with you.

TO MICHAEL HOWARD

Chopping's artwork for Thunderball *had been sent to Macmillan in the US for the attention of their designers. It was returned in a badly scuffed state.*

27th June, 1961

I am quite horrified with what Macmillans have done with the Chopping picture and I have no idea what can be done to rescue it.

Chopping originals fetch between £200 and £500 on the London market and God knows how much financial damage has been done to this one, let alone the sentimental value to me.

Since it was through your agency that this was sent to Macmillans I think it would be better for you to write to them as from one publisher to another, sending Al Hart a Photostat to demonstrate the damage.

By the way, something else horrible has happened! I took my son this afternoon to see the new Walt Disney film and it has a flying motor car which circles a church spire! Moreover "The Absent Minded Professor" builds it in his back yard.

This really is the limit.

Would you send one of your intelligence spies to have a look at the film and suggest what amendments we ought to make?

Personally I think we could get away with cutting out the spire of Canterbury Cathedral, but it really is pretty maddening.

TO GUY WELLBY, ESQ., 18 & 20 Garrick Street, Covent Garden, London, W.C.2.

Fleming thought a diamond might feature to advantage in Chopping's composition for the jacket and had asked a jeweller friend, Guy Wellby, to provide photographs. In the end it proved an unnecessary (and expensive) exercise.

12th July, 1961

My dear Guy,

Thank you very much for all the trouble you took over the diamond.

I have now put the whole problem firmly in the lap of Michael Howard, Production Director at Capes, and in due course, though not very quickly I expect, he will make up his mind about the jacket.

My own guess is that the diamond will not work very well for the present book but that we will keep the photographs for possible use in the future.

Anyway, thank you very much indeed and your friend, the owner of this wonderful stone, for your swift and kindly aid, and please in due course send me a bill for the cost, addressed to me in the name of my company, Glidrose Productions Limited.

Please don't forget to thank the owner most warmly for his kindness.

TO MICHAEL HOWARD

12th July, 1961

CHITTY-CHITTY-BANG-BANG

Trog says he is delighted with the two stories and is "terribly keen" to do the illustrations.

He is going on holiday from July 22nd to August 4th and cannot do anything before his return.

May I now leave it to you to contact him direct and carry the ball from there, making an agreement with Trog on the lines of my previous suggestions?

CHOPPING JACKET – THE SPY WHO LOVED ME

Chopping will be delighted to do a jacket but has upped his price to 250 guineas and cannot get going for about three weeks.

He scribbled some vague ideas and will scribble some more.

I think this may look a bit like a flower book, and I now suggest to you that he should perhaps cross the carnation with your commando dagger well polished up, with a cipher book background.

You may think the carnation should be pinned to the cipher page with a lover's knot brooch. I have borrowed some photographs of possible diamond brooches from Cartiers. They would be quite happy to cough up the brooches for this purpose if we paid the insurance. (Mr. Brown at Cartiers is the man to contact).

As to the cipher background, the specimen page I gave to Dickie Chopping is from a Bentley Code*, which they might not like to cough up.

On another page from this book, which I have had photographed, white on black to give a better background, is technical stuff which would not be copyright.

Dickie says that white on black would be very difficult for him and I see his point. But perhaps it could be technically fudged in one way or another.

I enclose specimens of all the possible pages, Dickie only has the crumpled one.

Apart from this possible design I have located in London probably the largest blue-white heart shaped diamond in the world. This belongs to a friend of Guy Wellby, the head of Wellby's, the jewellers in Garrick Street, and at my expense he has had transparencies made of it and also blown up replicas. (They could, of course, be blown up in colour). The name of the photographer is on the box.

I don't know if you feel that something could be made of this, either now or in the future, if in the future perhaps you would like to keep them for your files.

Now hurrying on with the corrections to the Spy and with a pile of other chores on my desk I must beg you please to take over from here

* A book of ciphers first published in 1909.

with Dickie, insuring [sic] that Tony Colwell informs Cartiers and Guy Wellby if we do not require their various jewellery, and otherwise coping with detail.

Personally, I think the carnation with your dagger is the right idea.

Sorry to transfer these two chunks of work on to your lap, but mine is not feeling very solid at the moment.

TO MICHAEL HOWARD

27th July, 1961

Here now is "The Spy Who Loved Me" cleaned up as best I know how and I hope to your satisfaction.

Could you give me any idea of when I am likely to have page proofs?

My present plans are to stay in London and Sandwich for the foreseeable future.

By the way, as you may know a vast film deal involving all the Bond books is in progress with United Artists spearheaded by Harry Saltzman who produced "Saturday Night and Sunday Morning" and "The Entertainer". It looks as if they will start with "Dr. No".

Saltzman has most grandiose ideas about book sales to be co-ordinated with the film due around April, and he is blasting hell out of Pan's because he can't find my titles even in Foyles or Hatchards.

He is talking of subsidising a print order in Pan's running literally into millions of copies of my titles, and it would obviously be a good idea for Cape's to ride on the back of this wave of Bonds in some way or another.

But perhaps it would be a good idea for you to keep in touch with Pan's and get them to let you know exactly what they are planning, particularly in respect of whichever picture Saltzman does first.

If this thing gets off the ground it will presumably be wise of you to have fairly solid stocks of all the titles on hand.

By the way, when your editress has finished tidying up the Chitty stories could you please let me have copies and I will then try and bend my mind to producing two more.

I have received tearful letters from Al Hart so I am sure that everything to do with the Chopping jacket will sort itself out. As to the next one, I feel more and more that it should be your commando dagger crossed with a carnation. A possible background instead of the cipher page might be a torn sheet of paper bearing the title and author's name, that would leave some corners for the famous wood grain you like so much!

TO JOHN HAYWARD, ESQ., C.B.E., 19 Carlyle Mansions, London, S.W.3.

Although Fleming's relationship with The Book Collector *remained uneasy he nevertheless valued the opinions of its editor.*

1st August, 1961

I am still proposing to descend upon you, but since I am being forced to spend most of my time at Sandwich this is not being easy to contrive. So please just expect me sometime this month.

Meanwhile I have been in lengthy correspondence with a certain Fritz Liebert of Yale University Library, who has corrected the Americanese in my next book.

In the course of our correspondence he expressed his highest regard for yourself and claims acquaintanceship both with you and with John Carter.

Anyway with his last letter he sent me the enclosed* and I wonder if you think it would be suitable for reproduction in The Book Collector, since, as you will see, only two hundred copies have been printed in America.

Personally, I find the story and the picture most attractive.

I have told Liebert that I am passing it on to you with my recommendation, but adding that you are a law unto yourself in these matters. At

* An article by Liebert on Samuel Johnson.

the same time I asked him for freedom to print in case the piece passed muster with you.

Please don't bother to answer, but when I see you you must tell me more about this Liebert man, who has, in fact, been exceptionally helpful to me out of the blue.

TO SIR WILLIAM STEPHENSON, 450 East 52nd Street, New York

16th August, 1961

In accordance with your instructions via the darling Miss Green I have the honour to report that my team of mechanics report that the engine, though less oiled than previously, is now running on at least eleven out of its twelve cylinders, and that the twelfth should start firing soon so long as I continue to obey their infuriating instructions, which are, broadly speaking, that I should do none of the things I want to do.

In fact, as possibly in your case, the whole business has been a timely warning not to try and pour a gallon into a pint pot, and I am taking the whole thing very philosophically.

In particular, I have not been siezed [sic] by what they call "coronary neurosis", which apparently is a very real consequence of one of these attacks. It results in people thinking of nothing except about their health and going about as if they were made of spun Venetian glass. Such people are an infernal nuisance, and since my malady got into the newspapers (in fact to my delight The Times had my obituary re-written by a friend of mine) I am regarded as fair game by all these morons who bore me to death with tales of their symptoms and of the pills and tests they have to take.

But I am, in fact, being reasonably sensible in following the instructions of my various mechanics. That is the reason why I did not come to New York last month as I had intended, and I am staying in London and Sandwich, where my more relaxed golf swing and an increased handicap (I happen to be on the handicapping Committee!) has confounded my enemies.

My strictly commercial love affair with the darling Marlow has gone slightly awry and I asked her to explain the circumstances to you. Briefly, a very big Bond film deal is in the offing and it could not go through so long as she had the option on my television rights, which I had given her over scrambled eggs and smoked salmon in Sardis East in a bemused moment.

She couldn't have been nicer about the whole thing and surrendered her option. I sent her a small token from Cartiers to signal my love and appreciation. But, in fact, as I have told her, I shall try and see that if and when the film series gets successfully launched and the moment for television series comes along, her name will in some way be linked with the television production.

But naturally I cannot actually promise anything, but only use my best endeavours with United Artists, who are the putative owners of the Bond properties under various options. If they do not take up these options and seriatim the whole property reverts to me, I would once more propose to offer my hand, at least in television marriage, to Marlow.

The deal itself starts with a minimum payment of $150,000 amounting by $100,000 with each further film U.A. makes. There is no object in my arranging a Bermuda company for all these, as the film rights are owned by Caspar's Trust and therefore avoid all tax. But, in addition, I get 5% of the producer's gross, which is very carefully defined, and if this should look like getting too big I would consult you again about a Bermudan gambit. But as you know producers profits have a curious way of melting like snow in summer sunshine when anyone else has a share of them, and I think the days of my becoming a millionaire are still some way distant.

Meanwhile I observe the Dows index and remember your dictum that it would be a thousand before the end of the year. Unfortunately you failed to tell me which stocks to buy, so here again I have failed to benefit, except through some minor holdings in Flemings Investment Trust.

By the way, should I now sink back into Caribbean Cement?

No other news except the minor item that I think England is in the process of slowly sinking beneath the waves. She had a very good run and I only hope she does her sinking gracefully.

I am sending you a copy of an article as I think it may amuse you.* It has just gone to M.C.A. with the suggestion that they offer it first to C. D. Jackson, though I dare say it will turn out to be too technical even for American publication.

Anyway I expect it will make you chuckle.

No other news except that if you bought some Drages shares at 120 you <u>might</u> be able to sell them at 200. But this is not five star guarantee but only from the mouth of two very reliable horses.

With best love to Mary.

TO MICHAEL HOWARD

16th August, 1961

My dear Michael,

Many thanks for your letter of yesterday about the new Courtelle advertisement.

I don't really mind these but they rather annoyed me by writing a patronizing letter offering me <u>one</u> sweater, <u>one</u> pair of slacks, or indeed any <u>one</u> object from their collection instead of begging me to come in and take my pick of their stuff – which I naturally wouldn't have done but which would have sounded rather handsomer.

In fact I would like them to invite me round some Tuesday or Wednesday afternoon to have a look at all this stuff I am sponsoring. I have absolutely no idea what it looks like.

In the present copy I don't think they should suggest that Bond wears suits from Savile Row, which he doesn't, or actually Courtelle shirts, etc., etc., though I don't mind them saying that people like James Bond wear these things.

* 'The Guns of James Bond'.

I don't want to make a song and dance about it and I entirely appreciate the points you make.

TO MICHAEL HOWARD

For the endpapers of The Spy Who Loved Me, *Cape had commissioned a black and white drawing of the situation in which the novel was set.*

10th October, 1961

My dear Michael,

I like Lee Vernon's sketch immensely, and I quite agree with you that it will admirably serve our purpose.

One or two small points which I had indicated in red:

The runaway car gets out of control and goes over the cliff to the right of the Motel. We do not need to see exactly where it went over the cliff, but could we move the rustic chairs and tables down to the right as I have indicated.

I forgot all about the swimming pool when writing the story, and as it would naturally come into the action if it is where Vernon correctly places it, could he please shift it to behind the Motel as I have indicated.

The saloon car should point towards Lake George.

I would rather do without the second sign board, as otherwise this also should have appeared in the book, notably during the fight with the gangsters where it would have been used as cover.

Otherwise I have no comments and I am much impressed with the sketch and particularly with the dark spikiness of the trees.

What a gift to be able to knock off something like this!

One last thought, could the artist vaguely indicate the 'No Vacancy' over the front door?

TO CAPTAIN E. K. LE MESURIER, National Rifle Association, Bisley Camp, Brookwood, Surrey

Fleming had invited Captain Le Mesurier of the National Rifle Association to comment on his short story 'The Living Daylights'.

31st October, 1961

Dear Captain Le Mesurier,

Here now is the story we discussed on the telephone, and I would indeed be grateful for any corrections or suggestions you may have, particularly on the opening pages about Bisley.

Please be extremely tough and critical and don't spare my feelings.

One particular point on page 25, half way down, is the expression "flash protector" correct? I have a feeling that my war time memory may have failed me.

It is extremely kind of you to allow me to take up your time and brains in this way, and I shall insist on sending you an editorial fee to cover general wear and tear, midnight oil and the heavy refreshment that I am sure it will call for.

This has nothing to do with the N.R.A. as such and I am consulting you privately and using your spare time, so please don't argue about accepting it.

TO GRAHAM SUTHERLAND, ESQ., O.M., The White House, Trottiscliffe, West Malling, Kent

Fleming had commissioned the distinguished artist Graham Sutherland to provide a picture to accompany his short story 'The Living Daylights' in the Sunday Times *colour supplement. In the end it was never used.*

7th November, 1961

My dear Graham,

The first reactions, while enthusiastic, are that the green is too gay giving the whole thing rather too much of a pastoral quality with which, I expect you have now read the story, you will agree is off-key.

Would you be an angel and take up your brushes again and try a background to the heart of perhaps a window frame or barbed wire and perhaps a gunmetal background.

Also the pontiffs think that the arrow should come from right to left.

Don't bother about leaving space for lettering as whichever way you do the design it will anyway leave plenty of room.

You are terribly kind to submit to this boring chore and all I can do in exchange, apart from the meagre hundred guineas, is to hand you over the whole bestiary idea without any strings whatsoever.

My pleasure of having thought of a theme that stimulates you is ample reward, apart from your kindness over this blasted jacket.

If you are both not too fed up with me by now I will in fact come by around midday on Friday for some more sausages and mash, but naturally countermand me if it doesn't suit.

I hear that Douglas is back at the chateau with Richardson.

TO SIR WILLIAM STEPHENSON, 450 East 52nd Street, New York

7th November, 1961

Many thanks for your chastening cable which actually fetched up at the right address. Please use it frequently.

Not much news from here. My host of medical advisers seem to be delighted with my recovery and, as you can imagine, I am losing no time in loosening up on their counsels of moderation in all things.

The film deal with United Artists is going ahead and they are going to film 'DR NO' in Jamaica in January and February, and the advance party has already gone out to prospect for location. But, as usual with show business, no actual money has actually changed hands yet.

I shall be coming out to Jamaica around January 18th and will be paying you my usual visit around the middle of March. So please warn The Pierre to lay in plenty of oysters.

TO ANTHONY COLWELL, ESQ., 30 Bedford Square London W.C.1

13th December, 1961

Dear Tony,

Very many thanks for the proof of the jacket which in general I think is splendid though, apart from the points you make, it does seem to me that the background wood has turned rather pink.

You are right about the spelling of Adirondacks, but this may have been my mistake in writing the blurb.

Should not the copyright line "Jacket design by Richard Chopping" be "Ian Fleming"? As it was with the last book and since the picture is my property.

One final point. On the back of the jacket I think typographically the joke slightly misfires. How about putting "Verdicts of THE TIMES!"

Incidentally, Victor Weybright has done a brilliant promotion pamphlet on the Bonds which I am sure will entertain all of you. Unfortunately I haven't got a spare copy, but perhaps you would like to get one from him.

P.S. And above the credit to Chopping mightn't we put "Commando dagger by the Wilkinson Sword Company" if that is their right title?

TO D. R. C. BEDSON, ESQ., Executive Council, Winnipeg, Manitoba

Mr Bedson had read The Spy Who Loved Me *while spending a weekend with Sir William and Lady Stephenson, and raised a few points. Stephenson, no doubt with some glee, insisted he write to the author. Which he did, stating that Fleming's description of French Canada and its various groups bore no resemblance to anything he had experienced. Also, if Bond was going from Toronto to Washington he'd have gone via Niagara Falls, Buffalo, then on to the highways through western New York and Pennsylvania. He'd have gone nowhere near Lake St George.*

19th September, 1962

Dear Mr. Bedson,

It is extremely kind of you to have taken so much trouble to write to me so helpfully about my last book.

I quite agree with you that I dealt very cursorily with the French-Canadian problem. I should have delved more deeply and not relied on a casual talk with a French-Canadian friend of mine.

You are of course absolutely right about James Bond's route, but I had to get him to Lake George somehow and I think we must assume that he was taking a leisurely sightseeing trip.

Anyway, it was very thoughtful of you to have written and I am delighted to hear from any friend of my hero, 'Little Bill'.

FROM WILLIAM PLOMER

6th April, 1962

My dear Ian,

How good of you to send me my special copy of <u>The S. who l. M.</u> Best thanks for this tenth knock-out. Of course I have dashed out from under my immense load of dung, & have beetled into a corner & begun to re-read you, which is fatal, because one goes on. "... and everyone froze" – and of course one freezes with them.

I notice the New Morality is beginning to appear. Perhaps you saw the letter in the Lit. Sup. about the new novel by Christopher Isherwood (wh. I haven't read). You must perhaps expect increasing attacks on the grounds of morality. Now that Non-Smoking is coming in too, you will soon find that you mayn't mention cigarettes. . .

I am hoping to see you – or should I say watch you – at the gathering at Bedford Square on Wednesday. In the meantime let me wish you as I always do, an enormous sale for this book.

TO MRS. FLORENCE TAYLOR, Ford's Book Stores Ltd., 9 & 11 Market Hall Buildings, Chesterfield

Mrs Taylor wrote icily to say that she 'did not care for your new book', that it was 'a great disappointment', and 'I do hope that this is not a new trend in your style of writing.'

18th April, 1962

Dear Mrs. Taylor,

It was really very kind of you to have taken the trouble to write to me and I was touched by your affection for James Bond.

The point is that if one is writing about a serial character one's public comes to want more or less the same book over and over again, and it was really to stretch my writing muscles that I tried to write like a twenty-three year old girl and put forward a view of James Bond at the other end of the gun barrel so to speak.

But this is a unique experiment and I have just completed the next Bond book, I think the longest yet, in which he appears from the first page to the last.

Again with many thanks for the kindly thought behind your letter.

The brickbats continued. 'What a let down', wrote a Canadian reader. From H. S. Baker of New Bond Street – 'in the sacred name of 'Casino Royale' and 'From Russia with Love', you hadn't oughta have done it.' From one David Ferney – 'Now look here Fleming, this catering to fifth form eroticism must stop. Do you hear?[. . .] It's inadequate Fleming, and you know it.' From an attorney in Chicago – 'This particular book does not belong in a library any more than a package of garbage does.'

Fleming was dismayed by these and other criticisms. As he wrote, 'The experiment seems to have failed and I am suffering from multiple contusions as a result of the onslaught of my critics.'

TO MICHAEL HOWARD

19th April, 1962

'The Spy Who Loved Me'

I am becoming increasingly depressed with the reception of this book although I don't think the TLS was as harsh as you gave me to think. But obviously reviewers and, as you know, some of the book trade are upset by two factors. Firstly that James Bond makes a very late entry into the book and, secondly, though this I think weighs less heavily, with the alleged salacity of certain passages.

It is the second of these criticisms to which I am perhaps overly sensitive.

Both I and all of you have treated the whole of the James Bond saga with a light heart and so, with one or two exceptions, have the reviewers, most of whom for the first nine books have been very kind. But in the reviews of The Spy I detect a note of genuine disapproval. This surprises me because of the genesis of this particular book which should perhaps now be explained to you.

I had become increasingly surprised to find that my thrillers, which were designed for an adult audience, were being read in the schools, and that young people were making a hero out of James Bond when to my mind, and as I have often said in interviews, I do not regard James Bond as a heroic figure but only as an efficient professional in his job.

So it crossed my mind to write a cautionary tale about Bond to put the record straight in the minds particularly of younger readers.

It was impossible to do this in my usual narrative style and I therefore invented the fiction of a heroine through whom I could examine Bond from the other end of the gun barrel so to speak.

To make this heroine a credible figure and one who would be likely to come into Bond's path, I had to explain her at considerable length and endeavour to make her worldly wise.

This I did by telling the story in her own words of her upbringing and love life which consisted of two incidents, both of which were of a strongly cautionary nature.

The trouble she then got into with the gangsters was of the normal American thriller variety.

Its verisimilitude and the language used were incidentally checked by a member of the University Library of Yale at his own request.

And, just to remove some further 'heroism' from Bond, he is depicted as making a considerable hash of his subsequent fight with the gangsters.

After the love scene with the heroine which Bond breaks off in the most cursory fashion, there follows the long homily from the chief detective warning the heroine and the readers that Bond himself is in fact no better than the gangsters. And on that note the book closes.

I haven't bothered to explain my reasons for writing this book before and I only do so now because the experiment has obviously gone very much awry, and I am in general being criticised for doing almost the exact opposite of what I intended.

This being so, and though we may get more understanding reviews later, I would like this book of mine to have as short a life as possible, and the subject of this letter is to ask you to co-operate.

In particular I would like there to be no reprints after your present edition is exhausted, and I would ask that it not be offered to Pan Books through whom, presumably, it would reach a more junior audience than your hard cover edition.

This will mean considerable financial sacrifice by both of us and I must just ask you to accept your share of this loss in as friendly a spirit as you can muster.

Please don't bother to reply immediately and perhaps we can talk the whole thing over when I see you after Easter, but I wanted to get this letter away to relieve some of the burden that is in my mind as a result of the book's reception.

14

The Liebert Letters

*I*N MAY 1961 *Fleming received a letter from Herman W. Liebert,* librarian at Yale University and a scholar on the works of Samuel Johnson. Having read Thunderball, Liebert was appalled by the language Fleming made his American characters use. Half the things they said simply made no sense in the US. He enclosed a long list of replacements for words like 'sponge bag', 'damnably', 'gammy', 'arse-end' and 'chap'. He was particularly acerbic on the use of 'by gum'. As he pointed out, 'I don't think an American has said this since the recent death of A. Lincoln.' And what on earth was a 'sixpenny sick'?*

Despite being hospitalised by a heart attack, Fleming was delighted. Nothing spurred him more than a challenge to Bond's authenticity. He replied with enthusiasm, and was intrigued to discover that Liebert was not only a book collector but owned a house in Jamaica and had been a member of the OSS, the CIA's forerunner. To have a fan of such erudition was one thing, but to find he was also a bibliophile, ex-spy and lover of the Caribbean was irresistible. Fleming wasted no time enrolling him as unofficial fact-checker and editor for his latest book The Spy Who Loved Me. They conducted a warm and witty exchange during its publication, for which Fleming paid Liebert with a Cartier pen set that had to be smuggled into the States by a friend to avoid customs charges.

The archive correspondence ends in 1962 but it would be good to think that their friendship continued, and that they eventually met,

---

* Variously known as Franz or Fritz.

whether in New York or Jamaica. As Fleming said, 'I have no doubt that fate will bring us together when the stars are right'. To which Liebert replied philosophically, 'favete astrae' – 'Let the stars decide'.

FROM LIEBERT

May 10th, 1961

Dear Mr. Fleming,

I am an insatiable Bondomane (what sensible man is not?) and found Thunderball one of the very best. But it was very nearly spoiled for me by the supposed Americanese of Leiter and Pederson.

A list of alternate readings is enclosed. A few are optional, most are not; that is, there are one or two an American might use, but most he would never use.

The Bond books are so very good that it hurts to find them at fault in any particular. Won't you get an American friend with an ear to vet the American dialect from now on? Then they would be perfect.

TO MR. HERMAN LIEBERT, Yale University Library, New Haven, Connecticut, U.S.A.

29th May, 1961

Dear Mr. Liebert,

Thank you for your absolutely splendid and invaluable letter of May 10th, but I only plead semi-guilty.

I particularly asked Vikings to clean up this story to spot anglicanisms and I can only suggest that through publishing Graham Greene and me they are beginning to forget their own language.

Mark you, I have set two or three books in and around America and this is the first time I have had such a dressing down, so I am taking the matter very seriously and passing your letter on to Vikings as they have a manuscript in the oven at the moment in which I suspect a great deal of the American gangster talk is very ham.

I shall accordingly suggest to Vikings, if I may, that they approach you with a view, for some miserly fee, to go over the Ms with your blazing eye. We will see what happens.

On the other hand I am not prepared to accept without further witnesses more than around 20% of your suggestions for the very good reason that Felix Leiter has been affected by his international work for CIA, and has picked up a good deal of English in the process. An example is "sixpenny sick", a very English expression for the kind of boat ride holiday makers take from the sea shore holiday beaches.

Anyway I am indeed grateful for your harsh letter and it was very kind indeed of you to have taken the trouble.

FROM LIEBERT

June 5th, 1961

Dear Mr. Fleming:

I am most grateful for your full, frank, and generous letter, and much concerned that mine gave you the impression of being harsh. Its emotional source was sorrow rather than anger – the sorrow of seeing what seemed a flaw in an author otherwise so sure and so stimulating that he evokes the wish for perfection. Language wouldn't matter in the host of bad books with which we are all surrounded; it matters desperately to me in books like yours to which I am devoted.

I would be delighted to comb any MS of yours and to offer a list of suggestions that you or Viking could accept or reject. For such a privilege I would not dream of accepting a fee, even the miserly kind publishers usually offer. And of course, if I were offered such a chance, it would shut me up.

I demur at the view Leiter has picked up more than one or two Anglicisms; of the 20 or 30 people I know in CIA (my wartime colleagues in

OSS) I don't think one has picked up any, except rarely in humorous quotes. But you are Leiter's parent, so I demur.

Delighted to hear there's a book in the oven; I would love a chance to baste it while it's cooking.

[PS] Good Lord, I have just done my homework and looked in <u>Who's Who</u> to be sure I shouldn't hang a couple of honors (sorry, honours) after your name, and suddenly realize it is you who publish the <u>Book Collector</u>. I suppose I have read the masthead fifty times without waking up. Now I am more than ever at your feet. Incidentally, Jake Carter and John Hayward are both good friends.

I also see you go to Oracabessa. I have a place in Runaway Bay. We must drink together sometime on that blessed isle. You must have known Peter Murray Hill: he and Phyl stayed at my place before he died.

TO LIEBERT

15th June, 1961

Dear Mr. Liebert,

Thank you very much for your letter of June 5th and I am most amused by the number of "bonds" we seem to have.

These, and your apparent enthusiasm, have decided me to take you at your word and ask you to go through the American parts of my next book with a microscope and a very sharp red pencil. I had already passed on your previous letter and notes to Vikings, but I am not sure that they will do anything about it and I would rather take the bull by the horns myself.

I am accordingly sending you by registered airmail a copy of 'THE SPY WHO LOVED ME' which, as you will see, is very different from the usual Bond but has considerable American angles which I am most anxious to have stringently vetted by an expert.

What I would pray you to do is to pay particular attention to the gangsterese – improving, re-writing, and even editing snatches of conversation wherever you think fit.

Any additions or amendments to the motel theme would also be invaluable as would any necessary brushing up of the local police procedure and nomenclature at the end of the book.

This is an uncorrected first typescript and you can assume that obvious mistakes have been picked up here. What I want badly to stiffen up are the points I mentioned above and if you decide to re-write whole pages or tear out chunks, I shall not be in the least dismayed – very much the opposite.

For instance, at the moment I feel the gangsters are three-quarters cardboard, and if you choose to change their names, clothes, or anything else about them I shall not object, for at the present moment they look to me rather like Mutt and Jeff.

This is going to be hard work, and I am afraid it must also be fast, as my publishers here are screaming for the corrected typescript at the latest by July 15th which means that I must have your amended and corrected typescript back by July 10th. Please don't bother about "suggestions", just write in your comments on the typescript.

So, as you see, I am taking your kind offer very seriously indeed and I am embarrassed to suggest what fee to offer you for this invaluable work. But if you can successfully bring about this vital piece of collaboration I propose to present you with a handsome present from Cartiers as a memento.

I am coming out to New York by the Queen Elizabeth sailing on July 20th and shall be about two weeks in the States, when perhaps we might meet and I could make the presentation!

I hope you will quickly get over the shock of this letter, and it would be most helpful if, on receipt of the typescript, you could send me a brief L.T. cable saying yes or no to the project.

I would also be most grateful if you could keep this whole affair a secret between us, though if the weight of your scholarship is as important as I think it may be, I will take the liberty of dedicating the book to you.

June 19th, 1961

Dear Mr. Fleming:

If, in the cable just now sent, I had given free rein to my reactions on getting your letter this morning, the cable would have bankrupted me. So I settled for "overwhelmed".

I cannot imagine an offer more exciting, or put in more generous terms. I will do everything I can with the script, and if you feel when it returns that I have done little, that will be because it seemed good as it was, and not through reluctance.

I must go west for a speaking engagement on 6th July, and I will airmail the script back before I leave, so you should have it easily by the 10th.

Grateful as I should be, I hope you will not indulge in a present, for the pleasure and pride I have in the offer to go over the book are more than sufficient reward. The fact that I am doing this work will be grave-yard so far as I am concerned.

If you could spare a day to come to New Haven while here (90 min-utes by train from N.Y.) we could meet and you could see both the Yale library and my own collections, and I could promise you food and drink fit for a Bond. If you can't spare the time, I would eagerly come to N.Y. In any event, let us meet.

Renewed thanks and cordial regards.

TO LIEBERT

21st June, 1961

Dear Mr. Liebert,

Thank you for your delightful cable and charming letter and I do hope you are not at this moment cursing your generous impulse.

But once again I abjure you to be as tough as hell with this book, as I am not at all satisfied that the peril represented by the gangsters is nearly powerful enough, or that the realism, though it may get by in England, will stand up to informed readership.

I am afraid it is bound to be a much heavier job than you could have expected, and I shall not be surprised if you are forced to rewrite whole pages.

But, anyway, there it is, and the gift is already on order from Cartiers so I am afraid there is no escape however powerful your nausea.

Incidentally, the Albany call sign is WGY.

Naturally we must meet when I get to America, but as I am semi-convalescent I shall be going straight up to Vermont to a millionaire's farm belonging to an English friend of mine, John F.C. Bryce [Ivar Bryce], who is married to an American and lives at Black Hole Hollow Farm just across the border from Cambridge, New York State.

Anyway we will fix up a meeting in due course and probably spend a great deal of time roaring with laughter over this extraordinary project.

With my warmest thanks and best wishes for your dreadful labours.

FROM LIEBERT

July 5th, 1961

Dear Mr Fleming:

Viv returns to you airmail registered under separate cover tomorrow. I fear you will find her not as much a changed girl as you hoped – partly because I have not been able to shake loose as much spare time to work on her as I wished, and partly because I am a much better editor than a collaborator. I would have liked to try some re-write, especially about the gangsters, which I agree is the place it is needed most, but by the time I had done what I knew I could do and so did first, the English/American transition, there was no more time.

A little about what I did do. There are two levels of correction, one in red (for the redcoats) of changes I think should be made both in the English and in the American editions; and a second in blue (for the Atlantic) of changes for the American edition only.

The changes are of several kinds: (1) matters of fact; (2) within dialogue by Americans, changes to American current usage fitting to the character speaking; (3) in Viv's story, changes of English expressions that would either mystify American readers or, though perfectly plain in meaning after a second's thought, would nevertheless obtrude on and slow the narrative pace. I have left Viv enough Anglicanisms of the kind most familiar to Americans so that they will remember she is Canadian and English-schooled, but have, I hope, pruned enough unAmerican from her so that most American readers will feel that she is simply speaking naturally.

I wish I could come up with better names for the gangsters, because here especially, I think, they have a literary flavor. 'Horror' seems to me a bookish word, and I am put off by the feminine ending in 'Sluggsy'. 'Slug' would be better, or 'Hot Shot': both are names of real underworld characters of the past, who were notable shots. One very tough thug a while ago was named 'Chiller', on the same ground as 'Horror', but I don't know that I like it much better.

My reaction to the whole book is that it is good but different. I like the Viv half of the book, and think the story is vivid, observant fiction; some of your Bond devotees may find it not the Fleming they expect. The second half is Bond enough for any devotee.

I suspect that when you see how little I have really done, in spite of many hours of work, you will want to send that item back to Cartier's and buy me a drink. I would of done more if I hadda chance, and certainly your very generous invitation gave me carte blanche to do more. It was the time, not the will that was lacking.

Sorry to hear you have been knocked up – a term of very different meanings on either side of the Atlantic. I hope your visit here and rest will repair the difficulty. Do let me have your American address, so I can at least get in touch with you while you are here. If there is a chance of seeing you, here or anywhere else this side of Calif., I am yours to command.

Tom Guinzburg of Viking, who was here at Yale a while ago, and whom I knew as a student, phoned the other day to ask about my work on the book. I tried to play it close, respecting your wish for confidence, and did not let on I was doing anything to it until he read me part of a letter from you telling them I was at work, so I presumed then that the secret did not extend to them, if you had told them yourself. He seemed pleased to know that I was working on the script.

No more now as I am off to Ohio for a speech to (rest my soul) a convention of librarians. If I make my address in Sluggsy dialect, it will be your fault.

Just a last word of sincere appreciation for the opportunity you have offered me, so fully and generously. No author could be more open-handed with his opus. What I have come to know about the man I.F. leads me to admire him as much as I have always admired the writer.

TO LIEBERT

12th July, 1961

Dear Mr. Liebert,

I really am most grateful to you for your splendid labours and for your charming and perceptive letter.

I shall pay close attention to all your advices and, from a quick glance, I already see that you have saved me from a thousand otiosities.

Regarding Tom Guinsburg's communication, I felt I had to tell Vikings that I had called on you for help to stop them hacking around on their own. I hope he was much impressed by the weight of the authority I had invoked.

Now, it's maddening, but the united medical councils of London have forbidden me to visit America next week. So the meeting I was so much looking forward to will have to be deferred and a small token from Cartier will have to come to you anonymously through whatever channel I can devise. Since it will reach you anonymously, this is to ask you to accept it as a memento of this curious literary association, which comes to you with my affectionate thanks.

I do hope that our meeting will not be too long deferred, and that if I do not catch up with you in America I may do so in Jamaica when, over a glass of flaming Old Man's Liqueur, we can discuss cabbages and kings.

Again with renewed thanks for your extreme kindness.

FROM LIEBERT

July 17th, 1961

Dear Mr Fleming:

How utterly rotten for you that your health will not permit you to make the trip here. I do hope this is a passing and not a chronic ailment and that you will soon be free of it.

I will, of course, receive the memento you are sending with warm appreciation, though the privilege of being "in" on the forthcoming Bond and of receiving such gracious and friendly letters from you are quite reward enough.

I am glad that some of my advices seem useful; I abjure you to abide by our understanding that they are only advices, and if you at last decide to reject all of them, I will be perfectly satisfied by their having been considered.

One thing I meant to say in my last, which you have already detected by now: I am a heavy hyphener, and you will probably want to neglect my many insertions of that mark.

Missing the chance to see you here makes me insist we meet in Jamaica. We will be at Runaway Bay from 15 December through 6 January, and back again sometime between mid-March and mid-April. I hope some part of our stay will coincide with yours. Though we have less reason to exchange letters now, I hope you will, toward the end of the year, let me know what your Jamaica dates may be.

Give my regards and thanks to the Hayward and the Carter when you see them; I am sure it was partly their vouching for me that encouraged you to make so trusting an offer as you did. I only wish I had had more time to tackle the larger aspects, but I felt my first responsibility was to the verbal problems, and when I had done those, the postman knocked.

I remain much in your debt for a stimulating experience backstage with my favourite fiction character. Let us now hope that your vitality (not I am sure broken down by torture or intercourse) will reassert itself as miraculously as Bond's.

Until we meet, when I will be able to express my gratitude and admiration in person, believe me,

Faithfully yours,

[PS] You must tell me one day what books you collect.

FROM LIEBERT

July 27th, 1961

My dear Fleming:

The chaste and handsome product of MM. Cartier has just arrived, and is so beautiful that it makes even signing checks a real pleasure.

I find my cyanide fits very neatly in alongside the ink-holder, and I think my thermite people will be able to make up a package just like the ink-tube, so you will see how handy it will be for everyday needs. And as soon as I have the Yale library filmed in microdot, I can close up shop and move to Jamaica with my pen and my swimming trunks.

Seriously, it is a very generous and much-appreciated gift, and I am proud both of its beauty and of its source. Adding it to the fun I had with the MS puts me deep in your debt. Thank you.

I hope your ailment has abated, and that if it does not permit you to come here, it will at least allow you to get to Jamaica later in the year. We will be there 15 December through 7 January and greatly hope this will synchronize.

I hope you will accept the enclosed piece about an item in my collection; I think you will like the fine photographs.

With renewed thanks and warm regards.

TO LIEBERT

1st August, 1961

Thank you very much indeed for your charming letters of July 17th and 27th, and I am glad that the pen has arrived and that you are pleased with it. In fact I find the ball points rather fine, but Cartiers were adamant that they could not get a broader one for you.

I have just this minute been talking to Jonathan Capes who are ecstatic at receiving the cleaned up manuscript so swiftly. And I do thank you most warmly again, not only for the trouble you took, but for your rapidity.

There is more I wish you had done to the book and I am still not very happy with the gangsters, but I accepted I think every one of your suggestions and now the little book must fly on its own.

Incidentally, I am also a great hyphenater and you picked up several I had missed.

I haven't had a chance to talk about you to Jack Carter or to John Hayward as I have been up to my uvula in miscellaneous mundungus since our correspondence began. I was warmly influenced by the kindness and perception of your first letter.

Alas, it is most unlikely that I shall be in Jamaica before January 10th, but I will let you know my plans nearer the time. In any event we will certainly meet in due course in one continent or another.

Thank you very much indeed for the Johnson's Head, which I shall take home and read this evening. I must say I am enchanted by the photographs of the bust, what a splendid face!

Having read it I propose to pass it on to John Hayward with a suggestion that he might care to reproduce it in the Book Collector. So please write if you would have no objection to this happening.

FROM LIEBERT

August 4th, 1961

Dear Mr. Fleming:

Footnote to Chap. I., requiring no reply.

I hope the garbridge (see OED s.v. mundungus,* 1st quote; a delightful spelling I shall always use) has dropped below the uvula, to the jeju-
num or even to the levator ani.

John Hayward is welcome to use the piece if he wants it, but if so I
would welcome the chance to make two small changes, so ask him to let
me know direct if he is going to print. He is indeed a law unto himself; I
always say he may have a weak constitution but his by-laws are iron.
Give him my love.

May the serious work prosper. May it and health allow you to come
south in January. End of footnote.

* Thank you for this lovely word.

FROM LIEBERT

January 16th, 1962

Dear Mr. Fleming:

The stars are indeed unkind to me, to take me away from Jamaica just
as you arrive. We had a wonderful month in Runaway Bay, and return
wondering why we insist on living so near a pole. Middles are so much
better than ends, in everything that counts: women, and bottles of
claret, and cigars, books, age, life, and even earth.

We saw in The Gleaner that you were filming "Dr. No" and we look
forward to seeing some of our favorite Jamaica landscapes in it. The
Runaway Bay caves and the phosphorus lagoon at Glistening Water
might supply good locations.

I hope the sun and the sea will restore your health, as it has ours. We
envy you the days ahead; drink a Red Stripe for us.

Don't trouble to reply. When we are next in London or Jamaica, we will inquire whether you are nearby. <u>Favete astrae</u>.

Signed with <u>the</u> pen.

FROM LIEBERT

April 30th, 1962

My dear Fleming:

I have just returned to find <u>the</u> book with its abashing inscription.

Like most of us, I do not allow my pleasure at flattery to be diminished by the mere fact that it isn't true. And I certainly greatly value the manifest kindness that prompted it.

I have also had the American edition, and am now reading the texts against each other to see what has been altered. I have found one typo and will write Viking about it and any others I find.

I hope the trip to Jamaica has restored your health. I am off to Italy this week, but only until the end of May. If after that you come Statesward, do let me know so we can meet. I have a Madeira solera 1808 that might tempt you; John Carter approved of it last Saturday, when we spoke much of you.

Liebert died in 1994 at the age of eighty-three, a man of many qualities. He was just three years younger than Fleming yet outlived him by another thirty. This says much for Yale, Jamaica and Madeira but may also have something to do with favete astrae – *'Let the stars decide'.*

15

On Her Majesty's Secret Service

GIVEN THAT HE had spent a formative period in the Austrian Tyrol, and with promptings from at least one of his readers, it was unsurprising that Fleming should choose the Alps as a setting for Bond's next adventure. Maybe, too, his memory of the mountains had been jogged by a brief visit to Switzerland the previous Christmas where, among other things, he had been delighted by the exclusive Corviglia Club in St Moritz. He began researching the project that summer and, by the time he went to Goldeneye in January 1962, he had all the material he needed.

On Her Majesty's Secret Service was one of Fleming's most intriguing books, offering as it did the closest insight into Bond's mercurial character since *Casino Royale*. Following his stylistic experiment with *The Spy Who Loved Me* he returned to tradition with an attempt by Bond's old SPECTRE foe, Blofeld, to destroy Britain's agricultural economy. Having surgically remodelled his features, Blofeld is posing as a millionaire research scientist based in Switzerland. From his mountain-top Alpine clinic, Piz Gloria, he uses hypnosis to cure farmers' daughters of their allergies before sending them home with canisters of lethal pathogens. His weakness, however, is snobbery: he would like to assume the title Comte de Blauchamps, for which he needs approval from heraldic experts in London. Impersonating a member of the Royal College of Arms, Bond infiltrates his sanctum and successfully prevents the canisters reaching their destination. Returning with reinforcements he destroys Piz Gloria's laboratories and very nearly kills Blofeld, too, but is defeated in a daredevil sled chase down an ice run.

The action was dramatic, and packed with all the sensation Fleming's readers had come to expect. The most important element, however, was Bond's relationship with Tracy, daughter of Marc-Ange Draco, head of the Union Corse, a criminal organisation whose power almost matched that of the Mafia. At the start of the book he rescues her from a suicide attempt, in return for which Draco uses his criminal network to help destroy Blofeld's lair. A strong character who knows her own mind, she can drive a fast car well, has no concern for danger and is a rebel. Quite possibly, Bond considers, this is the woman for him. Fleming builds her up so tenderly as a match for Bond, and pours so much angst into Bond's decision to exchange his 'marriage' to the Secret Service for a marriage in real life, that the reader expects 007's career to end in a rosy sunset. So it comes as a shock when Tracy is killed by Blofeld in a drive-by shooting on the first day of their honeymoon.

For anybody, let alone someone in poor health, it was an extraordinary book. Fizzing with energy, it captured the excitement Fleming had experienced in the Alps as a youth – Telemark, Sprung-Christiana and all – and his descriptions of the Swiss mountains would have brought tears to the eyes of any Alpinist. As for Bond's marriage, it made him fascinatingly human. Despite his image as a womaniser, Bond had teetered constantly on the edge of matrimony ever since Fleming first introduced him to the world. Now the moment had come, and it was no fault of Bond's that it had failed. If Fleming had dallied with the idea of ending Bond's career, Tracy's murder ensured he would have to follow it through to the end.

His zest for life was reinforced at Goldeneye by a Canadian film crew that came to interview him about Gary Powers, the US pilot who had been brought down while spying on Russia. Then there was the filming of Dr No which took place at Rolling River in Jamaica, and where Fleming met its stars, Sean Connery and Ursula Andress.

On his return to Britain he was cast down by the poor reception of The Spy Who Loved Me, and by the ongoing deterioration of his marriage. The former he was able to shrug off, but the latter weighed heavily on him (and on Ann perhaps even more). He retreated with increasing frequency to the Royal St George's golf course, where he amused himself by playing for unusual stakes: on one round he competed for a pair of pyjamas, which was then upped to include a monogram on the jacket. Adding further to the gaiety of the links he donated a golfing trophy to Eton College. His brother Peter had already established 'The Peter Fleming Owl' for the best-written item in the school's *Chronicle*. Fleming's contribution took the form of a silver chamber pot bearing the inscription 'James Bond All Purpose Grand Challenge Vase'.*

In July, as marital tension mounted, he left on an unusual summer visit to Goldeneye, where he started another Bond short story, 'Octopussy'. A throwback to the war, it features a retired commando officer, Major Dexter Smythe, living comfortably in Jamaica, his hobby being the study of marine life, in particular a favourite octopus. His peace is disturbed by Bond, who arrives with uncomfortable news. The intelligence services know that in the last stages of the war Smythe had befriended an Austrian ski instructor who knew where to find a hoard of Nazi gold. Having ascertained its location, Smythe had then killed him and taken the gold for himself. The choice Bond gives him is simple: face justice in Britain or choose his own fate. He has ten minutes to decide. Smythe swims out to sea and, having been stung by a deadly scorpion fish, allows his mask to be ripped off by his pet octopus.

Barely had Fleming got back than he was off to Japan, to research another Bond instalment. And then, in October came the film premiere of *Dr No*. It left him excited and weary but with spirit undimmed. In an address to students in Oxford that year he encapsulated his approach to writing: say whatever you want, research it properly, and write fast. Never look back, he said: 'If you interrupt the writing of fast narrative with too much introspection and self-criticism you will be lucky if you write 500 words a day and you will be disgusted with them into the bargain.' He cast a warning note: there wasn't much money to be made from books; it was only when you made a film deal that you could sit pretty. But if you persevered, a writer's life had its advantages: 'You carry your office

---

* This remarkable trophy, considered from the outset as in poor taste, is no longer awarded. But then, to balance the scales, neither is the more worthy Peter Fleming Owl.

around in your head. And you are far more aware of the world around you. Writing makes you more alive to your surroundings and, since the main ingredient of living [...] is to be alive, this is quite a worthwhile by-product of writing, even if you only write thrillers, whose heroes are white, the villains black, and the heroines a delicate shade of pink.'

In a foreword to a book titled *The Seven Deadly Sins*, published earlier that year, he dismissed the usual catalogue as part of everyday life and substituted his own: 'Avarice, Cruelty, Snobbery, Hypocrisy, Self-righteousness, Moral Cowardice and Malice'. He appended an Eighth Sin – 'that of being a Bore'. This he was determined never to be.

TO MISS JOAN SAUNDERS, 113 Fulham Road, London, s.w.3.

Joan Saunders ran the Writers and Speakers Research Agency. This rather attractive concept allowed authors to call her whenever faced with a tricky question of fact. She would then depute members of her team to provide answers. Fleming had already used her for Thunderball *and now he did so again.*

5th September, 1961

My dear Joan,

Before I begin I don't think you ever sent me a bill for putting me in touch with Wing Commander Dobson over my last book, and you are so unbusinesslike I am sure I am right. So do please send me a sensible bill because your help was quite invaluable.

I sent on to you Miss Ann Marlow and I gather you are giving her some help for some meagre fee. She is an extremely rich television producer in America and you really must charge people more!

Now, I have another problem for you.

Briefly, in my next book James Bond will foil a plot to bring England to her knees by the most direct form of economic pressure – the destruction of agricultural and livestock resources by the spreading of disease.

As you know, this form of "germ warfare" is in the arsenal of all the major powers, and I am sure much has been written on the subject outside classified sources if only I knew where to look for it.

Such diseases as anthrax, fowl pest, swine fever and foot and mouth disease, come to my mind, and there are doubtless other bacteria or pests such as the Colorado beetle for attacking crops and perhaps forests.

I think I can arrange the introduction of these various pests etc. into England, but what I need to know is which parts of the United Kingdom would be the best targets for which bacteria, etc.

So far as poultry and cattle are concerned obviously a good means to spread the disease would be to introduce the bacteria at the big horse and cattle shows (query Peterborough, Cambridge, Smithfield, Dairy Show) and poultry shows, if they have such things, and I would like to be instructed in such matters as the introduction of the diseases will be by human carriers and not by spraying from aircraft etc.

I realise that all this is very fanciful stuff, but with the help of expert advice I think I can make it more or less stand up, if I can get the ammunition right and the targets more or less credible.

Can you help me?

I also need to know whether there is a Corsican local dialect and where I can find a Corsican who can translate a few sentences of English into his native dialect.

Can you help me?

TO MRS. MALCOLM HORSLEY, L'Haute Ville, Calvi, Corsica

4th January, 1962

Dear Mrs. Horsley,

Your name has been given to me by Dr. Saunders of Writer's and Speaker's Research as being an expert on Corsica, and I wonder if you would do a little fairly simple research in connection with a passage that will appear in my next thriller.

I believe there is a Corsican dialect.

Could you please consult one of the locals and translate into Corsican the following conversation which takes place over the telephone between one shady Corsican and his headquarters in Corsica.

"Get me headquarters"
"This is the chief. Have we any news of
Smith? Where is he living now? You're sure of
that? But no exact address? Good. That is all."

This should be rendered in tough, slangy gangsterese.

Secondly, could you write me a brief essay, say 300 or 400 words, on the "Union Corse", which I believe was, and probably still is, run on the lines of the Mafia, the Unione Siciliano, – giving me as many facts as you can possibly discover both about their operations and habits inside Corsica and abroad.

I daresay you may find it difficult to get hold of this information, unless you have a friend in the police. But I would be glad if you could turn out something sufficiently mystifying and horrific!

If you think you could manage this chore I would be very grateful if you could possibly bend your mind to it quickly and air mail the results to me here [Goldeneye] together with your suggestion for a generous fee.

I hope this won't come as too much shock out of the blue, and I hope at any rate you will have some fun over the second question.

I do hope you can manage this.

P.S. Could you please also give me a good and villainous sounding christian and surname for my Corsican gangster.

TO MICHAEL HOWARD

From Goldeneye

28th February, 1962

Thank you very much for your two letters & the excellent bit of showmanship by Tony [Colwell], also for dear Daniel's amusing piece on Edwards. What a pity!

You continue to be splendidly obscure about the Joseph fiasco* but perhaps you will explain when we meet. If you need money, why don't you get it from people like me? I think it would be a fine idea for Caspar to have a stake in Capes!

Have just passed the 60,000 in my new opus. Quite tremendous bezants (look it up!) but at least JB is in from the first page to the last. Another 10,000 to go.

Fame is breathing down my neck. CBC flew a whole unit down to filmise me about Powers, the Tatler has visited again & of course the Dr No biz was a riot. By the way, Tony should have a talk with Saltzman sometime. Among other gimmicks he is turning out 5 million copies of a strip book on Dr No & I think you should climb on the band wagon.

No more for now as I have just had my hair cut for the first time in six weeks & am feeling rather light-headed! Back on the 20th.

Love to all on the Cape.

TO AUBREY FORSHAW, ESQ., Pan Books Ltd., 8 Headfort Place, London, S.W.1.

Forshaw, the head of Pan Books, was, like Fleming, a car buff. His advice was invaluable when it came to outfitting Bond with a suitable motor for the latest adventure.

28th March, 1962

My dear Aubrey,

I attach the passage in my new book which refers to Bond's fitting of a supercharger to his Mark II Continental Bentley to which he had fitted in Thunderball the Mark IV engine with 9.5 compression. He had also designed for himself a two-seater convertible body, but that is neither here nor there.

Would you be terribly kind and re-write this passage as you think fit, but including as much of your famous expertise as you can without clogging up the prose?

* An attempt by the firm Michael Joseph to buy Jonathan Cape had recently failed.

Sorry to beg this service from you, but it was as a result of your instructions that Bond changed to this car and the idea of adding a supercharger amused me.

I am also not sure if the Continental has a red line at 5000 revs.

With more apologies.

"He leant forward and flicked down the red switch [the moan of the blower died away] and there was silence in the car as he motored along, easing his tense muscles. He wondered if the supercharger had damaged the engine. Against the solemn warnings of Rolls Royce, he had had fitted, by his pet expert at the Headquarters motor pool, a supercharger. Rolls Royce had said the cylinder head [camshaft bearings] wouldn't take the extra compression [load] and, when he confessed to them what he had done, they regretfully but firmly withdrew their guarantees and washed their hands of their bastardised child. This was the first time he had notched 125 and the rev counter had been [hovered] dangerously over the red line at 5000 [4500]. But the temperature and oil were okay and there were no expensive noises. And by God it had been fun!"*

I don't see the need for maker's name, but if you feel it adds something, it should be Arnott supercharger controlled by a magnetic clutch. This has been done with a 4¼ engine.

FROM AUBREY FORSHAW

5th April, 1962

Dear Ian,

Extreme pressure following a long-weekend accounts for my delayed answer to your note regarding this Bond's Bastard Bentley.

I feel a bit of a hit-and-run daddy if the car born in THUNDERBALL was sired by any remarks of mine. My own idea of a special toy was an

---

* The square brackets above are Fleming's own.

R-type 1954 chassis with the latest series 2 engine – the Vee 8. The THUNDERBALL vehicle is using the chassis I would <u>not</u> have chosen – the S2 and an engine I've never heard of a Mark IV. But it's all so very 'special' particularly with a 9.5:1 compression ratio, that nobody is likely to crib.

However, let's get down to legitimising the bastard and meeting your wish to pour on more power by the casual flick of a dashboard switch.

I've got this planned and am entertaining the Rolls Tech. Expert next Thursday so that we can make this love-child a genetic possibility.

In your new copy you mention cylinder head (singular) so you have still the straight six engine – presumably 4.8 litres and I'm basing the engine treatment on this supposition although I'll cover an alternative for the twin heads of a Vee 8.

You mustn't add puff without lowering compression, particularly from your stated 9.5:1 – so the car should use 7.5:1 with a couple of Weber carbs, normally aspirated, which will give you lashings of docile power, but for le moment critique we will fit a by-pass to the manifolds, feeding from a Shorrocks supercharger the clutch engagement of which is effected by solenoid from your little switch. In fact, your bearings (big-end and main) are more likely to complain than are well-fitted cylinder heads but the proposition of a 'special' capable of, say, 140 or so is quite feasible, assuming a suitable back-axle ratio.

I imagine it is the B's sheer size and weight under unfavourable circumstances that will allow the girl-friend to get away in a less potent, but more wiggle-worthy machine – this could easily be, but she'd better have something pretty good; not so quick of course, not so accelerative, but with a better look and roadability.

I hope you can await my further thoughts and we will then put you in a position to confute any criticisms – always supposing that "Headquarters motor pool" enjoys happy relations with the Exchequer.

TO AUBREY FORSHAW

11th April, 1962

My dear Aubrey,

Thank you a thousand times for the priceless gen which I am afraid I find myself quite incapable of working up into prose as I must obviously start again and get the whole thing right from the beginning.

Would you be an angel and just take that extract from the book and dictate to the secretary how it should run, using your own choice of the R-type 1954 chassis with the series 2 engine – the Vee 8.

I know this is greatly imposing on you, but if I try and translate your high grade stuff into English I shall only get it all wrong again.

Please don't pay any attention to what I have actually written. What I beg you to do is to re-write the piece so that it is according to your specifications and technically possible.

Forgive all this labour I am asking of you and just put it down to the hazards of being my publisher.

Happy Easter!

FROM AUBREY FORSHAW

April 30th, 1962

Dear Ian,

I return your passage of motor mystique with the deathless prose intact but for detail additions which authenticate without inviting too many queries from the aficionados.

You may rest assured that Bond is now driving a Feasible Proposition (there have been stranger marques) the bits all being Bentley and susceptible of assembly into one car.

I am now off to the International Publishers Conference in Barcelona and shall not be back until third week in May. When I return I will furnish you with a kind of record card containing dimensions, ratios, revs. etc., so that questions to Headquarters Motor pool can be answered – but I'll undertake to deal with any such questions if you so wish.

Only one of your main requirements proved a bit difficult, namely the introduction of the Vee-8 engine. So you have an

'R' type chassis (1955)
the big 6 engine 4.9 litres
an Arnott blower
a 13:40 back axle ratio
16 x 6.70 wheels (Dunlop RS/5 tyres)
which would give a theoretical 126–162 m.p.h.
at 4,500 revs (the red line). Actually
about your 125 m.p.h. Max revs in <u>top</u>
would take an endless road to achieve without
a blower – so your addition is justified, and
your acceleration quite something.

Keep up the good work.

TO AUBREY FORSHAW

1st May, 1962

A thousand thanks for your letter of April 30th and for your wonderful help over the Bentley.

At last we will get Bond into the right kind of vehicle and he will damn well have to stay there until you let him out of it.

It was indeed kind of you to take so much trouble.

TO ROBIN DE LA LANNE MIRRLEES, ESQ., Rouge Dragon, The College of Arms, London, E.C.4.

25th April, 1962

My dear Robin,

I heard so late of the tragedy of dear Frances and am so bad at writing letters of commiseration, that I didn't write to you.

She was a dear person whom I came to like greatly and there is nothing I would rather have than some small memento of hers when you get around to sorting things out.

Now to the book. First of all many thanks about haemophilia, it was stupid of me to have got it wrong.

The book is a tremendous lark and while it has a bit of a rag at the expense of an invented Pursuivant called Griffon Or, Rouge Dragon then enters the story in fine style and plays a worthy part in tracking down the villain.

The text is now with the typist and should be ready in a couple of weeks or so. Then I would love for us to meet anywhere you suggest and slip you a copy sub rosa, which I would be most grateful if you would read for mistakes or improvements, making the freest use of your red ink.

You will find that your advices have been put to the most splendid use and the book is in fact dedicated to Rouge Dragon and a certain Hilary Bray, who, through you, makes a valuable contribution as a cover name for James Bond.

But please keep all this highly confidential and far away from the world of the College, who might prove stuffy about being dragged into a thriller, though they needn't worry and come out of it all most fragrantly.

I will get in touch with you as soon as the typescript appears.

TO WILLIAM PLOMER

9th May, 1962

Michael is coming to see me this evening about some drawings for the Chitty-Chitty-Bang-Bang series, so I am then going to deliver into his hands the gigantic volume, surely as long as the Koran, which I have just finished correcting.

Normally, as you know, I prefer you to see my oeuvres before anyone else in Capes, since it is always your verdict, and only yours, that I care about.

So please don't think that this break in continuity is a slur upon you, in fact it is sparing you an extra few days from the annual labour.

Thank you for your sympathetic note to Annie about the reviews [of *The Spy Who Loved Me*]. It has certainly been an uncomfortable two or three weeks having to digest a second breakfast every morning of these hommany grits – well deserved though they may be.

Only Wolverhampton and Bristol, bless them, have been kind. There live obviously the intellectual elite of England!

I hope at least some of OHMSS will bring a wry smile to your care-worn features, and of course I long for the sheets of green bumph.

Let us have lunch soon please. What about Wednesday, 23rd May at the Charing Cross?

FROM WILLIAM PLOMER

10th May, 1962

My dear Ian,

I am so pleased to hear that the new oeuvre has been handed over & I shall seize it as soon as it comes within arm's length. I think it a v.g. idea that we should lunch together at the Ch. Cross Hotel on Wednesday 23rd May. If you will ask Griffie to be kind enough to book a table, I will be in that room upstairs with all those armchairs at about 1 o'c. I hope by then I shall have read the new typescript.

I think you have had <u>quite</u> enough hominy (please note spelling) grits to be going on with, but, as my governess used to say, the higher one climbs, the thicker the clouds.

I hope you didn't think me tiresomely carping about the intro to the Hugh Edwards book.* It's simply that I want to protect you from laying yourself open to any more impertinence from reviewers. I didn't want them to say, "Look, he's telling us that he can <u>read</u>," or "Why does he tell

---

* Fleming had written an introduction to one of his favourite novels, Hugh Edwards' *All Night at Mr Stanyhurst's* (1963). Plomer felt his first draft was too pretentious.

us that about himself instead of sticking to the man & book he is introducing?" I was myself much interested in all you had to say, & I have a weakness for many neglected books & authors.

I am up to my clavicles in dung, but what are a dung beetle's clavicles for, if not for upholding many forms of that commodity.

Vive Wolverhampton! Vive Bristol!

TO LEONARD RUSSELL, ESQ., 14 Albion Street, London, W.2.

14th May, 1962

My dear Leonard,

You are always doing kindnesses for me, would you please do me one more?

Phyllis Bottome will be eighty on the 31st May and she is ill and low in spirits, and I thought it would be terribly kind if you could put a little paragraph in Atticus about her.

Her real name is Mrs. Ernan Forbes Dennis, and their address is Little Greenly, 95, South End Road, Hampstead, N.W.3. Telephone No. Hampstead 0579; in case an Atticus runner could have a word with him on the telephone to get some notes – the number of books she has written; copies sold; the most popular, etc.

A possible point of interest is that when Ernan was Vice-Consul for the Tyrol he took a few boys and taught them German for the diplomatic. It was our first contact with a 'famous writer', and it may be that by a process of osmosis we imbibed some of Phyllis's undoubted talent, because of the very few boys who stayed with them in Kitzbuhel three, myself, Ralph Arnold of Constables and Nigel Dennis have ended up successful writers, though in very different spheres.

So far as I am concerned I wrote my first story at Phyllis Bottome's behest when I was about nineteen, and I remember my pleasure at her kindly criticisms of it.

I am afraid this is rather straw bricks, but it would be terribly kind if you could somehow knit together a paragraph about her and cheer her up.

Forgive this chore but I promise to repay with a book review if and when you find anything appropriate.

TO MICHAEL HOWARD

24th May, 1962

My Dear Michael,

I am having my portrait painted – so is [racing driver] Graham Hill – by a man called Amherst Villiers who invented the supercharger on James Bond's 4½ litre Bentley. He has been taking a course with Annigoni* and we are obliged to sit for him out of friendship.

Now, he is a motor car and guided missile designer of absolutely top calibre and, in fact, designed the crankshaft for Graham Hill's B.R.M. which has been winning lately. I put to him our problem about getting a good car drawn for Chitty-Chitty-Bang-Bang, and he is amused and has agreed to have a bash.

We have obviously got to get this car right before either Trog or Haro can do the subsequent illustrations, and once they have something to copy it shouldn't be too difficult.

I guess Amherst will do a spiffing job and really make it look as if it will work. So I have written him the enclosed and sent copies of the stories, and we will see what happens.

TO AMHERST VILLIERS, ESQ., 48A Holland Street, London, w.8.

While sitting for Villiers, it occurred to Fleming that he might be able to assist with the illustrations for Chitty-Chitty-Bang-Bang.

24th May, 1962

My Dear Amherst,

Here are now the stories which it won't take you long to read.

---

* Pietro Annigoni (1910–88), Italian portraitist who had painted Queen Elizabeth in 1956.

The point is that while Jonathan Cape's have got one or two artists lined up for the figures, landscapes, etc., they can't find anybody with enough technical know-how and imagination to draw a suitable Chitty-Chitty-Bang-Bang.

What I and Cape's would very much like from you is a design for the cover to run right round the spine of the book for each story, again showing the car, but in the first adventure with its wings spread, in the second adventure with its wheels turned sideways so that it can motor across the Channel, and in the third adventure soaring up into the air with wings and perhaps some jet apparatus in the rear end.

Also on those centre spreads it would be nice to have one or two detailed little sketches of the dashboard, the radiator grill open with the fan belt extruded to provide a screw for air and water, and similar little imaginative details such as you might presumably add in the margin of any car for which you were doing a first rough design.

If you are kind enough to make the sketches, please make them as large as you like and then when we get down to actual book production Capes will talk to you about colour, sizes, etc., etc.

Although the guts of the car are supposedly antiquated, we would like to make it really snazzy looking to excite the imagination of children between about 7 and 10, so it can have every kind of entrail coming out of the side, air scoops, straps around the bonnet, etc. And, of course, the facia board will be crowded with knobs and switches, etc.

It is a long sleek sports car and I had in mind something between a pre-war Le Mans Mercedes and a 45 Renault. But you will surely come up with something more imaginative than this.

I think you can use up to three basic colours plus black and white. The chrome presents a problem, but these are only preliminary sketches and we can iron out these problems later.

It is terribly kind of you to suggest doing this and I am writing to Capes today telling them of the project.

See you next Wednesday at 3.30 for a further sitting in the dentist's chair.

TO WILLIAM PLOMER

24th May, 1962

My dear William,

I hope you will agree that this paper, foisted on me by the film company, will bring Spring to Rustington!

A thousand thanks for lunch and for the splendid green sheets. Naturally I agree with the majority of your comments, and I am horrified to see how much inward groaning goes on in the book. I will go back to school on these L.G.F.s* and see if I can't spruce them up a degree or two.

But to hell with you and Money [Manet],† I am going to go straight to Rothenstein‡ and see if I am not right.

The crankshaft designer, who turns out to be a pupil of Annigoni, is making me look like a mixture between Nehru and Somerset Maugham. As you can imagine I am longing for Annie's comments on the picture.

FROM WILLIAM PLOMER

25th May, 62

My dear Ian,

"O! O! 007!" I exclaimed when I saw your new writing paper. And what shall I say when I see your portrait?

About Manet & all that, it's just that that paragraph slightly holds up the reader and the action so near the beginning. It makes (I think) the take-off less smooth. One begins (at least this one begins) worrying as to whether the seaside landscape you are describing really is in the least like the one

---

* L.G.F. was Plomer's shorthand for 'Low Grade Fiction', a term that he applied to Fleming's more clichéd expressions.

† Fleming had described the beaches of Brittany and Picardy as being painted by Manet. Plomer remarked, 'One doesn't associate Manet with pictures of these beaches.' In the final draft it was changed to Monet.

‡ Sir William Rothenstein (1892–1945), painter, draughtsman and authoritative writer on art. He had belonged to the bohemian circle that Fleming's mother attracted in the 1920s.

painted by Boudin &c., in its human & incidental constituents. And also this sudden injection of art-history makes one wonder if there isn't some clue to a later development that one ought to look for. And, apart from heraldic information (which, as you happily point out, is a lot of bezants) I don't think there are any other allusions to art history &c., so this paragraph stands out too conspicuously. But you will think I am making a huge fuss about nothing & you may be groaning outwardly as well as inwardly.

I much enjoyed our Charing Cross lunch but of course missed you at your own table yesterday.

What is so good about your books is their sharp focus. Everything is <u>clear</u>, so makes a clear impression. I feel sure that OHMSS will rout the objectors.

TO MR. ROBERT KENNEDY, Hickory Hill, McLean, Virginia

The previous year President J. F. Kennedy had publicly endorsed Fleming's books. Now, in a reply to similar praise from his brother 'Bobby', Fleming reiterated his thanks.

20th June, 1962

Dear Mr. Kennedy,

Thank you very much for your charming note of June 1st, and I am delighted to take this opportunity to thank Kennedys everywhere for the electric effect their commendation has had on my sales in America.

My last book, The Spy Who Loved Me, has had an extremely mixed reception, due largely to the late appearance of James Bond. But I can now tell you that my next and longest to date, has James Bond in from the first page to the last, and all Kennedys will be receiving a copy around next Easter.

Incidentally, you may be amused to pass round the enclosed translation from Izvestia* of May 29th last. I am most amused to learn that I have been selected by the Russians as part of America's strong right hand!

* A Soviet newspaper that was often critical of Bond.

Over here we are all watching with fascination your gallant attempts to harass American gangsterdom. If James Bond can be any help to you please let me know and I will have a word with M.

Again with my warmest thanks for your kindness in writing.

TO MICHAEL HOWARD

31st July, 1962

Here is now the College of Arms final rendering of the true Bond coat of arms marked 1., and Rouge Dragon doesn't think there will be any objection to using it since the line is extinct.

I have no idea how you and Dickie are going to turn this into a jacket, but I think your idea of the thumb and forefinger holding a pen coming up from the right hand bottom corner is a good one. And it strikes me that the vellum on which Dickie would be writing could be perhaps turned up at one corner with brass drawing pins used to hold down the other three corners.

On reflection, I wonder if it wouldn't be better to get the whole title in however small, as otherwise the whole thing is going to look a bit stark.

Anyway may I now leave the problems to you as I am feeling slightly submerged?

I enclose the first copy, marked 2, for comparison, but if you don't want to use it could you please buzz it back.

Regarding the proofs, I have cut out all italics except the lines of Corsican dialogue and the names of newspapers, and I am sure this is the best formula to follow as otherwise we will have a forest of italics.

I have sorted out all the various problems and I don't think much more remains to be done.

FROM MICHAEL HOWARD

As part of their promotional campaign for On Her Majesty's Secret Service *Cape planned a limited edition of 250 copies. A handsome affair, it was quarter-bound in vellum, with a set of ski-tracks curving across the front board.*

8th October, 1962

My dear Ian,

I have to confess to being astonished by that film of DR. NO.* Judging only, I must admit, by the lamentable productions that have been made of most of my favourite thrillers, I had become convinced that it was really impossible to translate that kind of book into visual terms. Eon have certainly stacked the problem in the grand manner and, by pulling out all the stops, I rather think they have got away with it. It was a delight to be in that particular audience the other night, but up and down the country I should think the film will be lapped up. I do congratulate you on the magnificent billing you have secured in all the publicity and in the credits in the film itself. Are plans for distribution in the United States settled yet?

You remember mentioning in THE THRILLING CITIES the cover of Tiger Saito's THIS IS JAPAN. Would this possibly make an illustration to the book and, if so, do you have a copy we could reproduce: or could you get hold of one?

I have had two more thoughts about the limited edition of O.H.M.S.S. First, how about a frontispiece, viz. a portrait of you? If you favour this notion, have you a particular choice of picture? Would Amherst Villiers's portrait serve? Second, we plan to print at most 250 copies, of which only 150 would be nominally for sale, and I should expect that quite a few of them would be given away. Those actually sold would be priced at 3 guineas, but the revenue from them after trade discount won't go far towards covering the cost of quite an expensive operation, particularly if we pay a full royalty on them. As this is really a publicity gimmick, would you settle for, say, ten free copies of the limited edition in lieu of any royalty on them?

I hope that you now have a chance to turn your attention to the blurb for THE THRILLING CITIES.

* *Dr No* had premiered three days earlier on 5 October 1962.

TO MICHAEL HOWARD

10th October, 1962

I am glad you liked the film, it certainly had wonderful reviews and seems to be doing good business. Apparently it is to open in the States in April.

I'm afraid I haven't got a copy of Tiger Saito's "This is Japan", and I cannot find that I ever referred to its cover but merely to the fact that Tiger was its editor. I don't think it would make a particularly interesting illustration, but as it looks as if I may have to go to Japan in November I will get hold of a copy of the current issue and also look back through previous covers to see if there is anything suitable for us.

Regarding the limited edition of OHMSS, I think Amherst Villiers' portrait, which is just about finished, would suit you very well. But why not give him a ring and go and have a look at it. Incidentally, he is not very well off and I think should rate a generous fee.

I would be happy to accept ten free copies of the edition in lieu of royalty on them, but I don't see why you have to give so many copies away instead of selling them and then at least at four guineas a go.

Incidentally, why not put up the price of OHMSS? I am sure you could get away with it.

I will have a bash at the blurb of "The Thrilling Cities" forthwith.

TO PERCY MUIR

Percy Muir was assisting in the curation of a monumental exhibition, 'Printing and the Mind of Man', due to be held at the British Museum the next year. As part of the show he wanted to include some volumes from Fleming's collection of first editions.

10th October, 1962

My dear Percy,
This does indeed sound a magnificent affair that you are compering and naturally I will do anything I can to help.

Unfortunately all my books are at present housed at the Pantechnicon in large crates and I have no idea how you could find what you want without unpacking the whole lot.

The only hope is that we have built a small house not far from Faringdon and hope to get in some time after Christmas when the books will arrive and be installed in the shelves which have been prepared for them.

Meanwhile, have you got a copy of that rough catalogue you had done for me shortly after the war? If not I have a copy and could send it down to you.

I do wish we could meet soon as I haven't seen you for years. Do please give me a ring the next time you are likely to be up and come to lunch.

I have initiated the Fleming three day week but am nearly always here on Tuesdays, Wednesdays or Thursdays.

It was lovely to hear from you.

TO MICHAEL HOWARD

7th November, 1962

I gather you are panicking a bit for a blurb for "The Thrilling Cities".

To tell you the truth I simply cannot think of anything original to say about this book, and I do beg you to get one of your staff to write something suitable.

It may help to enclose copies of the draft prefaces I have written for the beginning and half way through, with the reservation that these are not final.

Sorry, but I can think of nothing in the way of a blurb except half a dozen boring clichés.

Off to Japan from November 14th to 21st researching for a new James Bond. My God, how I work for you all!

I shall be sending the corrected proof of 'On Her Majesty's Secret Service' off to you in the next two or three days. But I would like to point out here how many of my corrections are due to literals and other errors of your printers.

This is the first time I have had sloppy proofs from Capes and I hope you will take the printers' own errors into account in adjudicating the costs of corrections!

TO MICHAEL HOWARD

13th November, 1962

I would be quite happy for the 'The' to be dropped from 'Thrilling Cities'.

Incidentally, we must have a talk about pictures before Christmas and I have now corrected the proofs as best I can.

I have also had them corrected by a bright lad called Peter Garnham who works for 'Queen', but I am so fed up with going through the book that I would be very grateful if one of your minions could marry up the two versions, using his good sense.

Another small point. Since Amherst Villiers is likely to be off to America in the New Year it might be a good idea to get him to finalise, in your chosen colours, the drawing of Chitty-Chitty-Bang-Bang.

O.H.M.S.S. wasn't as bad as all that, but I am so used to getting really excellent proofs from your printers that I was only very slightly miffed.

Incidentally, Max Aitken of The Daily Express likes it very much and will almost certainly want to serialise it, straddling your publication date.

TO MICHAEL HOWARD

30th November, 1962

My Dear Michael,

CHITTY-CHITTY-BANG-BANG

I have no objection to Haro Hodson if you think he can do the job.

Mightn't it be an idea for you to pay Trog, say, a nominal ten guineas for the work he has already done and which might give Haro an idea or two.

But the truth of the matter is that I am now absolutely fed up with this whole series and have completely lost the mood.

I am tidying up Adventure Number 3, but heaven knows if and when I shall produce an adventure Number 4.

So would your machine now please take the whole problem over and cope with it as best they may?

I don't mind what alterations are made to the text, but I will do my best to discover a more delectable fudge and send the recipe along.

Sorry to put all this firmly on your plate, but such free mind as I have is now engaged in trying to devise another James Bond.

P.S. Would be quite happy to come to some joint royalty arrangement with whoever you choose, a la Trog.

FROM MICHAEL HOWARD

14th December, 1962

My dear Ian,

Very many thanks indeed for letting me see OCTOPUSSY and Cyril Connolly's parody ['Bond Strikes Camp']. I have shown them both to William, who will be writing to you about them before Christmas, and from the talk I had with him yesterday I think we both feel much the same about them.

I like your story very much indeed. I think it's rather better than the best of the stories in FOR YOUR EYES ONLY, but shares with one or two of them the disadvantage from the point of view of including it in a collection of Bond stories that Bond's appearance is fairly immaterial and the part he plays a negligible one, so that Bond fans might well react as they did to THE SPY WHO LOVED ME and demand more of their hero. It's rather like those alternate Simenons, the ones without Maigret: for my money they are often the better written of Simenon's books, more varied and interesting and with better character drawing: nevertheless it is really for Maigret that I read Simenon and I can't help slightly resenting the time he spends on the other books.

As to BOND STRIKES CAMP, this outrageous riot really deserves the maximum circulation and if the London magazine is really prepared to take the chance of printing it I think you should let them take it. It would become a collector's piece within hours and the much wider distribution would add greatly to the publicity value for Bond.

I hear that DR. NO has already reached the top flight of the year's most successful films.

FROM NOËL COWARD, Blue Harbour, Port Maria, Jamaica, W.I.

29th March, 1963

Mon Ever So Cher Commandant,

I really am very very 'Proudfull' of you. O.H.M.S.S. is, to my simple, unsophisticated mind, far and away the best you have done yet. In the first place there is much more genuine characterization than usual and I believed all of them. In the second place the 'action' parts although they go far, do not go too far and are terrifically exciting without straining the credibility to excess. In the third place it is really brilliantly constructed and all the Heraldic stuff and the discussion of biological warfare are very lucid as well as being most impressive. Whatever Mr Franklin may say I, for one, am extremely worried about the Great South African Land Snail even if he isn't.

Of course as an accurate picture of daily life in the Alpine Set it may leave a little to be desired. All jolly joking aside it really is very very good indeed and I only finally put it down so that Coley could pick it up.

Another thing that made the book especially glorious for me was my discovery, on page 34 of a gratifying bit of careless raportage [sic]. In the game of Chemin de Fer dear boy, unlike Snakes and Ladders to which you are obviously more accustomed, there are certain immutable rules.

Bond couldn't <u>possibly</u> have lost to a One with a Buche of <u>two</u> Kings. The English lady <u>must</u> have asked for a card as she would hardly stand on a one. In that case Bond would have turned up his cards and also drawn one so he must have had a 'Buche' – to coin a phrase – of THREE court cards or tens. I hate to have to point these little errors out to you but you are getting a big boy now and in writing about the gaudy pleasures of the Upper Set, which I have adorned so triumphantly for more years than you, you must <u>try</u> to get things straight. Incidentally there is now only <u>one</u> mention of Fairy Tale in my lyrics so sucks to you.

My time here is drawing to a close and I hate the idea of it. Joyce, Hopie, Coley and I drove over Hardware Gap and stayed at Strawberry Hill which we loved. It was redolent of proudfull memories of you and the Ex Lady Rothermere. It was staggeringly beautiful but a bit nippy after dark.

Listen now. Ed Bigg, my Chicago doctor who really is the most sensible doctor I have ever encountered, came to visit <u>with</u> me on a holiday – vacation – with his wife. We had a long discussion about smoking which he is <u>dead</u> against (He gave it up himself some years ago and there is a little conscious virtue mixed up with this). Anyhow I told him that, for creative people who had the habit badly, it was a really dreadful deprivation to have to stop it. Then he told me that the clever Americans manufacture a cigarette with virtually no nicotine in it at all called SANO. You can get them King sized or ordinary. The King sized are better. They haven't much taste but they most emphatically do the trick. I had two cartons sent from New York. Would you like me to bring you some on April 16th or better still cable to New York for some yourself. You <u>may</u> even be able to get them in London. Personally I never intend to smoke anything else. Of course they haven't got the kick of Senior Service or any of our Virginian cigarettes but they're very like Lucky Strikes or Philip Morris or any of the ordinary American brands. And you will soon get used to them. If you get the ordinary size smoke them with Aqua filters because they are not as tightly packed as the King size. Although I've been brave and heroic to cut down to five or six smokes a day it <u>has</u> been a bore and a strain, and to be able to smoke now without a sense of guilt is really a tremendous relief. Do have a bash. It is the demon Nicotine that is the trouble and buggers up the veins and arteries. I've been into the whole business with great care and am now as merry as a grig.

I shall be here until the 7th and then New York 404 East 55th street.

You were jolly sweet to send me the book and I would like to go on about it much more when I see you. I find that some dreary strangers are suffering ptomaine at Goldeneye and so I can't use the beach. What a bore you are.

Love and kisses to you and your poor old Dutch.

[PS] I would have preferred 'Pis du Chat' to 'Pis de Chat' but one can't have everything.

TO MICHAEL HOWARD

23rd April, 1963

It is really ghastly, I have never made so many mistakes in a book in my life as in OHMSS.

I am not blaming anyone but myself, apart from one or two very minor literals.

Anyway, I am being deluged with letters from people ticking me off because Raymond Mortimer said how wonderfully accurate I was in my books!

Here now is a total list of all the corrections which should go into the next edition, and I am hastily sending a copy off to Ed Doctorow,* who is editing the book in NAL, in the hope that he can check them all in time for the American edition, otherwise I shall get a fresh deluge of brickbats.

For your next edition would you please be very kind and see that all these corrections go in, and also make certain Pan has a list or, at any rate, the correct Cape edition from which to print.

So sorry for all this, and I have recently spent a couple of hours with one of the stupidest Japanese in existence trying to make sure that we won't get Arthur Waley† on our tail over the next book!

* E. L. Doctorow (b. 1931–2015), author of *Welcome to Hard Times* and *Ragtime*. He worked as an editor at NAL (National American Library) press in the 1960s.

† Arthur Waley (1889–1966) was a distinguished orientalist whose translations opened classical Chinese and Japanese literature culture to the general reader.

TO THE EDITOR, THE SUNDAY TIMES, Thomson House, Gray's Inn Road, London, W.C.1.

2nd April, 1963

Sir,

I am being deluged with enquiries as to why James Bond should dress his hair with pink tooth-powder. This misunderstanding arises from Mr. Raymond Mortimer's most generous review of my opuscula in which the late Mr. Trumper's "Eucryl" appears instead of his "Eucris". (In fact Bond uses nothing on his hair and the Eucris featured only in M. Draco's spare-room bathroom.) And your rendering of Bond's "Attenhofer Flex" ski-bindings as "Attenborough Fox" in Mr. Mortimer's most kindly reference to my efforts to achieve accuracy has resulted in one scornful winter sportsman suggesting I take a refresher course at Zermatt.

Could it be, Sir, that a sub-cell of SPECTRE is building up in your literary department?

16

You Only Live Twice

T HE WINTER OF 1963 was the worst Britain had suffered for more than 150 years. In January, the snow rose twenty feet high, blocking railways, roads and waterways. Ice extended so many miles from the coast that people wondered if the English Channel would freeze over. In February conditions deteriorated further, with more snow and gale-force winds. At Oxford somebody drove a car across the Thames. And in Goldeneye, at a steady 80° Fahrenheit, Fleming was writing about Japan.

Fleming had been fascinated by Japan ever since he visited Tokyo in 1959 while researching *Thrilling Cities*. During that first trip he had met the redoubtable Australian journalist Richard Hughes – 'Dikko' to his friends – who guided him through the niceties of oriental culture with blasphemous gusto. Another contact had been the journalist Torao 'Tiger' Saito. Both men were there to greet him at Tokyo airport when he arrived in November 1962 to spend two weeks collating material for his new book. The result, over which Fleming was now toiling cheer-fully in the Caribbean, was called *You Only Live Twice*.

Following the death of his wife Tracy, Bond is in decline: drinking, gambling and turning up late for work. As a last chance M equips him with a new number, 7777, and sends him to Japan on a diplomatic pass-port to effect an information exchange with 'Tiger' Tanaka, head of Japanese Intelligence. Instead, however, Bond finds himself on the trail of his nemesis Blofeld, now installed in a remote castle under the name Dr Guntram Shatterhand. Here, with his repellent assistant Irma Bunt, he tends a garden in which every flower, every bush, every ornamental pond, is deadly. Helium balloons surround the castle, warning people to keep away while at the same time advertising that here lies certain death. Month by month scores of people come to commit suicide. With the assistance of Tanaka and an Australian intelligence officer 'Dikko' Henderson, Bond is given a make-over as a mute coal miner from the north of the country and installed in a coastal village with the family of Kissy Suzuki, an actress turned pearl diver. With her help he infiltrates the castle and after several narrow escapes manages to kill both Blofeld and Irma Bunt before escaping on one of the helium balloons. Winged by a bullet from one of the guards he drops hundreds of feet into the sea. When rescued by Kissy Suzuki, it is as an amnesiac, with no recollection of his previous life. Settling down with her he works as a simple oarsman on her fishing boat. But at one point he sees the name Vladivostok in a newspaper. It stirs something inside him and he feels compelled to go there in search of his past. Behind him, though he does not know it, he leaves Kissy several months pregnant. Back in London he is categorised as 'Missing Presumed Dead' and is duly given an obituary in *The Times*.

While in Jamaica Fleming had a lapse in spirits. Pondering his ever weaker health, he wrote to Dikko Hughes that Bond had 'had a good run, which is more than most of us these days. Everything seems a lot of trouble these days – too much trouble. Keep alive.' When Hughes remonstrated, Fleming replied, 'Dikko, I promise. Don't worry. I'm not worrying any more. Down with death.' Despondent or not, Fleming managed to pull it off once again. *You Only Live Twice* was, like its predecessor, a splendid book and with its vivid set pieces – including a torture chair set above a volcanic vent, which Bond subsequently blocked to destroy Blofeld's castle – showed his imagination running at full throttle. The obituary, too, provided fans with their first full explanation of Bond's origins. After the box-office success of *Dr No* he could not have poised 007's latest adventure more perfectly.

The screen version of *Dr No* had boosted Fleming's standing to such an extent that he and his creation had become household names: in June he was invited to appear on the prestigious radio programme

Desert Island Discs; in Oxford a group of enthusiastic undergraduates had founded a James Bond Club; and across the Atlantic the *Harvard Lampoon* published a spoof Bond novel called *Alligator* which was so successful that it sold an astonishing 100,000 copies. Nor was there any sign of the acclaim abating, as, barely had the dust died down from *Dr No*, than Eon was on to the next one, *From Russia with Love*, which started filming in Istanbul that spring. Fleming, who flew there as an observer, was fêted with due reverence; but he must have reflected on the difference between this visit and his last. Back in 1955 he had been an intrepid reporter, roaming the darkened streets as all around him riots raged. Now he was a frail figure who struggled slowly over the cobbles, pausing every now and then to rest on a shooting stick.

In July came Percy Muir's exhibition, 'Printing and the Mind of Man', or, to give its full subtitle, 'A display of printing mechanisms and printed material to illustrate the history of western civilisation and the means of literary multiplication since the fifteenth century'. Fleming's contribution amounted to forty-four volumes, the largest showing by any private collector, and one of which he was immensely proud. An even greater accolade came when he was invited to be a member of the Committee of Honour. In a telegram to Percy Muir he wrote, 'A THOUSAND CON-GRATULATIONS ON YOUR WONDERFUL CATALOGUE AND PARTICU-LARLY ON HAVING ELEVATED OUR COLLECTION TO THESE FANTASTICALLY PROUD HEIGHTS STOP I TRULY BLUSH WITH EMBAR-RASSED DELIGHT AND WITH WARM MEMORIES OF THOSE DAYS WHEN YOU TOOK ME BY THE HAND STOP GRUESS DICH GOTT IAN'.

What was more, his collection having languished for so many years in storage, he now had a library to put it in. That month he, Ann and Caspar moved into their new home, Sevenhampton Place, where one of Fleming's first acts was to install a wall of shelves. Here he arranged his first editions, each in a black box stamped with the family crest of a goat's head, and with labels colour-coded according to subject. Despite Ann's valiant attempts to make it a home, Fleming was never entirely happy with the place. The surroundings were unkempt and overgrown, with a lake whose mists he said encouraged mushrooms on his clothes.

A bright spot in his life was a Studebaker Avanti – left-hand drive, spanking new and freshly delivered from America – which he had put through its paces earlier that year on a drive to Lausanne to interview Georges Simenon. But even this wasn't enough to shake off a gathering sense of mortality. As Ann wrote, he was in a state of 'permanent angry misery', and it was perhaps his own gloom more than anything else that cast a pall over Sevenhampton.

Professionally, he was a model of diligence. Despite instituting what he proudly described as 'the Fleming three-day week', he continued to pepper C. D. Hamilton with article suggestions for the *Sunday Times* and even found time to knock out a Bond short story, 'Property of a Lady', for Sotheby's house magazine *The Ivory Hammer*. The plot was simple. On finding an undercover spy in the department, M sends Bond after her paymaster. Her payment, it seems, is to be financed by a Fabergé egg, one of the few still held by the Soviets, which has been smuggled into the country and is due to be auctioned at Sotheby's. Bond scours the auction room and as the hammer falls at £155,000 spots the final bidder. Although it was perfectly well written, Fleming felt the piece wasn't up to standard and refused to accept any money for it.

Celebrity was taking its toll. *From Russia with Love* premiered on 10 October 1963 and was so eagerly anticipated that people queued around Leicester Square to gain admission. But for Fleming it was an ordeal. He insisted his doctor be present in the cinema and having arranged an after-party at his London home, Victoria Square, retired early, leaving his guests to face tables heaped with caviar.

There was a light-hearted moment at the end of the month when Fleming received an irresistible invitation: to present awards at the Romantic Novelists' Association annual dinner. But when it came to the speech he asked Evelyn Waugh to write it for him. This was the same Waugh who – himself approaching death – had visited the Flemings at Sevenhampton and written to a friend, 'Old Thunderbird [...] wishes to end his life and is determined to have his final seizure on the golf course or at the card table. Ann will be disconsolate.'

TO WILLIAM PLOMER

Plomer, who had lived for several years in Japan during the 1920s, was happy to supply Fleming with tips and recommendations before he embarked on his research trip.

11th September, 1962

My dear Wm,

A thousand thanks for the Japanese gen and I have already got the excellent Mariani Book. Will get the Horned ones.

I have no idea how Bond in Japan will turn out, but I have in mind an absolutely daft story in which Blofeld meets his match. The only trouble with killing off one's villains is that one has to invent new ones. However.

I was indeed rather low when I saw you, but this is largely because I am feeling tremendously stuck in an over mink-lined rut and I need to be booted off across the world in the old style.

However, I think I have the secret and I will report to you further in due course.

The main thing is to have your oaken shoulder available when necessary.

Anyway, the last thing I want to do is to heap more dung on the beetle's back and correspondence on this subject is therefore closed with the reflection that if one prays for the boot one very often gets it from the wrong quarter in the wrong place, so I must be careful.

In December 1962 Fleming came across a newspaper cutting that read, 'Mr. Ian Fleming won the Lord Strathcona and Mount Royal Challenge Trophy for the best collection of vegetables in the amateur class'. He wasted no time sticking it on a postcard, and with a stamp that bore the motto 'National Productivity Year', sent it to Plomer with the words, 'So please treat me with more respect in 1963!'

TO WILLIAM PLOMER

From Goldeneye, 22nd February, 1963

My dear Wm,

End of term report. I have completed Opus XII save for 2 or 3 pages and am amazed that the miracle should have managed to repeat itself – the 65,000 odd words that is, & pretty odd some of them are! Since it is set in Japan, every day I have heard you chuckling wryly (I know! Stand in corner!) over my shoulder & God knows what Arthur Waley et al will have to say. Lafcadio Hernia* – & you can say that again! But I think even you will glean some Japanese esoterica &, after all, when was it the last English novel about Japan was written? Just to give you an advance frisson, Bondo-san is about to pleasure Kissy Suzuki, the Ama girl, after she has stimulated his senses with toad's sweat – a well-known Jap aphrodisiac, as of course you know. But you have to take a long hike through Japan before this & similar mayhem are portrayed & I fear that only the soundest addicts of Japoniserie will stay the course. It is called "You only live twice", the first line of a haiku in the manner of Basho, 17th century itinerant poet whose works will be, I assume, on your bed-side table. Anyway, the Contemptible work is completed & will be submitted to honourable task-master shortly after my return.

Otherwise no news except far too much death & brooding bad conscience at not sharing the ghastly winter all our friends have been through. It must have been like this for those who were away during the blitz. I do hope you have breasted your way through without damage or too much dismay. Here it has been a shameful 80° throughout & perhaps the steadily best weather we have ever had. Haven't you arrived at the age when you should winter abroad? Your bed is permanently turned down here & TLC awaits you always.

Just had a long letter from Michael so please pass on the Contempt-ible Book news to him & save me an extra chunk of reportage.

---

* Lafcadio Hearn (1850–1904), Greek-American author who worked as a teacher in Japan during its emergence from feudal state to modern nationhood.

"Any message to William, Darling?"
"Just passionate love".
Back March 17.

TO JOHN GOODWIN, ESQ., c/o Magdalen College, Oxford

Following an unfavourable review of Fleming's books in the Times Literary
Supplement *John Goodwin, founding President of the Oxford University
James Bond Club, sent a spirited rebuttal. Having dealt shortly with accusa-
tions of snobbery and sadism he concluded with a perceptive remark about
Fleming's competitors in the field: 'One small point: if Mr. Deighton created
his hero to be "as unlike Bond as possible" he should not be seen with gar-
lic sausage and Normandy butter. Bond lunched off just such a combination
en route to Geneva for an appointment with the delightful Mr. Goldfinger.'
Fleming, who counted the* TLS *as one of life's necessities, undoubtedly read the
letter. Nevertheless, Goodwin sent him a copy to be sure.*

3rd April, 1963

Dear John Goodwin,

It was very nice to hear from you at last and thank you very much for
springing so entertainingly to my defence in the TLS and also for being
such a staunch supporter of James Bond at Oxford.

Naturally I should like to meet you all very much indeed, but I think
this will need a good deal of careful planning and tight security work, or
I shall end up dripping with stink bombs and the tyres of my Studebaker supercharged Avanti deflated.

If you are coming back through London why don't you ring up and
either come along here to my hide-out [Mitre Court] or come for a
drink to 16 Victoria Square, and we would try and make a plan for a
meeting which would amuse you and your fellow members.

Incidentally, I shudder to think how your Club will re-act to the April
issue of the London magazine!*

* In which appeared Cyril Connolly's lampoon, 'Bond Strikes Camp'.

I am much looking forward to meeting you and your Senior Member,* though if I was not already aware of his eminence I would find his name very suspect! Are you quite sure you haven't elected a double agent as your President?

With kindest regards.

Goodwin pointed out that it was a busy time of year academically, so a meeting might be difficult. At the same time, with some chutzpah, he asked if it might be possible to visit the set of From Russia with Love *which was currently being filmed at Pinewood Studios.*

5th May, 1963

Dear John Goodwin,

Many thanks for your letter of May 12th and I can appreciate the point of the "workers".

I think the best solution might be for us all to meet on one of the outing days of my son Caspar at Summer Fields, and as soon as one is coming up I will write and tell you and see if it will fit in.

Naturally I would be delighted to meet you all and I am only sorry that our house at Sevenhampton won't be habitable, I think, until July.

Anyway I will keep in touch.

Meanwhile I have stirred up the film producers and I think they will be happy to lay on anything you want so long as you keep in touch with them and find out how long they will be at Pinewood.

With best wishes for all of you who are preparing for their finals.

Thanks to Fleming's intervention, Goodwin had the enviable experience of being collected outside his college by chauffeur-driven limousine and taken to the studio where he posed for photographs alongside Sean Connery and Daniele Bianchi.

* Max Beloff, Fellow of All Souls, whose son Michael was at Magdalen College with Goodwin.

11th October, 1963

Dear John Goodwin,

Thank you very much for your letter and I shall certainly contrive to come over and meet your Society during the next few weeks.

How about, for instance, for drinks on Friday November 1st or November 15th? Please let me know if either of these dates would be any good.

I am looking forward very much to meeting you all and, as soon as the curtains are up at Sevenhampton Place I hope you will hire a bomb-proof char-à-banc and all come over for a déjeuner sur l'herbe.

Despite Fleming's cheerful outlook, the meeting never transpired.

TO P. MUIR, ESQ., Taylors, Takeley, Bishop's Stortford, Herts.

In preparation for 'Printing and the Mind of Man', Percy Muir retrieved some of Fleming's books from storage. He was deeply moved when he unearthed a first edition of The Communist Manifesto. *As he wrote to Fleming, 'I was delighted to see so many of the old friends again and to realize how well we had done all those years ago when we got this collection together. I really do not think that it would be possible to repeat at even something like ten times the price that they originally cost, which I need hardly say is a great cause of personal satisfaction to me.'*

17th April, 1963

My dear Percy,

Thank you very much for your letter of April 10th and I enclose the card duly signed.

I am greatly impressed by the valuation, but I am not in the least surprised and I think one day we would be in a position to sell the whole collection for a great deal of money.

You certainly invested quite brilliantly and we were lucky to go into the market when we did and also when you were cruising round Europe so fruitfully.

What fun it all was.

TO C. D. HAMILTON, ESQ., The Sunday Times, Thomson House, 200 Gray's Inn Road, London, W.C.1.

2nd May, 1963

My dear C.D.,

Here are one or two "bright" ideas.

1. I have just been down to Monte Carlo where I saw Graham Sutherland. He has spent the winter writing up a full account of the whole story of the Coventry Cathedral Tapestry together with very many sketches.

I mentioned that I thought this might interest you either for the Magazine or the colour supplement. And if you are interested his address is:

La Villa Blanche,
Route de Castellar,
Menton.

2. One of the exciting wartime stories that I think has not been told is the drama of the cross Channel battle between German and British coastal batteries. With photographs I think this would be very exciting.

This might be one of the long term projects you mentioned to me the other day and Antony Terry might be the man to do it plus David Devine to research the captured documents in the archives here.

3. I see I.C.I. in their Annual report refer to a sensational new heart drug. I don't know if we can get anything out of them about this, but the Chairman I think said it was equivalent in importance to the discovery of insulin as a cure for diabetes.

4. Gastronomically the least rewarding stretch for any visitor to France is from London to Abbeville, but there are still some excellent restaurants tucked away on or just off this route, and it would be a great service to tourists to give them a gastronomic tour of this route. How about getting Cyril Connolly to do it? I can give him plenty of ideas.

5. As a "Mostly for Children" feature how about rare pebbles on the English beaches in time for the summer holidays? The Natural History Museum can provide the dope and there are some beautiful colour photographs in a book called, I think, "Pebbles on English Beaches", published about three years ago. As an example, there are amethysts in Cornwall; Cornelians in Scotland; Amber at various places, and many other semi-precious stones.

Please don't bother to acknowledge this miscellaneous haul.

TO WILLIAM PLOMER

6th June, 1963
Wednesday

My dear Wm,

Thank you a thousand times for the charming green sheets & though I sense reservations it seems that you have swallowed your gruel with your usual good grace.

I note your various carps & will check & correct as instructed. Only one thing. If I start using italics won't there be too many of them in the text? I thought Capes were inclined to be allergic to them. Would you ask Michael what his feeling is.

But what the hell am I going to do with Bond now? I am feeling horribly lethargic about him and very inclined to leave him hanging on his cliff in Vladivostok. You *must* give me a powerful kick in the pants when we next meet at the CX [Charing Cross Hotel].

Just off to lunch with Allen Dulles! Perhaps he will inspire me. Ever seen him? I doubt his powers to enthuse.

Whether or not Allen Dulles was of inspiration he clearly had the power to enthuse. As Victor Weybright* reported on 11 June: 'You were a hero at the

* Fleming's new publisher at the New American Library (NAL).

*ABA [American Booksellers Association] not only because of your formidable
exhibit but because Allen Dulles repeated a half dozen times in the course of
his speech how much he wishes the CIA had a half dozen James Bonds! It
brought down applause from the rafters by the booksellers who were present.'
Fleming replied that he was delighted to hear 'that my Agent 008 spoke up so
staunchly on my behalf'.*

FROM MICHAEL HOWARD

10th June, 1963

My dear Ian,

As I am temporarily marooned in the country by a ludicrous accu-
mulation of medical misfortunes, I'm afraid this letter will go to you
unsigned. But I want to let you know that William, who spent the
weekend with us, brought the MS of YOU ONLY LIVE TWICE, which
both Pat and I read instantly and simultaneously, each fighting for the
next chapter.

No wonder you were a little mysterious in your monitory announce-
ments that there would be some strange surprises in the new story. This
makes a most brilliant diversion for Bond after the Tracy episode. It
takes an entirely new tack; but that should upset none of the addicts,
who get their full measure of 7777 (will the new number mean changing
the trademark?), and I congratulate you most heartily on making such a
skilful break from formulae. One novelty I notice with amusement is
the almost total absence of branded goods this time. Is this because you
decline to boost Japanese exports?

You told me Victor Weybright had commented that the start is rather
slow. That strikes me as a superficial criticism: it is the whole approach
to the story which sets the pace, and we find that one's interest and
attention are impelled from page one to the end with all the usual irre-
sistibility, or more. Except for the motorcyclist, and the climactic
encounter with Blofeld, strong-arm stuff gives way to a concentrated

course in Oriental culture, methods and attitudes to living and dying which will be unfamiliar and fascinating to your readers, few of whom would come across it otherwise. It will be unexpected in this context, but not unwelcome. Into snow, yes, I know it has happened. But something to soften the impact with the sea would be a help to the incredulous; and couldn't the balloon very easily be penetrated by one of those bullets and so subside less precipitously than Bond's free fall?

Apart from this, and a general suggestion about the very ending which I'd like to talk over with you when possible, I have no specific criticism to offer. But I have sent off the MS to the office to be read by all the usual sharp-eyed detail-hawks, and will present a summary of findings in due course.

For now, our warmest thanks and appreciation for the twelfth instalment of this astounding saga. It would be less than justice to say you've done it again – you've done so much more!

TO MICHAEL HOWARD

11th June, 1963

My dear Michael,

Thank you very much for your most heart-warming letter which gave me immense pleasure as I had feared that you all might jib at the amount of travelogue in the book.

But I also privately feel that it makes a good change from the usual formula, and I am glad that you feel the interest of the background made up for having to wait for the action for so long.

I was also doubtful about the 500 feet and we can easily cut it down.

Please ring me as soon as possible and discuss the ending because I have some doubt about it – not the least of which is that I have no idea how to get him from Vladivostok back into his early life, if I have the energy and inventiveness to pursue his career further.

We should have great fun with Dickie Chopping over the jacket. My first thoughts are in the direction of a vast white chrysanthemum being chopped in half by a very ornately-bladed scimitar but perhaps this time we might let Chopping read the typescript and see if he comes up with an idea of his own.

Anyway, thank you again for most encouraging letter and I do hope your medical misfortunes are miraculously cured as a reward for your kind words.

TO MICHAEL HOWARD

1st August, 1963

My dear Michael,

"You Only Live Twice"

I am getting on with the corrections and I think, with luck, you should have the finished article by the end of next week. But I would like to point out mildly that you have been sitting on the book for some two months and now expect me to do this rush job.

Another time wouldn't it be better for you to do the rush job and me to do the sitting?

I don't agree with you or William about the obituary and I would like it to stet. As for the Times masthead, I will try and get their permission to use it and I'm sure I shall have no difficulty. The main thing is that the whole obituary idea is a bit of a lark to which I am much attached.

TO C. D. HAMILTON

7th August, 1963

My dear C.D.,

I promised to let you have a note about my idea for a series called "Latter Day Adventurers", but I put off writing in the hope that I could think of more names.

Unfortunately I can't and all I can suggest are the following:-

1. The two Texas oil men who are the only experts in the world I think at putting out oil fires. They charge gigantic fees and are called in by all the great oil companies. They recently put out the great fire in the Sahara oil fields. Any oil company will give you the details.
2. There was a scheme afoot a year or two ago to salvage the Titanic. I don't know who the people concerned are but Elaine Greene does.
3. How about the Swiss guide who has just done the first solo climb of the Eiger north wall?

Sorry for this meagre list but I am sure the brains of the Sunday Times will be able to think up some more.

Off to Simenon on Wednesday and back in the first week of September.

TO AMHERST VILLIERS, ESQ., 547 Erskine Drive, Pacific Palisades, California

Villiers, although he was primarily an engineer, was also involved in rocketry and had been exploring an attempt to reach Mars with the aid of the wartime German rocket scientist Werner von Braun.

16th October, 1963

My dear Amherst,

It was lovely to hear from you and I am glad at least to have your new address at last. I wanted to write to you several times in the last few months but had no idea where you were.

Your news is very exciting, but I am much more interested in your and Charles work on the Bentley than yours on the Mars project, which I regard as a great waste of money!

The Avanti is doing all right mechanically, but there are a lot of small bugs in the coachwork and fittings and owing to bad paintwork it is having to be resprayed at Studebaker's expense. Also the windscreen has cracked. But it is certainly a good car and I shall live with it at any rate for another year.

The house [Sevenhampton] is more or less finished and we are installed and my life consists of cutting nettles and scraping mushrooms off my suits as a result of the proximity of the lake.

What about your London house, and who have you let it to?

When my book was published, the whole of England was plastered with reproductions of your portrait, and the doom-fraught eyes you gave me gazed out of practically every bookshop in the land. It is now down at the new house waiting to be suitably hung, probably next to a Sidney Nolan of a giant baboon!*

If I can find some excuse to come out to the West Coast I shall at once get in touch with you, but at the moment I am deeply involved in preparing for a maddening copyright case [about *Thunderball*] which is coming up on November 19th and is going to be a stupendous nuisance.

The first night of "From Russia with Love" was a majestic success and the queues formed all day round and round Leicester Square where it is showing at the Odeon. The whole film is a tremendous lark and I gather it will be coming to America before Christmas. So tell Nita [Villiers' wife] to watch the papers and drag you off to it when it appears in your locality.

The cartoon in the New Yorker will certainly have done no harm to my publicity in the States and Jock Whitney was kind enough to buy the original from the New Yorker and send it to me.

Not much other news except that I miss you both very much and would like to have you both back here as soon as possible, even if it means that I have to submit to another portrait.

Much love to Nita and a sharp pinch for Charles [their son].

Salud!

* Ann had just bought a picture of a gorilla by Australian artist Sidney Nolan (1917–92).

FROM K. W. PURDY, ESQ., Ridgefield Road, Wilton, Connecticut

The writer Ken Purdy had interviewed Fleming earlier in the year for an article commissioned by Playboy. *To mark the occasion he sent him as a memento his own Randall hunting knife. This remarkable object had a seven-inch blade, an ebony and ivory handle (the ebony being, as Purdy pointed out, impossibly slippery when covered in blood) and had seen hard service during two African safaris. It was capable of severing the head of a rhino, and to his certain knowledge had killed at least two men. Purdy being a motor enthusiast, his courier for this grisly gift was the champion racing driver Stirling Moss. 'I must tell you that Stirling is basically very shy, and if he tries to get out of having lunch, or tries to send you the knife, please do insist. I don't think you'll have to do, because I have told him I want the knife put into your hand. Of course he almost never makes any appearance of shyness. He is a master at concealing his feelings, and as complicated a personality as I have known. As lovable, too.' Whether or not the lunch took place is unrecorded.*

9th October, 1963

My dear Ken,

I have just got back from abroad to find your letters of September 22nd and 29th and, to deal first with that of the 29th, I am totally overcome by your generosity.

Naturally I would love to have the knife and I was most interested by your account of Randall. Please don't forget to send me his catalogue and any other literature he puts out. He sounds a fascinating man.

The knife itself will have a proud place on my walls, though I doubt if it will be put to any sterner use than cleaning my fingernails, but it's a wonderful gift and I am indeed most grateful.

Stirling seems to forget that we know each other,* and of course if he gets in touch I will give him a hot lunch or some similar celebration to mark the handing over.

---

* Fleming had visited the London Motor Show with Moss in 1956.

But now to get back to business. I'm afraid I can't help you over the book, not at any rate until next year. The books are in storage and the catalogue is missing, and although I was the second biggest contributor after King's College, Cambridge at the recent Ipex International Printing Exhibition at the British Museum, I have mislaid the catalogue of my collection and to help you with your piece, in the foreseeable future, would be a major enterprise.

When you get back to England I will explain all this in more detail, but, for the time being, please put the idea, which is certainly a good one, in cold storage.

I am sure Playboy will leave your piece alone, unlike the Herald Tribune who badgered me for something on the transatlantic telephone for their new magazine, and then cut it to ribbons.

This is a terrible fault in American editors, both in periodicals and book publishing, and I entirely sympathise with your firm stand against having your golden words turned to lead, which seems to be their purpose. What is the object of getting an original writer to write an original piece and then taking all the originality out of it? God knows.

Again with a thousand thanks for your generosity and come over here again soon.

TO C. D. HAMILTON

16th October, 1963

My dear C.D.,

Please see the attached.

My own feeling is that we could do well with a sophisticated diary from Paris and that Sonia Orwell* would do it well.

If you remember she tried it for us some years ago, but I don't think she ever really got into her stride and she is a much more mature person today than she was then and much more firmly established in Paris.

---

* Sonia Orwell (1918–80), widow of George Orwell.

The paper goes ahead splendidly and I am only slightly worried that the colour section has, by the nature of things, to contain so much art and archaeology. I will try and scratch my head for some alternative ideas, but I still think my suggestion of the great jewellers of the world would be a strong runner.

Sorry I didn't see more of you on Thursday night [at the film premiere], but I was absolutely exhausted and crept to bed pretty early. Hope to see you at lunch with Roy next Wednesday.

TO MRS. SONIA ORWELL, 38, rue des Saints Pères, Paris, 7e

16th October, 1963

My dear Sonia,

It was lovely to see you again and now to hear from you.

Personally I think you have much to offer The Sunday Times on the lines of the old Mitford monthly diary, but all this must rest with my good friend C.D. Hamilton, the editor.

So I am sending your letter on to him with a warm recommendation and I expect in due course you will be hearing either from him or from Frank Giles.

But you should remember that recently Stephen Coulter has been writing an occasional diary and I am not sure if they will wish to disturb this arrangement.

Anyway, best of luck, and it was lovely to see you again.

TO MICHAEL HOWARD

22nd October, 1963

My dear Michael,

Griffie has passed on to me your letter of October 21st and many thanks for the round figure.

Regarding Chitty-Chitty-Bang-Bang, I really hate the idea of having to do a blurb for it as I've forgotten all about the series after so much time. So could you ask one of your chaps to do a draft that I can scribble on? When will the pictures be ready, by the way?

You don't say what you think of Dickie Chopping's picture [for *You Only Live Twice*] and I am longing to hear from you about it.

Many thanks for the mock-up, which I return. This is exactly as I saw it but you might perhaps consider dropping the "Obituary" as it more or less repeats the chapter head.

Some lines have been dropped from the text, but that presumably doesn't matter.

Sorry I didn't get around to seeing more of you both the other night [at the premiere], but I was absolutely dead beat with grinning inanely at people, and how we got seventy people into our small house I simply cannot imagine. It mildly caught fire the following week and I am not in the least surprised!

Let's meet soon and have a tour d'horizon.

TO RICHARD CHOPPING

There had been some confusion over the copyright in Chopping's illustrations. For a long while Fleming had thought he owned the rights, having commissioned them and, to a large degree, designed them. But as Chopping pointed out to Michael Howard, he had never assigned the copyright in any of his works.

5th November, 1963

My dear Dickie,

First of all a thousand congratulations on the new jacket. It is quite in your topmost class and Anne loves it also. You and I really are a wonderful team.

Now I am delighted that you have raised this question of copyright which had completely escaped my attention. Naturally the copyright in all the jackets remains with you though the originals are my property.

I had assumed you were being paid a copyright fee for reproductions particularly in America, but I have now talked to Michael and find that this is not so. So I have asked Michael to have the accounts gone through to see what American monies have been paid to me for the use of your jackets and to re-credit this to you instead of me.

I am so sorry this hasn't been done before, but quite honestly both Michael and I forgot all about it. Anyway, it should come as a pleasant Christmas present!

You are quite right to have raised all this and I am delighted we shall at last get our accounts straight.

Yes, please do get the scroll a bit more scrolly if you can.

TO MICHAEL HOWARD

5th December, 1963

My dear Michael,
                           "You Only Live Twice"
We seem to be having the most tremendous arguments about what is a "tanka" and what is a "haiku", and I can't understand why somebody can't look it up in a dictionary and find the correct answer.

But at the present moment you have certainly got it wrong by changing my "syllables" for "letters".

If you will, as I have, consult Professor Blyth, Volume 4, 1952, you will find that "the haiku is the traditional Japanese verse of 17 syllables". [...]

Regarding the mention on Page 16, line 7, of "tanka of thirty-one syllables", which seems to have been missed in the general argumentation, I think this should also stet unless someone of high authority on either side of the Atlantic shouts me down.

I am sending copies of this to Phyllis Jackson, Victor Weybright and Playboy, and I hope we have now heard the end of Japanese poesy.

17

The Man With the Golden Gun

'I DON'T WANT yachts, race-horses or a Rolls Royce,' Fleming told journalist René MacColl in February 1964. 'I want my family and my friends and good health and to have a small treadmill with a temperature of 80 degrees in the shade and in the sea to come to every year for two months.

'And to be able to work there and look at the flowers and fish, and somehow to give pleasure, whether innocent or illicit, to people in their millions. Well you can't ask for more.'

It was a wistful vision of a future that Fleming knew was unlikely to materialise. By the start of the year he was in serious decline, and although Jamaica cheered him up as always, the end was written on his face. When the Canadian Broadcasting Corporation came to interview him at Goldeneye he spoke with intelligence and clarity but looked appallingly unwell. So tired and drooping were his features that it was hard to believe he was only fifty-five: he might have been a good ten years older. Nevertheless, he summoned enough energy to write what he had decided would be the last Bond novel.

The Man With the Golden Gun saw 007 transported once again to Jamaica. Having left Japan, where Fleming last stranded him, he reaches Vladivostok only to be brainwashed by SMERSH. When he returns, with murder in mind, the Secret Service foils his attempt to assassinate M with a poison-gas pistol. After intensive de-programming he is given one last chance: a do-or-die mission to kill the sharpest gunman in the business, Francisco Scaramanga. A ruthless character, Scaramanga does a nasty trade in drugs, prostitution and gambling, has murdered several British agents, and is cooperating with the Soviets to disrupt the Caribbean sugar trade. Naturally, he has all the attributes of a true Bond villain: he wields a gold-plated Colt 45 that fires silver-plated bullets of solid gold; and he has three nipples.

Using the pseudonym Mark Hazard, Bond wangles his way into Scaramanga's confidence as a personal assistant. When his cover is blown, his employer devises a colourful death on a tourist train. But Bond manages to shoot his way out of trouble, and, having killed a carriage-load of Scaramanga's associates, pursues Scaramanga himself through the jungle, where they meet in a final, deadly duel.

When Fleming sent the manuscript to Howard and Plomer, he was fairly confident that it worked – or could work, once he had polished it up. But the usual process of refinement proved beyond him. That Easter he played a game of golf in the rain, drove home in wet clothes and caught a cold which developed into pleurisy. On further examination it was found he had blood clots in the lung. He spent a long time in hospital and then in June was sent to recuperate, once again, in Hove. Visitors were discouraged lest they raise his blood pressure, but the few who were allowed found him sitting quietly at a window, cigarette in hand and staring out to sea.

Fleming's outlook was not improved by the death of his mother, who died on 27 July 1964. Recognising that he was the most fragile of her brood, she had always been a support. But now she was gone, and with her went what remained of his spirit. Her funeral was held at Nettlebed, the Fleming heartland, with a wake at his brother Peter's house, Merrimoles. Everybody noticed how ill he looked, and, when he asked for a glass of gin, Peter's housekeeper remonstrated that this wasn't what the doctors recommended. 'Fuck the doctors,' came his reply.

The shadows were gathering. When Michael Howard last saw him, 'on a dark and thundery afternoon a few weeks before his death, he told me suddenly that he knew how hostile I had been to his first book. It was generous of him never to have challenged me about it earlier.' This wasn't the first act of generosity. Despite receiving grander offers from other publishers he had stuck with Cape, and from being an annoying

upstart he had risen to become the mainstay of an increasingly mori-
bund publishing house. By Howard's admission, his books were by now
the only thing that kept Cape in profit.

In the following weeks Fleming smoked and drank his life to a
strangely symmetrical conclusion. He had moved into a house in Kent
at the start of his Bond career, and now that it was over it was to Kent
that he returned once again. That August he and Ann motored down
to Sandwich where Fleming was due to be elected captain of the Royal
St George's golf club. After dinner on 11 August he suffered a heart
attack. The following morning, on his son Caspar's twelfth birthday,
he died.

A memorial service was organised on 15 September by his sister
Amaryllis at St Bartholomew's Church, Smithfield, a spot she chose
not only for its central location but because it was said to be the oldest
church in London – and with its dense and massive interior it certainly
looked the part. Anticipating crowds, Amaryllis had arranged for
police cordons, but in the event they were not needed. She played a
Bach Sarabande on her cello, and William Plomer, Fleming's friend,
'gentle reader' and editorial companion, gave the address. Meanwhile,
if they had failed to appear at the service, the wider public had their
own memorial in the form of Bond. *The Man With the Golden Gun* was
published in 1965,* and the next year Cape produced *Octopussy and The
Living Daylights* containing the two stories they had to hand, plus
'Property of a Lady'.

Yet, as William Plomer remarked amidst the massive pillars of St
Bart's, this was only one aspect of the man. His envoi was heartfelt: 'Let
us remember him as he was on top of the world, with his foot on the
accelerator, laughing at absurdities, enjoying discoveries, absorbed in
his many interests and plans, fascinated and amused by places and people and facts and fantasies, an entertainer of millions, and for us a friend
never to be forgotten.'

---

* To help tidy up the manuscript, Cape approached Kingsley Amis, who had just submitted an outline for *The James Bond Dossier* – a slightly tongue-in cheek examination
of Bond's adventures. Amis would later be appointed to write a Bond continuation
novel, *Colonel Sun*, which was published in 1968.

TO ALAN WHICKER, ESQ., The British Broadcasting Corporation, Lime Grove Studios, London w. 12, England

The journalist and broadcaster Alan Whicker wrote in the erroneous belief that an approach had already been made, to enquire if Fleming might like to be the subject of a 50-minute episode in his investigative TV series, 'Whicker's World'. As an enticement he added that, 'I have interviewed Paul Getty; Baron and Baroness Thyssen; and have considered in depth the lives of such diverse groups as the Indians of the Guatemala and the Quorn [a British fox hunt].' Understanding that Fleming was currently in Jamaica, Whicker proposed he bring his film crew there in April. He received a stony reply.

23rd January, 1964

Dear Mr. Whicker,

Thank you very much for your letter of the 16th, but, if you will forgive me, I am not greatly impressed by being equated with any of your previous victims!

Moreover, I do not greatly seek publicity and I am daunted by the idea of working away for several days for the benefit of the BBC; apparently without payment.

And I leave here on March 16th.

Wouldn't you rather do the Battersea Dogs Home and forget about me?

TO WILLIAM PLOMER

From Goldeneye, 2nd March, 1964

My dear Wm,

Here is my end, nearly, of term report as usual.

I have somehow managed to write a, nearly, book. Not long, about the same as 'The Spy who loved me'. But it is nevertheless a miracle – in my opinion – because I felt empty as a Jamaican gourd when I left. It is called 'The Man With the Golden Gun', which I like & is set, once again, in Jamaica. I've no idea what it is like, but then one never does. I am not enthusiastic, but then I have lived with this joke, under your lash!, for so long, that the zest is seeping out through my Dr. Scholls. Anyway, I am proud not to have failed you, whatever your verdict! Perhaps I am getting spoiled by success. You must lecture me about this when I get back. Incidentally, & for your ears only, there is a big take-over bid for Glidrose underway.* A huge City company! Golly, what you started at the Ivy 13 years ago!

Annie sits & reads Keats & Quennell & moans about the 'Tristes Tropiques' but gets sleek. She sends her warmest love, as do eye.

TO MICHAEL HOWARD

From Goldeneye, 3rd March, 1964

Dear Michael,

One sudden, brilliant notion.

I am surrounded by books of reference here – about birds, fish, shells, tropical shrubs, trees, plants, the stars, etc. etc. – but every guest says "what does ganja look like?" (marihuana)

Why not do a cool, well-illustrated book on the "narcotic flora of the world"? Expensive. Definitive. With medical effects, etc. I would certainly underwrite it. You can't miss. Get cracking before Weidenpuss or Thames & Hudson do it. A £5 job.

I have spoken!

Thanks for your gen. Sorry about Monday but after the flight & signing all those books we will be in purdah. Anyway, why promote each other?

Now, get off the [launch] pad!

Cape did, in fact, investigate the possibility. But their enquiries were half-hearted and extended little further than the Royal Botanical Gardens at Kew

---

* Fleming had sold a 51 per cent stake in Glidrose, the company that held his literary rights, to his friend Jock Campbell, whose firm Booker Brothers, having acquired other literary estates, became famous as founder of the Booker Prize for fiction.

from whom they received a prim and slight disapproving list of plants in which the only curiosity – and one that Fleming would have enjoyed – was that lettuce (reputedly) had mild narcotic properties. But by then he was dead and they dropped it.

TO MICHAEL HOWARD

'57th Birthday', 28th March, 1964*

My Dear Michael,

Warmest thanks for your messages and the Googarty [sic].† He was in fact a great friend of my mother tho. she only gets a mention. He contributed to my first publication "The Wyvern", a one-time-only mag I produced at Eton containing my first piece of fiction – a shameless crib of Michael Arlen! But I made £90 out of my venture as a publisher which is more than many can say.

Out this weekend & then to Vic. Square for a week where I <u>promise</u> to finish correcting my book. Then to the country for a while.

I say, Cape's <u>are</u> in the news with their books these days! Many congratulations to you all.

Got some sweet peas from Andre Deutsch!!! Humpf!

Salud,

Ian

P.S. Happy B-day to you too.

TO VICTOR WEYBRIGHT, ESQ., The New American Library, 501 Madison Avenue, New York, 22

---

* Fleming was badly confused. It was actually his fifty-sixth birthday, and he was born in May not March.

† Ulick O'Connor's *Oliver St. John Gogarty* was published by Cape in 1963.

7th April, 1964

My Dear Victor,

I have had your comments on the title of my next book, "The Man With The Golden Gun."

I had thought of Algren's "The Man With The Golden Arm", but am I not right in thinking there is no copyright in titles? And, in any case, Algren's was in such a different vein of literature.

And was there not a man called Apuleius who wrote "The Man With The Golden Ass"! However, I have two alternative titles "Goldenrod" or "Number 3½ Love Lane", to fall back on in case of emergency.

But heaven knows when I am going to get around to correcting the typescript and doing a certain amount of rewriting.

I am absolutely deluged with junk from which I simply don't seem to be able to free up existence. So please be excessively patient this year.

TO WILLIAM PLOMER

While laid up with pleurisy in the King Edward VII Hospital, known as Sister Agnes, Fleming wrote to congratulate Plomer on the recently published diaries of Richard Rumbold which had given him, as editor, an extraordinary amount of trouble. Fleming also made clear that he was finished with Bond.

Chez la Soeur Agnes, 10th May, 1964, Saturday

My dear Wm,

Alas I am 'gisant parterre' here for the past 10 days with another 2 weeks to go – pleurisy. I thought only aunts got it, but no one will say how ill I am – the usual mumbo-jumbo – and in fact I feel totally 'remis' though not yet up to correcting my stupid book – or rather the last 3rd of it, but I shall get down to it next week and then you & I will plan whether to publish in 1965 or give it another year's working over so that we can go out with a bang instead of a whimper.

Your fine opus arrived just in time & saw me over the first 3 days. Oddly enough, on my first night, the night nurse exclaimed when she saw the picture on the jacket. She had been R[umbold]'s nurse at Midhurst in ? 1956. She had much liked him but said he was terribly 'mixed up' (indeed!) and his looks had gone (who's wouldn't have?) She remembered Hilda well (what a saint!) Odd coincidence.

I remember well, at the Charing X, was it 3 years ago? you telling me that this shower had emptied itself on your head – bales & cases full of letters & papers, & how I commiserated. Well, now time has passed & an infinity of labour (which you don't mention, of course, in your excellent introduction), and the work is done & the memorial stands. What a wonderful & good achievement! I read every word & shall now always remember this man I never knew OR heard of. Echoes of Denton Welch* – perhaps because of the introspection & Ceylon. What a monster that father was! One of the great ogres as you bring out in a few lines. Wish I had read 'My Father's Son'. And Ronnie Knox – really! Did this foul deed come in E[velyn] W[augh]'s biography? I bet not. Of course I adored your occasional asides & intrusions – rather like a Zen master with his stick! I would have liked a photograph of HOW he was at the end but that might have been unkind. Interesting his admiration for Paul Bowles whom I think a cold-hearted bastard but I can see that his compactness and discipline would have impressed R.

Anyway, enough of these maunderings. I must have my "sensitive areas" rubbed (bottom in hospitalese!) Thank you for the spiffing P.C. I am better without visitors but we will gnaw a string of spaghetti when I get out.

1,000nd congratulations on a beautifully accomplished task.

FROM SOMERSET MAUGHAM

Maugham, aged eighty-eight and nearing the end of his life, wrote a sad note to thank Fleming for his latest, You Only Live Twice.

* Denton Welch (1915–48), an intense and troubled writer.

7th May, 1964

My dear Ian,

Thank you for sending me your new book. I read it, as with all the others, with great delight and excitement. It was very sweet of you to think of me; I was touched and much pleased.

Forgive me for not having acknowledged it before now but I have been very seedy and distraught. I have just returned from Venice, but with the realisation that my travelling days are over – it is a great grief to me.

I hope we meet before too long. I think of you with great affection and should like to see you once more.

TO SOMERSET MAUGHAM, ESQ., C.H., Villa Mauresque, St. Jean, Cap Ferrat

13th May, 1964

My dear Willie,

A thousand thanks for your charming but rather triste letter of May 7th. Cease at once being "seedy and distraught". Move about as much as you can, even if it's only short distances, and don't forget that today's news wraps tomorrow's fish!

I have been seedy but without being much distraught, pleurisy and shut up in Sister Agnes for two or three weeks.

I shall be about again in a fortnight or so and I am going to try and persuade Annie that we might fly down to Nice and invite ourselves to you for a week-end, if you will have us. I would see that Annie did not exhaust you with her chatter and, as you know, I am as quiet as a mouse. But we both long to see you, particularly as you missed your London visit last year.

If you think this would be a good idea please scribble Annie a note and command her to your presence. She is your slave and will do anything you tell her to.

Now please don't treat yourself like a piece of Venetian glass, it is not your style at all and you have always had the courage and fortitude of ten.

With all my affection,

Dictated by Mr. Fleming and signed in his absence

TO AUBREY FORSHAW, ESQ., Pan Books Ltd., 8 Headfort Place, London, S.W.1.

Aubrey Forshaw of Pan Books wrote to invite Fleming to a party where he was to receive an award for having sold one million copies of Casino Royale.

20th May, 1964

My dear Aubrey,

I am so sorry that I missed our lunch and, alas, I'm afraid it may be another couple of weeks or so before I shall be fit to take part in this splendid beano you are arranging for me.

Griffie will let you know just as soon as I am back in circulation.

What the devil do these Oscars consist of? I assume they are at least 18 carat and the whole way through, unlike the Hollywood Oscars which are made of the basest of metals!

Anyway, it really is wonderful what you have managed to do with my books, and it certainly is a far cry from the day when you and Cape gingerly handled "Casino Royale" with a pair of tongs and gaze averted!

I don't think much of Harry Saltzman's new jacket for "Goldfinger". The golden girl looks like a man and there is far too much jazz about the film. Why the hell should we advertise Saltzman and Broccoli on one of <u>my</u> books? And on the back I see that Sean Connery gets at least twice the size type as the author.

Seriously, although Saltzman is a splendid salesman, do please keep a sharp eye on this tendency of his to use my books for advertising his films.

Longing to see you as soon as possible.

Dictated by Ian Fleming & signed in his absence.

P.S. By the way, Griffie just tells me you have a different cover in mind once the film is out of the way. She might have said so earlier!

Forshaw replied: 'Our PAN is 9 ¾" high – a replica of a 2nd Century statue owned by the British Museum. It is of bronze, as is the original, but is plated

with matt 18 ct. gold to prevent tarnishing. He stands on a 4" Mahogany plinth
bearing a plate engraved with your name, the title of the book and the fact that
the book has sold a million copies in our series.

'*Poor man you are now due to receive eight – i.e. all titles except "FOR*
YOUR EYES ONLY". Within two or three months this too will reach the
million and will be an all time record-holder, short stories being notoriously
difficult to sell in any numbers.' *He further pointed out:* '*Saltzman's films*
have done an enormous amount to spread the cult.'

TO WILLIAM PLOMER

20th May, 1964

My dear Wm,

Thank you for warming peecard & spiffing letter. I am satisfied with
your reviews [of Plomer's book on Richard Rumbold] except for that
pretentious booby Francis King. He reminds me a bit of Grigson* in the
way they PECK and denigrate. I would like to have read great accolades
for you, really great ones, but few people can know how much dung had
to be shifted by how staunch a beetle. I remember so vividly your throw-
away phrases in the Charing X and my immediate understanding of
what you had taken on. Odd!

Don't do it again! Write for fun now.

Have just been condemned to another week or so here – but by the
best mechanic in England – Stuart Bedford. I could have told him so
before he said it. One knows one's old vintage car by now. Reading
voraciously but I find I can now only read books which approximate
to the <u>truth</u>. Odd <u>stories</u> just aren't good enough. That's most of the
reason I shy away from Bond. Not good enough after reading 'Diary
of a Black Sheep' by Meinertzhagen[†] & even Francis Chichester[‡] with

---

[*] Francis King and Geoffrey Grigson were eminent writers and critics of the period.
[†] Richard Meinertzhagen (1878–1967), officer, spy and adventurer, is said to have
been a model for James Bond.
[‡] Francis Chichester (1901–72), British aviator and sailor who became the first person to sail single-handed around the world.

all its omissions. But in due course I will hack away & you will be honest with me. I don't like short-weighting my readers, myself or you.

Just finished Post's "Heart of the Hunter". Liked first third but got bogged down in Praying Mantis. You must bring me up to date with him one day. Also Deighton's "Funeral in Berlin" in proof. Amusing cracks but I simply can't be bothered with his kitchen sink writing & all this Nescafe. Reminds me of Bratby. I think Capes should send him to Tahiti or somewhere & get him to 'tell a story'. He excuses his ignorance of life with his footnotes & that won't stand up for long – nice chap though he is.

Please tell Michael to send me some books – any I.Q. but <u>good</u> ones!

Sorry for the long waffle but I've just had the extra sentence & Annie has a smart dinner party & I wanted to communicate.

Gruss aus Beaumontstrasse

P.S. Please read the Amis M.S. & put him right where you can.* You blew the whistle. You've <u>seen</u> the whole game! No reply <u>please</u>.

TO WILLIAM PLOMER

June 1964

Another 10 days, Brighton

My dear Wm,

You have calmed my temperature & blood pressure, reduced the albumen in my urine & sent my spirits soaring.

But I would still like to tinker with the book [*The Man with the Golden Gun*] & skip a year. We will discuss, but bless you as usual.

---

* The MS being of Amis's *The James Bond Dossier*.

TO LEONARD RUSSELL

15th June, 1964

Dear Leonard,

Forgive the typing and the signature, but I am still not firing on all cylinders.

I will certainly see that you have an early look at "Chitty-Chitty-Bang-Bang", but there is so much text that, apart from the brilliance of [John] Burningham's illustrations, I think you may have difficulty in finding room for it.

I wrote the three books three years ago when I got stuck in hospital and someone sent me Squirrel Nutkin which, apart from the illustrations, I thought was most terrible bilge – particularly the idiotic riddles.

Laid low again, I am now thinking of a musical called "Fizz-an-Chips", but I haven't got further than the title.

I'm afraid I entirely agree with your criticism of my critique of Norman Lewis's book, but I was not nearly as well up on the subject of the Mafia as you – strangely – appear to be. And though I never see him I am devoted to Norman and am sorry that he always just fails to come off.

But you are absolutely right, and it just shows that you must tell Jack never again to ask me to do reviews for him. My eye is absolutely out!

But be a good chap and lend me this definitive work in the "New York Review of Books" which I have never heard of. I promise it will come back to you safely.

Anyway it was lovely to hear from you and I now see that the only way to get more than a short paragraph from you is to offend your critical senses!

Salud.

Dictated by Ian Fleming and signed in his absence

TO DENIS HAMILTON, 25 Roebuck House, Stag Place, London, s.w.1.

15th June, 1964

My dear C.D.,

Forgive the typing and the signature but I am still not running on all cylinders.

It was lovely to get your note, but I am sorry you have been playing the fool in the garden. You must know that all forms of gardening are tantamount to suicide for the normal sedentary male. For heaven's sake leave the whole business alone, it is an absolute death trap.

Alas, next week won't work as with any luck I'm going to be allowed down to Brighton to play ring-a-roses with the Mods and Rockers.

So please let us make it the week after and I will get in touch.

You are a wonderful chap to take my broadsides in such good grace, but I have always felt that we have so much talent on the paper that just doesn't do its weekly stint and is not, from time to time, given the lime-light of the leader page.

There are some tremendous names there, often with axes to grind, off their usual beat and I feel it would be a great accolade for many of them to get on the leader page – and a stimulus and a challenge, for the matter of that.

But to draw them out of their shells might need something like a round robin letter or series of small luncheon parties.

But we will hack away at each other in a few days time, and in the meantime, for heavens sake keep away from that blasted garden.

TO PERCY MUIR, ESQ., Elkin Matthews Ltd., Takeley, Bishop's Stortford, Essex

22nd June, 1964

Dear Mr. Muir,

Thank you for your letter of June 19th. Alas, I'm afraid Mr. Fleming has been quite ill. He had a cold, played golf and got very wet, the cold turned to influenza and the influenza to pleurisy. All this of course has proved to be a strain on his heart. He was in Sister Agnes hospital for some weeks, then at home for two weeks, and last Wednesday he went to Brighton. I expected him back in London tomorrow, but I've just heard that he is not so well and will have to stay another ten days or so.

As you can imagine he is very bored and now he is only allowed to go out every other day. It's all very worrying. However, I know he would like to hear from you so long as you ask him not to reply. He gets exhausted very quickly and sends all his letters to the office, and I know he feels it is rather impolite not answering them personally.

I thought the Book Fair excellent, but the attendance was terribly poor.

Mr. Fleming's address is The Dudley Hotel, Hove, Sussex, so please write and cheer him up, he needs it.

Yours Sincerely,

Secretary to Ian Fleming

Afterword

A lthough Fleming died in 1964, Agent 007 did not. The Bond novels continued to sell in their millions – initially thanks to Pan Books, whose paperback covers were reinvented so often and so inventively that they became almost as iconic as Chopping's original designs. If the literary establishment had once looked down upon Fleming as a sensationalist, his contemporaries would now have given their eye teeth to achieve even a smidgeon of his fame. When Kingsley Amis's *The James Bond Dossier* came out in 1965 Evelyn Waugh wrote to his friend Nancy Mitford, 'Ian Fleming is being posthumously canonised by the intelligentsia. Very rum.' More importantly, perhaps, his books acted as a touchstone for a new breed of thriller writer.

Fleming's literary estate was managed at first by Ann, who guarded his reputation until her death in 1981, and by his brother Peter along with the agent Peter Janson-Smith. Caspar Fleming led a troubled life, which included a fascination for guns, drugs and Ancient Egypt before committing suicide in 1975. To safeguard the copyright in James Bond, Glidrose commissioned Kingsley Amis to write a continuation Bond novel, *Colonel Sun*, which came out in 1968, following which several other authors have since assumed the Bond mantle.

The grip Bond held on the world's imagination was enhanced beyond measure by his career on screen. Producers Cubby Broccoli and Harry Saltzman took a leap in the dark when they bought the film rights in 1961 (appropriately, they named their company EON: 'Everything Or Nothing') but their perseverance paid dividends. Fleming's credo had always been that if you wanted to make proper money from writing you had to get your books made into films. And he was quite right.

The first three Bond films – *Dr No*, *From Russia with Love* and *Goldfinger* – were produced while Fleming was still alive, though he lived to see only the first two. They followed, more or less faithfully, the novels – among the highlights were 007's game of golf with Goldfinger and his duel with Rosa Klebb and her poison-bladed shoes in *From Russia with Love*. Thereafter, Bond took wing, flying in a variety of directions yet always uplifted by a glamour and sense of excitement that reflected Fleming's original vision. The result, managed by the same family-run company, headed now by Barbara Broccoli and Michael Wilson, is a massive entertainment industry that shows no sign of diminishing.

At the time of writing, Fleming's books have sold more than 100 million copies (excluding translations) and it has been estimated that one in five of the world's population has seen a Bond film. All this from a man who in 1953 offered to flip a coin with his publisher over who should pay for a few extra promotional copies of *Casino Royale*.

The Works of Ian Fleming

Casino Royale (1953)
Live and Let Die (1954)
Moonraker (1955)
Diamonds are Forever (1956)
From Russia with Love (1957)
Dr No (1958)
Goldfinger (1959)
For Your Eyes Only (1960)*
Thunderball (1961)
The Spy Who Loved Me (1962)
On Her Majesty's Secret Service (1963)
You Only Live Twice (1964)
The Man with the Golden Gun (1965)
Octopussy and the Living Daylights (1966)†
The Diamond Smugglers (1957)
Thrilling Cities (1963)
Chitty-Chitty-Bang-Bang (1964–5)‡

---

* Containing the short stories 'From a View to a Kill', 'For Your Eyes Only', 'Quantum of Solace', 'Risico' and 'The Hildebrand Rarity'.

† Containing, in its first incarnation, 'Octopussy', 'The Living Daylights' and 'The Property of a Lady'. Later reissued with a fourth short story, '007 in New York'.

‡ Published in three volumes over the course of several months.

The James Bond Films

Of necessity, this volume concentrates on Fleming's literary output. Yet, for many people their first acquaintance with James Bond may come from a cinema rather than a bookshop. Here, therefore, is a list of the films, with their release dates. Most of them have been produced by Eon, the partnership created by Cubby Broccoli and Harry Saltzman, but as befits Fleming's tangled arrangements in this sphere, there are a couple of anomalies. The list is complete at the time of publication, November 2015.

Dr. No (1962)
From Russia with Love (1963)
Goldfinger (1964)
Thunderball (1965)
You Only Live Twice (1967)
On Her Majesty's Secret Service (1969)
Diamonds are Forever (1971)
Live and Let Die (1973)
The Man with the Golden Gun (1974)
The Spy Who Loved Me (1977)
Moonraker (1979)
For Your Eyes Only (1981)

Octopussy (1983)
A View to a Kill (1985)
The Living Daylights (1987)
Licence to Kill (1989)
GoldenEye (1995)
Tomorrow Never Dies (1997)
The World Is Not Enough (1999)
Die Another Day (2002)
Casino Royale (2006)
Quantum of Solace (2008)
Skyfall (2012)
Spectre (2015)

Also:

Casino Royale (1967)
Never Say Never Again (1983)

Acknowledgements

Many books have been written about Ian Fleming and this latest addition to the canon would have been a lot harder without the spade work of those who have gone before. In this respect I owe a debt of gratitude to Ian's two major biographers, John Pearson and Andrew Lycett (who battled valiantly to retrieve lost computer files), and to Ian's bibliographer, Jon Gilbert. Special mention, too, must be made of The Ian Fleming Estate who not only sanctioned the book but who own the copyright to Ian's letters and have been more than generous with their assistance throughout.

Thanks are also due to the following: The Lilly Library, Indiana University Bloomington, for access to its collection of Ian Fleming correspondence; the Franklin D. Roosevelt Library, New York, for copies of Ernest Cuneo's letters and memoirs; Ian Fleming Publications, London, for permission to use the occasional James Bond extract and for much else besides; the Jonathan Cape Archive at the University of Reading (Special Collections) and the Random House Archive, Rushden, which together hold the bulk of Ian Fleming's publishing correspondence; and the Beinecke Library, Yale University.

Letters by Noel Coward are reproduced courtesy of Alan Brodie Literary Agency; those by Aubrey Forshaw courtesy of Pan Macmillan; Somerset Maugham by permission of United Agents on behalf of the Royal Literary Fund; Raymond Chandler courtesy of the Raymond Chandler Estate via Ed Victor Ltd; and with thanks to the estates of

Geoffrey Boothroyd, Ernest Cuneo and Herman W. Liebert. The copyright in letters by Jonathan Cape, David Cape, Daniel George, Michael Howard, Wren Howard and William Plomer is held by Penguin Random House, of which Jonathan Cape is now an imprint.

Letters have been contributed most kindly by Jon Gilbert of Adrian Harrington Rare Books and The Ian Fleming Bibliographical Archive (Villiers); John Goodwin (The Oxford University James Bond Club); James Trepanier (Frewin); and Mark Davies (D. N. Davies). And, as so often in matters Fleming, many thanks to Mike VanBlaricum, John Cork and Brad Frank for their contributions and advice.

A special thanks to those individuals who have helped with the research. At Bloomington: David Frasier, Cherry Williams and particularly Erika Jenns for her transcriptions. In London: Corinne Turner, Jo Lane and Phoebe Taylor. In New York: William Baehr and Virginia Lewick. In Reading: Danni Corfield. In Rushden: Charlotte Heppell. And at Yale University, Michael Rush.

Occasional extracts have been used from Michael Howard's history of Jonathan Cape and Mark Amory's edited letters of Ann Fleming. In the absence of source notes here is a concise but informative bibliography.

Amory, M. (ed) – *The Letters of Ann Fleming.* Collins Harvill, London, 1985.

Gilbert, J. – *Ian Fleming: The Bibliography.* Queen Anne Press, London, 2012.

Howard, M. – *Jonathan Cape, Publisher.* Jonathan Cape, London, 1971.

Lycett, A. – *Ian Fleming.* Weidenfeld & Nicolson, London, 1995.

Pearson, J. – *The Life of Ian Fleming.* Jonathan Cape, London, 1966.

Finally, on matters of publication, Gordon Wise of Curtis Brown helped this book into the hands of Bill Swainson at Bloomsbury. Bill has been the most assiduous of editors: he has scoured the text with kind precision and any errors or omissions are entirely my own. In its final stages Anna Simpson gave the manuscript her stalwart attention and Alexandra Pringle brought the whole thing together.

Index

NOTE: In the index the abbreviation IF stands for Ian Fleming.

A Note on the Editor

Fergus Fleming is Ian Fleming's nephew. He is the author of several non-fiction books including *Barrow's Boys, Killing Dragons* and *Ninety Degrees North*. He is also the co-publisher of Queen Anne Press. He lives in Gloucestershire.